SEARCHING FOR STANLEY

SEARCHING
FOR STANLEY

UNFORGOTTEN HERO
OF WORLD WAR II

KAY HUGHES,
with contributions by HAROLD E. DWYER

iUniverse, Inc.
Bloomington

Searching for Stanley
Unforgotten Hero of World War II

iUniverse books may be ordered through booksellers or by contacting:

iUniverse
1663 Liberty Drive
Bloomington, IN 47403
www.iuniverse.com
1-800-Authors (1-800-288-4677)

Credit for the front cover photograph: AAF Training Command

Credit for the back cover photograph: JPAC photo—Derrick Goode, photographer

Permission to use the JPAC logo granted by the Joint POW/MIA Accounting Command

ISBN: 978-1-4502-9561-1 (sc)
ISBN: 978-1-4502-9559-8 (dj)
ISBN: 978-1-4502-9560-4 (ebk)

Printed in the United States of America

iUniverse rev. date: 07/07/2011

In memory of the thousands of servicemen and servicewomen who gave their lives for freedom.

When you go home, tell them of us and say, for
your tomorrow, we gave our today.
—Kohima Epitaph

CONTENTS

FOREWORD

This is a story about two brothers, both pilots of B-17s during the Second World War. One was eight years senior to me and thus in combat one year ahead. And therein lies the story between these pages: the unlucky one, Stanley Dwyer, MIA since 10 May 1944, and the trials and tribulations of the lucky one, Harold Dwyer, as we tried to recall Stan's last few minutes on this earth.

I say "we" with my tongue in cheek because it would not have happened without the many years of labor and the great dedication to the project by my daughter—and niece of Stan—Kay Hughes.

Kay spent thousands and thousands of hours on the computer, making telephone calls, and traveled to meet some of the survivors and an eyewitness to the actual incident.

It has also been quite a ride for this eighty-six-year-old man, and I know not how to thank Kay enough. I know my brother so much better than I did when he left home in the late '30s to join the merchant marines. But that is part of the rest of the story.

–Harold E. Dwyer
February 2, 2011

ACKNOWLEDGMENTS

I've heard Dad say time and again, "It's been an amazing journey." Dad, Mom, my husband, Rick, and I shared many incredible and memorable experiences in our search for Stanley, and we are deeply grateful for everyone who made our journey and this story possible.

Somewhere along the way, I knew our journey wasn't over until Stanley's legacy perpetuated. The story in my head needed to be put down in black and white. But only thinking about writing doesn't get the job done. With a giant leap outside my comfort zone and a new habit of writing daily, the pages added up. And praise God for his guidance in life's journey. The thoughts—and inspiration—that popped in my head in the middle of the night came from somewhere.

Dad's priceless background information filled in gaps of our family history, and his personal interpretation of the journey was essential and a vital part of the story. Mom always offered support and encouragement in every aspect, and I value her devotion, enthusiasm, and steady influence. And Rick, my husband, whether over a glass of wine or on our walks and talks, listened to me and reinterpreted my ideas, which stirred and clarified my thoughts. We traveled this road together on our shared journey through life.

We thank Deputy Commander Johnie E. Webb Jr., Joint POW/MIA Accounting Command (JPAC), for his patience and friendship and for his and the entire JPAC community's commitment, service, and sacrifice to bring home the missing. To the men and women of the two JPAC recovery teams we met, your Nebraska family thanks you for the photos, video footage, friendship, and unsurpassed dedication and efforts in searching for the remains of Stanley and John Boros. We will always remember your names and faces.

To our many friends in Austria, thank you for your willingness to help and share vital information in our search for Stanley. We feel fortunate that our lives crossed paths, and your continued acts of kindness add to our special memories of you.

Many family members, friends, and acquaintances—here in the United States and abroad—offered information as well as support and encouragement.

Several people read parts or all of the manuscript with special attention to factual details and accuracy. Thank you all for your interest, insight, and input.

We appreciate Aileen Groen, Mary Ellen Cameron, Karena Conley, and Sherry Grant for their contributions of memorabilia, observations, and help piecing together more of the story.

David Hughes and Martin Steinbereithner simply offered to help. We are grateful for their many significant contributions.

Several people translated information. Thank you for your talents.

Peter Soby, Brian Mastre, John Campbell, Harry Flansburg, Chuck Coleman, and Dave Hynek of sobyVISION are devoted to telling the story of Stanley in a short-form documentary. We thank them for their work, friendship, and interest in the story. We especially commend their motivation and dedication while balancing life's daily demands and challenges. Their interviews documented information which, for me, was invaluable in writing the manuscript.

Writing a book is one thing; publishing it is another. And editing is a reminder that we're human, not perfect. I am grateful for the professionals at iUniverse whose assistance eased the load. They are talented and friendly and were efficient moving the manuscript through the publishing process.

I thank computer-savvy Shayne Raitt for curtailing some technical challenges.

Also, heartfelt thanks to my friend Patty Scarborough, who was like a personal trainer. When the lazy right side of my brain "ached," Patty, an accomplished artist, assured me that the discomfort was normal.

Many thanks to English instructor Dorothy Miller, who played an indispensable role. She cheered me on with her knowledge and understanding of the writing process, and I relied on her keen intuition and masterful guidance for editing.

Personally, I am grateful to all the veterans who shared their stories and experiences of World War II. Thank you for your service to our country and for our freedom.

And I extend special thoughts of gratitude to my children, Sarah, Melissa, and Nathan, to my son-in-law, Jeremy, and granddaughters, Chloe and Allie, for their encouragement and patience with me—especially when my mind wandered and dust balls accumulated in the house. I say to them and my family, "Meet Stanley, and pass on his legacy."

PREFACE

"God Bless my dear friend's parents who have given so much to a harsh and bloody quarrel ... They just don't make medals heavy enough to fit men like my friend Stan. I came to learn that personal honor and integrity were to him as valuable as life itself. He proved that to me one day in a bomber over Austria ..." Ralph Lauper wrote this about Stanley Dwyer, a fellow squadron member, comrade, and personal friend.

At one time, Stanley Dwyer was, to me, simply a name on our family tree. Its branches extended and listed the offspring of my grandparents, Harold W. and Ellen J. Dwyer. The name of Stanley, their son, was recorded on a line between the names of his older sister, Aileen, and his younger brother, Harold E., my dad. Unlike Aileen and Harold E., who perpetuated their lineages, Stanley's legacy ended right there on that single line.

Growing up, I had the perception that our family was normal like everyone else. It was normal in the everyday sense of the word. But for decades, I was unaware of an invisible, unhealed wound. Unanswered questions about Stanley's fate nagged, but Grandma and Granddad never talked about him. The certainty of what happened in the "bomber over Austria" eluded his family. The mystery lasted their lifetime.

And as a young girl, I missed my cues in the rare moments when Dad mentioned Stanley, his brother. The most obvious clue, a subtle one at best, revealed that Stanley had flown a B-17, just as Dad had. But, it took several years and an unplanned journey to gradually peel away the layers of mystery surrounding Stanley's fate. Eventually, I learned that Stanley had flown with the Fifteenth Air Force from Italy, and Dad had flown with the Eighth Air Force from England. Stationed at different locations and at different times, both brothers served their country and engaged in daylight, high-altitude, strategic bombing. Bomber crews aimed to bomb, pound, and destroy the Third Reich's industrial and military targets. To put Hitler out of business, aircraft factories, rail yards, ball bearing plants, communication facilities, ammunition factories and storage arsenals, and oil refineries were directly under the crosshairs of the crews' bombardiers. And, as the name implied, daylight, high-altitude, strategic bombing was done in daylight to improve the accuracy of hitting the targets, which then exposed the ten-man crews to greater losses. Thus, there was a price to pay.

The price of freedom paid with human lives is incalculable. The cost compounds when the suffering families of the fallen are added to the equation. I discovered how costly a toll this was only after I transitioned into the inexplicable phase of adult life when history became more than a school subject, and I appreciated that family trees embraced personal lives—not just a fill-in-the-blank exercise.

I was paying attention the day my father stood in my kitchen and asked one single question. His question launched our ten-year, unimaginable journey. One coincidence led to another and then another, and together we searched for answers to Stanley's unresolved fate. We attempted to fill in the missing parts and piece together Stanley's last mission, the deadly mission of May 10, 1944, to Wiener Neustadt, Austria. And I discovered the physical and emotional remnants of war. Incredibly, the search uncovered tucked-away memories and mementos from the life of an unknown and almost forgotten man, revealing the essence of Stanley Dwyer.

Therefore, to complete our journey, we pass on the story of Stanley—the inspiring man behind the name on our family tree—telling of his place in history. He made a difference for friend and stranger alike and stands with a long list of soldiers and heroes who preserved freedom for millions around the world.

From Gettysburg, Abraham Lincoln said, "that from these honored dead we take increased devotion to that cause for which they gave the last full measure of devotion—that we here highly resolve that these dead shall not have died in vain ..."

Stanley N. Dwyer is not forgotten. This story, therefore, is a tribute to his life. This is Stanley's legacy.

INTRODUCTION

⌒✦⌒

Wednesday, May 10, 1944

Business is so good here that we seldom get to town to take a shower.
—Stanley N. Dwyer, from a V-Mail dated April 8, 1944

As much as I'd like to rewind the clock to rewrite the history of May 10, 1944, it's impossible. In May 1944, D-Day was "just around the corner." The world waited. Like the intense strategy of a chess game, the Germans could only guess the Allies' next move and where and when the hour would come. It came. On June 6, 1944, over one hundred fifty thousand Allied troops stormed the sandy beaches of Normandy, France, and penetrated Hitler's Fortress Europe. Hedgerow to hedgerow, village to village on a foreign land, the long battle to Berlin lay ahead for these liberators.

Meanwhile, in the months leading up to the D-Day invasion, the Allied strategy aimed to loosen Hitler's grip on Europe. So around the clock, Allied bomber crews bombed the Third Reich's mighty war machine. Decimating Germany's air force meant one less obstacle for the Normandy invasion forces. Therefore, on May 10, 1944, 2nd Lt. Stanley Dwyer and his B-17 crew flew with hundreds of Fifteenth Air Force bombers whose mission was to wipe out the aircraft factory in Wiener Neustadt, Austria.

The world was different in 1944. America wore different stripes. There are lessons in history, but textbook history always seemed one dimensional. However, our journey and search for Stanley took us down memory lane and meshed textbook history and family history—and history nearly came to life. We came to find out that May 10, 1944, for some people, was its own defining day.

Near Wiener Neustadt, Austria†—"On 10 May 1944 I was in school when the air raid alarm sounded," Augustin Stranz, village tailor from Pottschach,

---

†   Some dialogues in this book, whether originally in English or German translated to English, may not be verbatim, but every attempt was made to convey the intended meaning.

1

Austria, wrote to me in German. "Boys between the ages of six and fourteen went to school. Then at age fourteen or fifteen, boys were sent to the [battle] front. [On that day] my classmates and I had to go to an air raid cellar in a house about fifty meters away.

"It was about three kilometers from Buchbach [Austria], where I lived with my family, to Pottschach and the school. That was always taken on foot; there were no cars. On that day at about 11:00 a.m. the air raid forewarning alarm sounded on the radio, (like a cuckoo clock)—cuckoo, cuckoo, cuckoo. The loud rising and falling howl of sirens, a full air raid alarm, followed."

In 1944, the world was at war, in the midst of World War II. For the Austrians, it "began" in March of 1938, when their country was easily consumed as part of "Greater Germany." Hard times had fallen on the Austrians. Their struggles recovering from World War I were compounded by the hardships suffered as a result of the Great Depression. Life was burdensome for people in Germany, too, which is where Hitler rose to power in the 1930s. The empty rhetoric and solutions for prosperity feigned by the radical politician Hitler sounded promising. The unscrupulous dictator's propaganda seemed to mesmerize some people's minds. In Austria, political unrest was prevalent. Essentially, in 1938, the doors to Austria had been left wide open. Therefore, Hitler's army crossed the border and occupied his homeland.

Markus Reisner, born in 1978 and author of the book *Bomben auf Wiener Neustadt*, commented to me about his fellow countrymen, "There wasn't huge resistance from the Austrians against this occupation because a lot of people thought they'd get more. They thought, 'Let's see what the Germans will bring.' At the beginning, it looked very good for them; people were happy, and they got work, even if it was in the war industry. But after some time and war, they figured out, okay, some people—neighbors—are missing, and no one knows what happened to them. People realized they had welcomed the evil into their bed."

Yet people feared questioning the deception of their Nazi leader. Daring to doubt was done silently. Hitler was ruthless, and any form of dissent or suspected opposition was brutally crushed by his feared Gestapo.

Augustin Stranz said:

On the evening of Thursday, August 31, 1939, members of the Nazi party brought to my parents a food card along with the statement that, as of the morning of September 1, 1939, in all of Germany food could be obtained only with that card. We then first learned that on the next day, September 1, 1939, Hitler and his army had invaded Poland in the early morning hours. It was the beginning of the Second World War. The food card was for all food provisions. A supply certificate rationed shoes, paper, wood, coal, gasoline, fuel for gas lamps, soap powder, tires for bicycles, etc. The clothes card allotted clothing items, such as suits, jackets, pants, coats, shirts, blouses, and underwear.

Worlds apart, another version of that day, May 10, 1944, unfolded in Hastings, Nebraska. If it was around 11:00 a.m. in Wiener Neustadt, then a continent and seven time zones away in Hastings, it was approximately 4:00 a.m.

Chances were, at 4:00 a.m. on that spring day in 1944, Ellen Dwyer, my grandmother, was still asleep at home at 906 West Sixth Street. Granddad, Harold W., had departed the previous afternoon to work his four-state territory, selling livestock feed and supplements for Security Food Company.

After America was attacked on December 7, 1941, at Pearl Harbor, the landscape and mood across the entire country transformed. With a war to fight on two fronts, communities mobilized, and military training centers, airfields, and other military facilities and factories unexpectedly emerged where nothing before had existed. And it seemed the wartime industrial growth helped spur the nation out of the grips of the decade-long Great Depression. As towns and cities burst at the seams with the influx of servicemen and workers, people adapted the best they could.

Hastings, located in south-central Nebraska, the strategic heartland and breadbasket of America, is surrounded by prime real estate; consequently, our government found ways to develop the wide-open countryside and good farmland to sustain the war effort.

My father, Harold E., described,

I remember Hastings having a large amount of service people around. Harvard Army Air Base was just some twenty miles away, and the Hastings Naval Ammunition Depot was just a few miles out of town. The NAD had a huge workforce, and lots of navy and marine servicemen were stationed there along with the workers brought in to build and run the facility. The population of Hastings grew by over five thousand people during the war years. Nearly 40 percent of the shells fired by the navy in World War II were made in Hastings. The depot, I have heard, was on Hitler's hit list.

By 1944, the folks in that midwestern town faced unique and often controversial challenges, similar to folks in many other communities across America. When a town's population increased, it encountered housing shortages and overcrowding in some classrooms, and racial segregation was a fact of life. Nevertheless, people tried to live their lives as normally as possible while doing their part for the war effort.

Harold E. explained more,

Living in Hastings when the war broke out, and especially being a high school senior, didn't register as a big deal in my mind. We had gas, sugar, and many other things rationed. My dad, at the time, was a salesman on the road, so he was always working the angles to get a bit more gas. I really didn't know how he did it.

"May 10, 1944, was a Wednesday," Augustin Stranz said. "Normally, when the air raid siren started, I would run *away* from the houses—outside where I could see where the planes were coming from and where they were going. Just before we entered the air raid shelter, we had seen the planes from Wiener Neustadt."

And it had happened before. Like storm clouds, Allied planes rumbled through the skies over Austria, over twenty thousand feet in the air, their formations stretched for miles.

"Four hundred bombers of the Fifteenth USAAF with an escort of two hundred fighters bombed Wiener Neustadt," Mr. Stranz wrote. "It was the seventh air raid to Wiener Neustadt."

Author Markus Reisner told us, "The most defended city at that time in Austria was Vienna because it was the capital of Austria and there was a lot of industry. In second place [of most defended] was Wiener Neustadt [approximately thirty miles south of Vienna]. There's a ranking of the most destroyed cities during the Second World War. Wiener Neustadt was in the seventh place. It was smaller than Hamburg and smaller than Dresden. At that time, there were about fifty thousand inhabitants in Wiener Neustadt, and it was destroyed nearly 100 percent.

"The aircraft works in Wiener Neustadt produced during the war about one-third of the whole German 109 production [Messerschmitt Me 109 fighter planes], which meant eight to nine thousand out of thirty thousand German 109s."

Augustin Stranz noted that in addition to the aircraft works' production of 109s, a huge Luftwaffe base was located outside the city, and other vital facilities situated in or near the city produced steel, rubber, and parts for the deadly V2 rocket.

"It was clear that the city [Wiener Neustadt] had to be destroyed," Markus Reisner said. "The first attacks on the aircraft factory were done in 1943, and the Americans were able to damage the factory pretty bad, but the Germans rebuilt it. They [Americans] started with two new attacks in 1944, in April, but due to some bad weather and so on, they were not able to hit the factories again. Then they said, 'Okay, let's do one more, a full-scale attack.'"

That job fell into the hands of the United States Fifteenth Air Force. England-based Eighth Air Force B-17 Flying Fortresses and B-24 Liberators, along with Royal Air Force bombers, pushing the maximum range limit for a mission—approximately six hundred miles—targeted the Third Reich's military and industrial complexes in western and central Germany and occupied Europe. Austria, located deep within the European continent, was considered to be outside the Eighth Air Force's range. But the Fifteenth Air Force operated from bases in Italy and mostly bombed areas in southern and eastern Europe—locations including Italy, France, Germany, Austria, Czechoslovakia, Bulgaria, Yugoslavia, Hungary, and Romania.

"Hermann Goering, who was head of the German air force during the Second World War," Markus said, "promised the Austrian people that no enemy plane would cross the border and bomb one of their cities."

"No one expected Wiener Neustadt to be bombed; no one could reach it," Mr. Stranz stated. "Austria was declared the Third Reich's air raid shelter because the Allies were flying from England, and their range was only to parts of Germany. It was a surprise to the Austrian people when the Fifteenth Air Force from Italy bombed their cities."

But by 1944, war had escalated throughout most of Europe. The Fifteenth Air Force delivered their deadly bombs once more on untouchable Wiener Neustadt, reducing it to shambles, shattering the idea of Austria being isolated from bombings. It was quite clear: the country was no one's "air raid shelter." The ravages of war knew no borders and distinguished between no one.

The sun was shining in Hastings when Grandma awoke that Wednesday. She welcomed the warmth and anticipated the sweet fragrance of her budding lilac bushes. The house was, perhaps, a little quiet with Granddad gone, and she would have to see to it that the refrigerator got repaired. However, only four days earlier, she'd returned home from Denver on the bus, and Grandma probably basked in the memories of her new granddaughter, Carol Jean. Aileen, the eldest of her three children, lived in Denver, Colorado, with husband Bill Groen. On April 1, 1944, Aileen and Bill had been blessed with the birth of their first daughter. Ellen was thrilled to be a grandmother.

She reflected her thoughts in a letter she wrote to her son Stanley.

You have a niece that is a regular little doll. Or is going to be when she gets just a little more age on her. She missed her grandmother I'll

5

bet a penny. She got so the last few days I was there she would give me a big smile, and one day she had her mouth all puckered up to talk to me, but it didn't quite make the grade. It won't be long until she talks and will her folks think that is something wonderful. Much love, and much luck, and all of it good.

Mother

Stanley, her second child and the eldest of her two sons, had answered the call to duty on December 8, 1941. He was a B-17 pilot stationed near Foggia, Italy, with the Fifteenth Air Force, 463rd Bomb Group, 775th Squadron. Writing letters kept her in touch with family. Waiting for the mailman to deliver letters from her children was probably the highlight of any day as well as a great source of comfort. It took a couple of weeks or more for letters to travel from Italy to Hastings and vice versa; however, there were always old letters or V-Mails to reread.

V-Mail—Victory Mail—implemented during World War II, cut down on the bulk and weight of mail sent back and forth between the troops and the United States. Granddad and Stanley questioned whether V-Mail traveled faster than regular mail. Letters written in the allotted space on special forms were first copied onto microfilm reels, shipped, and then developed at a designated receiving center. The developed printed page was a condensed version of a regular page—just slightly larger than a postcard. The mini version, which almost required a magnifying glass to read, was sealed in an envelope and delivered with the regular mail.

A V-Mail dated April 8, 1944, from Stanley read:

Dear folks,

This won't be a letter, just a tracer, or an experiment on the mail situation. Until today I hadn't gotten any recent mail. Today I got one from dad of the 26th of last month. That should be about the average length of time. But his letter was sent to the old APO number indicating that you haven't heard from me for an age. The Red Cross letter you mentioned having received was sent an even age ago, and I have written umpteen since. A week is the longest time I have gone without writing and have been dropping you a note every four or five days here.

Business is so good here that we seldom get to town to take a shower. Well, maybe it's not that bad, but we have a day off today and are going in right away. So this will be brief. When we are there, I will try to find some place to send a cable or Mother's Day flowers in the hopes that you can have something from me that is somewhat recent.

Had a letter from Harold yesterday, but the squirt sent it free and was sent from primary. First thing I know, he'll be an ace, and I won't have him to basic yet. Your unc is now eligible for the air medal having done the required number of missions. 'Twas a breeze though.

Also yesterday received a letter from Lawrence Davidson from Ireland. And a couple of days ago one from Lynne. I think I told you about that, though, in at least one previous letter.

Everything here is lovely. Have no complaints to make. Am looking forward to coming back to the States before too long a time. You'd better begin saving up those points.

Pop, suspected that you folks would be back home after having visited Harold, but since the letter made such good time, I doubt that you have made it yet. I'll bet fun was had by all.

And pa, surely spring has established that beachhead by now.

Love,
Stan

Most likely, Grandma set that letter down and thought of "her other boy," Harold E., who, on May 10, 1944, was in pilot training with the Army Air Corps.

I enlisted in the Army Air Corps when I was eighteen. We were just getting out of the Depression when the war started, and it seemed to have been the background for the right attitude for young people to join the service and basically protect their families. A great bunch of young people stepped up to the task at hand and never thought much about it. You knew the possibilities of getting hurt, but most young people think it's always the other guy that's going to get it.

On the tenth of May, 1944, I was stationed at Marana Air Field in Arizona where I was completing my basic training. The folks had recently been down to Tucson to visit me. My training class had a chance to choose which aircraft we wanted to fly. At first, I took the P-38 fighter. My second choice, which I found out later didn't make my mother too happy, was the B-25. Of course, in the army, you didn't always get what you wanted. On May 10, 1944, I was days from being transferred to advanced training at Ft. Sumner, New Mexico.

There was a spirit of optimism across the country. Everyone was encouraged to do their part. Millions, mostly men, answered the call to duty to defend America and to preserve their way of life and the freedom they knew, which left women and others to carry on the war effort at home.

Almost from the beginning, most Americans took their part in the war effort seriously. By 1944, the citizens rallied for victory, pulled together, and the mood in the country was to win the war. The May 15, 1944, issue of *Life* magazine advertised various products and encouraged people with a popular motto "Back the Attack! Buy War Bonds."

A unity of purpose prevailed. Patriotism was in high gear.

In his book *Bomben auf Wiener Neustadt*, Markus Reisner, translated, wrote, "The weather on 10 May 1944 in the region around Vienna was ideal. Around 7:30 a.m., two P-38s of the Fifteenth Air Force flew a weather recon over southern Austria. The weather all along the flight path and the whole airspace around Wiener Neustadt promised to be perfect. The attack of the four-engine bombers on Wiener Neustadt could therefore proceed."

Wave after wave of American bombers from Italy—literally hundreds and hundreds of them—crossed the border into Austria and roared toward their target of the heavily defended Wiener Neustadt, about thirty miles northeast of Augustin Stranz's school.

Subsequently, bombs exploded. Clouds of thick smoke rose from the battered city. Any schoolboy standing on the hillside near the air raid shelter distinctly heard the booming antiaircraft guns blasting away in the distance. The blue sky blackened with smoke puffs from exploding, deadly flak.

"They were witnessing one of the biggest air battles yet to take place in the skies over Austria," Markus told us.

After the B-17s and B-24s came off their target, the German fighters, called "hunters," retaliated. They swarmed the four-engine bombers, and bomber guns blazed as the ten-man crews fought for their survival. Tantalizingly close to completing their mission, the crews pushed toward Italy, protected, too, by a defensive barrage of .50 caliber rounds fired from machine guns in other bombers of the formation—if they could stay in formation.

In order to protect their bomber formations, friendly fighter escorts swooped in and cut loose on the "hunters." The flight path for the bomber stream, going back "home" to Italy, took them near the towns of those young schoolboys. With a panoramic view of the skies, boys on the hillside were probably captivated as the swift fighters dueled it out—racing through the sky in a fierce and unrelenting dogfight.

"I saw very many American planes heading back to Italy after their incursions," Mr. Stanz said. "As children, we underestimated the danger. During the war, it was not so bad outside the city. The countryside felt safe."

Bombed cities across Europe turned out thousands of homeless civilians, starting with Warsaw, Poland, when Hitler's Luftwaffe repeatedly bombed the Polish city in the first month of World War II. As the war escalated and the raids intensified, the plight of a city's civilians worsened. As a general rule, U.S. airmen dropped bombs by day, and crews of the Royal Air Force had resorted to nighttime raids. Under the cover of darkness, tons of bombs carpeted a general area or city where vital facilities were probably located. But civilians paid the price, too, either way.

Precision bombing wasn't nearly as sophisticated or as accurate as it is today. In World War II, the Norden bombsight was a new device to put the bombs on the target. Under ideal conditions, it worked well. Reality was that bombs usually fell on and near the designated military or industrial targets, and sometimes we defaulted to secondary targets. Although the bombs were intended for the military infrastructure, many civilians living in and near the vicinity of the cities and infrastructures suffered casualties and destruction of their homes.

Moreover, Hitler's "stranglehold" on occupied Europe and the effects of the war became unmistakably obvious. "The Germans controlled almost every aspect of life in lands under their rule, from education to employment. The media were censored. Nazi officials supervised industry and agriculture and sent much of their output back to Germany. The economies of the occupied lands were left to collapse and their people to go hungry."[1]

Growing up in Hastings during the war years, my mom, Darlene, has told me time and again about the rationing of gas, sugar, rubber, and nylon— minor inconveniences in comparison to the hardships of the Depression. And parachutes, in high demand, required nylon.

"Instead of nylons to wear," Mom said, "we glamorized our legs by applying pancake makeup with a sponge. Then, to get the fashionable look of a true nylon seam, my sister or friend drew a 'seam' line on the back of my leg with an eyebrow pencil.

"Leather was needed for servicemen's boots, so people tolerated plasticlike shoes. We only had two pairs of shoes anyway, and we were willing to do without so the soldiers had what they needed.

"Troop trains came through town when crisscrossing the country. We walked almost everywhere. Our route to school took us past the main train depot located on First Street near downtown Hastings. Servicemen waved to us from the train cars and handed us envelopes out the window, asking us to mail their letters.

"One block from the train station, we walked past the Rivoli Theatre on Second Street. The Rivoli was one of three theaters in town during the war which provided entertainment. My sister and I, for eleven cents, started at the Rivoli for the first show, and then for another eleven cents, we'd go across the street to the Cornhusker Theatre for their show. If there was a movie that we really wanted to see, we'd walk down to the Strand Theatre for a third show. And always before the regular feature, Movietone News showed footage clips of wartime news. Otherwise, we listened to the radio for news and entertainment. We didn't have televisions in our homes. Candy and gum at the movies was in short supply because it was sent to the servicemen. After the movies, though, you could get a soft drink at one of the downtown drugstores or cafés."

At one café, Mom's friend Flossie had an after-school job peeling potatoes for two hours a day and a monthly salary of two dollars.

"Down the street from the Rivoli Theatre was the Carter Hotel," Mom said. "Across the street from the hotel, there was a USO club where servicemen and locals, if you were of age, could get something to eat, socialize, and have fun at the dances. Because of segregation at the time, there was a similar but different club for black servicemen a couple blocks away on First Street.

"On Saturday nights, the downtown stores were open. We'd sit in the car with my folks on Second Street and people watch. Occasionally, we'd do some shopping, and Dad would get a haircut. It was a form of entertainment seeing all the people, especially the servicemen and airmen that were in town for the night."

And after school, Mom and her friends walked around town collecting scrap metal for the war drive—recycling isn't a modern invention. Recycled metals helped make planes and ships. "Hested's store bought old 78 rpm records for 5 cents. Service stations took rubber for a penny per pound. Meat markets bought kitchen grease, which was ultimately used in gun powder."[2]

Mom's friend Rose lived through the war years on her family's farm near Trumbull, several miles from Hastings. "I was fifteen years old when my brothers left for the war. My sister, my dad, my mom, and I struggled to do all the chores and farming. There were no men around to rent the farm to. People didn't have much, but we made do with what we had and accepted it. We didn't get to town for a month at a time; we grew our own vegetables and were self-sufficient. There was no reason to go to town. I do remember making three trips with our townspeople from nearby Trumbull to the North Platte Canteen, which was about 180 miles to the west. We probably saved our gas rations to make those trips."

During World War II, when trains moved troops across the country and passed through North Platte, Nebraska, that town's residents decided to organize and operate a canteen in their downtown train depot. The North Platte Canteen was open, free of charge, around the clock from nearly the beginning of the war until the end. The story of the Canteen is told in the book *Once Upon a Town* written by Bob Greene.

Usually, three thousand soldiers per day—some days more—were allowed off their train for a brief layover at the North Platte Canteen, and so volunteers from North Platte and hundreds more from surrounding farms and communities made that brief layover a memorable few minutes.

As volunteers, Rose and her family pitched in and did what comes naturally to midwesterners. For over four years, the volunteers nourished about six million servicemen and servicewomen with plenty of food and goodies and with plenty of genuine kindness, appreciation, and support as the young soldiers traveled to an unknown future in unknown parts of the world.

"Scrimping with our own rations," Rose recalled, "we supplied the Canteen with our own food, including homegrown chickens—cleaned and fried—hundreds of ham sandwiches made with our homemade mayonnaise, and other goodies like deviled eggs, cream, cakes, and pies. Leaving a neighbor at the farm to tend to chores, we'd depart at night for North Platte, driving forty miles per hour for five or six hours, arriving in the morning, ready to meet the trains and greet and feed the young soldiers. We'd leave North Platte in the evening to get home for chores the next morning. We didn't think a thing of it; we were glad to do it. Even though the war was far away, it was our part of the war effort. It was very rewarding."

Americans everywhere got in the act one way or another and rallied behind the troops in the home front effort—anything to keep the morale high.

On May 10, 1944, thirteen-year-old Johann Piringer lived on a farm near Pottschach-Ternitz in the Gasteil region of Austria, southwest of Wiener Neustadt, near the tiny village of Prigglitz, also in the path of the returning bomber stream. "I worked on the farm besides going to school," Johann wrote to me. "During the war, most people, except farmers, had to work in the armament industry. Farmers were self supporters and exchanged food products with other people—who didn't have as much—for things like trousers and shoes. There wasn't much to eat."

His translation continued, "On the tenth of May, it was about noon. I just wanted to have lunch, and then I heard noises from the planes and from the bomb attacks. I was getting used to the bombings."

"After they [the bombers] dropped the bombs," Markus Reisner told me, "some of those bombers tried to follow the formation, but because of the loss of one or two engines, they were not able to follow. So they became what's called a straggler."

Several planes in the bomber stream were, indeed, stragglers. The crippled bombers struggled to maintain altitude and keep up with the formation heading "home." Without protective cover from the guns of planes in their formation, the crews counted on their own fighter escorts to help fend off the enemy. Nonetheless, some smoking, fiery bombers, guns hammering away, succumbed to the assault of the German fighters.

And one doomed, fiery plane flew alarmingly close.

"Just before we entered the air raid shelter we had seen the planes from Wiener Neustadt," Augustin Stranz stated. "[One] was very low to the ground, and the pilot tried several times to get the plane higher. You could hear the engine trying to rev up; several times they tried to restart. The engines just whined, and the plane lost so much altitude that they could not fly over the mountains.

"When the plane was near, we had to enter a shelter. After a few minutes passed, the women were still standing outside the shelter. The ladies were crying when they saw the plane flying so low. They didn't think they could ever be bombed. Now the war was very near."

Johann Piringer, standing near his farm, observed, "I saw a plane turning back; the plane curved around the area. It was smoking. He lost height and flew very low to the ground.

"There were not other fighter planes trying to hit the plane, but there were German fighter planes flying around. They didn't shoot at the plane because it was burning.

"I think the pilot figured out the landing path. The pilot was too low but went up higher again and continued to fly into the forest; otherwise he would have hit the house.

"Then the plane flew into the forest, and it crashed. I started to run. At the moment the plane exploded, I was already running. I felt great pressure from the following explosion. The concussion was so strong that it nearly knocked me over."

Like a big extended backyard, Johann knew the area. He'd probably explored the forest in the peaceful little valley dozens of times. Hidden from distant mountains, the valley was protected from a war-torn world, tucked away among the rolling, wooded hillsides and framed by slightly sloped patches of farmland. The pine-scented forest air was cool under the canopy of trees. Stately pines gracefully swayed in synchronized harmony, towering over the undergrowth of spindly trees, shrubs, and scattered green ground cover mixed together with fallen pine needles and leaves. The shallow waters of a stream, hidden from view by a tangle of shrubs, rippled across smooth pebbles and meandered leisurely here and there, carelessly diverging around a random boulder. The babbling stream disappeared into unseen parts of the valley, harboring her secrets.

But that day, this peace violently vanished. The once "safe" countryside became vulnerable.

"It was awful. I was very full of fear," Johann stated.

The concussion reverberated and blasted out windows in homes nearby. The pungent smell of fuel and a smoky haze hung in the valley. Snapped like toothpicks, the once stately tall pines were shredded, and the wooded area was strewn with foreign debris. Twisted metal scattered everywhere. Large and small pieces of jagged aircraft littered the valley and forest. One tire, violently ripped from the plane by the terrific force of the explosion and thrown far from the impact area, rested in the stream—near a propeller still hanging on the engine.

The once unscathed area of nature, that peaceful valley tucked away in a hillside in Austria, now wore the scars of war. The innocent sounds of nature would return; however, the order of nature in the forest had been shattered. It would never be the same. Not only had the peaceful valley changed, but the lives of many, some living their lives thousands of miles away on another continent, had also been shattered forever—only they didn't know it yet.

As soon as Grandma wrote "her other boy," Harold, she walked to the post office just a few blocks away and then picked up some groceries at the market right around the corner. With red meat rationed, chicken was the meat of choice.

Maybe she daydreamed of getting the family together for dinner on Sunday, May 14, Mother's Day. Those dreams readily vanished with the reality that her children were hundreds and thousands of miles, even continents, away from home. Anyway, Granddad wasn't due back in Hastings until the following Wednesday.

Rubber was rationed, and tires were hard to come by, but when Granddad was back in Hastings on Wednesday, May 17, he managed to get a tire on his car fixed. Plus, he was always trying to figure out how to get enough gas to keep him on the road. He had previously written a letter to Stanley, which Stanley never received, stating, "I'm rather on the spot. With things the way they are and Ellen feeling none too hot, I'm practically grounded for the time being. But there is plenty to do at home and not enough gas to keep me on the road all the time anyway, so there are no scalding tears splashing in the sand hereabouts. I hammer this thing [typewriter] a lot and am pleased plenty with the way it percolates since it was overhauled. Use the phone some and am getting in some good licks on my collection. Incidentally, it is about to where it will start to pay off some of these days. There is a lot more to it than when you saw it. I have a few pieces that will make the boys bat their eyes like a toad in a hailstorm."

Nevertheless, after about a week at home, Granddad hit the road again to put food on the table. On May 25, he headed west to North Platte, Nebraska, and then he headed south to Kansas. He was scheduled to be out for about two weeks. Whether working at home or out on the territory, Granddad seemed to always find time to write letters to his children and other family. And always eager to get the latest news from the kids, he'd often phone Grandma while out of town to get any updates.

Grandma, no doubt, did what comes naturally to most mothers—worry. The main source of any mother's worry is usually focused on her children and family. In addition to having two sons serving in the armed forces, as well as a daughter living hundreds of miles away, Grandma had a new granddaughter, and, well, the list was getting longer. Most likely, Grandma put in a little— probably a lot—of overtime worrying. She coped, though. Potluck dinners, garden club meetings, and playing cards, where she compared notes with other mothers whose sons were off to war, provided a source of comfort and support.

The local newspaper, the *Hastings Daily Tribune*, covered war news daily. Undoubtedly, Grandma noted the front page Signal Corps radio-telephoto and caption which ran on Monday, May 15, 1944. "Two B-17 crew member (arrows) are shown 'hitting the silk' over Wiener Neustadt after their ship was hit by flak while bombing the aircraft assembly plant on May 10. Shortly after the picture was made, the rest of the crew bailed out and the ship exploded."

Other newspaper coverage told of the impending "secret" invasion—what we know now as D-Day. As stressful and unsettling as it had to be, maybe that information left Grandma hopeful and cautiously optimistic as she anticipated the end of the war, dreaming of the day when her sons would return home, walk through her front door, and sit at her kitchen table.

We'll never know exactly how it happened. It was Saturday evening, May 27, 1944, two days after Granddad had departed. We presumed some young boy—dressed in the standard uniform pants with a belt and tucked-in shirt, dark tie, and the chosen uniform hat—came out of the Western Union office located down on Second Street in Hastings next to the Carter Hotel and hopped on his bike. He probably held several telegrams. Perhaps the first one to be delivered was addressed to 906 West Sixth Street. He biked through town, crossing intersection after intersection, and arrived at the duplex house located on the north side of Sixth Street. He probably compared the address on the house with the one on the telegram. The sweet smell of lilacs saturated the air as he walked up the sidewalk. A small banner with two blue stars was displayed in the window, representing family members serving in the armed forces. He knocked on the door. Surely Grandma greeted him and confirmed she was the telegram's recipient, Mrs. Ellen J. Dwyer. She occasionally received telegrams. Grandma closed the door, opened the envelope, and read:

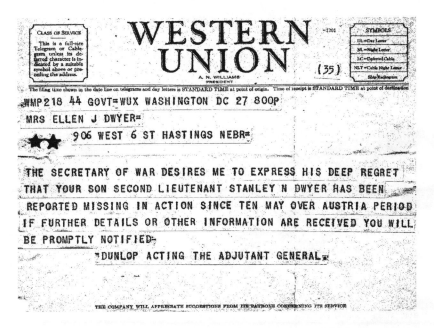

WMP218 44 GOVT=WUX WASHINGTON DC 27 800P

MRS ELLEN J DWYER=

906 WEST 6 ST HASTINGS NEBR=

THE SECRETARY OF WAR DESIRES ME TO EXPRESS HIS DEEP REGRET THAT YOUR SON SECOND LIEUTENANT STANLEY N DWYER HAS BEEN REPORTED MISSING IN ACTION SINCE TEN MAY OVER AUSTRIA PERIOD IF FURTHER DETAILS OR OTHER INFORMATION ARE RECEIVED YOU WILL BE PROMPTLY NOTIFIED=

DUNLOP ACTING THE ADJUTANT GENERAL=

"If further details or other information are received, you will be promptly notified." That was something to go on. We had a little crutch. Stan, my brother, was missing in action instead of killed in action, so that helped a little too. Of course, Mother hung on to that quite a bit, that glimmer of hope, a hope that would last her lifetime. Houses all over town had blue stars displayed in their windows. It was not known yet if she would have to change one of her blue stars in the window to a gold star, which would signify that she had lost a family member in the service.

What began as an ordinary day in May became more than just another spring day for my grandparents and the Dwyer family. Wednesday, May 10, 1944, a defining day, changed their lives and the lives of others forever. A nightmare came true; their world nearly stopped. Yet days turned into weeks and then months. Summer came and went. The seasons cycled. Year after year, for decades, May 10 had come and gone, and as strange as it may seem, I never knew the heartache connected to that date. All of that was about to change.

1

ᴄᴍ

The Beginning of a Journey

Everything here is lovely. Have no complaints to make.
—Stanley N. Dwyer from a V-Mail dated April 8, 1944

Etched in the recesses of my mind is the image of Dad standing in the kitchen at my home in Geneva, Nebraska. It was springtime 1998. All five feet ten inches of him stood between the end of the work island and kitchen table, and he wore cowboy boots. He studied the white piece of paper that he held in his rough hands. He glanced up and asked me, "Is there any way we can figure out the name of the crash site from May 10, 1944?"

From that point, it's vague. Maybe I looked over his arm to see what he was reading or else Dad handed the page to me.

I kind of remember the day. In Air Force Magazine *that I subscribe to, I must have read about Missing Air Crew Reports and the government releasing military information. Around 1990, I sent for MACR 4660, the report associated with my brother's crash. The report came to me in the form of microfiche film. Anyway, I took the microfiche to the library, which had a machine to blow them up so they were readable. Some of the information was not too clear. I had put this information in one of my files.*

Some of the words on the page from MACR 4660 (see Appendix A), Missing Air Crew Report 4660, were legible, and other words, especially the location of the crash site in Austria, were squished black letters trying to spell something important. We deciphered what appeared to be an *-of* at the end of the word, but who knew? I thought, *Well, let's grab the* A *encyclopedia off the bookshelf.* I flipped to a map of Austria—no luck. The map lacked detail.

Up to that day, I had only heard Dad mention his brother, Stanley, a few times. Dad once told me, when I was a young girl and complaining about

16

the natural red highlight in my hair, that Stanley had reddish hair, and his was a little curly. Stanley played the soprano saxophone, I knew, because the instrument case accumulated dust in Mom and Dad's closet until I asked about it and got it refurbished for my daughters—both alto saxophone players—to play. Somewhere along the line, Dad had commented that his brother had attended Kansas State College, and I was aware that Stanley was a B-17 pilot in World War II as Dad had been—but Stanley's plane crashed, and his remains were never found. In fact, when my older sister, Jan, and I were young girls, Dad reprimanded us, saying, "Never say, 'Hotsy, totsy, I'm a Nazi' around Grandma." But we didn't understand.

What happened to Stan had always been in the back of my mind. In the early years, we didn't know where to go or who to talk to.

As I recall, the reason Dad inquired about the crash site that particular day was because one of his grandsons, Chris, my nephew, and some of Chris's college buddies were headed to Europe over summer break to do some backpacking. Dad's thought process, I speculated, was that just maybe, if the boys went to Austria knowing the location of the crash site, they could nose around. As it turned out, the college boys' backpacking adventure bypassed Austria. Besides, I doubt Dad even mentioned anything to Chris.

Nonetheless, Dad's one question set in motion the journey we didn't know we were about to begin. Quirky things began to happen that we could have never planned. We now recognize that some things happened for a reason because of (a) timing, (b) chance or coincidence, (c) the choices we made, (d) divine inspiration, or (e) all of the above. In our case, the answer was (e), with a strong emphasis on answer (d).

Now, with a rearview mirror perspective, it's reasonable to think that we were led on this journey—and sometimes, it seemed, pulled and prodded along. At first, we didn't associate the connection between random events, but after a long while, it became apparent how unsolicited coincidences guided our search. Riddled with many coincidences, it seemed God initiated our unique journey, and like a knee-jerk reaction, we responded.

Soon after Dad asked that one question, I copied the page from the MACR at 50 and 75 percent zoom, and I even enlarged it 100 percent, examining it from every angle, trying to figure out that word. Time passed, and I set the page aside until one evening when my husband, Rick, and I entertained our friends Jeff and Helen Johnson. No one remembers how the conversation turned to the MACR page and the task of deciphering the illegible crash site town in Austria, but Jeff remarked, "I have a new home computer at my house with a great mapping system. Let's go see what we can pull up."

The mapping system on Jeff's computer was state-of-the-art for 1998—Microsoft Encarta Virtual Globe 1998 Edition. In 1998, the Internet was archaic compared to today. If MapQuest even existed, it was in its infancy.

Jeff and I were hunched over his computer desk. We squinted at the screen and studied a detailed map of Austria (see Appendix B). Other information from the MACR page indicated that three dead crewmen were recovered from the crash site and buried on May 14, 1944, in a community cemetery near Pottschach; that town's name was legible. We made a fair assumption. If we pinpointed Pottschach, surely the crash site location would be nearby. The -*of* ending of the place of impact offered our only clue. There on the map of Austria was Vienna, along with many, many names of places we could not even pronounce. We scanned the screen.

"Right here," one of us exclaimed, pointing to Pottschach.

Moving closer to the screen, we zeroed in on the center of the colored map of Austria. Close to Pottschach was a town named Vostenhof.

"Is that it?" I asked.

Then we could somewhat decipher what the black, squished letters spelled, and it seemed to fit and to make sense. We thought the line from the MACR read "Place of impact: 2 km SW of Vostenhof." Not until years later did we realized what a feat it was to stumble across *that* particular map and locate tiny little Vostenhof. Most of our accumulated maps—AAA Motor Club maps along with other road maps of Austria and even maps of Austria from Austria—do not list Vostenhof; it's too small. Vostenhof consists of a landmark castle and a couple of farms.

Essentially a door to the past had been unlocked. But Dad and I hadn't really contemplated our next move. What did happen was not on our to-do list, but it certainly breathed life into our search.

In the summer of 1998, Rick's cousin Dave Hughes, Dave's wife, Jane, and their five children drove through Nebraska from their home in Michigan to a summer vacation destination in Colorado. A dozen or so years had slipped by since we'd last seen Dave. His family's stay gave all of us a few days to catch up on everyone's lives. Previously, Dave and his family had lived in France, near the French-German border. During their stay in Geneva, we learned about their adventures and experiences living in France and more about Germany's history and World War II. So naturally, we showed Dave and Jane our computer version color map of Austria along with the page of the Missing Air Crew Report, sharing what little information we knew about the May 10, 1944, crash near Vostenhof, Austria.

Dave studied the papers, pointed to a city on the map, and added his thoughts. "I was an exchange student in Graz, Austria, when I was in high school, and I still know some people there. Oh, I also have a friend named Martin who lives near Vienna. If I may, let me take this information, and I'll ask Martin if he can do some research to find out any more details concerning this crash."

The next day, after we'd said our good-byes to the Michigan Hughes family, I reported what had transpired to Dad and Mom. Uncertain if Dave's offer would lead to anything and not wanting to get my hopes up, it was business as usual. Nevertheless, thoughts of Austria lingered in the back of my mind.

By then, the Rick Hughes family was up to speed with the Internet, but Mom and Dad had yet to enter cyberspace—that would happen sooner rather than later. And the Internet became a vital part of our search and journey. Often, an Internet search furnished a crucial link to help uncover and retrieve valuable information. If I surfed long enough, information I didn't even know existed was available at my fingertips. Communication and "conversations" with people all over the world became instantaneous.

So on September 22, 1998, one day before Dad's seventy-fourth birthday, those lingering thoughts of Austria in the back of my mind were tweaked. An e-mail from Dave Hughes (correspondence, including letters and e-mails, may be lightly edited) read:

Dear Rick and Kay,
Good news! The attached message is from my friend in Europe, and he has made good progress as you can read. Please consider what you'd like to do next, and let me know. Sounds like if you want to go there directly, there is someone interested to help and take you right to the site. You could also probably get in direct contact with them by e-mail or regular mail. They probably at least read English.

We're standing by to help. Just let us know.
Dave

And the attachment from Dave's friend from Vienna read:

Dear Dave,
My research has yielded the following. Indeed a plane crashed in the place and on the date indicated. The four people in it were:

- Francis Gillooly
- Peter Prescott
- William Olfins
- Stanley Dwyer

Do any of these names ring a bell? The first three were buried right in the neighbouring town and in '45 got exhumed, either to be taken to the U.S. or to the large U.S. forces cemetery on the German-French border. To find out more about their whereabouts, people recommend the U.S. Embassy in Vienna or some U.S. agency dealing with that kind of stuff.

Dwyer, the pilot, was never found since a bomb exploded with the plane, so people guess he just burnt to a crisp.

The place of the crash is known to the local historian (his grand-dad showed it to him when he was a kid), and he would be happy to meet an American who wanted to see the site and the town.

Let me know where to take this from here. I am sure we could arrange accommodations somewhere nearby and maybe even an uncle of mine to take them there and do a bit of translation.

I hope this helps
In Christ
Martin

PS: Speaking of history and dealing with it, I am off to see Auschwitz today.

Immediately, I called Mom and Dad, and with each of them on a phone extension, I read them the e-mail. I choked through the part about "burnt to a crisp."

"Take it easy," Dad said.

Well, up to then, I had never given any of it much thought. The whole scenario was new to me, and I chose to put out of my mind the consequences of a certain piece of information on the MACR. The line read, "Condition of airplane: 100% destroyed – (Plane detonated on impact with complete bomb load.)"

In fact, I knew nothing about May 10, 1944. *Nobody* ever talked about it, and it never occurred to me to question. I reflected back to my childhood growing up in Hastings and the memories of special times spent with my grandparents, Ellen and Harold W. Dwyer. However, in all those years, I never once heard them talk about Stanley, mention his name, or make any references to May 10, 1944.

I've had over sixty years to ponder my brother's fate. I really don't know why Stan's name never came up in all the years after the war. I don't recall it being mentioned in family conversations or extended family get-togethers. Perhaps it was and I have forgotten. My dad, being a military man himself, had probably come to terms with what happens in war. Mom, on the other hand, would not have been as prepared. It was probably hard on the folks, especially Mom. She never exposed her feelings much—at least I never saw her angry or cuss somebody out. The strongest word she used was "Oh, Kippee." She hid her thoughts way down deep and didn't want anyone looking in. Whether they talked about it when there was nobody around, I do not know.

I was beginning to understand that what happened to Stanley, as well as the events surrounding Stanley's disappearance, were decades-old, unanswered questions. And I assumed that my grandparents didn't know the location of Stanley's crash site.

However, we had a lead, and the question then was what to do next. Mom and Dad weren't wild about international travel—and, well, Rick and I thought maybe it would be beneficial if, with metal detector in hand, we went to the crash site, inquired, and snapped some photos. Rick, from the beginning of this journey, was just as interested in our family venture as if it were his own family. His support has been invaluable. He's the rock I leaned on.

But the question of what to do next wasn't the only question we contemplated. The e-mail from Martin in Austria had stirred up more probable questions, so we started a list. Once again, we turned to Dave for help. We e-mailed our list to Dave, who forwarded it to Martin.

On Sunday, October 18, 1998, I received an e-mail from David Hughes:

> Dear Rick and Kay,
> Thanks for your e-mail. I was out of the country so am a little tardy in getting back to you. Attached is a message from my friend [Martin] that answers most of your questions. Sounds like the best thing to do is pick a date and see if Martin's uncle is available. They are truly willing to help and would enjoy meeting you all. Since the local historian doesn't speak English, local translation is key.

The message from Martin Steinbereithner read:

> RE: Downed plane

Dave,
Happy to serve.

The names came from the records they have in the village archives, but they do not know how those records got there.

The historian does not have e-mail and does not speak English. However, my uncle and aunt would be very happy to help; so if your relatives came, I am sure my uncle would be happy to take them there and do the translating. The place is about 1.5 – 2 hours away from the Vienna airport. If they came, I would suggest getting a room in Wiener Neustadt, which my uncle would be happy to dig up, so they can spend a leisurely day doing it and maybe seeing some other things in the area. If we knew ahead of time (three months notice or so), we could time it so my uncle and aunt are there and not traveling (they are retired) when they come.

Let me know what you want me to do next.
God bless
Martin

We considered visiting Austria in the spring of 1999, since spring, Dave mentioned, was the best time to travel to Austria for our type of trip. But definite decisions pended. Feet were dragging. And sometimes, not to make a decision is your decision. Even if we had decided on an itinerary, a trip would have been put on hold. Something else happened that gave us the momentum to continue our search.

In the early part of February 1999, at about midnight, I was awakened by some strange noise. Darlene, my wife, was in Geneva babysitting some of the grandkids. I thought the noise was the garage doorbell, so I slipped on my pants and headed for the back door. As I looked out, I could see flames in the upper corner of the house and garage. I ran out the back door to see if I could turn on the hose. Frozen. Back to the phone. I had tried to turn the kitchen light on, and it didn't come on, so I had to feel the phone to dial 911. I told the operator the address and said "house on fire" and hung up. I'm not sure what happened next, but I was out front when the fire department arrived. For some reason, they couldn't get any water out of the fire hydrant directly across the street. After about ten minutes, they got something going. I can say that we lit up the north end of town pretty good. After about another ten minutes, all the neighbors gathered around, and my neighbor Pat Michaels handed me a pair of shoes. I had been walking around in the snow without realizing that it was cold. A few minutes later, a different neighbor handed me a coat. My chest was bare, and I hadn't even noticed. We all stood there and watched as about thirty-six firefighters went to work to put out the fire.

The house fire Dad and Mom endured destroyed a good share of the physical structure of their forty-year residence; however, it did not destroy family photos and memorabilia or their unwavering spirit. After sorting through and cleaning up what was salvageable in that stinky, charred, war-zonelike mess, Mom and Dad, true to their characters, and together with friends and family pitching in, spent a good year or more rebuilding their home. And looking back, one unique upside to that unfortunate event was what we found in the process.

Some of our things in the basement didn't get burned, but some of it was wet or damp. One day, I asked Kay to go through some of the trunks down in the basement and set the stuff out so it could dry.

Several trunks were stored in the basement. They'd been in the basement for decades. As a kid, I'd played Barbie dolls and school down there and never paid any attention to or was inquisitive about the trunks.

Up from the basement came a big, dark brown leather trunk held together with tattered leather straps. Stanley's heavy, suitcaselike trunk was plopped down on a table in the closed-in porch attached to the house—one of the few rooms not damaged by smoke or fire in what was left of my childhood home.

Stanley's trunk didn't look like a treasure chest, but it was a collection of a lifetime of memorabilia. Who would have known that, when his trunk was opened, we naively had walked through a door leading to the past? Already unlocked, the door opened wide, and we entered.

As I started to finger through the contents, it struck me. *This is what's left of Stanley's life, all jam-packed into this trunk, and that's it?* He was Dad's forever twenty-seven-year-old brother, a part of our family, the uncle I never knew and hardly knew anything about ... and that was all there was—all that remained of a man's life?

Stashed in the trunk were piles of papers—hundreds of pages of school assignments, exams, and class notes, especially from college. The tell-all report cards fell out from between the stacks of papers. Both high school and college graduation announcements were mixed in with the mass of papers. Copies of the *Mirror* and newspapers titled the *Kansas State Collegian* and the *Kansas Industrialist* had been saved.

Stanley dabbled in writing music lyrics, and he scribbled his ideas on all kinds of paper and envelopes. Along with several pieces of sheet music, proof he'd seriously considered getting his songs published, there were pencil sketches rolled up in a cardboard tube. A single hardbound book, *King's Log*, listed Stanley as editor.

There were baseballs, golf balls, golf score cards, playing cards, bus and train ticket stubs, theater ticket stubs and programs, Ban Johnson League ticket stubs, watches, shaving items, the stamp collection he started as a young teen, and old leather wallets. A 1941 Nebraska driver's license listed Stanley N. Dwyer as five feet eleven inches tall, 150 pounds, brown hair, and gray eyes.

Grandma and Granddad had clipped newspaper articles that told about their son playing baseball, basketball, and showing his 4-H livestock. They even saved the *Hastings Daily Tribune* article announcing to the world that their son, 2nd Lt. Stanley N. Dwyer, was missing in action. Every bit revealed a little more of Stanley's life. Digging deeper, I found saved birthday greetings, Christmas cards, Valentine wishes, and one Mother's Day greeting card signed, "Lt. Stanley N. Dwyer." The card was the kind attached to a delivered bouquet of flowers. There were small bars of soap—still wrapped—from the Hotel Strand in New York City, matchbooks from Jack Dempsey's Café and Restaurant, dozens of business cards, and a dollar bill with several signatures on it—a "short snorter." Other travel memorabilia included a pocket-sized, fold-up map of Shanghai, postcards from around the world, broken starfish, and silk souvenirs from lands far away. Inside one leather binder was a photo portrait signed, "To Stan, with love, Retta." Dad walked through the room to add a log to the wood-burning stove right when I held up another photo of a pretty girl.

It was a picture of Stan's girlfriend from college; Beatrice King was her name. They called her Bea, and she sure was a pretty girl.

Plenty of photos had frozen a moment in time—tangible evidence of places Stanley had visited and unidentified people who all touched Stanley's life in one way or another.

One day as I examined items in the trunk, I discovered the framed blue star Grandma had hung in her window and then another small banner that displayed two blue stars for two sons serving in the armed forces. I never found a gold star. A small box packed down near the bottom of the trunk contained Stanley's Air Medal, earned after flying five missions, along with the added clusters, each awarded after flying an additional five more missions. Inside another rectangular, black box—hinged at the back of the narrow side like a necklace box—was the Purple Heart, awarded

24

posthumously, along with the accompanying certificate signed by President Harry Truman.

Underneath everything else, carefully folded in a tissue-lined shirt box, was a blue baby blanket with scalloped edges and adorned with white chicks.

Somehow I sensed that that initial job of spreading the trunk's contents out to dry was just the beginning. In fact, that effort merely scratched the surface. For months, I drove back and forth from Geneva to Hastings, a one-hundred-mile round-trip, to help clean up, spending days sorting through Stanley's trunk. On the drive back to Geneva, I pondered, reflected, and thought about what I'd uncovered and learned. I shared my new discoveries with Rick, and I needed a shoulder to cry on.

I was sorry and sad that Stanley's life had ended at such a young age, yet I couldn't change what happened. What was he like? Where did the stuff in the trunk come from? What did those things tell about his life? Furthermore, I thought of Grandma and Granddad and couldn't even begin to comprehend their heartache, their devastating loss, their unanswered questions, and their grief packing away their son's lifetime belongings. They must have held on to everything: his belongings, the memories, and hope. At that point in their lives, wasn't that all that they had—hope? It seems it would have been impossible for them to have thrown anything of Stanley's away. Their son was missing, so in their anguish, did closing the trunk with his cherished memorabilia represent a type of closure for them? Memories and emotions weren't as easily packed away. But they never talked about Stanley.

"For your grandparents, it's possible that if they didn't talk about it, then they didn't have to admit it," a mortician friend, P. R. Farmer, explained.

And what about Dad and Aunt Aileen?

I almost dreaded going back to the porch and the chore at hand. I dreaded the feelings and emotions that were stirred up, but my sorrow only paled in comparison to what must have been a roller coaster of emotions Granddad and Grandma and the rest of the family wrestled with—a roller coaster that slows down but never completely stops. *And*, I thought, *when there are no remains to bury, what does that do to the mind? Is there ever closure?*

I had this compelling yet futile urge to rewrite history.

Nevertheless, the trunk was open; I was caught up in it. There was more to discover, and there was no turning back. So, I returned to the porch where I continued to sort through Stanley's life. One day, Mom got drawn in more than usual.

"Kay, during those years, it was not uncommon to know someone in town who had lost a family member in the war," Mom said. "Many families were touched with tragedy. Thousands of young men experienced the same fate as Stanley."

Then I removed from the trunk a stack of eight, smoke-tinged airmail envelopes postmarked with a three-cent "Win the War" stamp and bound together with a crusty rubber band. I showed the stack to Mom about the time Dad poked his nose into the warm room.

Those letters caused quite a stir for the folks. Every day, the folks watched for the mailman, and one day, they saw him put a stack of letters in the mailbox. Boy, their hopes went sky high. They got out to the mailbox and found it was all of their letters they had written and sent to Stan since he had been shot down. That stack of envelopes was all their letters that had been returned. What a huge disappointment for them.

Mom and I carefully examined the envelopes and read "Missing" scrawled next to the small, postal-stamped image of a hand with index finger pointing to the return address and the stamped words "Returned to Writer." Overcome with curiosity, we stood side by side and carefully slit open the still-sealed envelopes. I bit my lip and blinked hard. We sniffled as we read my Grandma's letter written after May 10, 1944.

Hastings—May 14, 1944
Mother's Day

Dear Stanley:

If you would step into my house right now, you would smell some scrumptious roses. They are beauties, and the smell matches their looks. That is some service that they are giving the boys, isn't it? All they have to do is put in their orders, and presto! There they are at the right time and right place. I do thank you a lot for them. I'm alone today, so I get quite a lift out of first looking at them and then at your picture.

Spring arrived here with a bang three days ago, and now, instead of freezing, we are smothering. I guess mostly because we are all soft and can't take it. I think we are all enjoying it for the sun feels good. And we are still getting rain every day and plenty of it. We already have had better than thirteen inches since February. I wish it would string out a little instead of coming in bunches.

The repairman came yesterday afternoon and fixed the refrigerator, for which I am very grateful. After a person gets used to one of those things, it is plenty hard to do without them. Everything was fine until it turned warm, and then it was something else again. I have been drinking so much milk since I haven't felt so good that I felt pretty forlorn after it turned hot. You can't buy it in pints anymore, and a quart is quite a lot for one person to get away with.

How is everything with you? I suspect that you have been doing quite a bit of flying here lately. Haven't had a letter from you since I came home, but I can imagine the reason by listening to the radio or reading the papers. I haven't had a letter from Harold, either, since the first of the week. I did have a big Mother's Day card from him Friday. I wouldn't be surprised if he has tried to call today, but I suspect it is almost impossible to get thru. Your pop called from Beloit this morning and wanted to know if we had heard from either of the sons. He was going on west, and I suppose he will be gone all week. He tried to call last night, but I was gone. Was invited out to a potluck supper, and then we played five hundred. It's been so long since I've played that game that it took quite a while for me to get started. I had a pretty fair time and didn't get home until midnight.

Had a card, handkerchief, and note from Aileen yesterday. Carol Jean isn't settling down like I was in hopes she would. Aileen will have her hands full for a while, and it will be good for her as it will give her something else to think about besides her own aches and pains. I may go back sometime this summer and help her out if Carol doesn't get to feeling any happier about things.

Remember the lilac bushes around the back of the yard? If they don't get nipped by frost, some of these days they are going to have a lot of blossoms on them. They are just full of buds. Last year they didn't have but very few and then they were frozen back. I hope they bloom for I love lilacs.

I would have gone to a show today if I had been sure Harold wasn't going to call. Pretty soon I am going to walk down and get a bottle of milk. That will be my Sunday walk.

I have felt quite a bit better the last three days. More like myself than for some time. In fact for several months. Haven't gained much in weight yet, but the way I'm eating now, it won't be long.

Right now would be a good time for you to come home on a leave. I've done a lot of figuring on how to get these walls washed. They need it badly, but it is too much for me, and it is impossible to get that kind of work done in a place like this. And I'm sure you would get a whale of a kick out of it. Harold E. washed the woodwork for me last spring. Do you remember washing the kitchen walls in Manhattan? It makes so much difference in the looks of things when they can be clean. In fact, it is right down discouraging to clean house and have to leave them the way they are.

In about fifteen minutes, I am going to listen to Drew Pearson. He is one commentator that isn't afraid to say what he thinks. Do you get to listen to any programs, or do you even have a radio? Oh, yes, if you are here in the morning, too, I'll let you help me wash.

The pictures we took in Tucson weren't any good. We forgot how really bright the sun is down in that country, so consequently, we had too much of it.

Much love, and heaps of good luck,
Mother

I gently refolded the letter, inserted it back in the envelope, and wiped my cheeks.

That letter was one of literally hundreds of letters uncovered in Stanley's trunk. There was correspondence to Stanley from friends and family, and there were letters from Stanley's crewmen's next of kin to Granddad and Grandma and letters Stanley had written to others, which the recipients eventually forwarded to Granddad and Grandma. And then the frosting on the cake—loose piles of Stanley's handwritten and typed letters to his folks. Grandma and Granddad had saved their son's letters—and what a treasure of memories. Many items packed away in his trunk hinted at what Stanley did; however, those cherished letters revealed Stanley the person.

And there was a wealth of information in those letters. Not until I delved into the trunk and thoroughly read and reread everything, which required time—actually years—did we appreciate their value. Like a telephoto lens on a camera, those three hundred letters zoomed in on details of Stanley's life. The essence of Stanley's character was imparted as he wrote, not only about events in his life, but also about his thoughts and feelings.

Prior to the fire, I was aware that there were a lot of letters from Stan in his trunk in the basement. However, I had never taken the time to dig into the pile to see what information they had in them.

Therefore, our unplanned journey continued to unfold. Prior to the revelations gained from Stanley's trunk, we focused on learning what we could about the May 10, 1944, mission and what happened to Stanley. Opening the trunk set in place a transformation. It was unthinkable to simply close his trunk, ignore it without another thought, walk away from the past, and get on with life. I was intrigued and inspired. Something deep inside me had been sparked and gripped my being. Energized, there was a wonderment to know everything possible about Stanley, the uncle I never knew, and a curiosity about his life and his place in history. My dad, too, felt a need to know more.

When I was growing up, I was just a kid with an older brother. I was only fourteen when my brother, Stan, left home, so I didn't have the opportunity to know him as a man.

Our search continued with a new fervor. Besides wanting to know what happened on May 10, 1944, our search embodied a deep desire to know Stanley as a person and a man. Who was our unforgotten hero?

2

⌒*⌒*⌒

Growing Up in Kansas

There were 100 men for every job every other place I've been.
—Stanley N. Dwyer from a letter dated June 14, 1938

After the contents of Stanley's trunk were dry, his trunk was put back on the shelf in Mom and Dad's basement—but not shelved permanently. Silently, I promised myself in 1999 to sort through it and make some sense of everything. I'd like to say that I started right away. Realistically, I've been digging through the trunk off and on for nearly a decade in an attempt to understand all the connections and piece together Stanley's life and the events of May 10, 1944, and their aftermath.

So in the years following their house fire, after Mom and Dad rebuilt their home and were once again settled, I sat in their family room and removed items from the trunk. Again I wondered how in the world I would ever figure everything out. I spread piles across card tables, coffee tables, chairs, the sofa, and the floor and categorized the memorabilia. The smell of smoke lingered on the papers. My hands felt gritty and were blackened from soot residue. Occasionally, Dad would join me. Different items triggered different emotions, along with hundreds of questions. Although Dad answered what he could, I wondered, *Who else would have known Stanley and could tell of events in his life?* I uncovered clues about friends and crewmen in the trunk, but the obvious and immediate resource was family. Clearly, no one was getting younger. Time was running short to find and talk to aging friends and even visit with family.

Dad had never talked much about Stanley, and come to find out—and not surprisingly—neither had Aunt Aileen, Stanley and Dad's older sister. An interview would broach unspoken territory, yet the idea was readily approved. Yet we procrastinated. After talking about it for a couple of years, I interviewed Dad and Aunt Aileen.

Five of us gathered in the small living room of Aunt Aileen's apartment in Denver, Colorado. My cousin Mary Ellen, Aunt Aileen's youngest daughter, opened a folding chair and sat next to Mom. A couple of years before the interview, Mary Ellen, along with her daughters, Karena and Sherry, had made their own fascinating discovery when they stumbled onto some old boxes in the basement of Aunt Aileen's house in Denver. The boxes, with still more letters and memorabilia, were another link to our family history and Stanley. And prior to their discovery, Karena and Sherry were also unacquainted with their great-uncle Stanley.

Mom smiled at Mary Ellen and said something. They laughed. Mom's unending support and encouragement were vital for that interview and many other aspects of research and the journey. Her memory is nearly impeccable. When it came to Dwyer family history, Mom remembered details others had forgotten, and she went the extra mile by contacting Dad's cousins for additional information and photos. She made the arrangements for the interview. I could count on Mom; she always followed through.

Even though she was tiny, Aunt Aileen's hunched frame sank into the soft sofa cushion as she peered over her glasses, looked at everyone, and smiled. She primped her hair and then alternated the positioning of her arms—either they were folded across her chest or relaxed by her sides. Sometimes, she clasped her smooth, ivory-skinned hands together in her lap.

Dad, arms folded across his chest, too, sat on another folding chair in front of the picture window. The rugged Rocky Mountains were visible behind him, the backdrop for that summer session. Then Dad leaned back in the chair. It squeaked. He crossed his legs and clasped his hands behind his head, elbows bent and pointed forward to frame his head.

I sat to Dad's left, Mom and Mary Ellen's right, and across from Aunt Aileen. The television was perched on a stand behind me. A colorful painting of a columbine flower hung on the wall above the television. The artist, Aunt Aileen, had captured the beauty of the delicate blue and white state flower of Colorado.

Aunt Aileen and Dad reminisced, remembering what they could of days gone past. Decades of living had clouded their memories; however, some memories were recalled as if they had happened just yesterday. Occasionally, Dad or Aunt Aileen remarked, "I didn't know that." They laughed as each enlightened the other with a tidbit of "new" information. We learned how their lives were intertwined, and we began to retrace Stanley's footsteps.

Stanley Naismeth Dwyer was born on Thursday, October 26, 1916. That date is easy for me to remember. My birth date was October 25, and then I associate twenty-*six* and *six*teen. Stanley was born near Asherville, Kansas, and Granddad wrote in a letter, "arriving 'out of the Nowhere into the Here' some thirty minutes before I could make it from Salina to Simpson and on out to the farm." We presumed that was the family homestead—the same place Granddad, Harold Winfield Dwyer, was born back on April 4, 1887.

Before Granddad was born, his ancestors had moved from Kentucky and homesteaded near Asherville, in Mitchell County, Kansas, and that was where Granddad grew up with his father, Eugene Kincaid "Kinny" Dwyer, his mother, Elizabeth, and two younger sisters, Pearl and Myrtle. Granddad was a Kansas boy at heart. In north-central Kansas, small, rural communities were and remain scattered eight, ten, or twenty miles apart, sustained mostly by agriculture. There, gently rolling hills and endless prairie cover the landscape.

"As one becomes acquainted, he learns to love the plains and its distant views and silent nights and the ever changing expression on the face of the sky," Granddad wrote about Kansas in his book *Uphill and Against the Wind*. "He thrills at the grandeur of prairie sunsets, and understands the whispering of the breezes thru the grass."

"Dad thought Kansas was heaven," Aunt Aileen said as she shook her head. "We didn't have air-conditioning then. The summers were hot, and then the winters were cold. I didn't fancy that.

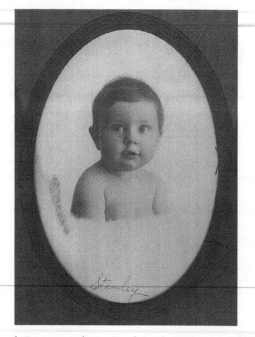

Stanley Naismeth Dwyer was born October 26, 1916, near Asherville, Kansas.

"Dad had an army friend by the name of Stanley. That's where my brother's first name came from. He was also named after Dr. James Naismith, the man credited with inventing basketball, a coach and teacher at Kansas University at Lawrence, Kansas."

Basketball, football, and baseball were favorite pastimes in the early 1900s. Granddad once told me that it was second nature for him to run down the railroad tracks to a nearby town, at least a five-mile jaunt, *just* so he could play basketball with his friends. And then he ran back home.

But basketball wasn't just for boys. A young lady by the name of Ellen Josephine Cristman had moved with her family from Iowa to the very small village of Scottsville, Kansas, a short distance—well, ten or so miles—northeast of Asherville. Born in Lorimor, Iowa, on October 13, 1894, Ellen was a young girl when her father, Frank, moved the family to Kansas where he worked in a mercantile store. Her mother, Jenny, tended their home and raised seven children: Ira, Clarence, Elizabeth, Gertie, Gayle, Ellen, and Claude. Ellen was left-handed, and she could play basketball. Harold W., several years older than Ellen, had graduated eighth grade, which was a milestone in those times. He attended high school and the Normal Institute in Beloit. As a young man, he taught school for a few years without a teaching degree, which was standard procedure in the "olden days." It was during those times that he refereed, as well as coached basketball, including the girls' basketball team from Scottsville. In his book *Uphill and Against the Wind,* published in 1963, Granddad wrote a story called "Friday the 13th."

Tonight I have been thinking of my first wife. A notice in the paper of a game at the field house, and mention of basketball, started the trend of thought in her direction.

Back in the dim and hoary, athletics in the smaller schools was not as well organized as it now is. There were no palatial gymnasiums with showers and lockers and heating systems. Much of the basketball was still being played out of doors, and no one thought of a shower after one of those games. There were no cozy buses to whisk the teams to far-off places for games, and bring them back the same night. Transportation then was mostly by horsepower—real 4-legged horsepower—or by train if the rails happened to run in the right direction. On basketball trips, more often than not one changed clothes in an unheated area and shivered into suits still damp or wet from the exertion the night before. More fun!

As a student in a small town high school and a member of the team, I found myself also coach of the girls' team. Girls played a lot of basketball in those days, and did it well. One day I accompanied that team to a town some twenty miles away via horse-drawn surrey. I was to officiate the game that night, and on the trip was substitute driver of one of the livery teams as well.

It is a matter of history that in due time we did arrive at the town, and that the game was played that night as scheduled. I recall that game was won, too.

It had been a long trip for that kind of getting-along, and we embarked on the homeward journey well knowing that the miles would be longer than they were the first time over—that it would be well along in the hoot-owl hours before we had counted the last of them. I was again at the controls to keep the horses pointed in the right direction and jogging along mile after weary mile. In all the rigs the players and others were sardined-in three to a seat to make the allotted expense money go as far as it would.

The player next to me was a little forward (noun, not adjective), who could run like a quail and whose aim at the basket was deadly. I had particularly noticed her playing—and the fact that her gym shoes were laced with white ribbons instead of shoelaces, and these tied in large bows. I might as well confess that I had noticed her personality even more than the way she could run and handle the ball. I just as well mention here that a horse-and-buggy trip of that many miles, then a hard game of basketball, this followed by an even longer trip over the same miles, was a man-sized day's work for a group of Freshman and Sophomore girls. We were a few surrey loads of utter weariness.

Maybe the unseen hand had been lining things up for me that night. Be that as it may, when one of those heads became so weary that something was needed to help hold it, one of my shoulders was right where it could do the most natural thing in the world without moving so much as a zillionth of an inch. To the sound of the rhythmic whomp-whomp whomp of horses' hoofs on the dirt road, up and down hill far into the night, I caught myself wondering, and even hoping that possibly it might not have been weariness alone that caused that head to nestle right where it did—that maybe she wasn't quite THAT tired.

Anyway, that did it. I wonder how much of what Destiny has cooked up for this old world down through the ages, has been influenced and started off at a tangent, or even caused to make a U-turn, by thrilly little sensations from a curl or wisp of soft hair blowing across a man's cheek. This much I know—they are nothing short of magic when it comes to shortening miles.

Following that game, coach and player relations improved right along as the days and weeks and months drifted past. The upshot was, as you may have guessed, that after a ceremony on a certain Friday the 13th a couple of years later, she and I were playing on the same team. She was still a forward and did the sharpshooting, while I jumped at center and ran the floor. That team saw some tough games. And it also played many most enjoyable ones for many seasons. We raised our own replacements, and in the natural order of things came up with a daughter to play the other forward position, and two sons for guards while I still bucked-off at center and ran an ever decreasing area of the floor. We didn't win all the games, but I'm sure no team ever had a better team spirit. And from where I sit now thinking of the scores, our position in the over-all Won-Lost column was quite satisfactory.

As I think of her tonight I wonder if she ever goes back along the years and recalls the events of that night, the game and the long buggy ride so many years ago, as do I. And if so, whether or not the play-by-play recollections affect her as they do me.

Also as I think of her and life's ups and downs, and what has happened since, I find myself most grateful to an all-wise Providence that that first wife of mine was one of the first-last-and-always kind that stays right in there through thick and thin, for better or for worse—and will still be there when the Timekeeper blows his whistle at the end of the last quarter. My urge at the moment is to go down stairs right now and tell her so. But on second thought I think I'll wait and let her read it when this appears in print.

So, on Friday, December 13, 1912, with little fanfare, the Harold and Ellen Dwyer team was formed, and by the end of 1916, they had two recruits—Stanley and his older sister, Aileen, born February 17, 1915.

"I don't know how those people survived that hard life," Aunt Aileen reflected. "Our mother just had a terrible time because we didn't have any home and no money. Fortunately, our relatives were very nice to us. When we weren't with them, we lived in rental houses. I'm sure it was hard for them too."

I've tried to imagine what daily life was like for Grandma, raising her two babies basically out in the middle of nowhere on the bleak prairie, before modern conveniences and before women could vote. Summers had their challenges, but winters in that part of Kansas were—and still are—frigid, snowy, and blustery. Before the faint glow of dawn, Grandma probably crawled out from under the warm covers into the chilly room. Feeling in the dark, she could have tucked the blankets around her sleeping babies. Shivering, maybe she hastily pulled on over her head the dress she'd worn the day before. Out of habit and necessity, she stoked the still-smoldering embers in the kitchen cookstove, adding a log from the stacked pile—logs Granddad had lugged indoors from the dwindling woodpile. Perhaps, wrapped in a shawl of some kind and clutching a kerosene lantern in one hand, she scurried to the outdoor privy, the biting wind nipping at her cheeks.

Back in the toasty kitchen, the cookstove did its job of warming the small house—especially the kitchen—heating water for laundry and dishes in a sort of water well, and helping with cooking the food. Maybe she opened a container of creamy milk, a scanty amount retrieved earlier from the cold cellar. Door-to-door milkman delivery was a future convenience; her milk came from their cow that she probably milked twice a day.

Perhaps Grandma's thoughts were interrupted by a small cry. Baby Stanley was awake—maybe he cooed and smiled as his mother scooped him out of the tiny basket. It's likely she tenderly wrapped the wiggly bundle in his soft, blue baby blanket, the one adorned with white chicks. Grandma kissed his sweet-smelling cheek, whispered in his ear, and since Aileen still slept, tiptoed out of the bedroom. I suppose Granddad, bundled up and ready for another day's work, gave both Grandma and Stanley his famous peck on the cheek before leaving the house.

It's possible that, with her baby in one arm, she finished preparing breakfast and thought about the day at hand. Ample water for chores had been pumped and hauled in buckets to the house. That water supply would suffice for more cooking, the wash—done by hand—and sponge baths for her babies, and maybe she took her weekly bath in the leftover water.

So Stanley's childhood began. Even though their lives were modest and meager by today's standards, the Dwyer family, like many others, thrived in northern Kansas. People lived their lives managing with what they had ... and they had each other, family, and fortitude.

Granddad did what he could to make ends meet. In his words, he was "always working to make a better life for the family." During their courting years and early married life, Granddad had been a rural mail carrier near Scottsville.

"I had the same route for six years, the first part of which I traveled by horse and buggy. It was only during the last two years of my mail carrying stint that I drove a motorcycle and car. I used to read every magazine and newspaper I had while making the deliveries. The horses knew the route better than I, so all I had to do was sit back and read," Granddad was quoted as saying in the *Hastings Daily Tribune.*

Times were uncertain, and jobs were scarce. On Stanley's birth certificate, Granddad's occupation was listed as advertiser. That was the time frame, we've assumed, when the family briefly lived in Salina, Kansas, where Granddad worked as an advertiser for an insurance firm and declined "membership" in the Ku Klux Klan.

"When we lived in Salina, I remember a player piano," Aunt Aileen recalled. "The folks made music together—Mom playing the piano and Dad beating the drums."

Meanwhile, war for America seemed imminent. Even though World War I had begun in 1914, President Woodrow Wilson was determined that the United States would remain neutral. However, due to unforeseen circumstances and threats, our country eventually entered the fray and declared war on Germany on April 6, 1917, two days after Granddad's thirtieth birthday. Granddad, a member of Company H of the First Kansas Infantry since approximately 1908, left home early one July morning in 1918 and answered the call to duty.

Granddad wrote years later, "I can still see most plainly how you two were lying on your pillows the morning I slipped each of you a good-bye kiss without awakening you, before your mother took me to the train to go into the service. Aileen was lying on her back and Stanley about half on one side and tummy with one leg drawn up, just the way he has slept hundreds of times since—and had before."

According to his letters about July 26, 1918, Granddad reported to Camp Funston, near Manhattan, Kansas. He wrote, "It is hotter than $700." Reveille at 5:45 a.m. was followed by mess, hikes, drills, and then lecture and study time. Granddad started out in the kitchen, but he didn't want to "juggle grease balls" through the war, so he put in for a transfer to the ambulance company. He preferred to "try hard for the training school."

"I owe it to you and the babes as well as myself, and I'm doing my best," he wrote to Grandma.

As part of Ambulance Company 239, Tenth Division, Granddad studied anatomy, physiology, and first aid, in addition to map reading and gas training. A flu epidemic, the worst in history, spread throughout the world in 1918–1919, killing more than twenty million people. Over five hundred thousand Americans succumbed. Published in his book *Uphill and Against the Wind,*

Granddad wrote how the exhausted ambulance company worked overtime to keep casualties at a minimum in a story titled, "The Night I Didn't Die."

"Do you suppose female flu germs are called flusies?"

The query came from a feverish face on an army cot next to mine in an emergency hospital during the influenza epidemic of World War I.

Not being an authority on the flu or flusies either, I was of little help. But coming from one who knew, as did I, that scores of our fellow patients would be dead in the morning, the question did send little ripples along my spine, and helped me to enjoy over and over the mental attitude of Uncle Sam's men in uniform no matter how rough the going.

We were in the 10th Division, training at Camp Funston, Kansas, in the early autumn of 1918. Our Company was Ambulance 239, commanded by Lieut. Caesar of Oakland, California. The training on this side was nearing completion. The "latrine grapevine" had us leaving for overseas the first day of October. Our advance detail had already gone across, and everyone was trying for a pass to get home and see the loved ones once more before the orders came.

Then out of the clear blue this flu thing had scored a direct hit. It was not considered serious at first. The boys reported on sick call, were sent to the hospital, had some fever three or four days, and in a couple more felt about as good as new. Three days after their temperature was down to normal they were sent back to their outfits where they went out to drill or maneuver or shoot on the range. What happened to them out there is history. And one of the saddest pages in that history.

New cases each day began to increase by hundreds. All members of medical units were pressed into service to man emergency hospitals. It was a dead serious matter now. Civilian morticians from most towns within a radius of a hundred miles were called in to help with the bodies. An ambulance driver just back from the Base the night before had told me they thought they were getting it about whipped in that only 65 had died the day before. Asked what the rate had been, he said 320 was the greatest number any one day.

Ambulance 239 opened this hospital in a rambling green building, a YMCA auditorium, on the Zone. This "Zone" area at Funston was a small business district running parallel to the parade grounds. Here were the theaters, shops and stores that catered to the troops, and the barber shops that turned out the rapid-fire "short pomps," the granddaddy of the "crew cut" and the "white sidewall." The building held 206 cots. These were filled in two hours after we were open for business.

We were divided into three shifts, beginning at 7 a.m. All were busy from 5:30 in the morning when we awakened the complaining patients to slip a thermometer under each tongue—until time to do the same thing the next morning. Feeding and doctoring and looking after the needs and wants and wishes of that many thousand sick men, some sick enough to die—and would within hours—added up to a right sizable chore. None of the workers got enough sleep to cause any bedsores.

When the number of new cases increased to thousands, the medical personnel force was enlarged by decreasing the depth. One 8-hour shift was taken out and the other two given 12 hours each. Patients were now being held ten days after normal temperature, and that also called for additional help.

I was on the shift taken out. I knocked off at 7, and at noon was told to take a detail of 6 men and report at the edge of the camp where a new hospital was opening in a barracks. We took over at 7 that night. The place was full of new cases, about 50 on the first floor and a hundred on the second. The doctor, a captain, divided his time between that and another barracks. One girl nurse did likewise. It was her first day in the service and she was having a rough time of it—in more ways than one.

We were under strict orders to call a doctor when a patient's temperature got up to a certain point. Cases with that much temperature were sent to the base hospital where they had the permanent personnel and better equipment. And besides it was near the other facilities to care for the bodies when the boys didn't make the grade. The officer in charge had the responsibility, and it was a bit rough on him if a man died in his emergency hospital.

During the past 72 hours I had had 8 hours of broken sleep. I doubt that any of the others on duty had had more. Sometime after midnight the orderly helping me on the first floor disappeared. Finally, when there was a minute I stepped across into the latrine. There he sat on the stool sound asleep where he had been for two hours.

Along in the wee ones I began to suspect that maybe all was not well with me. A thermometer under the tongue a few minutes verified that. My number had come up too. I was to be relieved at 7 o'clock. That was four more hours, but they turned out to be rather longish. The sergeant who relieved me didn't show up till 8:30. After he did, I had two miles to walk back to the barracks. The miles were as long as the hours had been, but I made it, sent word to the C. O. that I was a casualty, and took to the cot. It was good to be home and have a chance to sleep.

Luckily I was permitted to stay in the barracks and take care of myself, instead of checking through the infirmary to get a diagnosis tag wired to my shirt, then be sent on out, catch-as-catch-can, to a hospital. I could go to the infirmary and take my temperature and get aspirin or whatever I wanted. I appreciated this privilege and had ample reason to believe that under my own tender care I was in as good hands as any on the reservation, and better than most. At least in this case the "doctor" had a very personal interest in the patient getting well.

I was, however, handicapped some in the matter of food. Our mess was over at the hospital a mile and a half away. But I could buy milk and fruit and candy bars at the Canteen (maybe PX to you) and got along fairly well. My nose bled a lot and I pulled up old newspapers on the floor and hung the nose over the side of the cot and let it bleed because that took no effort. There was no one in charge of quarters, and no one to police up, so the old papers stayed there to be used the next time, and incidentally, to draw swarms of flies.

One afternoon I walked over to the Canteen to get a bottle of milk. It was closed! I had forgotten that this was Sunday! It was a cruel blow. The only other chance was an interurban station down by the highway. I made the quarter mile down there—and they were sold out of milk! I did buy two pears and ate them while I rested.

Then I started home. About half way to the barracks, spots a yard or so in diameter in the blacktop surface of the road would pucker up as though being squeezed by a giant unseen hand. Then these spots would flatten out, and others wrinkle up. Then the road began to sway. One side would tilt up a foot or two, then settle back and the other side go up. I knew who was doing the swaying, and determined not to go down out there alone. Then my two babies, Aileen 3 years old, and 2-year-old Stanley took me by either hand and kept me from falling as we went on up the road. I saw them and felt their hands in mine as plainly and vividly as I see the keys on this machine.

The last many rods of the way I have no recollection of at all. It didn't seem possible that two little tads that size could do what they had, but here was the evidence. The babies were gone, but I was on my cot on the second floor of the barracks as proof positive that they had finished the job before they left.

About 6 o'clock I went to the infirmary for a temperature check. It was a neat 103 in the shade. Later, and for hours that night it must have been two or three degrees higher. I imagined I could smell the blankets smoking.

It was a long night. I was too hot to sleep, and didn't want to anyway. I knew this was it, and didn't want to be caught napping when the showdown came. If the Grim Reaper came up those steps during the night I wanted to be able to look him right in the eye and tell him he had the wrong address. After what the babies had done, I certainly was going to do my part. That was one night I was in no mood to die.

But somewhere along the line, my plans slipped a cog, and I dozed off. How long I slept I have no idea, but when I awoke I was cold and shivering and my teeth chattering. God! What a pleasant sensation after the cooking earlier in the night! I swiped the blankets off the empty cots on either side and piled them on, and shivered myself to sleep, sure that the crisis was over.

In the morning I awoke with no temperature to speak of, but completely done in. The two pears, my rations for the day before, were getting pretty low. At noon a buddy came up for something and saw how things stood. He reported to the first sergeant that they had to get me to a hospital or I would starve, and they prevailed upon an ambulance driver they knew to bring me to this hospital without checking through the infirmary.

41

And what a ride! Barney Oldfield could never have shown that driver a thing. But we were headed in the right direction, and it beat walking. They stopped at the Kansas-Nebraska building at the end of the Zone, and started to unload. Being flat on my back on the litter, and a hitch-hiker besides, I was in poor strategic position to dictate terms, but I finally got them to understand that we were to go to the YMCA instead. They were none to pleased about it, but did drive on up and yank the litter out and lay me in the road back of the rig.

An orderly, Lloyd Coughenor, wearing a cheesecloth flu mask, dashed out, followed shortly by Lieut. Caesar shouting, "Put that man back in. We're full-up here!" But Coughenor who was nearer, recognized me and said, "It's Dwyer." Being "one of the family" changed the tune. Now it was, "Well Hell's Bells! Get him in here out of the wind!"

An hour before, the place had been full. But a man who was reported to have had spinal meningitis had chosen this opportune time to die and make some room. They were burning his cot, and orderlies were then mopping the floor area with a disinfectant, and my cot was set up on the spot.

My "entry" was kind of a triumphant sort. Seventeen of our own men were on the cots with the flu, and the orderlies on duty were men with whom I had been working four days before. The word spread, and as I was carried in, arms were waving and greetings called from cots in every direction. It was a heart warming home-coming, even without benefit of prancing majorettes or a duly chosen queen.

That had been yesterday. And here today, I was about as near Heaven as one could hope to be on this side of the curtain. Pajamas to wear, food to eat, sheets instead of army blankets! And under my head, a pillow instead of the rolled-up fatigue uniform I had used for months! And I was among friends.

All this, and nothing to do for the next many days but lie here and feel it heal, and help this young man figure out whether or not flusies is the correct designation for female flu germs. I could ask for little else.

We've often wondered if Stanley knew how he and Aileen "rescued" their dad from becoming another flu epidemic statistic that autumn day in 1918. Still recovering from the flu, Granddad tired of wearing the "blasted mask," and every waking moment he thought about getting a weekend pass home to see his family and celebrate Stanley's second birthday on October 26, 1918.

Granddad wrote, "That boy must be getting to be a real one."

Instead, in late October, Grandma made a day trip to Manhattan, near Camp Funston, and she was probably the only family to see Granddad before his company shipped out.

Granddad's company arrived in Detroit, Michigan, by train on November 2, 1918, where they received orders to drive a thirty-truck convoy, along with five cars, to Camp Holabird in Baltimore, Maryland.

Young Stanley growing up in Kansas.

Granddad faithfully wrote to Grandma. Decades later, my cousin Mary Ellen's daughter, Karena, found his letters to Grandma from World War I bound with string, sitting on a shelf in Aunt Aileen's basement. Granddad was a man of integrity—a quality passed on to his sons and daughter—and was loyal to Grandma. He addressed her letters either "My Darling Little Wife," "Dearest Little Sweetheart," or "Dearest Little Wife and Babes," and he signed off with "Lots and Lots of Love, Kiss the Kids." I blushed reading the "mushy" parts in his letters. Grandma, with her two small children—Aileen, who Granddad nicknamed "Pal," and Stanley, nicknamed "Scout"—lived near Grandma's family at Scottsville during those long months. Grandma's brother, Gayle, and his wife, Grace, took them under their wing.

"All financial matters will come out OK so cease to worry about them. Keep things paid up as well as you can handily, and enjoy life and be comfortable and cheerful," Granddad reassured Grandma in a letter.

Granddad, promoted to sergeant in the U.S. Army, received forty-four dollars per month.

He took care of his men and didn't approve of "loafing." With Granddad behind the wheel, the truck convoys, on their way to the East Coast, traveled hard-surfaced roads at speeds of eight to ten miles per hour, covering about seventy miles per day, if things went well. When driving through St. Clairsville, Ohio, a day or so before their scheduled arrival in Cumberland, Maryland, they heard that the war was over.

Granddad wrote to Grandma:

It would be hard to tell you on paper what happened between there and Wheeling. We were driving through mining towns, and all of the people were wild with joy. I literally saw "miles and miles of smiles." At least a million different people told us that the war was over, and they showered us with flags, candy, canned fruits, loaves of bread, and apples by the bushel. Then Wheeling was wild that night and surely showed the boys a fine time. We slept in an old mansion that had been used for a hotel years ago and was built in 1818. A Mr. and Mrs. Hoskins took McIntire and me over town in their Franklin Limousine (some boat) and showed us the burg. We were watching the crowd celebrate the end of the war, and one of our fellows showed up drunk, so I excused myself and took him to camp and spent the rest of the night looking for others to get them back to camp before the cops got them. The people were going to take us to their house and have some eats but—duty first. We have had a fine reception by the people of all the towns where we stayed, but I have been in on none of the social stuff. I figure if I drive a truck all the way that some of the other fellows should be willing to take care of the chickens, etc.

Even though the war was over, more liberty trucks needed to be delivered to the coast. Granddad made a total of three convoy trips, spending nights and leisure time at local YMCAs. He saw mountains, the ocean, forests, mining towns, and all sorts of landscape for the first time and even mailed home pebbles from the Chesapeake Bay. But, with the extra trips, he knew a

December 13 wedding anniversary reunion in Kansas was out of the question. On December 13, from Columbus, Ohio, he reminisced about their life.

> They've been nine [including courtship] mighty happy years for your Uncle Sassafras. I don't like to think of some of the things you had to put up with while we were so darned hard up, but it might have been best for all of us. Of course we're not so well off just at present, but I don't mind it at all as its part of the war game, and we haven't been touched to what millions of those overseas have. More than that I know what I can do when I get out, so I don't mind at all. I never cease to be glad that I volunteered and never think of it, but I thank my stars that I had a wife that was made of the right stuff and every inch a good sport. I couldn't stand to be there when the boys came home had I not done my part. The longer one is in the service, the less use he has for slackers.

"What one hears amounts to very little," he wrote when explaining rumors of men voluntarily signing up for six months of overseas work. Since the war was over, Granddad opted out.

For nearly two weeks, the company waited in Columbus, Ohio, for orders either to take more liberty trucks to Baltimore, Maryland, or return to Camp Funston in Kansas. Orders were to return to Baltimore, and Granddad realized that Christmas at home was only going to be in his dreams. Often, while lying in bed, he built "air castles" before getting up; his mouth watered thinking of Grandma's brown cake, oatmeal cookies, and waffles.

Grandma's news from home told about Aileen with her dolls and Stanley's black eye, throwing stones, and playing with his wagon. Granddad had seen a cute girl on the screen at a picture show that reminded him of "Pal." One evening, Granddad met some folks on the street with a young boy about the size of Stanley which made him "sweat a little around the eyes."

"I miss you fellers so badly I can taste it," Granddad wrote Grandma.

He stayed until the army was done with him, and Granddad informed Grandma that farmers in the service could probably get discharged with five affidavits attesting their help is needed at home. Granddad reminded Grandma that being married to a farmer had benefits too. He returned to Camp Funston in Kansas on January 12, 1919, and was honorably discharged on January 24, 1919. Now it was time to make a living and make up for lost time with his family.

"I started school in Asherville," Aunt Aileen said. "Stanley went over to the school when I started and tried to talk the teacher into letting him start, too, but he didn't convince her. Dad's father was a farmer and lost their farm when crops were so low. He also lost a leg in a sandpit accident. They moved to the small town of Asherville, and their house wasn't much—no plumbing. Asherville had a business district only one-half block long with a bank across the street. When we were in Asherville, Aunt Pearl would march us off to church often."

Some time after returning from the war, Granddad moved his family to Iola in southeast Kansas, so he could work in the oil fields. If Stanley hadn't started school by then, that may be where his schooling began—first grade.

"Basic survival was the most important thing in those days," Aunt Aileen said. "So we didn't really have hobbies. Stanley and I didn't get along very well. He loved to rag me, and I didn't take very kindly to that. He matured over time, a little by the time Harold came along."

While the family lived near Iola, the last "recruit" joined the team on September 23, 1924. Harold Eugene was born near Council Groves, Kansas, at Fred Martin's home, probably one of Granddad's relatives.

"We didn't live there, though," Aunt Aileen said, laughing. "We just went there for Harold's birth. In those days, people that lived in small towns and on farms seldom went to a hospital to give birth."

"Babies were a bit out of the ordinary when he came along," Granddad mused years later in a letter.

By the time Harold E. was around four years old, Granddad accepted a job with Chicago Casualty Company and worked in advertising in Chicago.

I remembered a little about Chicago. I remembered swimming in Lake Michigan.

"You wondered why the water 'shakled'," Aileen said, laughing.

Dad and I were Cubs fans. He pitched me a ball in the apartment where we lived, which wasn't any bigger than Aileen's living room. I hit the ball in our apartment. Mom was reading the paper, and I put the ball through the paper and into her lap. That ended the ball game.

"You were with the folks in Chicago, and Stanley and I were stuck in Asherville," Aileen remarked to my father. "When you got back, I suppose you were glad to see us, but I suppose we were jealous of you because you were having a great time in Chicago, and we'd been having a miserable time in Asherville."

Stanley wrote in a paper for a college assignment in about 1937:

I had a most promising background. I had traveled throughout my life—not just vacations, but a frequent moving life. I went to seven different schools before I graduated from high school. My father was as independent as any man could be. When he tired of one job, he had half a dozen others of which he could take his pick. He had a very likable personality—from which a personality of my own should have sprung. My father was forced to quit a job in Chicago to be with my grandmother during her last days. It was the height of Depression, and following her death, he took the first job offered him—newspaper. He had a chance to buy a paper of his own shortly after. He did—in a Catholic town miles from civilization—a town of about five hundred population.

"Dad came home from Chicago dead broke," Aunt Aileen remembered. Some merchants at Tipton got together and scared up enough money to start a newspaper.

"We moved to Tipton, another tiny little town with nothing to do, no place to go. It had maybe three blocks of business district. The Depression was more of the same for us."

Stanley's paper continued:

This town consisted of a colony of foreigners who cared not to mingle with the world, to seek happiness other than that which they found around them. I was most interested in sports and tried every means possible to find expression along those lines, but to no avail. Every desire I ever had was suppressed. I became silent and uninteresting. I lived in an imaginary world of my own.

My first recollections of Stan were when we lived in Tipton, Kansas, and our dad had the weekly newspaper the Tipton Times. *It was the latter years of Prohibition, and it was the middle of the Depression, the dry years. Money didn't just exactly grow on trees during that time. We lived in a metal building right on Main Street, next to the water tower. The print shop was in the front part of the building, and we lived in the back part. During those days, it was very common for the temperature to get over one hundred degrees outside. I don't know how in the world we stood living in a metal building, but it didn't seem to bother us any because nobody knew any different at the time. The print shop had a great big glass window in front of it and an awning over that. I picked up a big clod and threw it up on the roof so it would roll back down and I could catch it. Well, I undershot, and it went through the plate glass window instead.*

Stan played basketball, baseball, and was in the band, along with all the other things a youngster did in a small town in the "Dirty Thirties." I don't think he was ever a Boy Scout even though Dad started one of the first Boy Scout troops in Scottsville in 1912. Kay discovered Stan's stamp collection in his trunk, which dates back to the time when we lived in Tipton.

Stanley liked sports.

I started school in Tipton. Stan was eight years older, so we didn't chum together much; however, my earliest memory of Stan was when our neighbor's house was on fire. Of course, all the kids had to go have a look. The smoke was pretty heavy, and a bunch of guys—volunteers—were in the basement fighting the fire. Right down in the middle of the group was my brother, Stan. He glanced upward, and our eyes met. I had a feeling for his safety, which was probably why I remembered the incident.

"Stanley and I went to Tipton High School," Aunt Aileen said. "We played in a band at Tipton. I played the tenor saxophone, and Stanley played the soprano saxophone. We didn't take lessons; we just taught ourselves. I think the Knights of Columbus sponsored the band, and they built us a bandwagon so they could haul us to different places. Later on when we lived in Glasco, Stanley borrowed my saxophone and played with a group for fun."

I sat in the Catholic school at Tipton for one concert. The band was playing, and I wanted to say something to whoever I was with. So, I yelled at him so he could hear it. The band stopped playing, and my voice was louder than the band.

Aunt Aileen said, "Stanley enjoyed radio programs like *The Lone Ranger* and *Amos 'n' Andy,* and he enjoyed the popular music of the day and would keep track of its popularity as it ebbed and flowed. He had a high school girlfriend and a great sense of humor. Stanley told me once that when he was out and about, he couldn't keep from making wisecracks."

Stanley and his sister, Aileen, were members of a band.
Stanley played the soprano saxophone.

Another memory I had of Tipton was when I had to go to the biffy—outdoors, of course—and they were not made very tight. There were cracks between the boards on the door. Stan and a buddy saw me go in, so they proceeded to throw mud balls at the cracks so that some of the mud would splash inside. It quieted down a bit, so I opened the door and caught a mud ball right between the eyes. I don't remember the consequences, but I suspect there were a few well-chosen words between Stan and Dad.

Among all the piles of papers in the trunk was a copy of the *Dawn*, a newsletter published every six weeks by the students of Tipton High School. Aileen Dwyer was listed as editor, and Stanley contributed as a staff reporter. Stanley wrote a poem for the senior class of 1933 titled, "Seniors, All."

The pleasures and toils of the life in the past,
    In the Tipton Parochial High,
Will soon be mere memories to this certain class;
    Mere memories which never shall die.

This group joined as one many long years ago,
    Enduring much hardship and pain;
(With a few dropping out and a few coming in)
    In an effort great heights to attain.

But suffering is naught, when compared with the joys
    Which are had by each one of the class;
For the hardships are met with the strongest of will
    And are conquered by each lad and lass.

And so through the years in the lifetime to come,
    Till to rest they are called one by one,
May each do his share in the duties of life,
    And join this same class when he's done.

After Aileen graduated from Tipton High School as valedictorian in 1933, we moved about forty miles down the road to a farm about three miles out of Glasco, Kansas, where Stan attended a larger high school. There's a little story about Aileen being valedictorian. She was upset one day after school because she didn't think she would be selected as the student with top honors. Dad went up to the school and asked to see the grades. She was the top student. Dad asked the monsignor if Aileen would be chosen valedictorian or if he needed to run a story in the paper. Case closed. Dad wouldn't have to worry about that with Stan or me.

We lived near Glasco on a farm, but Dad worked in Clay Center, Kansas, for the paper there. He commuted about forty miles, while Aileen attended Kansas University for a short time, and Stan and I went to school in nearby Glasco.

"Dad wanted me to go to college, but he didn't have the money," Aileen said. "I went back home to Glasco briefly before I moved to Colorado Springs to attend business college."

Aunt Aileen married Bill Groen in 1939 and lived the rest of her life in Colorado.

Glasco, Kansas. Several months after the interview, as one Memorial Day approached, Mom and Dad made their yearly pilgrimage to Kansas to decorate graves, and I tagged along that day as I sometimes did. Glasco wasn't the scheduled destination of the day, but plans changed, and it turned out being a short stop on our unscripted journey. The first stop was Scottsville, Kansas, where Grandma grew up, about ninety minutes from my home. The town was nearly boarded up. Dust from the main street collected in vacant, run-down buildings, but one church and the grain elevator were still open for business. The 1916 State Bank of Scottsville building still served as an office. The one-time landmark gymnasium and school half-stood, the Kansas limestone structure crumbling to its foundation. I imagined Grandma, her shoes laced with white ribbons, running up and down the basketball court in that building. Dad pointed to the house where his Granddad Cristman had once lived. Dad, as a boy, had played there with his cousin. The overgrown weeds in the yard obscured the broken-out windows. The siding was bare.

We drove to the Scottsville Cemetery on the edge of town. After weeding around family headstones, especially the Dwyer headstone where Grandma and Granddad were buried, Mom grabbed the white, crinkly sacks of flowers in the back of the van, and we decorated graves with red, white, and blue silk carnations.

Every time I went with Mom and Dad to the Scottsville Cemetery, we discussed the same idea, erecting a headstone for Stanley on the reserved plot alongside his parents. There, years ago, Granddad had mounted a postcard-sized brass plaque on a wooden stake designating Stanley's killed in action status over Austria on May 10, 1944. A headstone for Stanley never made it past the talking stage.

On the road again, Dad gripped the steering wheel. Dust billowed behind the van. From the backseat, I gazed out the window. Kansas is known as the Sunflower State, but beyond the limestone fence posts dotting the roadside ditches, a sea of waist-high, green wheat fields emerged, topped with heads that rippled in the wind like tame ocean waves. We stopped at East Asher Cemetery atop a gentle hill on Highway 9. A black wrought-iron fence enclosed the small area of grass, weeds, four pine trees, and headstones—some leaning, some broken. Outside the van, we stretched our legs and stared off into the distance—an unobstructed, panoramic view of 360 degrees. As we looked to the horizon, we saw miles of tree-dotted hills, rolling prairie, and endless, green wheat fields. Mom carried another crinkly sack. We followed the same routine, paying our respects to Granddad's deceased ancestors, adorning their graves with red, white, and blue silk flowers.

Back in the van, I studied the Kansas map and realized that we were about forty miles from the geographic center of the forty-eight states. We learn something new every day, and there was more in store for that day. I looked at the map again and calculated our distance to Glasco—about fifteen miles.

"Do we have time to make a side trip to Glasco before going to the cemetery in Beloit?" I asked.

So Dad drove the back road route to Glasco. Mom pointed out the front window to the southwest and said, "Somewhere over in that direction is where the Dwyer homestead was located. Aunt Myrtle showed it to us one time."

Then the van slowed down. Dad glanced back over his shoulder.

"What's the matter, Harold?" Mom asked.

Dad answered, "The house back down the road looks familiar. It reminds me of the house we lived in while Stan attended high school and I was a kid."

There was no place to turn around, so I drove for three more miles to Glasco. I planned to drive back to the house after we checked things out in town.

And in Glasco, Kansas, as in most small towns, it's almost effortless to locate the main street, the town bar, the city park, churches, and the schools. Glasco High School remained as Dad remembered it, but a new building had replaced the old elementary school Dad once attended.

Dad explained to Mom and me as he parked the van, "I had a pony that I rode to school—a Shetland pony named Daisy. While I was at school, I kept her in a barn near the elementary school. It was about three miles to school from the farm. When the weather was good, I rode my pony; otherwise, we hoofed it. It was the 'Dirty Thirties' back then. One day in school, the sky filled with dust. It was as black and dark as night. Our teacher had to turn on the lights in our classroom."

We walked through the open doorway into the brick, two-story Glasco High School building, and the secretary led us down the hall to the picture display of past graduates. Twenty-three pairs of eyes, the class of 1934, stared back at us from under the protective glass. Some smiled, and others like Stanley gazed solemnly. We bent our heads sideways to study the photos that had slipped out of place and rested on their sides. Stanley and his senior class graduated from Glasco High School on May 22, 1934, inspired for the moment by their class motto "The horizon widens as we climb."

Dad told us, "The night Stan graduated from high school was a doozy. I had my pony in town and had forgotten all about the graduation services. Here the folks came in the car looking for me. Dad took me home to get cleaned up, and Stan rode Daisy three miles to the farm—'twas a quick ride, as he galloped her all the way. Anyhow, we made it to the ceremony in time, but the poor, sweaty horse probably wondered what the heck brought that on."

And how many from Stanley's graduating class might still be alive? The secretary directed us to the elementary school next door.

Dad held the door while Mom and I entered the brick school building. Two young women came out of the office. Dad talked to them.

I asked them if they knew where the ladies were that could tell us about the upcoming alumni reunion. Those two gals were the ones we were looking for, so we followed them into a classroom and briefly told them what we were interested in. One left the room to print a list. Darlene could strike up a conversation with anyone. The other young gal's last name was Dwyer, but she was no relation.

So we wrote down the information we needed, thanked the ladies, and they mentioned a collection of historical information in a building down on Main Street operated by a man named "Squeak." Glasco's Main Street was mostly boarded up, downsized from a town of a bygone era that had a half dozen filling stations, a few cafés, a couple of grocery stores, and banks. As we drove through town, we checked out the historical "museum." It was closed.

I stepped out of the van in front of the "museum" and asked a fellow on the street, "We're looking for a man named Squeak. Do you know him and where we might find him?"

The man lit a cigarette, puffed it, and said, "You're looking for Squeak? Well, that's me. What can I help you with?"

He unlocked the door to the building, showed us around, and helped us find some information. We thanked Squeak and were on our way again.

I drove out of Glasco and back down the road to the house I'd seen. When the drought ended in the middle 1930s, the river that ran between town and the farm flooded. The water was about two miles wide. As I drove over the road, it seemed impossible to even think there could have been that much water, but I had seen it years ago.

I pulled in the drive, studied the yard and house, and decided to go to the door. I explained my presence to the homeowner, a very cordial man. We stood on the sidewalk outside the back door near the porch, and it occurred to me that it was the sidewalk I'd ridden my bike on. It wasn't very long—not what I remembered as a kid. The sidewalk went down the hill, past the shed where we raised pigs, and stopped at the windmill. If I didn't get my bike stopped first, the windmill did the job.

Looking east up the hill, I remembered when I first climbed up there. There was a big truck tire lying there. My first thought was that I could crawl in the thing and ride it to the bottom of the hill. Second thoughts prevailed. The tire went like heck, got to the bottom of the hill, hit a little drainage ditch, and went airborne. Then the tire slammed through the side of the barn and wiped out the horse stall inside. But when I looked in the direction of the barn, the only thing there was a red tractor. The owner explained that the building had to be torn down. I told Kay that the barn was where Stan kept his 4-H livestock.

Another piece of Stanley's life fit into place—an "ah, ha" moment. Now the 4-H certificates and the curled photos from the trunk made sense. In one black-and-white photo, Stanley is dressed in a three-piece suit with light shirt and tie, handkerchief in the breast pocket, and armband on his arm. The handsome 4-H showman wore a felt-brimmed hat—a fedora trimmed with a dark band of cloth. Two ropes dangled from his hand, the other ends tied to the halter straps of the two ribbon-winning Herefords, Tommy and Toby. When I first found that photo, I checked the back side for any information, smiling when I read the animals' chosen names written in pencil. Rick and I had a family dog with the same name—Toby.

Stanley, a 4-H showman, and his livestock, Tommy and Toby.

Dad looked off in the distance and said, "The Davidsons lived about one and a half miles to the northeast, over those hills. Stan and Lynne Davidson were good friends, even after they both joined the service."

That name registered—and another connection in Stanley's life became clear—Lynne Davidson and Stanley's friendship began as neighbors. I had already checked—Lynne Davidson was no longer living.

We had a collie for a farm dog that was pretty smart. When Stan and I were roughhousing around, old Shep would stand around until he thought I was getting the worst of it and then would proceed to take a nip at Stan's rear. Worked every time!

In addition to playing basketball and baseball, Stan took up golf when we lived in Glasco. We still have some of his left-handed clubs. I shagged balls for him in the hills around our house on the farm. I tried to catch one once, and it was the last one I tried to catch.

Dad worked on the newspaper in Clay Center and was gone a lot. I recollect he was home just on weekends. We had a lot of love and a lot of respect. We didn't think about him being gone; it was just the way life was. We did the normal dad-boy thing together. He bought me a .22 rifle when I was about nine years old. At the farmhouse near Glasco was where we learned to shoot it—inside in the wintertime. There's still a couple of holes in the casing there where we missed the target. I don't imagine many people take a .22 caliber rifle and practice shooting it in their living room this day and age. That's where I learned to shoot. It was a single shot. All my buddies had lever-action repeaters, so I had to learn to make my first shot count, because it was the only one I was going to get. I used to hunt birds in the grove of trees about one-half mile from the house. The cat got smart and followed me when I went hunting.

Once, when we lived at the farm, the outhouse filled up, and we had to move it. We dug a new hole and moved the thing over and filled the old hole up with loose dirt. If you weren't careful, you might step in the hole and find yourself up to your knees in you-know-what. Stan made a sign to stick in the loose dirt—Don't Step on the Grass. It was fair warning!

Eventually, we made it to the Beloit cemetery that day and laughed along the way. Never knowing what was around the next corner or what was waiting for us down the road, our journey and search continued, and somehow, more memories bubbled to the surface.

From Glasco, we moved to Manhattan, Kansas, so Stan could live at home and attend Kansas State College of Agriculture and Applied Science, now Kansas State University. How Stan or the folks came up with the tuition money for him

*to go to college must have been quite a trick. He enrolled for his freshman year in
the fall of 1935. So he probably worked for a year after high school graduation,
maybe with a wheat harvest crew, before his college career began.*

Over the years, Mom, Dad, Rick, and I have made a few road trips to
Manhattan, a college town nestled in the Flint Hills of Kansas, eighty miles
east of Glasco. Each of those trips served a different purpose in our quest to
retrace Stanley's footsteps. Each trip revealed more. Dad's self-guided tours
through Manhattan shed light on faded memories, memories of an ordinary
family—a married sister and two brothers living their lives.

Stanley and his brother, Harold E., in Manhattan, Kansas.

*Manhattan was a great town to grow up in. We lived on Leavenworth Street,
which is about six blocks south from the edge of K-State campus. We had a pretty
good hill in front of the house—the best sledding hill in Manhattan. Eugene
Field Elementary School, where I attended, was at the bottom of the hill, but they
wouldn't let us sled to school. My buddies and I built a bobsled about ten feet long
that would seat about eight to ten people. Of course, we didn't have a car to pull*

the sled, so we approached the fraternities and sororities and asked them if they wanted to borrow it. The only catch was that we would get to ride along.

When Stan attended Kansas State College, student enrollment was about four thousand, and approximately two dozen fraternities and a dozen or so sororities housed some of the students. Stan did not belong to a fraternity but lived at home. We shared a bedroom. He was a member of the Independent Student Union.

In the piles of college papers tucked away in the trunk, there was a yellowed paper titled "Driftwood" by Stanley N. Dwyer. He wrote:

It looks very much as if the Greek Organizations already are taking a back seat for the Independents. Constitutional law of the school declares that these Greek organizations must be in the form of fraternity and sorority houses, separated one from another by at least eighty feet of space, and that the members must abide by the rules governing the time that a person of the opposite sex be allowed to enter the house. The Independents have a house in the possession of both men and women of the college and no regulation as to which sex has control of the house at any certain time while it is open.

Stan studied broadcasting and journalism. He wanted to be a radio announcer. During his senior year of college, he worked as an announcer at radio station KSAC in Manhattan. He was going to follow in Dad's footsteps. I've often wondered how far he would have gone because that segment of the industry grew by leaps and bounds after the war. It would have been interesting.

When I dug through Stanley's trunk, it was like stepping back in time, back to the 1930s. Events of the 1930s hadn't yet been recorded in history books. Instead, they were studied as current events. The people lived in the Depression, not knowing when or how it would end. The words *Pearl Harbor*, *World War II*, and the *Greatest Generation* meant nothing. One of Stanley's journalism assignments debated whether the United States should implement a silk boycott on Japan for its aggression toward China.

Another assignment asking, "What did you get *out of* the course?" prompted Stanley to write:

That expresses better the general outlook on grades than anything else that can be said. Grades are gotten in various ways other than earning them. Apple polishing and cribbing are two of the many devices used to influence this herd of blind, unsuspecting professors.

If the future employers of these bribers are as blind as the professors, some of the students should begin their careers with fat salaries.

He concluded:

> So the question remains: what shall we do? We fellows with not an oversupply of that gray matter will fail after we get through college if we spend our time bribing our grades, and we'll fail before we get through if we continue to let the Ds and Fs go down on our records.

Stanley wrote some poetry and scribbled song ideas and little love notes on class assignments or scraps of paper. He had some thoughts about "fizz-ed."

> If you don't enjoy playing drop the handkerchief, ring around the rosy, thirteen kinds of tea party races—any kind of games except the major sports—under the direct supervision of some of your senior classmates, we suggest that you take physical education by correspondence in your spare moments during the summer.

Along with his studies, he was in the middle of everything—YMCA member, Crack Patrol, and on staff at the K.S.C. Fourth Estate. *During his sophomore year, he became a member of the KSC Quill Club to add to his literary pursuits. During his senior year, he became editor of the club's publication, the* Mirror. *To become eligible to join the Quill Club at KSC, besides the initiation, you had to write a little ditty that you could keep track of. Stan's little ditty went like this: "I saw a girl upon a bike upon a windy day. And when I say that I saw the girl, I mean just what I say." That was pretty risqué stuff back then.*

Dad wore many hats in his lifetime. By 1933, he'd "retired" from the Kansas National Guard. Dad, at one time or another, owned five papers across Kansas, including weekly papers in the towns of Selden and Woodston. Woodston was approximately 140 miles west of Manhattan, and some summers, we stayed there in an apartment but still lived permanently in Manhattan. I recall that Stan worked at the grain elevator in Woodston. Also, during the hot Kansas summers, Mom and I visited Aileen in Colorado, staying long enough for me to work a busboy job at Bauer Cafeteria in downtown Denver.

Around 1937, Granddad found another outlet for his creative talents. Granddad wrote a weekly column—his first—called "Along U.S. 24," which ran in newspapers across Kansas and other states for about fifteen years. Granddad once wrote in a letter:

I was older than the hills before I rattled a typewriter any. And had always done something I disliked. At forty I had about written myself off as having made one mell of a hess of the whole job and thought about all there was left to do was to scrape up subsistence for the bunch until the end, squeak a couple of times and pass out of the picture, and then hold a lily in one hand as they filed past and remarked about how natural I looked (as tho a man were supposed to look like a bale of hay or something as soon as he stopped breathing).

Also in 1937, my dad began a twenty-five-year career in advertising and sales with Security Food Company of Minneapolis. He traveled through the Nebraska territory selling feed while Stan was in his last years of college, but we stayed in Manhattan. Dad came home one Friday night off his territory and gave Stan the keys to the car. Dad had a quarter in his pocket, maybe a half dollar—that was all—which he gave to Stan so he could take his date out on the town. Stan had a date with his girlfriend, Beatrice King. She was a nice-looking lady. I don't know what ever happened to her.

And from the looks of the memorabilia in the trunk, Stanley and his date attended spring formals, winter formals, sporting events, movies, and hung out at the local campus canteen, which served fifteen-cent hot fudge sundaes. One lone, distinct envelope stood out in the crowd of papers in the trunk. The letter, written to "Miss Beatrice King," was postmarked June 14, 1938.

Dearest Bea,

Well, I am in Attica [Kansas] for the moment but don't know how long I will stay. I have a chance at a job this evening, but I'm not sure of it. It depends upon whether or not the wheat here is ready to combine. I sure had a bad time even finding a place where there was a chance for a job. I've been clear to Oklahoma, farther west than here even.

As far south as Kingman, the wheat wasn't ripe, and farther south than that, it wasn't worth a darn. The farmers were singing the blues and weren't hiring anyone, and the streets of every berg I've been in were lined with bums looking for work. In Hazelton, where I was this noon, there were twenty men who left town at once because they couldn't get jobs. Some had been there for two weeks.

I just stumbled upon this town, and because it didn't have quite as many harvesters lining each side of the street, I decided to look around. If I don't get the job, I will let you know tomorrow. If I do,

I will let you know the first chance I get, which might be tomorrow. Don't feel hurt if you don't get a letter in every mail because I'll have to do my writing when I can. I'll write as soon and as often as I can though. When I give you my address, you can write as often as you like.

I wish I could jump in with this and come up to see you. It's best for both of us that I battle it for a while.

Things were looking pretty black till I got here. There were 100 men for every job every other place I've been.

I slept in Harper last night. Using the ground for a mattress and rain clouds for a blanket probably didn't help my disposition any.

Well, honey, I better get this in the mail. I'll give you my address as soon as possible. Be good, and have a good time.

Lots of love, sweetheart, Stanley

In Stanley's senior year of college, the College Student Employment Project of NYA, National Youth Administration, approved him for employment. A brochure found in Stanley's trunk explained that NYA provided federal funds to aid eligible college students, and Stanley, for a rate of thirty-five cents per hour, worked twenty-five hours per month.

Included with his job application to NYA, Stanley wrote:

The job I would like very much to secure is the work at the radio station under L.L. Longsdorf. I will take any other work, but the radio work is actual practice in my future business. I have taken many hours of radio work and shall take more this year. However, my voice is not perfect, and no matter whether I get NYA help, it will be necessary for me to spend time every day in voice training. Hence, the time spent at the radio station will not be taken from my study hours. Financially, I do not rate very high. My college expenses are met only by what I earn in the summer and money that I have been forced to borrow.

From papers saved in the trunk, I surmised that Stanley—recommended for the position by Program Director L. L. Longsdorf and Harrison Summers, professor of public speaking—joined the team of students who participated in actual one-hour weekday student broadcasts. Selected collegians prepared and presented informative, fifteen-minute programs on topics of interest— including national news and world affairs—on the *College of the Air* program over the KSAC radio station in Manhattan. A letter from Professor Harrison Summers indicated that he entrusted Stanley to "take charge of radio debates" and stated, "It's your baby and your job … and thanks for taking over." Stanley's voice carried a radius of over 125 miles. "You've been listening to KSAC, the voice of Kansas State College at Manhattan, Kansas. At this time, we leave the air until 4:30 this afternoon, making way for WIBW at Topeka. This is Stanley Dwyer. Good afternoon."

On May 29, 1939, Stanley earned a Bachelor of Science in Industrial Journalism from Kansas State College of Agriculture and Applied Science in Manhattan, Kansas. Stanley and other students gained experience broadcasting programs that carried over the radio waves of KSAC.

Stan played semipro baseball while he was in college. Manhattan had a baseball team, the Chastains, which was part of the Ban Johnson League. After a while, they played at the new Griffith Field, often before hundreds of cheering fans. Stan was first baseman, and I was the batboy. He was left-handed, and his first baseman's glove was getting pretty old. To keep the ball from rolling out of the pocket, he cut some oak boards to slip in the fingers. During one game, he went high over his head to spear a line drive that was headed to right field. When he came down, he had to look to see if the ball was in the pocket. It was, but the boards had been broken in about three places. His coach later told him that the ball was headed "over the fence" in right field.

We spent quite a little time together during those times. One time, I was playing catch with another fellow, and Stan saw me flinch when a ball landed just in front of me in the dirt. After we got home, we had a little lesson. Stan told me to get my glove and follow him. He led me to the inside corner of the house and garage for a little practice. He instructed me to catch the ball or get hit. "Keep your eye on the ball," he told me. "Don't turn your head away from it." He proceeded to burn the balls in at ankle height or just below. It didn't take me long to learn to watch the balls until they were in the glove, and then it was a cinch. Years later, when I was first baseman for the Hastings High School Tigers baseball club, it paid off. Coach Eldon Miller wrote in my high school annual, "Not many guys dig them out of the dirt like you do." I attribute that all to the little session Stan and I had down in Manhattan.

Stanley and his father, Harold W. Dwyer. While the family lived in Manhattan, Kansas, Stanley played semipro baseball with the Chastains.

Stanley Naismeth Dwyer, promising journalist, poet, songwriter, radio announcer, and—more importantly—son, brother, grandson, nephew, cousin, brother-in-law, friend, teammate, and boyfriend, graduated from Kansas State College of Agriculture and Applied Science on May 29, 1939, with a Bachelor of Science in Industrial Journalism.

My brother, the red-headed, all-American kid that enjoyed what he did and was positive and always upbeat, left home after graduation. I was fourteen. Jobs were scarce to unavailable, so he set out to see the world and get some experiences to talk about in future years.

3

⚜

On the High Seas

The biggest job aboard ship is spending the other 16 hours.
—Stanley N. Dwyer in a letter dated February 24, 1940

One day, during the aftermath of cleaning up the 1999 house fire, I was reading some papers as I removed various damp items from Stanley's trunk. Dad rummaged through the charred rubble in another part of their house.

I went looking for him. "Dad, I'm confused," I said. "What is a merchant marine, and what does it have to do with Stanley? I thought Stanley was a B-17 pilot." Dad stopped what he was doing, held some tool in his hand, and answered my questions.

Stan was both—a merchant marine first, before the United States entered the war, and then he was a pilot. Soon after Stan graduated from Kansas State College in 1939, he and a buddy, Theron Newell, hitchhiked to New Orleans. The country was still in the Depression, and there were very few jobs to be had. Stan and Theron decided to become merchant marines, but before they could get a job with the American fleet, they had to get their seamen papers, which required a trip or two on a foreign tanker.

Merchant marines were the seamen that manned cargo ships and tankers. Those unsung heroes hauled supplies to various countries all over the world. Early in the war, even before U.S. involvement, Hitler tried to defeat island England by cutting off its supply of food and war materials. America became the lifeline for England—they desperately needed supplies, and we had them. So cargo ships— and later troop transports—sailed the dangerous waters of the Atlantic Ocean for England, eventually sailing in convoys as prime targets of German U-boats. In wartime, the job of the merchant marine was one of the most dangerous.

Dad stood there and thought a minute. As he scratched his head, the proverbial lightbulb went on.

One of the ports of call for Stan's tanker, the SS India Arrow, was in the Philippines. My recollection was that Stan watched Manila burn while he sat on a hillside on the island, and he wrote a manuscript about his experience, possibly with intentions of further publication. After Stan turned up missing, the manuscript was returned to the folks with all of Stan's belongings, and as I recalled, Dad sent the one and only copy of the manuscript to Theron.

What happened to the manuscript, and could Theron, Stanley's good friend, tell us more about Stanley and their friendship? Theron Newell became the first person I tried to locate after I got into Stanley's trunk.

Three cheers for the Internet. Before all the privacy restrictions, it was easier to locate a person and retrieve vital statistics, such as death certificates, etc. I located Theron. A newspaper obituary notice from Marin County, California, stated that his ashes had been scattered over Mount St. Helens in 1993. Darn! His wife had survived him, and they had had no children. It wasn't as easy to locate Theron's wife or any extended family. Nevertheless, after hours of "surfing" time, plenty of cold phone calls, more dead ends than I'd like to admit, and eventually some willing assistance from West Coast acquaintances we'd casually met out of the blue—all over a period of time—it turned out that Theron's wife had moved back to Oregon from Marin County. She passed away in 1997. But what about the manuscript? Without hesitation, Aunt Aileen—well, Dad too—clued me in that Stanley's manuscript was considered by them to be a sentimentally valued piece of writing. A little more digging in Stanley's trunk offered some clues. Piled among the hundreds of letters in Stanley's trunk were a couple of letters from Theron Newell. Theron wrote to Granddad:

> For several months Stan was working on a novel based on an experience of his in Manila. Do you have Stan's novel or could you get it? Is it finished? If not, sometime I would like to finish it just so that Stan's biggest undertaking will be completed ...
>
> I still have Stan's letter in which he described what he was planning for his novel. I think I could appreciate what nerve it must have taken to go through his belongings. I dread what feeling will come over me when I get the ms. [manuscript] and start reading it. I know whose presence will come into the room and help me revise or finish it. But in spite of that dread, I wouldn't want to miss it for anything. It is something I must do for him.

Nonetheless, it took years to get to the bottom of the hunt for the manuscript. Finally, one afternoon, after hours on the Internet and a stiff neck, I was frustrated and thought the session—one of many—had been a waste of time. Google this, click here, click, click, click, and click some more. Not knowing how I had even gotten there, I was lost in cyberspace. However, my eyes hadn't completely glazed over; I recognized a name on some newspaper page I'd willy-nilly pulled up on the screen. An old society page from a newspaper in a town in Oregon stated Mr. and Mrs. Theron Newell were guests of so-and-so. So-and-so didn't happen to be just anybody; it was Theron's wife's family. I recognized her maiden name—thus, the connection to her extended family. After more searching, a few cold phone calls and more leads, one very nice lady, a niece of Theron's, listened to my story and request and offered to help. Everything remaining from Theron's estate was in her possession. She knew of Theron's published writings, but did not recall anything like the manuscript I'd described. However, she took time and went through the remnants of Theron's materials. No trace of the manuscript. Darn it again.

Dead ends were part of our journey—no manuscript and no Theron to tell us about Stanley and their adventures. But, the more I rummaged through the trunk, with or without a manuscript, I realized the magnitude of all the letters and what they alone revealed about Stanley. Mixed in the stack of over three hundred letters Stanley had written home from June 1939 to May 1944 were a few rough-draft letters Stanley wrote to friends. The essence of Stanley emerged from that whole collection of correspondence, along with what remained from who knows how many letters he'd written to his sister.

So when Stanley set off for the merchant marines and to explore the world, he wrote home often. Here's a copy of his first letter home, complete with evidence of smoke and water damage from Mom and Dad's house fire.

Along with Stan's letters in his trunk, there were copies of some radio programs he'd put together after he left the merchant marine. We're getting ahead of ourselves, but in the fall of 1941, Stan worked for the KGNF radio station in North Platte. He wrote a travelogue for broadcast based on his travel experiences. I had read the travelogue programs before, but I'd forgotten about them. Now, I like to sit down sometimes and read Stan's radio programs. It's like having a conversation with my brother.

Those radio scripts, woven together with Stanley's letters—which have been lightly edited for clarification, including omitting some sentences and paragraphs and combining some letters in composite form—portrayed his character, recounted stories of his life, and made it possible for us to retrace his steps beginning with his merchant marine days.

New Orleans
Sunday

Dear Folks

Well how's everything up in the mid-west? I'll bet the swimming pool has been getting plenty of patronage.

We stayed all Thursday with the kid at Little Rock. He lives up on "mortgage hill." We sure had a big time. His family was gone and we just layed around all day. We left about 8 Friday morning. We stayed that night in Vicksburg. We looked over the forts guarding the Mississippi river the next morning before we left. We got here at N.O. late in the afternoon Saturday. Don't know anything about shipping conditions yet because everything was closed up when we got here, and is also closed today. From what we can pick up tho, things look pretty favorable. Tomorrow we'll start after my seamans papers, then if we decide to join the union we'll do that.

If you folks will save _all_ these letters, and guard them with your lives, I'll just write all the description I want to save on them, then I'll have me a valuable diary when I get home.

We sure have seen some pretty country since we left home. We could see a difference in vegetation as soon as we crossed the Missouri line. In Mo. we were impressed by the timbered hills, and in the south by young tobacco crops.

We had a notion to pass Little Rock
up, but decided if we went that
way we could see the Ozarks, so we
did. They're sure beautiful. We came
through them during moonlit night.
The wild, timbered hills reminded me
of the black hills, tho they're not
so large.

I got my first glimpse of Spanish
moss in Little Rock. That is sort
of a fern-like growth that hangs
down from limbs of trees. It is
gray-green, and is really
beautiful. We saw oodles of share-
croppers and their abodes in Ark.
and south. It's really terrible the
way they live. Some in delapidated
shacks, some in tents.

Plants that I have seen that
were new to me include cotton,
rice, Spanish moss, magnolia trees
date, fan, and cocoanut palms,
olive, sugar, banana trees.

We went to the top of Huey
Long's capitol building at Baton
Rouge and looked the town over.
It's a beautiful bldg, 30 stories
high. We could see Louisiana
State University.

Here in N.O. I have seen Ocean
going vessels, canal street - which
is about a block across, the St.
Louis cathedral which is 200 years
old, and very beautiful, the bldg. where
the Louisiana purchase was made,
and gobs of other things.

There's lots of what we'd call
timber here in Mississippi. They
say its not much good tho. We

Stanley's travelogue began, "First, I don't want you to have the idea that the trip I took was a cut and dried affair sponsored by some rich uncle. I worked my way from place to place never knowing where I'd find myself next. I know that being a vagabond offers a thrill that no planned trip could ever give. Another fellow from Kansas State started the trip with me. He was probably as influential as anyone in my deciding to travel. He had done some traveling before, and some of the stories he told only served to rouse my curiosity that much more.

"When I left home I had nine dollars and sixty cents in my pocket. My home was in Manhattan, Kansas, and I left the day after I graduated from Kansas State College. I knew if I postponed my trip I never would take it. Just as soon as a person gets into business, he's there for life. So my partner and I started out for the ocean. At eight o'clock in the morning, we were at the edge of town hitchhiking to New Orleans. We were lucky that day. We spent the first night in Little Rock, Arkansas, about six hundred miles away.

"I really enjoyed myself for those two years. Many times in those two years my folks didn't have the least idea where I was. And you know, especially for mothers, that's not much fun. And of course, I gained lots of knowledge that I couldn't get out of books. Really, the greatest thing I learned in college was just how little I did know.

"New Orleans has been called the crescent city because the city was built on the curve of the Mississippi River. I suppose the thing that caught my eye first was the subtle charm of the old French section of New Orleans with its half-hidden courtyards, narrow streets, odd appearing buildings with overhanging balconies and iron lacework. Two centuries of French and Spanish influence were plainly visible. I was a little disappointed in the great Mississippi because it didn't look as wide as it really is. I've noticed that same optical illusion a lot of times on the water. Out on the ocean you'll see a ship pass and it looks like it's about a mile away. Really, though, a ship you think is a mile away is probably five miles off.

"We had enough to live on for a few days by doing our own clothes washing and buying food in grocery stores and eating it in our room. I remember a sign in a café window that attracted our attention. It was an advertisement for an eight-course dinner for fifty cents. The two of us decided that, after we got to making money, we were going to have that eight-course dinner before we left town. But we never had the opportunity to do it. One hour after we got a job working our way on a ship, we were sailing down the Mississippi River. Frankly, I had never seen an ocean-going vessel before I got to New Orleans. And I'm sure I didn't know what kind of work a person did on a ship.

"We decided that the quickest way to get a job would be to find a vacancy on a foreign ship. Lots of fellows from foreign countries disappear from their ships when they get to the United States. They've heard so much about life, liberty, and the pursuit of happiness in the States they want to find out what it is all about. Our opportunity came when there were two vacancies on an old Norwegian tramp freighter. We didn't care what the jobs were or where the ship was going. We just wanted to get to some foreign country.

"The first ocean trip wasn't very long, just to Cuba. It was four days from New Orleans to Cuba. I have an idea I'll remember that trip longer than I'll remember some of the long trips I took. First of all, I was impressed because it was my first ocean voyage, and I really got a big kick out of it. Yes, I got seasick and was almost dead when I got off that ship. The worst part of it was the living conditions on that old scow. We ate boiled potatoes three times a day. Once in a while we'd have lamb stew for dinner or supper. The bread was cooked on the ship, and if the bread wasn't bad enough to begin with, the men on the ship would grab the loaf in their greasy hands leaving black handprints on the loaf. I didn't eat any bread.

"We slept on mattresses made of wood shavings, without pillows, without sheets or blankets. I should explain that the ship, the SS Novasli, though it was

Norwegian, is not typical. The Norwegians are noted for their cooking and their high standard of living. That ship was Norwegian only because it was built in Norway and most of the crew was Norwegian. By the way, I shoveled coal eight hours a day. I worked from 4:00 p.m. until 8:00 p.m. and from 4:00 a.m. until 8:00 a.m. and made thirty-two dollars a month—not much, but I got three squares a day, a place to live, and a very good education.

"The thing that impressed me most in Cuba was buying large pineapples for twenty-five cents a dozen. A native showed us how to peel them. We ate two or three each day. We also ate grapefruit and mangoes and drank green coconut juice. I did have lots of fun there, other than eating, and the weather in Cuba was ideal.

"We were docked at a small village called Nuevitas in the wilds of Cuba, and of course, there were no beaches. One day my vagabond pal and I decided to go swimming. We jumped into our bathing suits and waded cautiously into the ocean where sea vegetation had probably never felt the touch of a human foot. And I know two feet that that sea vegetation will never touch again. We had to wade out into the ocean about a hundred yards before we could get into water deep enough in which to swim. And in that hundred yards there were more big crabs, sand dollars, and other sea life than I thought inhabited the whole world. We'd take one step and a vicious crab, about eight inches long, would grab a toe with its big sharp pincers. In the attempt to get rid of the crab, we'd stand on the other foot, and upon doing so, we'd feel the sharp prongs of a sand dollar push through the skin on the bottom of the foot. Those prongs on the sand dollar broke off just like a sticker does sometimes, and they're really hard to pull out. So, you see, we didn't have a picnic. We didn't know what kinds of animals might be hiding in the seaweed, and we expected every minute to see some monster start after us. But we had to have our swim, and then we got back the same way we went out. Only going back was worse because we knew what would happen.

"Back on dry land in Cuba I walked through a jungle for the first time. The growth of trees and brush was thick, and we followed the beaten path through the jungle because we didn't know what wild animals were there. From some of the sounds that came out of the jungle, we didn't feel like venturing very far in, especially with nothing to shoot except a camera. Nuevitas is a typical dirty, poor town of probably ten thousand people who live on the income from pineapple and other tropical fruit and what little iron ore can be found there. The streets were paved with some kind of stone that was about three times the size of bricks. Instead of having grown smooth with years of traffic on them, they had grown rough. The cementing material between the rocks was poor quality, and the weight of iron wheeled wagons wore the edges of the rocks off, leaving the center of the rock sticking up above the rest of the surface. Needless to say, what few cars, mostly Fords, were in Nuevitas got shaken to pieces very quickly.

"All the stores had open fronts. Most of the front was a large double door that was closed during the night. The homes in Nuevitas, if they can be called homes, were built together like our stores. Many homes were second floor dwellings above the stores, a dingy two-by-four frame house with neighbors on each side using the same walls for their house.

"I didn't realize how lucky I was to be born in the United States until I took that trip. That was my first visit to a country across the sea. It was a very good education, and I was thrilled from the time I arrived until I left."

"And what Spanish I remember came in handy," Stanley wrote home from Cuba. "Some of the motions we go through to help us speak to the people are wows. I'll probably have to fly to get the guy to realize I want this sent airmail."

Meanwhile, the SS *Novasli* loaded iron ore in Cuba and started a six- or seven-day voyage up the East Coast to Philadelphia. After disembarking, Stanley and Theron made their way to New York City via Washington, D.C.

July 2, 1939

Dear folks,

Well, here we are in New York City, and what a city it is! It has everything. We went to a show at the Roxy, the most beautiful theatre in New York. I think we'll go out to the World's Fair on the fourth. Then we'll settle down to a little shipping business. We had to quit the other ship because it was going to Norway, and they didn't know when it would return, if ever.

In Washington, D.C. we saw the House in session and sat through the senate session. Of course, I saw the vice president in action. And here's the big thing of that day. We went to the Library of Congress to see the originals of the Declaration of Independence and the Constitution, and there examining them was none other than the exiled president of Czechoslovakia, Eduard Benes! We shook his hand and talked a little with him. Was I thrilled.

We spent some time in the Smithsonian Institution, and went through a few other buildings, then walked up the stairs at the Washington Monument ... went to see the Lincoln Memorial ... and Arlington Cemetery. We got to the amphitheatre, where you have seen so many pictures of Decorations Day programs and the grave of the Unknown Soldier nearby, just in time to see Benes decorating that. Wasn't that a coincidence? We saw the Ford Theatre where

Lincoln was shot and the building where he died and called it a day. We hitchhiked here yesterday.

We are staying in a rooming house. It doesn't cost much, and it's just a block from Times Square. Last night we gave this part of the city the once-over, including Radio City. We were in the Empire State Building today, and we saw Jack Dempsey's Café and Bar a while ago. And the lights at night are something never to be forgotten.

Food is reasonable here. There are all kinds of stands where you can buy malted milks for a nickel, and a while ago I had a hot dog and a root beer thrown in for good measure for a nickel.

Well, give my love to everyone. Have a big time this summer.

> Lots of love,
> Stan

The Royal Norwegian Consulate issued Stanley's seaman papers, and then he and Theron parted ways. Stanley served as crew messman on a tanker, the SS *Japan Arrow*, for a few trips from the East Coast to Beaumont, Texas, and he considered his options.

> Tuesday, August 22
> Coast of Florida

Dear Folks,

We were in quite a storm the first day out. The wind blew a gale, and the rain beat hard against the ship. The ship rocked and rolled, but your young son didn't get seasick. Ain't that a shame?

We just listened to the Ambers-Armstrong fight in the second assist. engineer's room. I didn't get very excited over it.

I have quite a deal up my sleeve. I hate to tell it because it is sort of embarrassing when you tell everyone about things that might happen and then they don't. But I can't hold it any longer or I'll burst, so here goes. More and more it is being impressed upon me that when a person wants a thing bad enough, he gets it. With that thought in mind, while we were in New York, I went to the shipping office of the Isthmian steamship lines. I visited them often the first time I was in New York hoping I might sail for them, but all the time I never even saw anyone shipped out. For that reason I came to the conclusion that there was an inside track. I determined to get on that track. He, the boss, told me to come back and to bring a recommendation from my Steward (that, incidentally, is the key to that inside track).

But I haven't told you why I'm so eager to sail for Isthmian. Here it is: They are a freight line, and they carry spices, and in doing so they sail around the world. It is a four-and-a-half-month trip, and I guess it's a biddy. The ships go from New York, down through the Panama Canal, over to Hawaii, then to China, through the China Sea to India, through the Red Sea and the Suez Canal to the Mediterranean Sea, then back to New York. A chance on a deal like that is something. I hope the European situation doesn't ball things up.

Lots of love,
Stan

In the 1920s and '30s, Europe teetered with uncertainty. After World War I, in President Woodrow Wilson's words, the "war to end all wars," treaties were signed, borders in Europe were remapped, and other attempts were made to renew peace. In hindsight, those treaties only established a temporary solution for world peace and seemed to provide the catalyst for the next world war.

With unrest in the German government, the stage appeared to be set for Fascist Hitler's masterminded entrance. The impoverished and dejected German people, suffering morally as well as economically, were inspired by the extremist Hitler and his deceptive propaganda. He envisioned the Thousand-Year Reich. So as the Nazi dictator rose to power in the '30s, Germany's economy rebounded somewhat while he schemed. Rejecting signed treaties, it was only a matter of time before Germany's rebuilt army reclaimed the Rhineland, annexed Austria, and occupied the Sudetenland and eventually all of Czechoslovakia. Germany's unprovoked attack on neighboring Poland set off World War II—about the same time Stanley's sailing ventures began.

Stanley, back in New York, assured his folks about the safety of an around-the-world venture in a paragraph of a letter dated September 8, 1939.

> Your uncle Pedro would be made after a trip like that. And with a war close by, that trip would be much safer than any trip on a tanker. Not even Hitler would waste a bee-bee on a harmless spice ship. Spices will never win anyone's war. And besides, if and when I do get on, the ship goes westward, and peace might be declared a dozen times before we would get around that far. And with that much value involved, no company is going to stick a neutral ship's nose anywhere it might get cut off. (This last paragraph was for you, ma.)

And, Stanley wrote more on September 13, 1939.

> And here's a little note that should ease your fears, ma. Since the war started, Isthmian has redirected their ships from India down

around the southern tip of Africa, thence back to N. Y. That keeps us clear of hostile waters, and if anything, adds to the educational and entertainment value of the cruise. Dad, I think foreign-going on a freight ship is less dangerous than coastwise on a tanker.

Stanley, when in New York, "graduated from rooming houses" and stayed in the Coolidge Hotel, one-half block east of Times Square, with a view of the "tallest building in the world" from his ninth-floor window. His college professor from Kansas State, Harrison Summers, whom Stanley called "Doc," happened to be working in New York at that time. In fact, the whole Summers family was in New York, including Bob and his younger sister Dorothy. Bob probably introduced Stanley to Gerv; the three often played golf, and Stanley wrote, "during which time I made quite a name for myself."

Stanley wrote:

Gerv and I went to see "The Rains Came," and then Gerv took me out to meet the family, the Keoughs. They're Irish as Irish can be. New York is Ireland's greatest population center. Was there ever a New York cop that wasn't named Pat? Just one, and that was Mike. Great people, the Irish. I had supper with the Keoughs. Then we gabbed and gabbed. And the Summers are sure nice. They make me feel as if I were in my own home. I've been up to their house a number of times; they have taken me riding. Gee, I practically know everyone in New York now. I know three families. Well, maybe four or five, including the landlord.

Wednesday [September, 1939]
N.Y., N. Y

Dear folks:

Howdy. This is your wandering son speaking again. And when I say wandering, I do mean wandering cause I'm at work again. The only catch to it is that it is for Standard Oil again. I don't know whether it was a dirty trick or a bit of good luck. There wasn't to be any Isthmian ships in for a few days, and I had been here two weeks, so I strolled down to Standard Oil to apply thinking that it would be a couple of weeks more before my name got to the top. By that time, if I wasn't out for Isthmian, I'd be glad to take another Standard Oil ship.

Within three hours of the time I applied, I was packed and aboard ship. This time it's the same address, except the India Arrow instead of the Japan Arrow. I guess they had been putting a lot of ships back to work and had run out of messmen. I'm crew mess this time. I guess the crew really dishes out the tips. Rumor has it we are going to Beaumont then to Portland, Maine, but of course, it's not sure.

I guess I'll never know whether or not this was the right jump, but I'm not going to feel very bad about it. After all, fate has done some queer things to steer me the right way. Now that I'm here, I think that I will turn my firsthand attention to paying that debt at school. If everything goes right, I should be able to get that done by the first of the year.

Incidentally, this couple of weeks has done me alright in the eyes of Isthmian. If everything is right for me to try to make that trip later, I shouldn't have a lot of trouble. (You are saving my letters, aren't you?)

During the next several months, whenever Stanley ported in or near New York City, he chummed with friends to, in his words, "head for the tall buildings and run around." He "had a big time," with what spare moments he did have, experiencing a city's culture. He made time for "mundane affairs" like getting a haircut, but better yet, he filled the hours at the World's Fair, attended radio programs at NBC and shows at the Paramount, ate out, and enjoyed just "shooting the bull." He said, "We went up to a place called Fiesta Danceteria where you can pay sixty cents, get a meal and dance to Ben Bernie to your heart's content. We surely did some tall listening and talking."

Stanley's letters home, starting on September 23, 1939, disclosed more.

It looks very much like you are going to get a letter in pencil. I don't seem to be able to locate my ink, and my pen is dry.

Low and behold, I'm afraid that today is Harold's birthday. I didn't think of it until we were far out on the high seas. I'm quite unable to do anything about it now. Maybe I can pick something up in Beaumont that is worthwhile. If I can jar loose with a little cash, I might call you mugs up when I get to Beaumont.

We're getting down where it is getting hot. I'm sweating now. I'll probably sleep up on the lifeboat deck.

Oh yes, will you send me a copy of the football schedule? You might send me some copies of the "Collegian" if you can get a hold of them. If nothing more, Harold could get me some by going to Anderson Hall on campus and getting one out of the wastepaper basket at the entrance to the post office. There are always lots of them there.

My job is fine. I work a couple of hours less than I did on the other ship. I feed twenty-two men. That's nine more than on the other job, but I don't have any rooms to make up, no salads to make, and one doesn't have to be so particular with a crew. Financially, the job is better also. A crew tips better than the officers. And when the crew gets in a poker mood, the crew mess can pick up a couple of dollars a night by waiting on them. They pay well for the messman's kind attention and service.

I'm getting a big kick out of my radio. It has a little something wrong with the volume control; it turns itself off sometimes. I'll get that fixed in Beaumont. I sure got a swell filter for the set. I suppose I have told you that aboard ship a filter is necessary to eliminate electric machine noise. In spite of the fact that our room is very close to the generator, not a speck of noise gets to the radio. As you probably know, reception is stronger at night than day, which is really when I want to listen. It's swell.

P.S. By the way, mom, I seem to have no driver's license, except the one that expired in 1938. Do you happen to know where my later one is? If not, will you call up the right party and try to get me another? I might need one badly sometime. I'm sending my pictures with a short description on the back. Guard them with your life.

Once the SS *India Arrow* docked in Beaumont, Texas, Stanley continued his "education." He wrote home, "At last I've found someone that I can run around with who is interested in something other than wine and women. He's the saloon mess. He has been on passenger ships and has been all over the world." Over time, to "break up the monotony of being on the ship," Stanley went roller-skating or ice-skating—on an indoor rink—or he rented golf clubs for twenty-five cents and, for another twenty-five cents, played a round with friends—old and new. And Stanley also told his folks, "I'm a sucker for seafood. It beats terra meat ten ways."

During the fall of 1939 and early months of 1940, Stanley made several voyages on the SS *India Arrow* from Texas, down the Sabine River from Beaumont, across the Gulf of Mexico, around the tip of Florida, and coastwise to New York. He may also have gone to Baltimore, Maryland; Boston, Massachusetts; Providence, Rhode Island; Portland, Maine; or Paulsboro, New Jersey.

"I had the thrill of sailing up the Hudson River to Albany, New York," Stanley wrote in his radio travelogue. "It's a beautiful trip—mountains on both sides, beautiful country—and we saw the home of President Roosevelt in Hyde Park, right across the river, incidentally, from the retreat of Father Divine, the Negro revivalist."

If time allowed, Stanley rode a bus or train to New York—"Staten Island docks are about an hour from the City"—to call the Summers and "hook up with friends." After one or two days in port, and sometimes after only a few hours in port, Stanley was back on the tanker for about a seven-day return voyage—depending on the weather—hauling cargo back to Texas, which was approximately two thousand miles. It appeared he collected overtime pay if they were in port on the weekends.

Stanley explained:

Again the time has come when I must get to writing letters, or I'll get caught with my panties down. We are three days out of Beaumont. We had a strong wind in our rear that just sent us sailing along. It lasted a couple of days. It's fall on the high seas now. Altho there are no yellow leaves falling from the trees around here, it is quite obvious that winter is just around the corner. The ocean is restless. Waves are thicker and bigger, and there are more and larger swells. There's more chance for a storm now than there was a month or so ago, and no one feels too pert when the ship is tossing a lot. We got into the roughest water I have been in so far. I would say the waves were about fifteen feet high. One minute the waves would be a couple of feet from the deck, and a couple of seconds later they would be twenty feet below. Then, of course, we'd have to go down and meet them. Great fun.

In another letter to his folks, Stanley commented:

We missed our overtime in Beaumont. We got in Friday afternoon and out Saturday morning. Can't miss them always tho.

I didn't go ashore with the boys, or get drunk with the boys, or play around with wild women, but I'll bet I had more fun than any one of them. And I spent less money too. Were you surprised when I called, mom? I've been contemplating doing that for a long time, but this trip was the first one on which I felt financially free to do so. It's too bad that Harold wasn't there and also that it wasn't Saturday night so Dad might have been there. We'd have made a family affair of it. Wouldn't that have been the cat's pajamas? Too bad we couldn't have talked for an hour or so.

Stanley received letters down south or up north and then wrote his correspondence while at sea, stating, "I'm practically in the same place when I write."

23 years later
N.Y. bound [1939]

Dear folks:

I take this occasion, the twenty-third anniversary of the birth of a bouncing little brat to the H. W. Dwyer family, to write a letter to the grandest parents and brother in all the world. And who is in better position to judge than I, I who have talked with presidents, traveled extensively, acquired a Bachelor of Science degree, been in half a dozen businesses of my own, labored for others, ridden in boxcars with tramps, and sailed the seas with the sailor? I have been given freedom of thought and action, leaving me to make my own decisions, having been given before each decision only the unbiased interpretation of the good and bad points of each path I may choose from. Yes, others have been given freedom, but the choosing of the right path comes not from the final decision only, but from goodness of mind and body of generations previous.

I doubt if anyone has gotten a bigger kick out of the first twenty-three years of their life than I have. Ah, yes, money is fine; it will buy fine clothes and cars, etc., but it can't buy the satisfaction one derives from accomplishments through his own efforts, the thrill of seeing one's self work gradually from the bottom to the top. And I am far up the ladder, and my life has hardly begun. Nothing short of a torpedo could stop me now. These sailors and many others cannot see my point in what I'm doing now. These fellows can't see how this broadens one's mind. And no wonder. When they hit port, they don't go, see, or think farther than the nearest beer parlor to the ship.

We are certainly being watched this trip. A day out of Portland a U.S. destroyer stopped and inspected us. Since then there have been two more ships and at least a half dozen airplanes look us over. I guess they are afraid we will discharge cargo into a ship of a belligerent country.

Believe it or not I had a couple of dates down in Beaumont. A kid that joined the crew in Beaumont the trip previous got me the date with a girl that used to double date with him and his wife before they were married. We took in three picture shows and danced a little during the two evenings. The best show we saw was Judy Garland and Mickey Rooney in "Babes in Arms." It was swell. The four of us practically made two full nights of it. The place the ship was docked was so lousy with mosquitoes that one would get eaten alive if he tried to sleep on the ship, so we ran around most of the nights then came back to the ship in time for him to go to work at four.

Incidentally, the last paragraphs are being written the 29th, Sunday. I'm supposed to see the Summers tonight, but I doubt if we'll get in in time.

I suppose you are saving my letters like I asked you to. Dad speaks well of the business. Hurray for our side. Have you folks drawn names for Christmas? At present it looks very much like the family is going to have to spend Christmas with this son "in absentia."

That is some picture of the airplane. If the airplane is half as good as the picture, it is quite a machine. Can I take a ride in your plane? Don't break it up before I get to see it. Do high schoolers write letters?

Don't forget my address.

Love,
Stan

I started high school in Manhattan, Kansas. I had always messed around with model airplanes, and Stan and I used to fly them all the time his senior year in college. We had a vacant lot right next to our house in Manhattan, and at that time, the planes were rubber band–powered flying models. You'd turn the plane loose, the rubber band would wear out, and it would go down someplace. I'd fly the planes, and Stan would run them down for me.

As I read Stanley's letters and learned about his life as a merchant marine, I had a notion to Google SS *India Arrow*. Subsequently, I corresponded with a man, Charles Seerveld, who first sailed on the *China Arrow* in 1940 and 1941 and also sailed on the *India Arrow*—but his service was in the months after Stanley was discharged.

Mr. Seerveld sent me a letter and wrote, "A civilian ship like the India Arrow is listed as SS India Arrow. Navy ships are listed as USS."

He stated on a website:

I was sent to the India Arrow, a sister ship of the China Arrow. There were 10 Arrow boats in all. They were built in the twenties for the oil trade to China. They were different from flush deck tankers in that they had a covered 'tween deck that we walked through in heavy weather ... In merchant ships we never wore uniforms ... American ships were not in the war yet and sailed with all lights on at night. Some ships even had a large American flag painted on the side of the hull with a flood light shining on the flag at night. [3]

The 8,327-ton tanker was owned by the Socony-Vacuum Oil Company.[4] According to the website www.us-highways.com/sohist1941, "Standard Oil Company of New York (Socony) merged with Vacuum Oil Company in 1931, becoming Socony-Vacuum." The names Standard Oil and Socony Oil are often interchanged, and Stanley usually referred to Standard Oil in his letters.

Stanley conveyed his impressions.

This ship is a few feet less than five hundred feet long. It has a crew of thirty-eight. Its capacity is ninety-two thousand barrels. How long it takes to load and discharge depends on the weight of the oil, the temperature, and the distance is has to be pumped in the case of discharging. In Albany it took almost two days to unload. And the beauty of it is, Sunday overtime in port began, which put nine bucks in the old sock gratis. My pay was raised to sixty-five, from sixty. The sixty-five is for P.O. messman, but I'm getting it because I've been on the ship the longest. And I still do the same work.

Standard Oil is the granddaddy of the companies. I don't know about living conditions in the other co., but on S.O. ships they make living as much like living in a home as possible, cleanliness, recreation, and things like that being stressed. As time passes, we add little comforts that make this room more and more like home. Until a few days ago, we had a swivel chair in here. That, of course, exaggerated many times the roll of the ship. Now we have one of those big straight chairs with a curved back culminating in arm rests.

This tub does a lot of vibrating back here where I write; it's near the propeller. I surely have the letters to answer too. I got five from you folks, one from Aileen, one from Dorothea S., Bea, Lynne, Aunt Gertie and Uncle Lou, and oh yes, I got a letter from Theron. He has another novel finished. By the way, are some of the relation begrudging me because of this trip or something? Some have owed me a letter since about the first of the trip. If there is such a thing in the air, I'd like to know about it – in detail and without a soft peddle. How about it?

And the ritual continued. Stanley, on board the SS *India Arrow*, sailed across the Gulf of Mexico, up the East Coast, and then the ship reversed order. Stanley wrote:

> Lately, believe it or not, I have been getting a lot of good song ideas, so I started putting them down on paper. I wish I had started making a few notes sooner because I've had some good ideas that I have forgotten. Anyway, in the last three or four days, I have written two songs and have ideas for two more. Just between us girls, they are pretty darned good and have hit making possibilities. They both have a few rough spots yet that I'll have to iron out, but that is something that takes an unlimited amount of uninterrupted time. I have lots of time, but interruptions are frequent throughout the day. I could hardly be situated better for the actual song writing. Half my working day I am alone, and as my work takes no thought, I can compose as I work. If some of the sailors would see me drop my work and run for a paper and pencil, they would throw me over the side for a hopeless case of tankeritis. I guess that is a mental disease in which one does abnormal things in an effort to keep the monotony of the sea, and time, from driving him nuts. Many times the "escape" is itself a form of insanity, but not this one. This old buzzard's escape is productive and perhaps profitable.
>
> About the best friends I have on ship now, believe it or not, are the Captain and the wireless operator. Officers usually think they're too good to have anything to do with the lowly crew, but once in a while you run into one that takes a man for what he's worth and not his position. The other guys are alright, but they just have different interests than I have.
>
> Someone on the ship got a Chinese checker board in port, and your uncle Pedro is the champ. The rest play to see who will be second when I play. When the boys have spent their bills in port, they play poker with change, and they dig up a lot of it sometimes. And I ought to be able to pick up a few stray coins for the collection. I suppose you know there is, I think, a 1913 nickel worth $250. Well, write soon, and often, all of you (incl. Harold)

I discovered pages of handwritten song lyrics in Stanley's trunk.

> Afraid to dream
> I'll see you there with someone new
> Afraid to find another one caressing you

And tho you promised me
That this would never be
It's the thot of losing you
That makes me so afraid to dream.

Another day, he wrote:

It's getting near Christmas, and I, like all good girls and boys, find that time is heavy on my hands. My spare time aboard ship continues to produce fruit. Whether it is green fruit, ripe fruit, rotten fruit, or fruitless is hard to say as yet, but if nothing else, the law of averages should make a song hit once in a while. I have two more this half trip which makes four for the round-trip. These two are "Love Has Come Your Way" and a good tear jerker "Crying My Tears Away." There's nothing dry about that last one, is there?

Yes, butch, you can use the skates. All I ask is that you dry and oil them, steel and leather, as quickly as possible each time after you use them.

Dec. 24, 1939

Dear folks,
'Tis the day before Christmas
And all thru the ship,
Every sailor's awaiting
The end of the trip.

And so's your old man. It would be a washed up holiday if we had to spend it out here on the sea with nothing but white caps to make it a white Christmas. It was snowing to beat four of a kind this morning, and the temperature was playing around the freezing mark, but for some reason, not a bit of it stayed, not even in the grass or behind the buildings. There was enough up on deck for a few snowballs, but of course, that didn't last long either.

We can feel mighty lucky that we'll be in port tomorrow. There are plenty of ships that didn't have it timed just right. And incidentally, fate tried its darndest to keep us out here too. Down on the coast of Florida we lost one of the three propeller blades. But with the help of the Gulf Stream, which runs up this way as far as Cape Hatteras before turning east, and the fact that the officers of the ship have families that they want to spend Christmas with, we're going to be able to limp in anyway. Of course, a fog on the river or some such thing could keep us out yet, but we're ignoring such possibilities. We'll be at the bar about ten tonite then at the dock at nine or ten in the morning. We'll probably pay off right after dinner, which will be turkey, then I think I'll be off for the rest of the day. If so, I spect I will take a bus into Philly, which isn't far away, and give 22 a ring. If I don't get off, I'll have to call from the dock, in which case I'll be putting nickels and dimes and quarters in the slot till midnight.

Don't know just how I'll spend the rest of the day. In any case, it won't be like any I ever spent before. I wonder if Aileen and Bill will be with the rest?

As you probably know by now, I didn't get much shopping done down there. I looked for quite a while for something for Aunt Myrtle, but because I knew so little of what she could use, I gave it up as a bad job. I did mail a few Christmas cards.

The song writing has progressed at the usual speed. Had a couple of good inspirations, but they're ideas that will take more than the shallow, interrupted thought I can give them here. Then today "Why Don't You Speak For Yourself" came over the inspiration wireless and has good possibilities.

Can you imagine, I'm out of something to say? I can say "Merry Christmas," but by the time you get this, you won't know whether I mean this Christmas or next.

Under such circumstances, I guess the usual procedure is to scribble the handle. Sometimes "Write Soon" is added and also "Love"

Stan

P.S. Just called you on the telephone, sort of a round-robin affair. And it didn't cost much either. Also called the Summers, and they wanted me to come over. I guess I will cause they're leaving soon. I can go over for little more than entertainment would cost me here. And Christmas comes only once a year. Merry Xmas

Stan

And the adventures—on and off shore—continued into the winter months of 1940. "Had a big time in Philly," Stanley wrote. "Rode the bus to the city, went to the Stanley Theatre from which network shows originate, and saw 'The Great Victor Herbert.'"

Stan Dwyer
S. S. INDIA ARROW

Dec. 27, 1939

Dear folks

Cast an eye upon some scrumdumptious stationery, will you? Had I guessed for a century I never would have even given a thought to individual ship stationery. I'll bet even the captain doesn't have such a thing. I don't know of anything that you could have sent that I would have appreciated more.

I sure had fun talking to the Christmas congregation. I didn't know I was going to get to talk to everyone - there's some more of that Dwyer novelty I guess.

I called Summers after I called you and they insisted that I come over. We went down to Keogh's for turkey, and I sure enjoyed it. Bill K., who goes to K.S.C. was home for vacation. After the meal I ran over to Brooklyn to Russels to see if Theron was in. To my disappointment and his fortune he wasn't.

Stanley's letters read:

Not long 'til mail time again, so I better spread a few drops of ink to put into the box. Also, I cut recently from "Look Magazine" a two-page, six-month calendar and hung it above my bunk. So today, all I had to do to find the date was turn my head a little instead of the usual census of guesses. It makes so little difference aboard ship what date it is that I can hardly keep track.

I'll bet a fur-lined bathtub that it's colder than a wet undershirt out in your neck of the woods. I heard on a newscast that there was a foot of snow over Nebraska, Kansas, and Oklahoma. That should provide a little moisture to the soil. I wonder if dad got caught in it somewhere. If I remember right, the last car we wore out let us down on the coldest day since hell froze over. I haven't gotten thawed out from that yet.

We've been missing storms, both cold and wind, all winter. Things have gone on as usual this trip. I usually play pinochle for a couple of hours in the evening, work eight hours a day, listen to the radio or write songs between watches, and listen to the radio for a couple of hours before going to sleep. I have two more songs added to the stack. I don't know whether it's coming easier for me now or whether these just wrote themselves, as some verse does. I got the idea for one while doing supper dishes, and by the time I had finished, I had all but the last fourth of the song done. That was nite before last, then last nite, I finished it while taking a stroll on deck.

> If my dreams come true
> I'll be seeing you
> Skies will all be blue
> If my dreams come true.
>
> If my dreams come true
> When you say "I do"
> I will say "me too"
> If my dreams come true

Stanley wrote:

'Tis spring, and a young man's fancy turns to such lighter things as sunshine, warm breezes, and a shirtless afternoon up on deck. And I'm not kidding about the weather. This is the kind of day that at Kansas State there's a parade of men headed for the picnic grounds with a blanket under one arm and a gal under the other. I can't enjoy it to the fullest tho because I haven't been thru a week of winter yet.

We have a new second cook on the ship, and he's quite a fellow. He's almost human, and that's quite strange around here. Sometimes he and I throw the bull a couple hours each evening.

These miles are bad things to have between a person and his family and friends. [You] could make new friends but never a new family. I suppose I have told you that after six months on a ship a person is entitled to a ten-day vacation, with pay. My six months will be up in a couple more trips. I expect to spend it in New York, the vacation. I have a mouthful of teeth to take care of, and I think I shall see about my sinuses. Also, I'll see what I can do with my songs. And I know pretty much about the racket now. I invested $2.50 in a book that tells all about writing songs, selling songs, evading song sharks, popularizing songs, etc.

I wonder, dad, if whoever you talked to about the draft can tell you the exact time that I'll get my questionnaire and how long after that I'll be called. If you could give me the info, it would help me make definite plans.

Yes, I guess I'm a bit restless. The biggest job aboard ship is spending the other 16 hours. Very few stay on this long. There are eight of all the crew that started when I did that are still here. There have been over a dozen and a half messmen so far.

I enjoyed and appreciated very much the papers, mom. But I'm going to paddle a youngun if he doesn't write! See you in the funny papers.

March 6, 1940

Dear Peoples:

Rumors are flying thick and fast around the good ship India Arrow, and the suspense is terrific. Word has been received that she is going foreign next trip, but it wasn't stated where. We are supposed to take on six-month stores when we get to Providence. I don't know whether we will know where we are going before we get in or not. I hope so, so I can make a few plans and preparations.

This surely upsets my previous plans. I had one more trip before my vacation. Now it might be quite a while before I get off. On the other hand, it might only be a short trip, little longer than coastwise. If it's a long trip, I spect I will call you before I start. If it's only a short one, I'll add it on the south end of this letter. In either case, it's silly for me to write my guesses and the rumors here cause I'll know more before this is sent.

I guess I am never going to see any of the kids. I was sure of seeing Theron in New York during my stay there. I still had one more chance to see Lynne down south in Beaumont, but I spect that's out.

I had quite a time down in Beaumont this time. The utility man served my supper, so I was off as soon as we docked in early afternoon. I called Cliff as soon as I got to town, and we went golfing. Then I had supper at their house. Home cooking sure tasted good. I don't know what I would do to a meal back Dwyer way where cooking is a natural art.

P.S. Providence, Sunday

It looks like you guys were going to get a phone call tonite. Guess where—to Aruba, off the northern coast of South America, then over to Dakar, French West Africa, then no one knows where. Because of the war, we don't get orders very far in advance. Of course, I'm not signed up yet but will be tonite unless something drastic happens. The trip will last a minimum of two and one-half months.

Love,
Stan

March 15, 1940
Aruba bound

Dear folks:

I'd play heck throwing a rock onto the shores of the U.S. now. We have been traveling south and a little east for four days. This sudden turn of events is as much a surprise to me as you. I thought my days on the India Arrow were about over. Now I don't know whether it will be a month or six. At any rate, I'll be seeing lots of things shortly. And when I get to Africa—that will be the day! That's the last continent I expected to see. Course I haven't seen her yet. I was very much surprised, mom, that you gave even a thot to worrying. I assure you there's no reason for it.

Sure had a big time with Theron; just threw the bull the whole night.

The four of us messmen together bought a radio with short wave so we could keep in touch with the world. I can't answer all the questions, Harold. I've been taking pictures and will take more now since I got a new camera.

Aside from that, this trip so far is just another trip. The waves here look about the same as on the coast. But I should have lots to say Monday.

Love,
Stan

In fact, Stanley had lots to say about his trip in his 1941 radio travelogue broadcast. The radio announcer called it, "The world through your loud speaker."

"Aruba is a small island off the South American coast," he wrote in the radio script, "and it is the top of one of the partly submerged mountains that form the Dutch West Indies. The land, as is the land of all good mountaintops, is rocky, hilly, and of very poor quality. That, in itself, is enough to make crop raising difficult, but on top of that, Aruba is in the path of the northeast trade winds as they make their way across the Atlantic from the coast of Africa. Consequently, practically everything is one sided. A tree, for instance the divi-divi tree, about the only kind of tree that grows on the island, grew all on one side of the trunk. Normally the divi-divi tree grows about ten to fifteen feet tall then branches out eight or ten feet each direction. But in Aruba, the limbs were all one direction because of the trade winds that blow every hour of the day, every day of the year. So the divi-divi tree looked like an "L" stood upside down.

"And you can't guess what the natives used for fences, tall tubular cacti planted close together like hedge trees in Kansas. And I dare say that cactus grown close together makes a wonderful fence, whether or not there are any animals to keep in or out. There were a few goats and a few chickens and some kind of a sturdy grass, and that's the size of the crops on Aruba. Practically everyone, the twenty thousand people living on the island, worked in the oil business or worked serving those who are oil workers. You won't find oil derricks there as thick as corn stalks on a Nebraska farm—there wasn't a derrick on the island. The oil was transported from the South American mainland by what is called a mosquito fleet, a fleet of small flat bottom tankers."

In a letter home, Stanley wrote:

You should see my new spring outfit. It consists of a pair of white trunks rolled up to the lord knows where from the bottom and down to the same place from the top. Such an outfit wouldn't do for you women tho. I should be black from sunbathing when I get back, and I don't mean just where my sleeves are rolled up either. Everyone is wearing practically the same thing. I don't wear much more than that to work, a pair of light pants abbreviated to the knees and a silk shirt (three for a dollar at Aruba). It is a duty-free port known by sailors all over the world as a place to buy Japanese silk cheap.

The travelogue continued, "We then headed for Dakar, French West Africa, the farthest point west in Africa, about fourteen or fifteen degrees north of the equator. A few days out of Aruba we saw the islands of Martinique and St. Lucia. It took nearly two weeks crossing the Atlantic, and the only other land we saw was a couple days from Dakar when we passed the Cape Verde Islands where I saw my first crater, extinct, but you could distinguish the ravines where lava once flowed down and hardened.

"We heard lots of war news on the radio, but somehow we didn't seem to realize just what was taking place. Radio helped to bring upon us the grim realization. I remember the time [in early April] when news came that Norway had fallen. That was a shock to everyone. Then I heard later about the reaction of that news to a shipload of Norwegians who had left their homeland just a few days before heading for America. I'll bet there were different emotions shown on their faces when they realized that they had not fallen with their country. They were free as long as the ship remained on top of the water.

"I also saw firsthand the grimness of the war. A French passenger liner that had been bombed in the North Atlantic limped into the harbor at Dakar with a big hole in the side near the bow. The crew had boarded up the hole so she wouldn't sink. Her name was 'Haggar.' I'll never forget the looks on the faces of the passengers and crew as well—the look of fear and hate, together with thankfulness that they were still alive.

"When we were there [in Dakar] France was still a free nation. We were there about three months before the trouble started—when the English and Free French, under their leader de Gaulle, attempted to get a foothold at the naval base, after France had fallen to the Germans.

"When we were going across the ocean, our short wave transmitter was sealed so that no one could pick up our position from a broadcast. We were carrying oil to the naval base in Dakar, and Germany or some other opposing nation would have liked to have had that oil. There was no actual fighting, but the attention of the war leaders had turned toward Africa at that time making it quite dangerous to be on that side of the Atlantic. The harbor was enclosed with miles and miles of submarine nets. As we sailed into the harbor, I saw the first floating mines that I had ever seen. They were strung across the harbor from shore to shore. The mines looked like huge black balls—the waves washing over them kept them shiny. On the top side there were openings where the dynamite was inserted. We were guided through secret gates.

"We were docked inside the boundaries of the naval base at Dakar, on the side nearest to the city but farthest from the only gate to the base. There was a bay about a mile in diameter between us and the city, so none of us felt like trying to swim across. The captain received orders from the French government that no one was to leave the ship while we were in port. In fact, a guard was stationed at the gangplank so that we couldn't even set foot on terra firma. We, of course, could understand the attitude of the French government because someone with a bomb or even a match could do a lot of damage to a naval base. But, we had been on water for about eighteen days without seeing land, and there was no one on the ship that relished the idea of being so close to land without getting off the ship for a few hours.

"So all during the day we plotted and schemed to find a way to get ashore. By night fall, no one had concocted a surefire method of getting to town. Darkness descended on a gloomy crew of men. So very quietly we climbed over the railing around the main deck, and hand over hand, we climbed down the mooring lines hoping with each movement that we wouldn't fall into the water below or that we wouldn't be seen by the guard at the gangplank. There were about eight of us in the group, and after we were all safely down the lines, we began making our way toward the gate, following the darkest shadows, on a route farthest from the traveled walks and roads.

"After about fifteen minutes we came in sight of the gate. The only trouble was that we, too, could have been seen by the armed guards at the gate if they had been looking in our direction. They'd have shot immediately if they'd seen us for they were protecting French naval secrets. So we had to move while they were turned in another direction, and we didn't know what we were going to do when we got to the gate.

"Finally, we got close enough that we could see how the wall and the gate were laid out. We could see that there was a ledge along the waterfront, about thirty feet from the gate that had been built to keep the waves from washing away the wall and the guardhouse. The ledge was about a foot wide, and on one side were stone buildings and on the other was deep water. We decided to make an attempt to slip out that way, and we crept, one by one, to the ledge. I'm sure that if the guards had seen us they would have used us for targets. You know, slipping through the guard around a naval base is a serious offense in time of war. But to make a long story not quite so long, we got past the guards by following along that ledge for about two blocks. Then all of a sudden, we realized we were free, and we broke into a dead run in the direction of town.

"We were pretty glad to get to the city, and we felt pretty smart for having gotten out, until we realized that before daylight we would have to get back into the base and onto the ship without being seen by guards. While we were in the city, we met some English pilots who were on a British plane carrier also docked in the naval base. They were dressed pretty much like we were, and we found out that they went in and out of the base without written passes. The name of their ship was His Majesty's Ship Hermes, and all they had to do was to say HMS Hermes as they passed the guards, and they were allowed to go on. So when we got back to the gate before daylight, we repeated HMS Hermes and hoped the guards would never know the difference. Well, they didn't, so we passed unmolested, but of course, when we got back to the ship, we had to climb a rope ladder hung over the stern rather than going up the guarded gangplank.

"We spent four days in Dakar. The city of Dakar is built around the water's edge, on the opposite side to the naval base. It is a city of red roofed, one-story wooden buildings, inhabited, of course, by the native Negroes. It sure seemed strange to walk up a street in a town where there wasn't a handful of white persons.

"I scoffed when I was told going over that one couldn't tell the difference between the two sexes of the natives. But I don't laugh now. There was no difference in their hairdo, no difference in their dress, and no difference in their looks, at least to a stranger. Their hair was cut short, and they wore anything they could get to hang on. Clothes were scarce. Those people would work their heads off for something to put on their backs. In fact, I hardly turned a finger in port. I just sat around and watched native boys do my work. I paid them off with old clothes, and they were tickled to death. They preferred clothes to money, and it was good riddance for me.

"I found a native African boy who could understand the English language, so I used him as my interpreter. While he was with me, he took me to the house of an old lady who sold parrots. I bought one for a souvenir, after going through some mighty dark and uninviting alleys and passageways to get to her door. He was a good parrot and so tame he walked all over me, but he spoke French, and I couldn't tell whether he was cussing me or asking for something to eat. I knew before too long a time either I could teach him to speak English or he would teach me to speak French.

"We made the trek back across the Atlantic Ocean, during which we hardly saw land, and arrived at a port in Venezuela called Guiria. Incidentally, that was not La Guaira, the capital of Venezuela [Vargas state], but a small village between the mountains and the ocean where oil from that nation was loaded onto oil tankers.

"The water was so shallow near shore that there was a flexible pipeline running three miles out into the water through which the oil was piped to the boats. The boats were moored to buoys out there while loading. Well, needless to say, we wanted to go ashore, especially those of us who were on the ship just to travel. And before we had been there any length of time, we received word from shore that we would not be allowed to leave the ship. You know we were thrilled at that message, so long before dark we were making plans to get ashore.

"By night fall we had our plans pretty well developed. We took two air tight oil drums, put a plank on them and tied the plank firmly with a rope. Then we let the homemade raft down to the water, taking much care that we didn't make a suspicious noise. We put on our bathing suits and life preservers and put our clothes and belongings in a basket on the raft. There was a half a dozen of us in the crowd, and we climbed down a rope ladder, slipped quietly into the water and started ashore, pushing the raft ahead of us.

"It was three miles to shore, and before we got there, we thought it was three hundred! It would have been a much longer journey if there had been a current there running away from shore because it would have taken us right with it! Anyway, after long hours of swimming and pushing that raft, we finally reached land. And as we did, each of us fell on the sand, exhausted. Pretty soon our desire to see the town got the best of us, and we dressed, leaving our life preservers on the raft. The town was just a village of a few hundred population, all of which probably made their living in the transporting operation of the oil to the ship. We saw about all there was in the town in a few hours, and after buying a few souvenirs, hired a native to take us back to the ship.

"The captain of the ship didn't miss the life belts until about two weeks later. It seems that we had landed our raft on the shore during low tide. When the tide rose, the raft that we had pulled up on shore a little way was again in the water, and after floating for a few days, got caught in the Gulf Stream that runs from the Gulf, up the Atlantic Seaboard, and over toward Norway. The Gulf Stream runs about three or four miles an hour, and before long, the raft had traveled hundreds of miles to the north.

"Well, naturally, the United States Coast Guard, after seeing a raft in the water with half a dozen life preservers on it, made an investigation. The name of the ship was on the life belts, and I have an idea the Coast Guard was relieved to find that the ship, off of which the raft had been taken, was still on top of the water. But realizing that the raft would be seen by other vessels and maybe taken for a floating mine, a wireless was sent out from Washington to the effect that a raft had been found on which there were life preservers belonging to the SS India Arrow. And so, the plot that we thought had been so well executed was reported to every captain in the area.

"I had to give my parrot 'Oscar' to a fellow in Venezuela. I wished I could have brought him home, but the Captain had different ideas. There have been other people who brought parrots back from Africa and South America, and the parrots brought disease to birds in the States, so the parrots were not allowed."

93

New York bound on April 21, 1940, Stanley wrote home:

I've been to South America and that makes three continents. Venezuela is nothing but mountains and jungles. Consequently, it's just another country where people scratch out a meager living, another country where people worship us folks from the States and wish they could get into the U.S. When I settle down, I'll be a midwesterner by choice, not by inheritance or something else.

Far up in the wilderness mountains [in Venezuela], probably twenty miles from this small town, and probably fifty miles from a large town, and probably no connection but a mule trail, I saw a light at night. I've wondered a million times what that old gent could be doing up there. I'd like to share his camp with him for about a week. That man is either the happiest or the unhappiest person in the world.

And the songs have been doing quite well. Not so many completed songs, but good quality. Today I finished "In the Shadows of My Heart," which is the prettiest song I have written. And not long ago, I did a novelty number entitled "Little Onion" which I'll compare with any of these light numbers that have taken the country by storm.

About a week later he informed his folks:

We're leaving at six in the morn for Texas. I put my application in for vacation. I will be relieved on the next trip north. By then I will have been eight months on the ship, and that's about long enough for one stretch. Yes, I guess I'm a bit restless. I have outlasted practically everyone on the ship, including half a dozen captains. Do you think you could stand me for a few days?

Stanley sent a telegram from Beaumont, Texas, on May 10, 1940.

Mom: Decided at last minute to take vacation here. Am trying to get in touch with Lynne so it may be Monday or Tuesday before I arrive in Manhattan. Stan

That telegram was followed by another.

I'll be home in a few days to greet the best mom in the world in person. Stanley N. Dwyer

4

~

Opportunity Knocks

Maybe some people think these are hard times, but it seems to me
that a person has to be as blind as a bat to overlook the opportunities
that pound on one's door every time he turns around.
—Stanley N. Dwyer in a letter dated July 20, 1940

Stanley, now a world traveler, returned to Manhattan, Kansas, to see his folks, relatives, and college chums and stayed until after Kansas State College's May graduation. In a newspaper interview found in his trunk, Stanley was quoted, "If I hadn't left America last summer, I'd have been a midwesterner by force—now I'll be a midwesterner by choice." Even so, he boarded a bus for New York in early June 1940. After a stopover in Indiana to visit relatives, he continued to the city, intent on pursuing a plan he had up his sleeve.

Stanley previously mentioned his plan in a letter home to his folks.

For the free use of sailors, there are about a dozen marine hospitals in the country. They are of a quality surpassed by few, if any, hospitals in the U.S. They encourage seamen to enter and be treated. I need some dental work done, and then, too, there are sinuses and hypodermic needles that just might as well be looked after as long as that will have to be done sooner or later, and as long as it's gratis. If I'm near New York, I have a couple songs to peddle sometime, and I may be able to kill a couple birds with one pebble.

When my dad had the newspaper at Tipton, Kansas, during the '30s, he took Stan to Cawker City for some dental work. I don't know how extensive it amounted to, but in the process, the dentist broke off the hypodermic needle he was using, and the end piece was in Stan's jaw. The dentist proceeded to cut around, trying to find it. From what Dad said, he cut things up pretty good with no luck finding the needle. I guess Stan carried it with him all the rest of his life.

Family photo taken in the early 1940s.
From left to right: Harold E., Ellen, Harold W., Stanley

And Stanley's plan proceeded, and we continued to follow his footsteps. In June 1940, Stanley started out in New York City, but then he corresponded with his folks from Portland, Maine.

Dear folks:

I didn't get any satisfaction in New York. I made some dental and sinus appointments and saw a skin specialist. The specialist was the best in N.Y.C. Of course, I had to throw a couple quacks out the window before I made it clear that I didn't want to play games. They had so many patients there they couldn't take me into the hospital. I stayed at the Strand Hotel, and it was costing me to live, so I got a transfer up here. So here I am, clad in pajamas and bathrobe, tucked away in the hospital, letting my fifty-million-dollar-in-debt uncle worry about my food, clothing, shelter, and medical care.

They don't have as extensive a supply of possible cures here, but they are taking an active interest in my case, and that's half the battle.

But my stay in N.Y. was definitely not a waste of time. The music publishing racket is the hardest thing on Broadway to crack, but your uncle Pedro, with the aid of fate, a few friends, and a bit of red tape pulling, has done just that—no doubt not a large enough crack to jump through as yet, but still cracked. The rest is pretty much up to time and fate and my future song writing.

Remember a few months ago a company, Broadcast Music, Inc., organized in an effort to break the ASCAP monopoly? So far they have done right well. All they lack now is songs.

I took three songs to BMI, and they tried them out. After a thorough going over, they made this decision: my lyrics were excellent; my melodies were good but not outstanding like they must be for hits. Consequently, they told me to type the lyrics, bring them in, and at the first possible moment they would put one of their two company composers on them to see if they could come out of a huddle with some saleable melodies.

I didn't have verses to the songs, so Sunday I went up to Central Park, found a lonely tree, sat down in the grass, wrote the verses, then typed them and took them in Monday morn. I took up "Little Onion," "The Man in the Moon," "In the Shadows of My Heart," and "Do your Lovin' Tonight" (see Appendix C). Out of that list something might happen. They told me to come in when I got back to town, and they'd know more by then. If ASCAP wins the battle, they will take the composers, songs, etc., so no matter who wins, I'll be on the winning side if I get some songs published—sort of a Mussolini deal, whoever wins, I'll be with them.

The days are pretty much the same—temperature and pulse count at 6:30, breakfast at seven, letters or songs, dinner, songs or letters or cards, supper, reading and radio until lights out at nine. We have earphones here so we can listen to the radio at any hour without bothering anyone.

I've a notion to send a telegram just to make someone peddle up the hill with it. How's the job by now?

Send the mail here, including that in your own handwriting, till I tell you to cease firing.

Love,
Stan

Stan was referring to the job I had taken as a Western Union delivery boy in Manhattan. But before we moved to Manhattan, I sold the pony I had on the farm and bought a bike, the necessary mode of transportation for the delivery boy job. The bike was a dandy. It had Texas cattle handlebars, streamlined fenders, and all the goodies. Pretty spiffy stuff. If Stan had sent a telegram home, I would have had to navigate one of the many hills in Manhattan to deliver it. The first day I wore my new uniform, I had a delivery in the west part of town where we lived. I was headed down a hill with a rather sharp turn at the bottom. I had picked up speed on the hill, negotiated the first half of the turn, and was getting along just fine until runoff water from somewhere covered the other half of the street. Besides the holes in the knees of my new uniform, I survived that episode. But my singing voice was squeaky and shrill, at best, so when Western Union brought in the singing telegram, it was time to part company.

After two weeks, Stanley checked out of the Portland, Maine, hospital— the doctor who was to treat him went on a three-week vacation—and transferred to the marine hospital in Baltimore, Maryland, his arrival delayed by a two-day stopover in New York City. There, Stanley delivered his "three Maine creations" to BMI and met Theron's ship at the dock coming from South America. The old friends spent a day catching up.

Stanley had this to say about the Baltimore Marine Hospital:

Sometime when you want to do less than nothing for a few weeks, just jump into a marine hospital. This is some hospital. It is a block long, and in three places—the ends and the middle—it is a half block wide. It is seven stories high. There must be a million patients here, and across the street is John Hopkins University. I have a nice single room with bath, and my food is brought to me on a tray. I suppose if I were an old man of seventy or eighty I could appreciate all this generosity. But with all the hay I have plans for making during the next year, this is a monkey wrench in the wheels of progress. I'm doing the best I can by remote control, but it's not too satisfactory. I can't do much financially or in the line of travel while I'm here, and the sooner I get to making money, the better. I need a typewriter as bad as I need my eyes.

Stanley explained the situation in a letter:

There was a skin specialist here who diagnosed my case and came to the conclusion that I had two skin diseases, one more or less on top of the eczema, sort of like moss growing on trees. From the top of my head to the tip of my toes I was covered with grease, or should I call it salve. It takes five days to kill the stuff with it. The more mature growths began to keel over, so half the battle is won. However, it's the other half that has a twenty-three-year head start.

July 22, 1940
Baltimore, Maryland

Dear folks:

Cast a glance at my new style of handwriting. Pretty snitz, isn't it? It is a noiseless Underwood. I rented it for a month. I sure ought to be able to make hay now, even if I can't get out to the field. I went uptown the other day then came back and got permission to have it here.

I have a date with the dentist in half an hour though, so it will have time to cool off after this first warming up. This is the third tooth session, so I ought to have them fixed up before many moons. The guy wants to put in partial plates instead of bridges in the vacant lots, but he's going to have to be a darned sight bigger than I before he gets the job done. Can you imagine me, at the ripe old age of twenty-three, running around with half my teeth in my shirt pocket?

Your uncle Pedro made a ten dollar bill the other night, very much unbeknown to him. Some old gent was about to kick the bucket, so they rounded up a bunch of us who would give him a transfusion. My juice came as near matching his as any, so I was chosen. Just when they were ready to begin, they said to sign a paper so I could get my ten bucks. And with that I nearly keeled over. Any transfusions that I ever heard about were donations, as far as I knew. At least that was the angle that was always played up in the papers. It took about a half an hour, and it had no effect upon me whatsoever.

I took a stroll around the Hopkins campus yesterday evening, once I was out of solitary confinement. I didn't see all of it tho; it is so big that it would have taken an airplane. By the way, I wonder how the airplanes are coming and the Western Union. Are you a company official yet?

I have a start on a couple more songs. I've heard it mentioned that Tommy Dorsey was looking for amateur songwriters. I don't have any more dope on it.

When I finish this (and that won't be long, according to the quality and quantity of these contents), I am going to type my index to Doc Summers's mimeographed radio book. I wouldn't trade that stuff for a lot of money.

I got another letter from faithful pa. He and this Oklahoma gal I met on the bus really make letter writing a pleasurable pastime. And it's sure appreciated by one so far from home—especially a shut-in.

So from all of ussens to all of youns,

Love yelnatS

In 1940, World War II, as Stanley wrote, "was somebody else's war." World War II broke out with Germany's premeditated invasion of Poland in September 1939, and by the spring of 1940, the countries of Denmark and Norway surrendered to the Germans. Hitler didn't stop—Belgium, Luxembourg, and the Netherlands fell to the Third Reich. Hitler's next calculated move was to occupy France. The French army proved no contest for the Third Reich's highly trained and well-equipped Wehrmacht and their *blitzkrieg* tactics. Stunning the world, by mid-June of 1940, most of France, including Paris, toppled to Nazi control. The Battle of the Atlantic escalated, and merchant ships sailed in dangerous water with alarming casualties. But, even though the fighting seemed contained to a continent an ocean away, the fallout of war rippled across the pond and affected the lives of Americans. The United States—assuming a neutral stance—continued to debate in Congress what would become the Selective Training and Service Act of 1940—in other words, the draft. The act was signed into law on September 16, 1940. Stanley was then required to register, which made him eligible—if chosen in the lottery system—for twelve months of service.

July 28, 1940
Baltimore, Md.

Dear guys and gals:

One score and three years ago my father—with the help of my mother—brought forth on this continent a new youngin', conceived in liberty, etc. etc. Then Prexy Roosevelt came along and said, "Look here you, I don't give a damn whether you have the next few years already planned or not, and I don't care if it is the best part of your life, you're going to join the army, for practically nothing too. If Hitler can do this, I'm going to, too. And I'm not interfering with your liberty—you have your choice of a year in the service or five years in the jug."

All in all it looks like I'm going to have to do some fast thinking in the next few weeks to outwit the brains in the machine. Course there's always the chance that I can prolong my stay here till after the draft. Then, too, the merchant marine might need men bad enough to get us exempted. Or I might be able to jump in as an officer. If I do get caught in the draft, I'll be drafted at home so I can see my peoples once in a while. Course the bill isn't thru yet, but it seems to be headed that way.

Piles,
Stan

Stanley continued with other letters in August.

Dear folks:

Operations run a close second to the weather as a boring subject, but I must tell you about mine. They grabbed a couple of hatchets, a butcher's knife, and a pair or two of tin snips the other day, ran me down, and yanked about a pound and a half of excess cartilage out of my nose. Consequently, I haven't been kicking very high since. It wasn't at all bad while they were at it, in fact, it was quite interesting, but after the dope wore off, it really went to town. Everything above my shoulders ached like thunder, including, believe it or not, my teeth and ears. But all I had to do was to give the nurse the high sign and she'd give me a pill that would put me to sleep in no time.

They had been watching my nose for a couple of weeks and came to the conclusion that the cartilage was bent enough so that when there was any irritation at all, causing swelling, it would stop up my right sinuses. So maybe I've helped myself physically as well as eliminating my nasal twang. And it wasn't a bit hard on my billfold.

Seems the draft bill is hitting a few snags. I've been trying to figure out some way to make a little cash on the side if I am drafted. I've considered column writing, script writing, and what have you. I had in mind starting off with a few "Forgotten Heroes" radio scripts. Got any suggestions, pop? How's the feed business and the poetry coming?

Which reminds me, do you know what the calf said to the silo? He said, "Is my fodder in there?" Pretty dad-gummed clever of him, wasn't it? Must have been Toby.

And so, with the ringing of the dinner bell, we bring this edition of the seen behind the scene to a whirlwind finish. Don't forget the address.

Urine, with Love,
Stan

P.S. Got a letter from pop today. Congratulations, old topper, on the new auto. Wish I were home to give it a trial. Maybe this will be one I don't bend up. Suppose? Maybe Harold will do the job for me. Or maybe the army will drag me home in time. Wouldn't that be tough? Jest like I wrote Aunt Pearl and Uncle Dusty, if I didn't have such darned good folks, I wouldn't be hankering to come home all the time. So there too.

Lovestan

And that explained one of the billfolds in Stanley's trunk, the black one filled with dollar-bill-sized newspaper clippings titled "Forgotten Heroes." Stanley must have clipped the columns from Granddad's newspaper, the *Tipton Times,* and slipped them in the paper bill compartment of the billfold for future reference.

August 26, 1940

Dear folks:

This will be short cause its about time for lights out. I just want to feel xx you out on a subject that has come up lately. It's like this: I was up xxx to the recruiting station the other day finding out how I could get by without having to be a lowly private on out. They suggested that I try to get into the air corps. I didn't think anything of it when they suggested it, but I've been looking over some of their dope on it and it looks xxxx like a pretty good deal. In the event that I didn't get washed out I would serve nine months in training then I think three years in active service, and at x quite a price. My college degree eliminates my having to pass an educational exam, so if I can pass the physical I will be on the way. They are taking men pretty fast for it and the guy said with my recommendations I xxx could get in in a month or so. I would serve three months at an elementary school somewhere, then go to Randolph and Kelly. Of course I don't want anyone but you to know it yet, so don't spill it.xx I'm not sure I want to do it but I've been thinking about it a lot. What do you think about it? I'd like to know your opinion on it right away. I would have to get some recommendations and other stuff before I could make application, so I'll have to get going on it before I start for the Lord knows where again.

So let me know in the next few days will you? As far as danger goes any more I think it is about as dangerous as driving a car on the highway. So there should be no reasons for grey hairs. So whatcha think?

Everything oke. Will write later.

Love
Stan

August 30, 1940

Dear folks:

I would have been very much surprised if I hadn't gotten your letter yesterday afternoon because I knew that subject would cause quite a stir when you read mine. And the reply was just as I expected—the answer that I have always gotten when problems confronted me, the answer that has so well prepared me to meet the really big problems that I am and will be stumbling over for the next hundred or hundred-fifty years. If everyone else's parents were of the caliber that mine are, if everyone else's had the common sense tucked away between their ears, there wouldn't be any war preparations or any dictatorial steps, which cause one to take steps toward self-preservation defense instead of the offense toward happiness.

I got a letter from Jim K yesterday. He said that there is a Public Relations Department at Randolph Field that is sort of an advertising agency for the field. He says they do feature writing, as well as other, for magazines and newspapers, and picture work such as a Paramount movie that is being made for the field. I don't know how a person gets into that angle, but I'm going to find out. So the Air Corps, which I haven't decided about yet, I'll postpone at least till I feel this out.

I don't think I will do anything about the navy band deal, though I appreciate you going to a lot of trouble to tell me about it. In the first place, I'd have to do a lot of brushing up [on the saxophone] before I could try out, and I don't have the cash to live on during that time. Also, I don't want to get involved any way with the navy. I've seen too many guys go to the devil because they got in the navy and couldn't get out. This sea life as a vocation is the worst thing in the world a person can get into. A person can't live a normal life, and he gradually goes to the dogs. They're calling for men to enlist for a four-month training course to become a naval officer. One has to be a college grad to get into it; and as far as money is concerned, I'd be on easy street the rest of my life, but as I said, I wouldn't get into it for anything.

Or I may just go ahead with my travel plans and take a chance on Uncle Sam letting me go as a member of the merchant marines, an indispensable service to any government.

It sure would have saved me a lot of trouble if I had taken a few minutes off sometime in the last few years and gotten married. Maybe I could have done that if I hadn't been so darned eager to tell all the lassies it would be years and years before I would be in position to do so. As it is, I guess I scared them all away. Guess, tho, if the

103

right one had come along, I wouldn't have been so eager to run her off. The things I have gotten in the last few years would have been impossible had I been hitched, and their value is immeasurable, so the tears I'll shed will be few and far between and dry.

The other thing is that if I got dad's description of the two missing nickels, I have them here and will send them in this letter. There are a lot of Philly 1940 nickels around here, but I didn't find a '38 until last night. I was out again last night fulfilling my social obligations. This fellow and I went out to some friends of his for the evening when I got the '38 coin. Hope they're the right ones. If not, you can get a couple sticks of licorice for mom, a few onions for dad, and a school pencil for Harold. Don't know anymore news and not news, so I'll slide this into the mailbox.

evoL

yelnatS

Stanley wrote his folks and sister, Aileen:

I have typed two book-length manuscripts while I've been here at the hospital and got paid twelve cents a page. So my stay here hasn't cost me much. Part of the rash is gone and the rest improved. The eczema on my leg is pretty much dried up. If I get a little medicine anywhere except on the rash, the skin peels off like when it's sunburned. When the eczema is raw in any place, it burns like I imagine the turpentine on the cat does. My nose is coming along fine, and I sure will have a good set of teeth when I get out of here.

"By the way," he asked Aileen, "a radio friend of mine said there was a Radio Employment Agency in Denver. I wonder if you could find it in the phone book, and if so, if you would give me the name and address. It would sure save me a lot of time and money when I get ready to enter the field."

A few rough-draft letters found in the trunk that were written to friends conveyed extraordinary insight of Stanley's personal thoughts and future plans.

Sept 4, 1940

Baltimore, Md.

Dear Doc:

Unless you changed your plans, you should be "resting up" from the vacation about the time this arrives. I don't like to add to the stack of letters that will be staring you in the face, but on the other hand, I owe you thanks for the letter of recommendation. I typed the manuscript for the fellow and another one for a minister in the meantime. So I haven't had much time to think about all the things I should be doing while I'm here.

I've wondered many times, Doc, how you and a few other professors whose interest in the students doesn't stop at the classroom door get repaid for post-curricular help. I really appreciate the favors you have done for me since graduation to say nothing of all you did for me during school. Sometimes I wish I had entered it [radio field] when I got out of school, but this jaunt has been of great value to me, and I'm sure I'll never regret it.

Uncle Sam has caused me no little bit of worrying and floor pacing. I had some pretty definite plans until this draft deal came along. Now, I'm pretty much undecided. I've considered going ahead with my plans and hoping that something would turn up so that I wouldn't get the call. And I've considered, tho not very strongly, the Air Corps, which would eliminate me from radio for at least four years and probably forever. But whether a person with only a passive interest in aviation can make the grade, I don't know, or whether it would be advisable. I might develop an interest in it, but if I didn't, it would be a long, hard trek. Seems to me that if a fellow is in a business that he enjoys, he can enjoy all of life, otherwise the few pleasures he can find are overshadowed by drudgery. Also, I've thought of using some form of draft elimination, such as being a passive farmer while holding down a radio job. I don't feel that would be at all unpatriotic because I know that if this country were attacked, I'd be a first line of defense volunteer. If we should enter someone else's battle, I'm not at all interested. Wonder what the other kids think and are doing about it?

As I've said, I'm in a dither. I'll be moving from here soon, and as I see it now, I'll go to sea for a while not only to further my travels but to fatten my billfold so I'll be in a position to do whatever I choose. Sailing opportunities look great for the winter, then in the spring, I think I'll bid farewell to the seas.

Dear Theron:

It's been many a green moon since I got a letter that was nearly three thousand words long, and I don't know what I've done to deserve it all, but you can bet your boots it was welcome.

Since I received your first letter the other day, I have given a lot of thot to joining you out in Portland. There are a few things that will affect my final decision that I have not been able to weigh yet, such as songs, which I won't know about till I get to New York, but from my perch here, I see it this way:

If I should come out there now, I'd have to start from scratch. It would be much harder and would take much longer to elevate myself to the standard of living I could reach if I would go to sea at least a few months longer.

I took one long chance to eliminate that angle the other day. You'd never guess how, either. It was wicked. I went to the races and gambled! Of course, it would have surprised me more if I had won than if I had lost. With my small investment, I took a long chance of winning a few hundred. My two long-shot choices both came in second. I won my money back on other races, tho, and came back with as much money as I left with. So I still have a little.

Then there's a little detail that you didn't even mention that is going to affect the life of a lot of us youngsters, all of us who don't figure a way out of it. That is the army draft. I've done a lot of tall thinking on it, but until Congress settles a few controversial details, I couldn't come to any conclusions.

Something else that might have weight if a move to Portland were permanent—it is a seaport. I've sworn that I'll never pick a wife or raise a family in a seaport, near an army reservation, or near active oil fields. It would be bad enough to live there myself. Also, reports from West Coast sailors here say that Portland is rainy about five months a year, and I wonder if a Kansan, especially a radio announcer, could accustom himself to that.

The last thing I would do would be to take a job from you that you had lined up. It wouldn't be fair to you, and I would feel like a parasite, more than I do already. Besides, the radio job that you have lined up probably isn't the job I want for my entrance into radio. If I came there, I would start on that one-horse station and learn commercial radio from the ground up.

I don't mind telling you that, much credit due to Doc Summers, I can be a credit to what station I go to work for. And, incidentally, I have hundreds of pages of material with me prepared by Doc that you can have to study, if you like. It is wonderful and will do you good besides helping you.

So I haven't come to any definite conclusions yet. I'm going to pull out of here shortly. Then, if by any miracle, such as advanced royalties on songs, I should get my fingers on a couple hundred bucks, I might be out there shortly. I don't know where I'm going to settle down, but the Rockies are getting their share of thought. I'm giving thought to eastern Texas too. There's weight in the fact that the big money in radio is in the East. I think I'd like your country, and radio means so much to me that sitting here writing about it has gotten me worked up into a nervous dither.

I can see that sea life hasn't hardened you like it seems to me it would do to one. But even at that, I am afraid of it, and that's one reason I'd like to get back on dry land as soon as possible. Theron, if I could start out there before long, buy a fair car in Detroit, stop to see the folks, the school kids, and a football game on the way out, I'd be the happiest mug in the world. I'd do most anything for that opportunity, but where the hell is the two hundred? I'll be damned if I'm not slightly homesick as I write about seeing the folks.

Meanwhile, the stay at the hospital ended, and Stanley returned to New York City by mid-September 1940. He described the big city as a great city and observed:

Certain parts of New York leave the impression upon one who has never been there that the big city is the one place where a man can live to the fullest extent of his dreams, the "Shangri La" of the earth. True, the heart of the theatre, the heart of radio, night clubs, music, bright lights, tall buildings, art, science, and what have you lie there. But therein also lays the heart of the other side of the picture—poverty, distress, filth, broken hearts, broken dreams.

New York is overflowing with a money-mad group of people. If you have money, money you don't need, New York is at your feet. If you haven't, you're an outcast. And that is why New York, with its eight million people, is conceded to be the loneliest place in the world. One thing that the big city does not possess is the heart of America. That we find out in the small town, out where people are human beings, out where the friendship of one's neighbor means more than all the money on Broadway, out where a businessman respects his competitor and treats him as a friend. Yes, "Shangri La" lies in the small town. It lies dormant to those who crave to leave "this dead berg" for the lights of the city. But to those who have seen the lights, the small town with typical American people, its rickety buildings, its grassy yards, its sunlight and pure air holds something that cannot be matched on earth.

Stanley checked in with BMI to submit his patriotic song, "A Job For Every American," (see Appendix D) and dropped in on friends. He wrote:

> Gerv and the Keoughs were thoroughly shocked at the deepness of my voice since the operation. Har. Har. I'd like to have Doc Summers get an earful of it now. He always razzed me about my western Kansas twang. Dad, I found an old coin shop the other day, so if you'll jot down the coins you'd like to have, we'll see what we can do about it.

Gervase Keough—an unusual name, therefore an easy name for a simple Internet search. Maybe Gerv could tell me more about Stanley. When the hyped Y2K glitch never materialized, the clocks on our computers kept right on ticking and rolled our search into the twenty-first century. In fact, an Internet search helped locate Gerv. Unlike Lynne Davidson, Gerv had lived beyond the twentieth century. So I dialed his number. My heart raced as I talked to Stanley's old friend, only Gerv didn't remember Stanley.

Stanley relocated to the Sloane House YMCA, temporarily living there for half the cost of his room at the Strand Hotel. Time was "hanging heavy on my hands," he wrote. Stanley took in more shows, *Dodge City* and *When the Daltons Rode* while he "waited for a ship that hadn't come in."

About one week later, his ship came in—the *Yorba Linda*, another Standard Oil ship. Stanley was promoted to officers' mess, and he made about one hundred dollars a month. He wrote home:

> I'm a workin' man these days,
> And a good workin' man at that,
> And if I'm a lyin' to my folks,
> I'll eat my 'ole straw hat.

However, it was a short sail for Stanley from New York to Providence, Rhode Island, where the *Yorba Linda* met the end of the line, the boneyard. Still on pay, crews lived aboard ships while they waited for yet another ship assignment.

In the fall of 1940, the folks and I moved to Hastings, Nebraska. School in Manhattan hadn't started yet because of the polio outbreak, so when we got to Hastings, I was about a month behind the others in the class. It took a little catching up, but it was a good move for us. Dad's sales territory covered much of Nebraska, and it was the start of many years of social activities that my mother enjoyed.

Stanley commented:

I was surprised to hear that you folks are contemplating a move to Nebraska. Spect it will be a lot better for you, and you won't be so much farther from the rest of the folks. In a way, it will sorta sever my connections with Manhattan, but I guess that doesn't make a lot of difference this late in the game. Hope you can move my stuff up without discarding any of it until I can go thru it. We had some good times in Manhattan. And I, for one, will be glad to cast a couple of glances around the haunts whenever the opportunity presents itself. What school is in Hastings? Are there any good looking women around? I see and hear Nebraska wherever sports are being discussed, even here in the East. I listened to the Nebraska-Minnesota game Saturday, but no one here has ever heard of Kansas State.

"I can hardly keep up with this modern, speed-minded age," Stanley wrote home. "Just think. Pa wrote me a letter on the 9th of this month, he sent it the seventeen or eighteen hundred miles in one of these new fangled air machines, and in only six days, I got the letter. The postmaster must have thought you meant it should be sent hitchhiking, you know, 'air you going my way?' And guess where I'll spend the near future—India Arrow."

October 24, 1940
2 days from Houston

Dear folks:

With your kind permish, I will write to you in pencil. My pen is in my locker, and the boys in there are asleep, so I won't bother them.

I never thought I'd be back on this tub again. There are about fifty ships in this company, and it is quite a coincidence that I'd get this one again.

But here I am, and I don't care a bit. I'm making folding money again, plate over dishpan, and that's an important little item in my life. By spring I'll be able to take off on something ashore and at the same time be able to live like I had been in business for ten years.

This tub just got back from Honolulu. Had I been on it, I would have gotten to see Lynne [stationed in Hawaii]. It is generally agreed among those in the know that she will be going foreign again before the winter is over. That's just prediction, of course, but pretty good.

I'll be celebrating my twenty-fourth birthday in Houston. And so I figure you gave me a pretty good start, and you are to be complimented on the way you've handled things since.

By the way, if I didn't tell you before, I registered for the draft as living in Hastings.

And it's midnight, so I better fly up.

> Love,
> Stan

Subsequently, Broadcast Music, Inc. returned Stanley's submitted lyrics and suggested that he get in touch with some composer to put notes to the words. A letter in the trunk from Robert B. Sour of BMI stated, "Songs in complete form give themselves a much better break."

Therefore, Stanley pursued a composer and continued to scribble down lyrics. He stated, "I started a song that came easy, is good, and has a natural time to go with it. The boys on board have been suggesting lots of things I could write, but I don't think any of it would be fit to print. And I'm sure it wouldn't be fit to read."

Stanley made one uneventful trip after another on the SS *India Arrow*, back and forth across the Gulf and up and down the East Coast. "Wish I could crawl in this envelope and come along," he wrote. Stanley adopted a similar routine as before; he served meals to the men, ran their poker games, corresponded with family and friends, and dealt with "channel fever, the fidgety feeling one experiences as you near port. You can't sleep because of nerves caused by something you are awaiting." No matter which port, there always seemed to be friends to look up, which helped "break the monotony of being on ship."

"I can enjoy most anything [in port] no matter how trivial after being at sea a week or so," Stanley wrote. "It's sure good to spend an evening with a human being now and then."

Thanksgiving came and went, and with Christmas around the corner, Stanley wrote:

> Well, it's nigh on to Santa Claus time, and I've been making some stuff for the family. I figgered maybe youse guys would like to have something really from me instead of from a store. They don't amount to much, but as you will see, they're wealthy in elbow grease. I have Harold's done and will do dad's on the way back to Texas.
>
> I think that I'll just turn my Christmas shopping over to you folks. As it is, I never get all I want to do ashore done, and if I'd take four or five hours off to shop, I wouldn't even have time for my marshmallow sundae. Living on a ship, a fellow's "musts" when he gets ashore are really burdens.

FORM P. S. 59
3.38

MENU

S. S._____India Arrow._____

DATE Thursday, Nov. 21st. 1940

Thanksgiving Dinner.

Shrimp Cocktail.

Iced Hearts of Celery.

Clear Consomme.

Roast Vermont Turkey - Giblet Gravy.

Cranberry Sauce   Old Fashioned Dressing

Baked Virginia Ham - Raisin Sauce.

Green Peas   Sugar Corn

Asparagus Tips   Candied Sweets.

Mashed Potatoes.

Pumpkin Pie.   Hot Mince Pie.

Plum Pudding - Vanilla Sauce.

Fruit Cake.

Grapes   Oranges   Pears

Apples   Bananas.

December 22, 1940

Dear pipples,

We'll be in tomorrow about noon. I guess you mugs will have to wait another trip for your presents. I just can't stretch my days enough to work on them much. How's your curiosity?

The fact that we're getting in a couple of days before Christmas may hinder me from calling if you folks should be on the road then or be somewhere there's not a phone. But whether or not I get to talk to you, I'll surely be with you in thought on Christmas. One who has never been away from home, especially on such an occasion, can't realize how completely one can be at two places at once. Pa knows how possible it is, I'm sure. And tho I won't be there physically, I'll sure be watching you open the presents. And I'll enjoy your dinner too.

The idea of spending New Year's Eve in N.Y. is a bit of consolation. Spending the 25th on the water won't be quite so bad with that thought in mind.

So, with best wishes to you folks and all the others, we'll have to let it stand that way this year.

Love,
Stan

> 1940 has one leg in the grave
> and one foot on a banana peel

Dear folks:

Near as I can tell, it's about three hours until 1941, and this old tub is still a long way from Times Square, damn it. What a trip this has been. We let a sick man off in Miami on the way down, another in Key West on the way back, then a few hours after the latter stop, guess what—we lost another propeller blade. So we didn't have a chance to make it, especially after being slowed by the storm. And if that wasn't enough, one of the tanks sprung a leak, and we had to stop and put a plug in it so we wouldn't lose a lot of oil before getting in. So, we'll get in the second.

The year 1940 proved to be a great cog in my life wheel. I saw Africa, South America, made a bit of money, spent it, spent a few months in the hospital, made new friends, saw others scatter from brell to heckfast, started saving again with the idea of living a secure life while getting a start in my life's work, and above all, added a lot to my store of knowledge.

I can look back upon what I've learned in the last 365 days, and adding that to the better than average start that I had previously, derive great satisfaction in knowing that I have an edge on most people. And with that in mind, I'm sure I won't have any trouble in selling myself to some potential employer before long.

It's not with regret, tho, that I bid the old year good-bye and greet the new, for I feel that the next will be even better. And part of that is seeing my folks a bit more.

And it's bedtime, so, so long.

Love,
Stan

A letter home on January 3, 1941, stated:

I had Christmas today, and some Christmas it was too. I got a package from you folks, Aileen, Clarks, Gayle and Grace, and a card from Pearl saying she'd sent a gift to Beaumont.

The kids have surely been swell to me while I've been away from the family, friends, and relatives. It makes me realize what a big difference it makes in one's life to be a part of a family that is so human. And the things from you folks, they really hit the right spot. Had I made a choice of my own presents, I couldn't have picked anything more pleasing and useful. I wondered when I opened the presents what I had done to deserve it all, and it's appreciated clear from the bottom.

Yesterday I spent the first half of the evening with Gerv and the last half with the Summers. Gerv works for "Time" and "Life," and Doc is in the Public Relations Department at NBC. Sure had a swell time. If we're still in town tomorrow night, I'll have to see Tommy Dorsey at the Paramount Theatre.

On January 30, 1941, Stanley informed his folks:

At last! Santa Claus is about to come to your house, anyway to the male representatives of the species. The other third will have to wait a little longer. The fellow who was going to show me how to make the other present was one of the two that got sick and had to be taken off in Florida. However, he showed one of the guys here in the Steward's department, so after we get the necessary equipment tomorrow in Beaumont, we'll try our hand. If we can get the job done, swell, but if we can't, maybe mom would like one of these I made for the men. Sorry these are so late, but I spect there's more of me tangled up in them than something I might have gotten at a drug store.

> N.Y., N.Y.
> February 25, 1941

Dear folks:

Just between the deep blue sea and you and me, another trip is about over. Forty-eight hours from now I'll be chewing the rag with Gerv. I plan on making a few more trips on here yet. Then I'm not sure what. I won't be home, tho, for a while 'cause I want to do everything I'm going to beforehand, and I have a jillion things to do yet. Also, I think I have a thousand pounds of junk. If I got off now, I'd have to hire a truck.

Don't know what the heck to talk about anymore. The trips are all about the same. I've sat here trying to think of something to say for so long that my rear is about numb.

Love,
Stan

P.S. Yes, I'll add. It seems I've hit the jackpot again. This trip we're going to Pedro, California, by way of the Panama Canal. So I'll have to blacken the face of another country and another state on my map. It's about a twenty-three day trip out, so don't be looking for another letter for a day or two …

Ta, ta.

Once again, with his lightly edited letters and more parts of the radio travelogue, Stanley served as our travel guide, and we experienced his foreign adventures firsthand.

"I always wondered what the Panama Canal looked like," Stanley told. "During times of war, no pictures are allowed to be taken of the canal, and I have an idea that Uncle Sam prefers to have visitors to the canal forget most of what they saw. Soldiers board the ship for the journey through the canal to act as guards and prevent sabotage.

"The Panama Canal is really a wonderful engineering feat. Some imagination the gent or gents had who dreamed up the idea of cutting a ditch between the two American continents. In many places the canal is dug right through stony mountains. I have heard it said that during the digging of the canal, one of the chief engineers was driven partially mad while attempting to blast through one of the larger cuts, the Gaillard Cut to be exact. The hill at Culebra was the greatest obstacle the canal builders faced. It is formed of soft volcanic material, and excavating was a heartbreaking task. When a hole was made, more rock and dirt would slide into it from the side or be thrust up from below by the weight of the hills. Even after the canal had been opened, the slides continued, and the canal was blocked from September 1915 to April 1916. Three times as much earth was taken out of the cut than had been originally planned. In fact, it is said that enough earth was removed to make a pile as high as a New York skyscraper with a half-mile wide base.

"It took about ten hours to make the trip through the approximately forty-mile-long canal—the isthmus is about thirty miles across. There is a short channel from the city of Colon to the first set of locks. This set hoists the ships up thirty feet or so to the level of the lake beyond. From the lake to the other side, the channel is cut through mountains, during the transgression of which the ships are lowered to the sea level by means of two more sets of locks, the last just inland from Balboa and Panama City.

"An approaching ship enters the lock at the same level as the water in which it sailed. After the ship is in the lock, two gates close and the water is raised by means of many pumps in the bottom, I would guess at the rate of about an inch a second. Then when the water around the ship is at the level of the lock or the channel ahead, the gates ahead automatically open and the ship is towed ahead by the track tugs which provide the locomotion through the locks. The ship proceeds from one lock to the other until the elevation of the water ahead is reached. The locks are constructed with cement bottom and sides. A ship going through the Panama Canal moves under its own power, except at the locks.

"Contrary to popular belief, the canal runs south and east to the Pacific side. Crossing Gatun Lake—which is a distance of ten miles or more—we were going straight east, believe it or not.

"We were in sight of Panama for a day after going through, then a day off Costa Rica, then the next land we saw was Mexico. We sailed through a school of porpoise over a mile long. A fish on one end would jump out of the water, then the one next to him would jump—almost at the same time so that starting at one end of the school and running clear to the other end, half a dozen porpoise would be out of the water at the same time. It reminded me of the way we stood dominoes on end, close together, and then after knocking the end domino over, the others—one after another—fell into the next one until they were all down."

Stanley wrote home:

Dear folks:

And I just as well tell you where else we're going, although the orders are indefinite until we get to Pedro. We're going to the Philippine Islands. Incidentally, it is a seven-thousand-mile jaunt across and will take thirty days. That's quite a jump without hitting land or maybe even seeing it. But, unless this tub takes wings and flies, the shortest length of the trip will be four months, and that's quite a payoff.

Each of us had to fill out a government card asking for a draft postponement in case we were called before we get back. I don't suppose it will be my time, though, by then.

I'm not sure what I'll do in Pedro. I've thought a little of going to Hollywood, which is a couple of hours away, or to Long Beach, which is just a step.

I'm going to send a box of junk home from Pedro. In it will be mom's Christmas present, and I wouldn't be surprised if she kinda likes 'em. I suppose you're still saving the letters for me?

Pedro – Orders received today state that we are stopping at the Hawaiian Islands. Ain't that sumpin? I'll get to meet Lynne in the middle of the Pacific after all! And so, adios for a longer stretch this time. But keep the home fires burning cause sooner or later, I'll be seeing you.

Love,
Stan

And on the voyage to Hawaii, Stanley wrote his folks:

In Hollywood we visited the Brown Derby bar, Melody Lane, the Plaza Hotel and then went to the Earl Carroll Theatre. I met Jackie Cooper and saw Carroll himself ... It's calm now and it's warming up considerably. It smelled like spring today, even out here in the middle of nowhere.

His radio travelogue described more. "The one day I spent in Hawaii was the most interesting day of my life. My friend Lynne, who is stationed in the army near Honolulu, gave me the royal Hawaiian welcome including fresh flower leis and even a kiss from his girlfriend. I was dumbfounded and probably acted the part perfectly. I dare say that a person feels quite conspicuous with a number of leis draped around his neck all day, even though he realizes it is the customary thing.

"Lynne showed me practically the entire island, and we spent a lot of time at the world famous Waikiki Beach near the famous reddish-pink Royal Hawaiian Hotel. Thousands of people were sunning on the white sand beach, swimming or surf board riding in the blue Pacific waters. I'll admit, it was a little different from what most people expect. For instance, it was very hard to find a real Hawaiian native there, and the only grass skirts I found were in a ten-cent store.

"In the mountains above Waikiki is Schofield Barracks, Lynne's 'home' and the 'home' for many military men. There are hundreds and hundreds of soldiers and sailors on the streets of Honolulu at all times. Pearl Harbor is alive with navy ships and airplanes that form the islands' first line of defense.

"The sentiment of the Aloha Tower, the leis, Diamond Head—towering above the island—and the welcoming and farewell ceremonies is what I'm reminded of each time I hear a steel guitar or listen to the strains of a Hawaiian ballad. Upon leaving the island, I threw a lei in the water as the ship passed Diamond Head. It is said that if the lei drifts back to land, the visitor will return to Hawaii. So for good measure, I threw two leis in the water. I kept other leis for over a month, until they were withered and shriveled. Even then, I hated to throw them away."

April 29, 1941

Dear Aileen and Bill:

I haven't heard from you since Adam was a yearling. We'll be in the Philippines in three more days. We lost a propeller blade right in the middle of this big pond, and that will have to be replaced after we've unloaded the cargo. We were a million miles from nowhere when the blade came off. We were about at the 170th meridian, this side of the International Date Line. Since the mishap, we've been limping along at 150 or 175 miles a day. We've seen one ship and no land. Consequently, this has turned out to be a long jump, but the weather has been perfect, making it a very pleasurable cruise. We left Honolulu on the sixth of April, and we'll be in Manila on May 3.

As ever,
Stan

"I guess a book could be written about things I saw and did in and around Manila," Stanley told in his travelogue. "One of the most exciting things happened the first day we were there. We arrived in Manila in the morning, and that afternoon a fire broke out in a poor section of Manila that burned a hundred square blocks of the city. Of course, we had a ringside seat to the excitement. The fire started in a district where penniless natives had built houses out of tin or boxes or anything else that would shed water. The houses were so close together there was no chance in the world to stop the fire, so the fire burned to the sea. Twenty thousand people were left homeless by that fire that burned those hundred small blocks.

"We stood across a small stream that had stopped the fire from spreading in that direction. Spectators jammed the streets. In the stream, a stream of green stagnant water, boys and men were swimming across with rescued furniture and other belongings. One boy dragged his pig into the water to keep the pig from being burned to death. On the side of the stream where we stood, frantic men threw water onto their shacks with buckets. More than once I got soaked with that stagnant water (from a poorly aimed bucket of water). A block behind us, on an unusually large street, dozens of women and girls carried their few pieces of furniture and then sat down on the curb waiting to see if the fire would spread to their homes. It didn't, but I'm sure if the wind had been in another direction, it would have and much more of the city would have burned.

"I met a Spanish senorita at the Santa Ana, the largest cabaret in the world. Her name was Emilia and she could speak a little more English than I could Spanish, so we got along fine. Time meant little to people there. She thought nothing of talking a half hour on the phone. We and another couple went to the Casa Manana then to the roof garden of the Hotel Great Eastern. It was the most novel date I've ever had. She was my guide for seeing the town.

"Seven thousand islands make up the Philippine group, and Manila, located on the island of Luzon—farther north than where the wild men live—is situated on the east edge of the bay with its outlet to the west. I did read about the antics of a tribe of wild men, the Moro headhunters, attacking an army battalion farther south.

"Practically all of Manila had a putrid odor. Nearly the whole town is what we call slums. There were Spanish people, Filipino people, Chinese people, and of course, a few whites and other nationalities. The natives of the Philippine Islands looked forward to the day when they would achieve full independence. According to the Filipino, the American businessman became rich through industries there using the Filipinos as slaves. Even the educated natives don't think some other country, such as Japan, will take over as soon as the United States steps out, but they admit it would be very easy to do. When the American army, marines, and the navy leave the islands, there won't be enough military protection to quell a street riot. Rice and tobacco used to be the main farm products, but the American businessmen provided a market for sugar cane and paid the natives well to, shall we say, 'raise Cain'? There will be plenty of reason to 'raise Cain' in 1946 if the cane market is not turned over to someone else when the islands gain their freedom.

"The first thing to catch the traveler's eye as he enters Manila for the first time is the walled city. The walled city is the original Manila. A wall about fifteen or twenty feet high was built around that Spanish settlement to protect the residents from headhunters and other warriors. The wall, about a mile square, is made of stone and has seven gates for entrance into the old city. Manila's six hundred thousand inhabitants—the population had doubled in ten years—hid the walled city.

"The streets were just wide enough for two vehicles to pass, and there was a narrow sidewalk on each side of the street. Jammed up against the sidewalk were two-story houses, most of the architecture, of course, was Spanish. The bottom story was used for business houses and the top story for living quarters. There were stores full of souvenirs influenced by the Moro headhunters—arrows, spears, knives of all sorts, and even skulls of dead men.

118

There wasn't a spear of grass growing inside the walled city, but just outside it was lush with grass, shrubbery, and palm trees.

"Besides cars, street cars, and busses, they used what is called the caramata. It is a cart, something like the buggy used in this country, only it was shined and polished until you could see your reflection in it. It had all kinds of shiny ornaments on it and was pulled by small Arabian horses. When we were on the way to the fire that we talked about a while ago, we were riding in a caramata, and as if that wasn't a slow enough way to get to a fire, we met a farmer coming to town in his wagon pulled by a caribou, so we stopped to take pictures. The caribou is just about twice as lazy and shiftless as a Missouri mule.

"One day we took a taxi up into the mountains east of Manila, past grass-roofed houses, or huts, built on stilts. We hired the taxi for the afternoon. I guess I should say that, aside from paying our taxi bill, we had a great time. As we got into the foothills near the mountains, we saw some of the mountain terracing like in the north end of the island. The Igorot tribe, uncivilized people who aren't vicious at all, live in the mountain wilderness in northern Luzon. We call them uncivilized, but I don't suppose their description of the so-called civilized people would be too complimentary. The Igorots live in the mountains and grow rice for a living. Don't tell me I'm mistaken, that you can't grow rice in the mountains, because what you'd mean is we civilized persons can't do it. But the Igorots can, not just on the mountains, but right up on the very top of the mountains. They do it by using a very complex system of terracing. Not only are we so-called civilized people unable to grow rice on top of a mountain, but some of the greatest engineers sent over to inspect the Igorot system of terracing couldn't understand it. To the Igorots, it's just an art, handed down from generation to generation. One odd characteristic of the Igorots is the fact that a boy, to be able to marry a girl, must carry her one hundred meters through that mountainous country.

"Anyway, on our taxi trip to the east of Manila, I saw similar terracing, but it was the wrong time of year to see rice growing on the foothills. There was only rice stubble left from the crop just harvested. We met a farmer woman walking along the road carrying supplies on top of her head that she had just purchased in town. In her arms was a small Filipino baby. We stopped at a village to get soft drinks. I don't suppose there have been a handful of white men stopping there, and everyone in town stared at us as if we were in a museum. Some were afraid of us; others just looked at us as oddities.

"The main reason for that trip was to see a dam across one of the mountain streams. It is the famous Ipo Dam, where half of Manila's water supply begins its journey by tunnel to the city about thirty miles away. I wish I could describe our view from where we stood at the top of that particular peak. Down below us, between two beautifully colored mountain slopes, a blue stream lazily wended its way downward. Then when the water got to the dam, it was brilliant silver flowing over the dam. As it passed over the dam, it disappeared into the tunnel leaving just enough water continuing down toward the valley, keeping it thick with foliage. Winding through cuts and down other valleys, the cement tunnel carried water to the city of Manila."

Stanley wrote home:

We were two days at the Olongapo naval dry dock in the Philippines located north and west of Manila about a hundred miles. There isn't much there but the navy and the marines, and of course, plenty of jungle. The town is two blocks long and is hidden in beautiful foliage with the bay in the front and thickly timbered mountains in the background. The climate is much hotter than in the States, and the Oriental atmosphere soon loses its romance when one can't get away from it.

I spent my evenings fishing. One peaceful evening I wandered out to the end of this floating dry dock to sit and think and maybe even throw a fishing line into the water. For a man with his underpants as the only bit of protection, the weather was perfect. There was a cool breeze, white clouds drifting across the sky, a million stars, and beautiful mountains rising from the mile-wide bay. I settled down to meditate, and low and behold, what happened? I caught a fish; a red snapper. He wasn't nearly as surprised as I. Then I caught an angel fish. It was a brilliant silver color—it was well named—and was about eight inches long and was as tall as it was long but very thin. When we were fishing, we could look far down into the water and see fish that were larger than we were.

I talked with a marine there from Oklahoma. I haven't talked with one American stationed in the Philippines who didn't regret having been sent over. We ran into bargains on summer suits over here (sharkskin), so I had one tailored to fit the bones of this old carcass.

Our next port of call was Miri, Borneo, four short days from Manila. It's just a little berg located about at the equator. We've gotten a long way from the highways. As Hawaii had no hula girls in skirts, so Borneo had no, or very few, wild men. I didn't see anything nearly as wild as the wild men from Borneo in the circuses. The English and Dutch have done wonders in educating the natives of Borneo … I got your airmail letters in Manila.

April 23, 1941
Hastings, Nebr.

Dear Stanley:

It's been so long since I have written you a letter that I may have to take some lessons on how to write letters to a wandering son ...

We were certainly surprised and thrilled to get your Easter greeting from somewhere in the Pacific. We almost weren't home that day ... Oh, yes. I must tell you about some mats that I received as a Christmas gift from a boy who makes his home on the ocean for the time being. You had me guessing that it was about everything except what it was. They are all beautiful, especially the orange and black one. I like the white ones very much too. There wasn't anything the matter with them except tying a few strings together on the edge so they wouldn't fall apart. I get such a kick out of them—more so knowing what kind of a guy you are. If you were a sissy, I wouldn't enjoy them nearly so much ...

The head of the draft board called up the day he got your card. He said he wasn't going to do anything about it as they weren't any ways near your number yet. They only do ten a day and are now a little past 1500. So you see, it will be a while. They are not taking them in the army very fast right now either. Then, too, I saw where there was a shortage of seamen, and they would like to have the draft boards pass those who were working in this line.

I get a big kick out of your mentioning that you smell spring out where there is nothing but water. Spring isn't arriving here very fast ... I went to a bridge party the other night and didn't get home until 11:30. Had a big time and also a nice dinner. I've been going quite a bit since I came to this town, and I enjoy it. I plan to join the American Legion Auxiliary in about two weeks. Last week I went to a newcomers' club meeting and came home with a nice slip as a prize. Then the next day I went to a group meeting of the Presbyterian Church ...

Harold started to write this letter, and then a friend came by and took him to another boy's house ... Wish I could have been with you in Hollywood ... Take good care of yourself. I know you are having one swell time seeing all these new places. Take several looks for me too, will you?

Lots of love,
Mother

Stanley wrote his sister, "I thought it would be a shame if we came this far over, twelve thousand miles, without touching the mainland. Apparently, Standard Oil thought so, too, cause we're headed for Shanghai, China."

"Shanghai's a lot of town to put into a few words," Stanley wrote in his travelogue. "It has a population of four and one-half million, and after attempting to get through some of those crowded, narrow streets in a hurry, I don't doubt it a bit. Many factories and other buildings were situated between the place we docked and the heart of town that had been bombed by the Japanese back in 1937. Very few of the buildings had been rebuilt. We were docked on the Whangpoo River which flows into the Yangtze River. I rode across the river once in a sampan. The Mrs. rowed in the front and the Mr. in the back while the little bare-reared youngin' enjoyed his few short years of freedom from the oars. I saw little tots of three and four years of age helping row.

"Those people lived night and day in the boats. A meager meal was sometimes prepared right on the sampan; the woman washed clothes in the dirty river and hung them on a makeshift clothesline on the boat, and of course, there was no entertainment for those poor people and no education for their youngsters. A baby born to a family making their living in a sampan was destined to spend his life at the same trade.

"Rice was grown in the fertile valley on each side of the Whangpoo River where the ground was low and moisture plentiful. During the growing season, the deep green of the rice plants added a beautiful touch to a naturally beautiful landscape. The few houses that could be seen were made of rice straw, were about fifty feet long, and looked like a haystack on a Nebraska field. We saw no windows. Clear to the mouth of the river, there were plenty of sampans and junks. A junk, of course, is an overgrown sampan propelled by sails made from strips of cloth woven together with bamboo rods.

"Shanghai is about as Chinese, as far as architecture is concerned, as is North Platte, Nebraska. Shanghai is divided into three sections: the old Chinese settlement, the international settlement, and the French settlement. The Chinese settlement, where no one except the natives lived, was old and dirty; the streets were narrow and literally cluttered with Chinamen. The old Chinese section didn't have the Chinese architecture, and don't ask me why because I haven't the least idea, unless during the many years of the city's existence, the Chinese people have migrated from one section of the city to another occupying the districts vacated by foreign residents.

"Few visitors to Shanghai venture far into the old Chinese section, but of course, we had to satisfy our curiosity— although it's much better to be a live person with a curiosity than a dead person with a satisfied curiosity. Some of the places we were taken to by guides and interpreters ran cold chills up and down our spines. He'd take us up dark, narrow alleys, up or down a few flights of blackened stairways and hallways, and we'd wind up in an attic or a basement where some Chinaman, with an exceptional command of English, had convinced us that we could get the best bargains. And all the time we were walking past hungry Chinamen who couldn't make as much money in a lifetime as we had on us. The rate of exchange in Shanghai when we were there was twenty to one, and, incidentally, we were unable to find any Chinese bills larger than ten mex. One can feel pretty fortunate he's an American and lives in God's country.

"The international and French settlements had modern buildings, clean stores, sometimes with advertising in English. There were probably a half dozen theaters in town that showed movies in English. At one I saw "Gone with the Wind." We spent many hours at the navy YMCA placed there primarily for use of the American military. At the YMCA we could get ice cream, milk shakes, and soft drinks the way they're made in America. And, I dare say, that was one of the most welcome things a person could find when he'd been away from the States for a few months. We would have enjoyed finding American people, but shortly before we arrived, most Americans had evacuated the city due to government orders."

For years, Japan's aggressive and sometimes violent empire building stirred things up in Asia. Japan sought raw materials to sustain its economy as well as to exist as a world power. Since 1937, Shanghai was one city along China's east coast that was controlled by the Japanese. So America had imposed sanctions and restricted crucial exports, especially oil. Such embargoes predictably created not only economic hardships for the Japanese, but tensions between the two countries intensified. And then, with most of Europe occupied and bogged down with war, European colonies in Southeast Asia and the Pacific were in jeopardy. Japan awaited the opportunity to expand its empire. Prior to Stanley's arrival in Shanghai, Japan had entered the Tripartite Pact of 1940 with Germany and Italy. And as Japan aimed to expand into Southeast Asia, the island nation entered a neutrality pact with Stalin, hoping to thwart possible aggression from the Soviet Union. A showdown between Japan and the United States brewed.

"Along the streets of Shanghai were cars; first-, second- and third-class street cars; busses; and the coolies trotting up the street pulling their jinrikisha, commonly called just rickshaw," Stanley continued. "At first it was quite amusing to have coolies with their carts, lined up at the curb for a half a block each way, shout the few English words they knew to you. Before long it got tiresome, and you hated to step out on the street. I must say though, it inflated one's ego to be catered after in such a manner.

"One has to use his sign language, devised on the spur of the moment, when two languages are so totally different. I lost all traces of timidness or self-consciousness while performing the art.

"One day when I was in a hurry to get back to the ship, I took a taxi out to that section across the river. Part of Shanghai was under Japanese control and was patrolled by Japanese policemen—Japanese policemen, who I might add, had no love for an American. The part of the city across the river from where our boat was docked was controlled by the Japs. A Japanese officer stopped us, and if my Chinese interpreter hadn't told the policeman that I was a German off of a German freighter anchored in the river, I probably would be trying to get across the river yet."

"Your son is smiling to everyone," Stanley wrote his folks. "I had all my missing teeth replaced in Shanghai, so I'm sure giving the grub a workout today. The whole lot cost me less here than one tooth would in the States. San Pedro was rumored as the next port, but I doubted it. We are going to Palembang, Sumatra. It means that after having gotten so close to the equator, I'm finally going to cross it"

On June 2, 1941, Stanley's letter home stated, "The engines labored heavily, the ship lurched, then we seemed to be coasting downhill. At last, after hundreds of thousands of miles of travel to many corners of the globe, I had crossed the equator. Here we are on this half of the earth, and it seems about the same as the top half."

The radio travelogue continued, "The island of Sumatra is part of the Dutch East Indies; it is flat, and vegetation was thicker than hair on a dog's back. We sailed up the Palembang River about one hundred miles to the city of Palembang. It was night when we went up the river, so we had to use our imaginations about what was on each side. The river was about a quarter of a mile wide, but the aroma of flowers was as strong as in a greenhouse. The moon was full that night; the breeze was cool, and if ever a night was romantic, that was it. The native folks enjoyed the nights, but there's sure plenty of room for other people.

"Along the river, wedged between the water and thick vegetation on land, were many villages. The houses, made of bamboo and grass, were on the edge of the river. There were no streets, no cars or any other means of land transportation. Small boats parked in front of each native hut. Each house was about fifteen feet long—from front to back—and that was the width of the entire town. Can you imagine a town fifteen feet wide and a mile long?

124

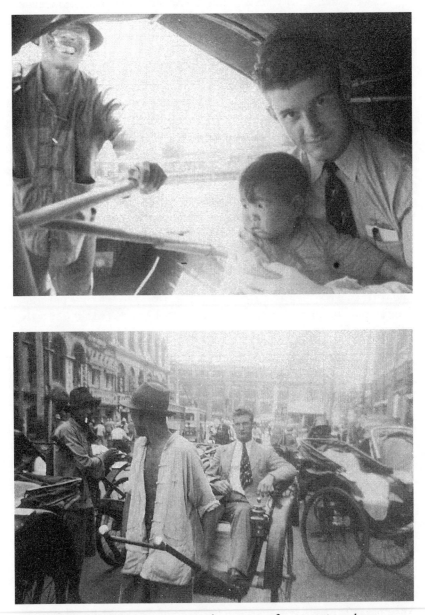

Stanley sailed the ocean as a merchant marine for approximately two years. These photos were probably taken when he ported at Shanghai, China. One photo shows Stanley as a "passenger" on a sampan. The other photo shows him as a "passenger" on a rickshaw.

"As we neared the city, we saw the reflection of thousands of lights above the tops of the trees between us and town. Then as we rounded a bend in the river, there before us was what I thought was the most beautiful city in the world. Every one of the lights was white, and each building was outlined with those white lights. That night I thought, when I get rich, Palembang would be my winter home. But my dreams were shattered the next morning. The next morning turned my beautiful white city into an oil refinery across the river from the town. So when we got ready to go ashore, we had to go across the wide river in little boats propelled by native kids and then take a taxi into town a few miles away. The road to town was cut through the woods, and on each side were palm trees, grass and shrubbery, and hundreds of varieties of wildflowers.

"Palembang was a nicer city than most in the tropics, over a hundred thousand in population. The Dutch had done a marvelous job of making the cities and villages on the island pleasant places to live. Buildings were made of white stone, and native houses were made of wood and unpainted. Farmers sold loads of fruits and vegetables, many I had never heard of or seen, and curio shops and jewelry shops stood side by side with trinkets for sale, trinkets shipped there from the United States or Japan. The natives, having prospered because of the oil and refineries, took on the air of lords. The wealthier a native was, the louder he dressed."

"We're taking on a half a load here in Sumatra," Stanley wrote home, "half a load in Singapore, unless orders should change. Then back to Shanghai. Pedro is rumored next, but I'll believe it when I see it. Anyhoo, I'll see you soon."

On June 7, 1941, he added, "Cast an eye on that address, Tandjong Oeban, Rhio Archipelago. Ain't it a honey? It took us a day to get here from Palembang. It's a small island twenty miles or so from Singapore. Singapore is a city on the southern tip of the Malay States. I wanted to run over to Singapore, but I guess it's impossible to get through the minefields. So we had to be content to spend our shore leave in the jungles."

In his travelogue, Stanley told, "The island itself was quite small, and much of it was jungle. I don't suppose there were five hundred people on the island and three or four cars. Four hundred fifty or more were natives. The white men there were Dutch. There, too, the Dutch had shown much effort and success in raising the standard of living of the natives. We docked at a port called Tand Jangoeban [Tandjoengoeban], which was an oil refinery. Incidentally, the 100th meridian runs through the Malay States—the hundredth meridian that is just exactly on the opposite side of the world to the 100th meridian that runs through Cozad, Nebraska. So we were on the other side of the world to the folks living near Cozad.

"On the island, most of the newer homes were stucco or cement houses. The older houses were just the plain, unpainted frame structures typical of the tropical native. There were a few grass-roofed houses, too, but not many. A couple of us wandered past the village along a small path cut through to the other side of the island. To return, we cut through the jungle where a drainage ditch had been dug. Much to our regret, we followed a path worn there by animals at night. The ground was soaked with oil, then there was swamp water which ran along the ditch. The two together didn't smell like a bed of roses. Sometimes the path would cross the drainage ditch, and not being able to jump as well as the animals that had made the path, we sunk into the slimy mud halfway up to our knees. Then added to all this were the weird noises that came from the dense jungle on each side of the path. Needless to say, although we enjoyed our little hike, we were glad to reach a road that led back to the village.

"About 2:00 a.m., on my way back to the ship the night we were to sail from the island, I decided it would be a shame if I left without climbing a coconut tree and picking a nut. With the light of a half moon, I shed my coat and shoes and began what I thought would be an easy task—to shinny up about sixty feet to the top of a coconut tree. I had no way of holding myself to the tree except with the grip of my arms and legs. Each foot I climbed upward was harder than the foot before, and by the time I was half way to the top of the tree, I realized I had undertaken quite a task. I couldn't think of quitting with the task incomplete; my conscience wouldn't allow it. And, I never would have lived down the shame if the fellow down below, watching me and having a much jollier time than I was, had seen me come back down the tree without a coconut. So inch by inch I climbed upward. My arms and legs got so weak they would hardly grip the trunk of that palm tree. And on top of it all, it was so dark I couldn't tell whether there were coconuts at the top of the tree or not. Anyway, just as I felt my arms and legs would give out any moment, I reached one of the palm leaves at the treetop. I hunted in the dark with my hand for a coconut. I had just about decided there were no coconuts in the tree when my hand touched something big and round. With my left arm holding on to the tree, I twisted the nut off and let it fall to the ground. I suppose I could have found other coconuts if I had groped longer, but I was out of the mood to pick them. And on my descent, I didn't climb cautiously back to earth. I just wrapped my arms around the trunk and slid to the ground. For the next two weeks, I doctored a chest that didn't have enough skin on it to keep a gnat warm. When I dropped the coconut, it cracked, and about two weeks later, out in the middle of the ocean, my roommate gave me the choice of throwing that smelly thing overboard or swimming the rest of the way myself."

The SS *India Arrow* sailed with a load back to Shanghai. The half trip was, according to Stanley, a "bit unpleasant." He wrote home, "We had a stern wind all the way blowing about the same speed that the ship moved. Consequently, the flag has hung down like a dishrag, and the perspiration has poured. Orders are still Pedro."

Stanley glimpsed the Japanese islands and an active volcano on his way "back to the other side of the world."

In the travelogue he described, "When we were on the side opposite the sun, the sun reflected on lava flowing down the gullies of the volcano." But it was yet another month before the crew touched the shores of the United States.

"When we were on the ocean," Stanley continued, "one of the things I enjoyed most was going up on the bow of the ship just after dark. There wasn't a sound up there, except the rolling waves ahead of the ship, and very seldom a light, even to the horizon. There was some substance in the water in some places that, when the water was stirred, that substance burned. It's some kind of organic matter. I could look down into those rollers ahead of the ship and see millions of little lights that burned for a second and then disappeared. Some of the fellows called it phosphorous, but technically, I didn't know what it was [phosphorescence]. Anyway, sometimes it was so bright it lit up the bow of the ship from the waterline to the top of the bow."

The SS *India Arrow* sailed the Pacific waters while German U-boats sank cargo ships in the Atlantic Ocean. When Stanley resumed sailing as a merchant marine in the fall of 1940, his travels coincided with an escalating war in Europe—France had fallen, and Hitler resolved to invade Britain. But first, the Luftwaffe bombed England's military facilities and then unleashed the Blitz on London and other British cities. However, under the determined leadership of Winston Churchill, the suffering Brits rallied to fight the Germans and won the Battle of Britain. Yet, during the war, indiscriminate buzz bombs and V-2 rockets wreaked death and destruction in England's cities and countryside.

So Hitler "settled" for a German-occupied Western Europe, without the conquest of England. But that wasn't enough. The Nazi leader set the stage to invade Russia, advancing the Eastern Front. While Hitler's Afrika Korps fought in the sands of North Africa and rescued Mussolini—his Italian army in over its head—emboldened Hitler manipulated and battled for the occupation of the Balkans. Controlling the Balkans gave the Nazi war machine possession of the vital oil fields of Ploesti, Romania, and backdoor access to Russia. Devious Hitler turned on his Communist ally, Stalin, and marched his troops into Russia in June 1941. Operation Barbarossa was underway.

A conquered Russia meant plentiful oil, land, and other resources and living space for the Germans. In addition, the Fascist Hitler was motivated by his hatred of Communism.

Hitler loathed Communists, as well as Jews and other "subhumans." And with visions of preserving what he believed to be the master race, Aryans, the fanatic dictator obsessed about eliminating from the face of the earth those he labeled inferior. Jews especially were denied citizenship. They were also demoralized, persecuted, and, behind the closed doors of Nazi Europe, were ruthlessly and systematically exterminated. Not until the camps were liberated at the war's end in 1945 did the world totally realize the truth of the disgustingly horrific atrocities of the Holocaust.

Against that backdrop, and almost in another world, the SS *India Arrow* retraced its journey back to the East Coast. Stanley wrote home:

> All in all, I've had a big time, learned a lot, and there are many places I want to visit. I wouldn't regret a return trip. It's been great in every respect, except that I wanted to go on west to encircle the globe. But I guess a fellow can't expect everything. As it is, I lack 120 degrees—the distance from Singapore to Dakar—of having gone around the world. And there's darned few people who have done even that.
>
> I might mention that I'd like to lay away a couple of square meals of mom's home cookin'. And I intend doing that before long.
>
> From all reports in Pedro and Panama, there must be plenty of jobs to go around in any field of endeavor, so I shouldn't have to try very hard to piddle my services. My traveling days are about over, and I will be getting acquainted with terra firma. If I get off in Paulsboro, I could see the N.Y. people once more. It'll be a chance to see the big city, and it might be the last time for a long time. Plans are to make the half trip to Beaumont before I get off. So I should be home about the first of September. So far, that's what I plan to do, but my plans are changing often these days, and it depends on what the draft has in store for me too.
>
> I'm planning on buying a car soon, and after a good while at home, I'll start out job hunting, taking a turn thru Kansas and Colorado and winding up in Oregon where I know I can work, if I don't stumble onto a job in the meantime.

Stanley got off the SS *India Arrow* in Texas, and before heading home, he visited one more country. He stated in his travelogue, "I had seen its shores many times but had never touched Old Mexico. I went to Juarez, just across the line from El Paso, Texas. Technically, across the river, but more technically across the creek. I had heard all my life about the beautiful Rio Grande. And when I got to it, I had to ask a guard if that little stream was the Rio Grande. I guess if I had wanted to be more impressed with the Rio Grande, I should have seen it nearer to its mouth."

Concluding his travelogue, Stanley said, "I couldn't get back to see my folks soon enough."

We didn't live in Manhattan anymore, so Stan went home to Hastings, Nebraska. It was the fall of 1941. While at home, we both went down to take our driver's tests—my first and his renewal. I beat him on the written, and I remember the look he gave me that maybe I had grown up since he had last seen me. I don't remember much more about him being home. He got a lead from the Radio Employment Bureau in Denver for a job at KGNF radio station in North Platte, Nebraska. The announcing position was filled, so he wrote scripts, mostly, and had some airtime. The position was for a "man who can announce and write continuity." The station in North Platte had a running program about Stan's travels, and those were the scripts packed away in the trunk.

Stanley's job at KGNF filled a temporary need for both the employer and employee. In early December 1941, Stanley drove to Longview, Washington, in his 1940 Plymouth that he'd purchased for six hundred dollars, joined his friend Theron, and planned for his long-awaited radio career.

On December 3, 1941, from Longview, Stanley wrote, "I've done quite a bit of running around since I got here. Mt. St. Helens is about fifty miles from here, and Mt. Hood, fifty miles south of Portland, is famous for its skiing. I think there were an even jillion people skiing there last Sunday. We rode up the mile-long ski lift and walked back getting our feet half frozen in the snow but got so warmed up elsewhere it made up for the cold feet. Looks like skiing would be a lot of fun, but durned if I would like the walking back up. Lots of the skiers walked part way up the hill and then skied back down—I think that's dumb. I guess it's a good way to walk off a lot of steam.

"Yesterday I went to Seattle and talked with a fellow that used to be at KGNF and through him had a good interview with the boss at KOMO. The turnover there is very slow. It's a station where, if you get on, you stay until doomsday. That's the kind of station that I'm going to be looking for when I feel I'm well enough experienced to handle anything that big. At present, I'm about ready to make the grade with KWLK here in Longview. It's not definite yet, but I was up there this morning to see the manager, and he asked me to come back day after tomorrow [December 5] for something definite."

Friday, December 5 was two days before the grim Sunday morning at Pearl Harbor. Sunday, December 7, 1941, in the words of Franklin D. Roosevelt, "a day that will live in infamy," set in motion a new future for everyone.

5

◦✥◦

Answering the Call to Duty

Private Dwyer is the name.
—*Stanley N. Dwyer in a letter dated December 25, 1941*

By December 1941, the Japanese calculated that the U.S. Pacific fleet anchored at Pearl Harbor posed a threat to their conquest of Southeast Asia and the South Pacific—and that threat needed to be eliminated. In response to Japan's intimidating empire building, the United States imposed more economic sanctions, stoking almost insurmountable tensions between the two countries. Consequently, the surprise attack on Pearl Harbor was Japan's military response to the impasse in negotiations between the two nations.

Early on Sunday morning, December 7, 1941, ships of the Pacific fleet of the United States Navy were moored in the calm waters of Pearl Harbor on the picturesque island of Oahu. Without warning, hundreds of Japanese planes zoomed in for the attack, and the rest is recorded in pages and pages of history and the memories of the survivors. It must have seemed like hell on earth. The next day, the United States declared war on Japan, and three days later, Germany and Italy declared war on America. World War II lived up to its name. The conflict stretched around the globe and encompassed most of the world.

Most people of my generation remember where they were when they heard about the bombing of Pearl Harbor. I happened to be two months into being a seventeen-year-old kid on December 7, 1941. I was a senior at Hastings High School, standing on the corner of Second Street and Burlington Avenue. Years later, I happened to be standing at the same spot when I heard that John F. Kennedy had been assassinated. In 1941, I was with some buddies, in line to go to a show at the Strand Theatre, when someone in line said something about the bombing of Pearl Harbor. The significance of the bombing did not register with me because I didn't even know where Pearl Harbor was located.

I certainly didn't think about what effect that event would have on me, my family, our country, and our world—I had too many model airplanes to build. What started out as just another Sunday in December became a day that affected my life and those close to me. The country and the whole world changed. December 7, 1941, set in motion the course of our lives that made a life for a lot of people that they hadn't anticipated—some good, some bad.

Japanese Admiral Yamamoto feared Japan's attack at Pearl Harbor had "awoken a sleeping giant." They underestimated the resilience of the American people. America did awaken from its isolationist "slumber" and geared up for war—a war to be fought on two fronts—in Europe and in the Pacific. After World War I, the army had basically downsized to a bare-bones operation. A display at the National World War II Museum in New Orleans notes that, in the late 1930s, America's military ranked eighteenth in the world. But, in 1941, confronted with a war on two sides, the home front in this country began mobilizing to an extent never seen before. The Depression era was left behind.

The country was just getting out of the Depression when the war started. It seemed to have been the background for the right attitude for young people to join the service and basically protect their families. For my older brother, Stan, who was twenty-five years old on December 7, 1941, the prospect of him being drafted was already reality.

If they qualified, millions of ordinary young men and some women—from all walks of life, from towns and cities and farms across the United States—enlisted for service. Millions more were drafted. Deferments were sometimes issued to men operating farms or working in the war industry. A small minority resisted the draft. A sense of duty seemed to be the overriding response. Americans selflessly put their lives on hold, answered the call to duty, and served a cause greater than themselves. They put their lives on the line to defend America and our country's way of life and ultimately preserved freedom for people they didn't even know. And little did the World War II soldiers know how their collective efforts would change the course of history and the world.

Stanley's postcard to his sister, Aileen, on December 11, 1941, read, "I'm in the army now, tra la. Had a job at KWLK, Longview, starting tomorrow. Probably will be shipped by train this aft to Ft. Lewis, near Tacoma, Wash. Don't know where from there. Will write when I get settled. Sold my car last nite. Have been witnessing black outs the last few nights."

From Ft. Lewis, the next stop for Stanley was Camp Roberts. Christmas consisted of a turkey dinner at camp and a letter home.

Dear folks:

So darned much water has passed under the bridge since I wrote to you, I don't know which log I sent the letter on. Reckon you're having a Merry Christmas even though I'm sure I didn't do anything to make it merrier. This letter is a substitution for presence and presents.

After taking a number of intelligence tests, which turned the mass back, but not me, I was placed in radio communications. After a couple months of technical training, I'll probably be sent some place else. We are learning the international code now.

I doubt if I'll be needing anything that isn't stamped "U.S." for a long time. Don't seem to have much use for my lifelong collections of clothes and souvenirs, so box by box, I'm getting them all home.

Private Dwyer is the name.

Love,
Stan

Everyone was required to do basic training, including KP duty. After five weeks of drilling, hiking, rifle firing, and a little technical radio work, "then we'll go into radio in earnest."

Stanley wrote home in January 1942.

Dear folks:

Today is Sunday, as you can tell by looking down the rows of bunks in the barracks and seeing the large number of fellows writing letters. You needn't worry about my stay in the army. I'll get along; you can bet your boots on that. I got acquainted this week with a transceiver, a combination miniature sending and receiving set.

Did I tell you that radio com. gets the men with the highest intelligence ratings? What do you suppose I'm here for? Not my money. If a college education ever quits paying off, I'll be surprised. And I'll ever be grateful to those who made it possible for me. Wish Harold could go on. But maybe Uncle Sam already has a place for him in the army or industry. Whatever it is, I'll bet it is run by propeller.

Wish some of the gang would scram so I could think. They are discussing, again, the merits and demerits of each state. In the two squads occupying the downstairs of the barracks, there are well over a dozen states represented. Of course, we've got our clown. Any group of men, especially in the army, wouldn't be complete without him. The whole gang is swell; practically all the fellows here have degrees.

I plan to take a run into Paso Robles after while. Don't have anything to go for, but think I need a change now and then. The popular soldiers' hangout there is a new USO club. One can play ping-pong or write letters or read there. The people in charge put a lot of effort into making one feel at home. They invite girls from surrounding towns to come up to dance on Sat. evenings. In the daytime, women's organizations serve coffee and cake. There is a USO building on the camp. It has game facilities, a library, room to entertain visitors, and so on. Then the USO brings shows to the camp. Night before last the great violinist Jascha Heifetz was here, and it was free. Tomorrow night there's a variety show. If you weren't my sister and brother, this would sound like the build-up for a donation, wouldn't it?

I'm sort of toying with the idea of getting into the Air Corps after I complete my radio training, and if such is allowed. Flying is something that can be used after the war is over. So, ta, ta. See you in the funnies.

Love,
Stan

Stanley joined the U.S. Army on December 8, 1941,
and first served in the Signal Corps.

"Yesterday I should have written," Stanley wrote, "but I found a new hobby and spent the day at it. The hobby is hitchhiking. It's wartime now, and folks think lots of their soldier boys. Consequently, a fellow can't even plant both feet on the highway before he's picked up."

Weeks became routine, and technical training included four hours a day of code practice. "This first week in radio I'm taking 14 w.p.m. in code," Stanley reported. "Code words are just a jumble of letters, five to a group. They are encoded before reaching the radioman and decoded after being passed along. Yesterday we got acquainted with the different types of equipment we'll handle, including four types of sending and receiving sets (one a car radio), a telegraph set, et cetera."

Dear folks,

It rained or misted all week, but the way the army dresses you, you couldn't get wet if you jumped in the lake.

About the most exciting thing I can think of to tell about happened last night. I lowered a window from the top, then getting down, hung myself on a nail. It ripped a hole in my pants, my underpants, and scratched my rear. Went over to have the doctor patch me up, but it wasn't because it was so bad, but rather because I wanted to clear myself lawfully if it should become infected or something. And I've taken plenty of razzing today from the gang!

Tomorrow night I have a date, the first, I think, since I got in the army. She's a telephone operator. Don't know why I always pick on operators. That's one way to tell the type of girl you're going with though. Anyone that works for Bell Telephone must be tops. The company sees to that before they hire. The North Platte operator I dated who was transferred to Denver was checked on plenty before the move. They even went out to see what kind of place she was going to live in and even if it was in the right section of town.

The other big news of the day is an appointment with the company commander on the subject of officer's training. I have my letters of recommendation in hand, as well as my transcript from K-State. Now all I have to do is to pray that I pass the physical and that I get all the red tape cut before I get sunk deep into something else. I hope it's possible—in the event that I make the grade—to get back into radio. The deeper I get into it, the better I like it. Don't know whether or not I told you, I am taking 18 w.p.m. in code.

I haven't the cash necessary to have a whale of a time, but Jack, a lawyer in civilian life, and I are planning a weekend in Frisco, if we get the passes. They're rather hard to get, but we have a pretty good chance this week. We've nothing to go for in particular except just to break the routine.

And ma, when you get to feeling chipper, I'd like to have you make some cookies or candy. We're well fed, but many of the other fellows have gotten stuff from home and passed it around, and I don't think it's more than fair that I do the same.

And Harold, each of the family and relatives has told me that you had to have my clothes lengthened before you could wear them. Don't you think you'd better start wearing a weight on your head?

About the India Arrow, I didn't know anything about it till I got your letter.

Thought I'd get a letter from home today, but I guess the mailman is out cutting down a cherry tree. So dit dah.

Love,
Stan

Stanley had stepped off the SS *India Arrow* for good in August. Charles Seerveld, the man I located with an Internet search, the man who sailed on the tanker after Stanley's service, wrote in his letter to me, "After 12-7-41 we sailed blacked out."

It seems Pearl Harbor was a turning point. Prior to Pearl Harbor, the United States assumed a politically neutral stance while aiding merchant shipping. Nonetheless, U.S. ships were targets and victims of German U-boats. After Pearl Harbor and Germany's declaration of war on the United States, our involvement in the Battle of the Atlantic became "official." The Atlantic supply route was crucial to winning the war.

"Most of our sailing [across the Atlantic]," Mr. Seerveld explained, "was in convoy with other ships. Anywhere from ten to eighty ships … There would be a destroyer up ahead and usually one on each side of the columns, and one in the rear. If one escort suspected a submarine, he would hoist a solid black flag and maybe even drop a depth charge. If one or more ships were hit, the rest were supposed to keep going. The escort in the rear would pick up survivors … Moonlit nights on a calm sea were good. No lights were shown except a blue light on the stern of each vessel. Stormy nights in heavy seas were near disastrous."[5]

Convoys protected merchant vessels in the North Atlantic, but closer to home, it was a different story. After Pearl Harbor thrust the United States into the war, German U-boats, more than before, lurked in the unprotected East Coast sea-lanes and proved to be a shocking and deadly menace.

Mr. Seerveld continued:

[On February 4, 1942], the tanker, India Arrow was sailing north, blacked out, about fifty miles off Atlantic City, New Jersey, on a voyage from Corpus Christi, Texas, to New York, carrying crude oil. German Captain Werner Winter, on the submarine U-103, had the tanker in his sights. At exactly 7:00 p.m. he fired one torpedo. There was no chance of a miss. The sea was calm and the lights on the Jersey shore put the tanker in a sharp silhouette ...

I could hear the six bells for seven o'clock being struck by the man at the wheel on the bridge. I was dressed, sitting on my bunk reading when there was a terrific thump. We half expected something like this, but this early in the war, not many people knew what a torpedo felt like. I ran out of my room and up the companionway ladder. I saw a huge mass of flame on the starboard side of the tanker back aft. It dawned on me immediately that we would have to abandon ship. I also realized that I had no life preserver, and I was not a swimmer. I ran back down to my room and grabbed my life preserver and came back on deck and ran back to the bridge. I had to go up the ladder to the boat deck.

There were two lifeboats on the boat deck of the midship house and two back on the stern house, but the flames were too high to go aft. There was no point in going to your assigned boat. A loaded tanker is low in the water to start with. The only buoyancy is the open engine room aft and the open space of the bow compartment. Apparently, the torpedo blew a hole in the side of the engine room and the incoming water caused the ship to roll to starboard. By this time I had reached the lifeboat and it was afloat, but still in its davits. The air tanks in the lifeboat kept it afloat. I held my nose as the ship rolled to starboard. It came right up and I unhooked the ball on the stern of the lifeboat. Somebody else must have unhooked the front ball.[6]

"The ship went down in ten minutes," Mr. Seerveld wrote me. "Twelve of us were able to get into the one lifeboat, twenty-six were lost. We sailed in the lifeboat for 36 hours. The India Arrow sits on the bottom [of the Atlantic Ocean] in 135 feet of water."

Mr. Seerveld noted that the same German submarine sank a sister ship, the SS *China Arrow*, the day after sinking the *India Arrow*.

The war was closer to our shores than most people realized. A tiny newspaper clipping floated around in Stanley's trunk, which read, "The SS

India Arrow is about the eighteenth ship attacked by enemy submarines off the United States and Canadian coasts in recent weeks."

And Stanley thanked his "ma" for the goodies.

If I added herewith all the compliments from the boys, I wouldn't have room to write anything else. Anyway, from them all, and from me, thanks heaps. We've been doing a lot of work with radios in the field. It's great fun, and I'm not going to cry if I don't get the green light on the officer's school. And here's a bit of dope for ma. Practically all radio work is done behind the line of scrimmage.

Stanley wrote more another day:

At last! Two minutes to myself. Wish I could put a stop watch on time for a while. I owe more letters than I can shake a rifle at. Hope my chair at the home fireside hasn't been carried out to the barn.

The officer's training board failed to recommend me for training. Too bad they can't detect a man who can produce the goods. Personally, tho, I don't care a lot, except that it sort of shrinks my pride. I'm sure I can still make it if I decide it's worth fighting for.

Up to now, the car deal in Oregon hasn't gotten to a head enough for me to get money out of it, but I intend to see that it is settled shortly.

Don't believe I've written since last weekend. One of my North Platte operators, now in L.A., spent Sunday with me. So between such and the car deal, pop can readily see that the second five was welcome and put to good usage. I reckon the matter of pride would have kept me from asking. Thanks heaps, tho the rate of interest will pile up a little before I get it paid back.

Stanley wrote:

We've been doing a lot of work in the field lately setting up and conducting field nets. Our hike Monday night included that too. Today, on the way back from the field, we stopped long enough to run an obstacle course twice, once without rifles, then with. The obstacles included a ten-foot wall, a Tarzan swing rope over water, and ten- and twelve-foot broad jumps. And anyone who doesn't think I'm getting into great physical shape, just step forward. I've never been in as good of shape in my life, and I feel like a million dollars. If they'd give me an unlimited mileage pass, I'd run home for a game of pinochle tonight. Our training here is fast drawing to a close, and we're all getting anxious to know where we're going.

He wrote again:

Everything here is in an uproar with the news this evening of a few of us leaving tomorrow, most of the company leaving Wednesday, and the rest of us leaving shortly. So far, I'm not on the list. There's probably a fourth or less of us who are not assigned yet, and it keeps one's curiosity at a peak. A couple of fellows who have passed the officer's training board since we got a quota are urging me to try again. So ta, ta. Letters have been flowing in from home at a good clip.

Stanley replied to his sister, Aileen, and her husband, Bill:

Was I surprised when I got a carton of cigarettes from you, darned near passed out. But they were very much appreciated, and the brand was right. Thanks heaps. And about the insurance. I admire your ability to see into the future. I'm sure I can't see that far. However, I have already taken out five thousand, payable to mom and changeable. It costs me about four a month, which leaves me all of seventeen dollars to live on. (You folks act like you had lived through a couple of wars and know what it's like to try to exist on twenty-one dollars a month.)

The USO clubs are leaning over backwards to make us feel at home. And the people in the communities around are cooperating. Slowly but surely folks are learning that the wartime soldier is the boy whom their daughter dated a few months ago. And as a result, the respectable girls are coming out from hiding.

Keep the home fires burning, and maybe I'll get to come see you ere we grow old and gray.

Stanley and Grandma and Granddad commented back and forth about the mail service. Stanley would write, "Darned if I know why it should take mail a week to travel halfway across the States," or "Hope the next place I go to can get mail service," or "Don't know where in heck all the mail goes." Stanley corresponded with people all over. His cousin Beth was on the list, as were friends from KGNF in North Platte, Doc Summers, Gerv, Lynne, Dorothea, and, of course, Theron, to name a few. Theron lived in Vancouver, Washington, and at one point, worked on the newspaper and worked a shift at a shipyard. Stanley told his folks, "He is making over one hundred bucks per week. If a man who doesn't have the health to get in the army can do that, what could a perfect specimen do? I'd like about a week to find out." Whatever the "merits and demerits" of the postal service, mail usually caught up with him wherever and whenever he transferred.

April 7, 1942
Camp San Luis Obispo

Dear folks:

I am now at Camp San Luis Obispo, a town of about fifteen thousand population forty miles south of Camp Roberts. The neat and legible letters of a typewriter should give you an inkling as to the sort of work I'm doing these days. One hour a day we drill, which serves only to limber one up, and the rest of the time I'm doing office work. Said office work is being done in the Adjutant General's department.

I don't know what kind of record I made during the series of many aptitude tests shortly after my enlistment, but apparently it wasn't so worse. First of all, I wouldn't have gotten into radio communications unless I was in the upper bracket. There were nine of us sent here from the 140th Inf. where the rest of the men landed. The two lawyers, of course, settled in the Judge Advocate's office. Six of the men were given clerical work, having been assigned to duty by the master sergeant, but not your uncle Pedro. I was ushered in to see the Lt. Colonel. He decided that since I had radio experience, he would see that I was placed in Public Relations. He suggested that, while I was waiting for such a placement, and because I'd probably be applying for officer's training again, I should flit from office to office in the AG department to get an idea of what goes on in each.

Then the payoff. To make it short, he's an alumnus of dear 'ole Kansas State College. So I guess I'll fare well. Don't you think? Incidentally, pop, there's a ghost of a chance that you might know him. He was a Kansas man and was in the world war. He probably held a rating then similar to yours. His name is Arthur A. Alexander. And by the way, should we ever discuss the subject, it probably would be well for me to know what outfit you were in. As if I hadn't heard it a thousand times.

There are gobs of Kansas and Nebraska men here. I've run into quite a few I know, including a couple from Tipton. It's surely different here. Those of us working here at division headquarters live in the HQ and MP company. We stand no guard, do no KP, we have no nightly bed check, and can, if we like, stay out till reveille the next morning.

In spite of all my freedom here, I must stand retreat, and that happens in about five minutes, in which case I better shake old fanny pronto. The sergeant over in the company area is itching to blow his pet whistle. Oh yes, that's another thing I can do. I stroll to and from work like a civilian.

evoL,
yelnatS

Meanwhile, Stanley adapted to a new routine. He wrote, "Right now I'm in the message center department recording all outgoing mail and sending it on." He was granted the privilege of using the office anytime he liked, and he explained, "With the events across the Pacific making perfect material for the novel I began on my last trip, I have begun writing again. I have, in my mind, cut off some of the last that I got done to replace it with this more interesting material. I will knock off a couple thousand words of imagination tonight. I see no reason why I can't finish it if I stay here long enough." Nevertheless, movement of the AG office temporarily disrupted his work.

For the first six months or so after Pearl Harbor, it was almost all defeat for the United States in the Pacific. The Japanese were on the move in the South Pacific to expand their regime, and there was no way this country could stop them until we got geared up. Many of the places Stan had visited—the Philippines, Borneo, and Sumatra—Japan conquered. The Dutch, English, and French lost control of their colonies in the Pacific.

Doolittle and his force of B-25s raided Tokyo in April 1942, but not until the Battle of Midway two months later—a turning point of the war in the Pacific—did the Americans go on the offensive. From that point on, our troops battled the Japanese from island to island. We developed a strategy to island hop, regaining strategic island locations to eventually invade Japan.

April 26, 1942

Dear Aileen,

Surprise! I'm not dead after all. In fact I'm very much alive in comparison to your mailman. I wrote to you ages ago after receiving the requested twenty-five. So long ago, in fact, that I've even forgotten what I said. I suppose I took my hair down and dissertated upon how grand a sister and brother-in-law I have. I remember that I added that, in spite of your offer to make the money a gift, I shall repay it as soon as I can. And I shall repeat, thanks a jillion.

We've moved again and are now located on the grounds of the Coliseum at Exposition Park in the village of Los Angeles. We're living right in the Coliseum for a few days until the remainder of the previous outfit clears out. Then we will occupy the tents in the surrounding area. The Coliseum is the stadium of Southern Cal, a measly little grandstand that holds about 115,000 people. Yesterday we were invited to a track meet in which a number of notables performed, including the world's highest pole vaulter. He cleared fifteen feet yesterday, seven inches less than his world record. Finally, I'm located in a camp where there are a few civilians to break the monotony of the sight of a uniform, et cetera.

We went out to the USO club at the Beverly Hills Hotel, the swank of the vicinity, stayed a little while, and decided to go to the USO at Hollywood. We stepped on the street to wait for a bus, and within two seconds a fellow stopped and asked us where we were going and invited us out to his house. He turned out to be one of the "400" of Beverly Hills. We chatted most of the evening, visited his little baby a moment who was sick in bed with a cold but who just had to see the soldier boys, then the fellow took us out to dinner.

I reckon as how I should do a little work. There's not a lot, but I don't want the boss to think I'm not worth even the buck a day. Write when you have time.

Love,
Stan

May 4, 1942

Dear parental and fraternal branches of the Dwyer family tree:

Another day, another dollar, and I ain't just kiddin. But the day was just as much like yesterday as the two dollar bills were similar. Or I should say like day before yesterday, because yesterday was Sunday, and though I made my dollar, the day was spent differently than most. Yesterday morning I went up to see Irma, since I have been so busy fulfilling my social engagements that I hadn't yet gotten to see her. I came back to camp for dinner. Oh yes, I might add, I've seen everything now. An elderly lady picked me up to bring me back, and as I got out of the car, she asked me if I would get mad if she asked a personal question. Of course, I said that I wouldn't, and she asked me if I had all the spending money I need. I've had everything else offered to me here, and now that completes it.

Anyway, to continue the ventures of yesterday, after a ham dinner, with all, another fellow and I went up into north Hollywood to see a couple of women we met at a USO dance recently. We bowled, saw a show, ate, then went riding with the parents of the girl I was with.

Of course, it wasn't the first date I've had since we pulled into town, but I dare say it was the most pleasant. Margaret is very nice looking, is a lot of fun, and has had one of the finest upbringings I've seen. She's all of eighteen years old, and judging from other girls around here, I'd say she has been fully matured for four or five years. We have another date Saturday night, and the two couples of us have a standing invitation from Margaret's folks to come up anytime we like for a steak fry or sumpin'. They have a very nice home, and I think the car's a Cadillac.

We were scheduled, those of us who are detached from the 140th Regt. which is now in San Diego, to go down there on the first of the month for our pay. The powers that be, however, decided that it would be much easier for us to get paid on a supplementary payroll here sometime this week. When we'll get paid now seems to depend on the desire of some ham in headquarters down there. So it might be next week; it might be next month. Let's hope that we don't just have to wait for the filthy another month. This is a poor town in which to be broke. If there were not so many strings attached to making out a requisition, said strings of which take so much time to be cut, I should fill out a form #132-78-42 in which I would request a five-dollar bill. Instead, I'll just hope that the folks back home take matters into their own hands and make such a loan within as short a time as possible. A typical letter from a son at college, don't you think?

I suppose a person could get along fairly well here without cash, but on the other hand, when people are breaking their necks to show us a good time, it's well to not be so flat that one cannot show his appreciation in any way other than a "thank you" when the thing is over. A fellar doesn't feel like making everything a donation.

Assurances to pop that I haven't forgotten about the coins he wants. One of these days, I'll get those I don't have and send them on.

I think I'll do about one more letter then maybe a couple thousand words on the often interrupted novel. I haven't settled down to working on it since we moved.

Hugs and kisses,
Stan

"Gee, how we are abused here," Stanley quipped. Stanley's letters recapped entertainment provided at reduced rates at the Palladium and Glenn Miller broadcasts at CBS, shows starring Bob Hope and his crowd, weekly USO dances, legitimate stage performances, afternoons at the beach, golf games— green fees waived for servicemen—bowling, and a dance in a radio studio with a two-hour broadcast. Stanley commented, "There was audience participation, so of course, I had my fingers well into it."

Hard to imagine the country was at war. But millions of men—and some women—in uniform were evidence otherwise. Most servicemen and servicewomen were a long way from home and their families, many for the first time in their lives. Between working hours and social engagements, they probably entertained thoughts of home and holidays. Mother's Day reminded them of what they'd left behind.

Stanley wrote:

> Guess you know you got called over the telephone yesterday [Mother's Day]. The call was made possible by a woman here who gave a soldier the yearly call she makes to her mother. Her mother had suggested that she not call this year because the lines would be so busy with soldiers calling home. Don't know how it came to be me; any one of the guys in this company might have wanted to call his mother. Enjoyed talking to you a whale of a lot.

Whether they offered a small gesture of patriotic kindness, served on the front line, or worked in factories and shipyards on the home front, Americans contributed to the war effort—and unemployment lines all but disappeared. As factories were built and began mass-producing planes and other military equipment, women—traditionally homemakers and teachers and nurses—stepped forward and filled job vacancies left by men who were fighting the war. You name it. Women filled the void of almost any job customarily held by men.

Moreover, USO clubs opened across the land of the free, and their orchestrated efforts catered to servicemen and servicewomen.

The Hollywood Victory Committee and the National Broadcasting Company presented a radio show entitled *The USO Show*. Besides Stanley's radio travelogue from station KGNF in North Platte, another script from another radio broadcast turned up in his trunk. Reading his letters placed the radio script in context. As he stated, Stanley, no doubt, had the "inside track on participation on a coast-to-coast NBC broadcast," which took place on May 30, 1942.

I recalled that Stan had participated in a radio show in California with Don Ameche and Mary Martin, but the details escaped me.

The cast of characters listed were Don Ameche, Mary Martin, Lana Turner, Edgar Bergen, Charlie McCarthy, Fanny Brice, Bob Burns, Spike

Jones and his City Slickers, Meredith Wilson and his orchestra, Max Terr's chorus, and Stanley.

AMECHE: Well, ladies and gentlemen, here's what this radio program is all about. You see the USO people have asked me to be their spokesman to tell you about the job the USO has been doing the past year. One of the first things USO did was to send special companies, featuring the latest Broadway shows, orchestras, and vaudeville acts, to 260 army camps and naval bases. And then the USO arranges for the appearance of big radio and movie stars who have given their services absolutely free … After a fellow's been hiking his feet off he doesn't want to just sit around the barracks all evening feeling homesick. So, he goes to see a USO Camp Show …

Now let's get to the heart of the USO, the 695 clubhouses and service units in towns and cities near the camps. The USO is a home away from home for the boys. A place where there are comfortable chairs to sit in, comfortable people to talk to. The fellows have a place to write letters, play games, and get a bite to eat. Every now and then someone may drop in to entertain the boys. Out here it might be the lovely singing star Mary Martin. Mary, what's the boys' favorite song at the USO clubs?

MARY: They've got lots of favorites, Don. But I think they like "Embraceable You" best.

AMECHE: Take a whack at it, huh?

MARY: Okay.

MUSIC: (Mary Martin singing "Embraceable You.")

(APPLAUSE)

AMECHE: That was swell, Mary, and now here's somebody who wants to meet you. He's Private Stanley Dwyer.

MARTIN: Well, how do you do?

DWYER: How do you do, Miss Martin? That's a swell song, and you sing it all right too.

MARTIN: Thank you, soldier. What outfit are you with?

DWYER: I'm sorry, I can't tell that. It's a military secret.

MARTIN: Oh, dear. I ought to know better than that by now.

AMECHE: You certainly should.

MARTIN: Now, Don! Let's see, soldier, can I ask you, how you like the army?

DWYER: I like it fine, except it was kinda lonely at the outpost I just came off. You see there were only ten of us there, and it's a good long hike to town.

AMECHE: Where is that post, soldier?

DWYER: (Laugh) Sorry, That's another –

AMECHE: Military secret. Okay, Mary. Do you want to kick me?

MARTIN: No, Don. You'll learn. Private Dwyer, what does the USO do for a soldier when he's at a lonely outpost like that?

DWYER: Well, when I first got out there I wondered too. But one afternoon this truck they call a mobile unit came around with cigarettes and candy and some magazines. Then the girl got out a little screen and motion picture projector and started showing us pictures, the latest movies. And I'm telling you even if it was only a picture, I never was so glad to see Rita Hayworth in my life. And this girl on the truck told us she goes around to a lot of little camps that way.

AMECHE: Well, soldier, maybe it would interest you to know the USO is spending over half a million dollars a year on mobile units like that.

DWYER: That's swell. But I'll tell you something, Mr. Ameche. I sure was glad to see the USO clubhouse here in Hollywood.

AMECHE: (Laughing) Well, I don't think anybody blames you. Say, there are a lot of fellows in uniform here in the audience. How about giving our listeners a little bit of the flavor of a USO club on a quiet night?

DWYER: What do you mean?

AMECHE: Well, you know how the boys gather round the piano and give out. Let's get Mary Martin to lead off with a song right now. What'll it be, Mary?

(APPLAUSE & WHISTLES FROM THE AUDIENCE)

MARTIN: Let's make it "Pound the Table" boys. Sing along with me in the chorus. Here we go.

The show incorporated other stars in "skits" and ended with Ameche plugging for donations, seeking thirty-two million dollars for USO clubs which would triple in number. "This year the USO will operate 40 clubhouses at strategic places outside of the United States for our soldiers, sailors, and marines," Ameche said. "Remember, the money you give the USO will work for Victory because it will keep up the fighting spirit of our fighting men who are going to win that Victory." The show closed with the singing of "The Battle Hymn of the Republic."

Pasadena, Calif.
June 3, 1942

Dear Aileen,

I was afraid when I got a letter from the folks saying that static was awfully bad the night of the broadcast that probably none of you heard it. So I was quite surprised to hear that you did. Sure was exciting. I have the script to save for posterity, so you can see it some time. Mary and Don endorsed it, or I should say autographed it.

We've been on alert the last few days and will be for a few more, which keeps us confined to camp or nearby. Unless the bombing of Alaska extends our alert period, we'll be free until the next alert period.

We are now located in the swankiest hotel in the west, the Huntington Hotel here in Pasadena. We moved here yesterday. It's just a skip and a jump to L.A. from here. We're still close enough to be in the swim of things there, but I have an idea that the folks here will welcome us similarly, especially since there are no other outfits in the vicinity.

Poor mom. I told her that Dorothea was coming to California for a visit, and now mom's afraid that I'll up and marry the girl. If she only knew how needless her worries are. There are women in L.A. a dime a dozen that appeal to me more than does Stratton. She's nice and all that, but hardly what I'd be looking for.

Gotta hit the chow line.

Love,
Stan

At that particular time, caution prevailed for those on the West Coast. On the alert, they had no idea of Japanese intentions as Japanese forces overran the islands of Attu and Kiska in the Aleutian chain extending from Alaska, which brought World War II to North America. Japanese submarines also prowled the Pacific Ocean. They even shelled an oil storage tank near Santa Barbara, California.

I graduated from Hastings High School in May or June of 1942. Stan encouraged me to pursue a college education. He wrote about an announcement he had heard that "a fellow in college who joined the Air Corps would be allowed to finish school." He thought I should look into it, especially since I liked flying. But before I had to make any final decisions about college, the folks and I drove to California to see Stan. We got in the car and went, and Aileen was along, so I presumed we stopped in Colorado to pick her up. A couple of black-and-white photos showed Stan and me at the beach. Then there was the family photo where the five of us stood in front of a car on some street in California with Stan in uniform. I don't remember much more, except that it turned out being our last family vacation together. That probably meant a lot to the folks.

"I remember how Dad swore most of the way to California because the roads were covered with gravel, and it wouldn't be good for the tires," Aunt Aileen commented.

In letters to Aileen and his parents, Stanley reminisced about the family visit:

All in all I think we had a mighty fine time. All except the dance we didn't go to. I suppose we should have gone to it anyway, but you can't even get in the damned place after nine o'clock in the evening. And by ten or eleven when we would have gotten there, the sides are bulging out. A couple must be madly in love or stewed to the gills to be able to stand it at all. You get shoved and pushed and squeezed till you're black in the face. So I really don't think you missed much other than to be able to say that you had danced in the Palladium.

This is the last family photo. It was taken in Pasadena, California, in June 1942. From left to right: Harold W., Aileen, Harold E., Stanley, Ellen.

Dear folks:

The weather was hot, and it was dry, or else it was cold or rainy—I don't remember which. It was typical Midwest weather, and a certain family had been on the West Coast visiting their soldier boy. They had been on the coast just long enough to find out what the weather was like in God's country, and so the Midwest weather felt even worse than it had before. Right? I'll bet my last nickel on it.

But anyway, we had fun out here, didn't we? I think it would be a good idea if you'd come out each week. Next time you come out, you are to dash right up to the Wells' home. I had a date with Margaret last night, and I sure caught hell for not bringing you out. I told her that I had had no invitation to do so. Then her ma came home and informed me that it was assumed that I would do so anyway. Last night was the first time I had seen Margaret for about a month, so I had to make up for lost time. The family donated the automobile, and we stepped out in style. I don't think it would be wise to tell what time I got in this morning—I mean last night. They're sure good people. So good that, in spite of the fact that Margaret is practically engaged to some other guy, I much prefer her company than that of the jillion women between Pasadena and Hollywood.

I have not been sleeping useful hours away since you left. I was called before the Aviation Cadet Examining Board, and after a hectic day of standing in line here and there—which is the hardest part of any service examination—I passed the mental and physical examinations. So I'm in a different branch of the service than I was yesterday morning. There are more men waiting for training than the Air Corps has room for, so I'll stay here on detached service until I get the call. It will be a minimum of a couple months, I think. I'm now assigned to a stable unit and attached to this job, so if the Division should happen to pull stakes some night, I'll stick around and wave good-bye to the boys.

Today is Sunday, and it's my Sunday to be on duty all day, but there's not much doing so far. Tonight is my night also. But this thirty-six-hour stretch will be another of the easiest and most pleasant that anyone ever stood through. Right now the master sergeant is working a jigsaw puzzle, and the other sergeant is shining his brass buttons. I don't know how we'll live through this ordeal.

Mailing address is about the same. So do me a line one of these first rainy or hot days, huh? See you in the funnies.

Love,
Stan

Several photos surfaced showing Stanley in uniform, posing with Aunt Pearl and Uncle Dusty. When I was younger, we occasionally visited Aunt Pearl and Uncle Dusty, the Schoutens, in Beloit, Kansas. Aunt Pearl (technically, as Granddad's sister, she was my great-aunt) had no children and was a dainty lady, prim and proper. Uncle Dusty, always joking, had a good, hearty laugh. Unknown to me, during the war years they moved from Kansas to California where Dusty looked for work. I had no idea Aunt Pearl and Uncle Dusty had known Stanley so well.

"Pearl and Dusty are down here at Compton," Stanley wrote his folks. "I hiked down to see them a couple of nights ago. They're well and good, but Dusty is a little worried about getting a job since the unions seem to be impregnable. Too damned bad the Japs don't make a special trip over and blast hell out of the whole union business. It's doing more to aid the Japs than the Japanese army and navy."

Dear Aileen and Bill:

I look back upon what has happened since you were here and I find that period has been quite void of anything worth telling. The folks around here are still mighty swell to us, but after a while, a person gets tired of GI entertainment (Government Issue) and prefers to make his own. So the bright lights and the big names and stuff have, to a great extent, been traded for human beings and homes, et cetera. Don't know who I was going with when I wrote you last, but my present interest is in a harem—a family of five girls over in Los Angeles—all within the desired age limit. They're all mighty sweet, but my more intimate attentions are being showered upon the oldest of the girls, Bernie. Incidentally, she's even a little older than I. I seem to be going from one extreme to the other; Margaret in Hollywood was quite young. I just go over and make myself at home, which is mighty fine with me, and they don't seem to mind in the least.

It won't be long now before we'll hit the pay line again. And this one will be good as far as I'm concerned. In fact, I'm going to pay you mugs off in full. I still won't be so bad off. In fact, I'm thinking seriously of setting a bit aside each month for war bonds.

Everything seems to be hunky-dory at this end of the line. I haven't heard from the Air Corps yet and probably won't for a good while.

Love,
Stan

Dear ma, and eventually pa and Harold:

I just et. I'm eating like a horse and not doing too much hard work.

I got ma's letter and one from pappy shortly before to the effect that the tire situation has gone from worse to worser. Reckon your trip out here was even more expensive than anticipated.

We have a small yellow kitten over in the company area—one of three or four mascots. A couple of nights ago I woke up and the kitten had crawled in bed with me. He wasn't just on the bunk but under the covers and down in the middle. The next night I woke up and he was there again. I have a couple of scratches on my arm that I can't account for, so I have an idea that I must have laid on the critter sometime during one of the nights.

The more I think about the Air Corps, the better I like it. In the first place, that pilot training will be something that I can use after the war is over, whereas infantry training is of practically no value except during the war. Then there's the thought that when one is seated in a cockpit, he isn't bound by water or by the enemy. He doesn't have to sleep on the ground nor is he at the mercy of communicable diseases that flourish where men are grouped together in adverse living conditions. Nor does he starve to death as did many of the men in Bataan, for instance. Off hand, I'd say it was a pretty good deal. And there's a commission to reward one who is successful.

I finished the novel and am now ironing out the wrinkles. I'm doing a lot of changing of the first half since it doesn't fit too perfectly with the part that was plotted and written afterward.

And that is the news to this moment, as well as the hot air. Thanks, pa, for the horticulture instruction. You should be a college instructor. Only I dare say you would create more than one major revolution if you joined the ranks of those ordinarily narrow-minded creatures.

Hope Harold is making all kinds of cash in the wheat fields and that tires are growing on trees.

yoursonstanley

Dear family:

This is the day after, after the three-day pass. And I dare say a three days that were enjoyably spent. I went out to see Pearl and Dusty the afternoon of the first day then spent the evening with Bernie, one of the five sisters. I slept at Pearl and Dusty's that night then went back to the harem the next afternoon since it was Bernie's day off. I think we bowled a couple of games in the evening. Then I spent that night here in camp, put on some clean clothes, and went to Pearl and Dusty's again yesterday afternoon.

Dusty and Pearl had moved before I went out yesterday. And I had a hand in the movement, not laborily but otherwise. It began when I found out that Dusty was having a little trouble getting a job since all the places he had tried he met up with the union situation where the industries can't hire their own men, and the unions won't give cards to a person unless he has a job. Well, to make a story short, I got a ride the other day with a fellow from Consolidated Steel. He turned out to be the president. So he gave me some inside dope on getting a job there. Dusty went out the next day and landed a job. So they moved closer to the plant.

Spect Harold is head over heels in wheat and making more at it than I ever did. There's plenty more to be made if he will do a little studying in the meantime. Or did I say that before? I guess I have a half dozen times. I think, though, that Harold will probably not be satisfied unless he's up to his neck in airplanes.

Mighty snitzy letterheads youse guys have these days.

Love,

Stan

"If I had a carbon copy of the last letter I sent you," Stanley wrote, "I would just mail it because the happenings preceding it were the same as those of the time since—nothing. Except that we've raked in another paycheck, and that always gives one a new outlook on life. I've been bowling almost every night since payday to see if there is any possible way in the world to get out of the slump I've been in for an age. Don't know what is wrong unless I've suddenly gone cross-eyed.

Dear folks,

The time has come again when all good boys should write to their family. Saw Pearl while I was on a twenty-four-hour pass. Pearl is slightly homesick for the relatives. I took the letters I had received from you folks for her to read. She gets a big kick out of reading mail from back there. I took the pictures that you folks sent of ussens when you were here. She enjoyed looking at them. Bernie and I went out to her married sister's for supper that evening and chatted till about eleven then came home. Wasn't that exciting?

I reckon I won't be going over to the Ruleys quite so often from now on. Bernie just got a job with an aircraft plant and works the swing shift. It would take a pretty good woman to get me to come over for a date at midnight. And I reckon Pearl will speed up the process somewhat of getting the coins you wanted. I don't seem to have a minute while I'm off in the daytime.

I have about five minutes of work to do for a change, so I better get at it. Will see you in church.

Love,
Stan

Stanley told Aileen, "We are getting fifteen-day furloughs now, but I doubt if I'll be fortunate enough to get one of them. There are plenty of fellows here who have been in the army longer than I and naturally deserve the first furloughs. By the time mine comes around, I'll probably be in the Air Corps."

Pasadena, California
21 September, 1942

Dear Harold:

Didn't think I'd remember it, did you? Anyway, Happy Birthday, and about eighty-two more of them. I went out to Pearl and Dusty's for dinner yesterday, and it was during the ensuing conversation that we decided that a birthday had darned near slipped up on us while we weren't looking. We went to Long Beach after dinner and spent most of the afternoon there. It's too bad that Dusty couldn't have been a fish instead of a person. He swam across the lagoon before we left; it's probably a mile across and back.

I'm afraid a present for the birthday will be a bit late. And even then it will be more of a present to me than to you. If plans are not messed up by the proverbial monkey wrench, it will arrive sometime after the first of the month. It really doesn't amount to much, but the freight charges will be enormous. It's big and hard to handle, but that's what transportation employees are getting paid for. It's not very good looking, and you probably won't want to keep it around the house long, but you might enjoy having it around until the newness wears off. What is it? Now you wouldn't want me to give a birthday secret away would you? Maybe, though, I should tell you so that when it arrives you won't be too shocked. Well, of all things, it's me! Yep, I made an arrangement with the Warrant Officer in charge of furloughs in this section that, if none of the fellows applied who have priority over me, then I would make application at the deadline. No one did. So my request has been approved by everyone except the company commander, and I see no reason why he would disapprove, unless it would be because I'm in the Air Corps officially now and subject to call.

I don't know yet how I'll come. First, I'm going to see if the Red Cross can get me a berth on an army bomber flying to Denver. From all reports, that's not too hard to do because they are flying east all the time. And it doesn't cost a penny. In fact, it saves the pilot the trouble of loading that much weight in sandbags. If that doesn't work, I'll hitchhike, get a ride through a travel bureau, or take a train. So of course, I don't know when I'll arrive or where I'll wind up, but I'll probably make the first stop in Denver in any case.

And I suppose I should tell you what you're in for when I get there. A fellow over in Los Angeles gave Bernie and me some bowling lessons a while back, and shortly after I was doing right well. Then I got in that slump and couldn't get out. It gave me the desire to change my style from the accepted professional form, but I was bullheaded enough to stick with it till I mastered it. I average about 150 now, and I bowled 210 the other day. So there too.

There's a bit of work piling up this morning, so I better get at it. I shall keep you posted on developments.

Love,
Stan

Stanley's furlough started at midnight on October 1, 1942. A telegram he sent to his mom on Sunday, October 4, read, "Barring unforeseen and unavoidable circumstances, we should arrive late Monday."

Stan got to Hastings either before or after—I don't remember which— another telegram arrived at the house. The telegram dated October 5, addressed to Sgt. Stanley Dwyer, read, "Return immediately by October eighth you have been accepted by the Air Corps to report October ninth." I'm sure the folks were glad to have him home, if only for a day or two.

He left on the Burlington Zephyr that came through Hastings. We took him to the station. As the train pulled out, I can still see Stan standing on the platform, between cars, waving. A chill ran up my back, and I had the strangest feeling that I would never see him again. How true it proved to be. It seemed strange because, at that point, the war really hadn't been on my mind. I don't recall ever sharing my premonition with the folks. It's just something I never forgot, and it crossed my mind once in a while. As we progressed with our search, I verbalized it.

6

◁₩▷

The Wild Blue Yonder

Guess all that is just another chapter in the life of an eager kaydet.
—Stanley N. Dwyer in a letter dated March 30, 1943

As mentioned earlier, before our search for Stanley began, Dad rarely talked about his brother. And as our search progressed and the journey evolved, different things sparked his memory. I was caught off guard the day I heard him tell about seeing his brother for the last time. When I read and reread Stanley's letters, I was able to take whatever tidbits of information Dad disclosed and make the connection to what Stanley wrote.

Also, there had been one other subject Dad talked about even less—his own military service. I knew Dad had been a B-17 pilot in World War II, stationed in England with the Eighth Air Force. That was it. However, there was a reason why I never heard him talk about that subject. He, along with most of his comrades, didn't think they did anything special. They served their country in the military, did as they were ordered, and they longed to go home. Shortly after our journey to find Stanley was underway, I was fortunate enough to sit with Dad and some of his crewmen in a hotel room at one of their 34th Bomb Group reunions—four surviving crewmen out of nine.

A B-17 was designed to carry a crew of ten. Near the end of the war, some crews had one waist gunner taken off the list. I flew with a crew of nine.

Years before, those soldier boys' lives crossed paths when they were randomly assigned together as a bomber crew, their lives in the hands of each other. Consequently, the camaraderie forged under combat circumstances survived the test of time. In a rare moment at that reunion, pilot, copilot, radioman, and flight engineer reminisced about the war. More particularly, they reminisced about the cold, rainy weather in England, their sparse living

157

The Wild Blue Yonder

conditions in the Quonset huts, snitching more than the allotted amount of coal for the meager stove that warmed their living quarters, passes to London with German deadly buzz bombs exploding near their hotel, and their close-call flight back to the United States after the war.

Someone mentioned the mission to Austria at the end of the war to fly French POWs back to Paris—how the prisoners were so weak and emaciated that the crew practically lifted them into the plane—and then the cheers from the Parisians when their countrymen were repatriated. That's what they casually talked about. And Dad and his crewmen made it crystal clear that they weren't the heroes—they were the lucky ones. The heroes, well, the heroes were the men and women who didn't come home—the ones who gave their lives.

And there were hundreds of thousands of heroes, over four hundred thousand from World War II alone.

At another one of Dad's reunions, Rick and I sat in the back of the tour bus waiting to get off. We watched out the window as the veterans—some accompanied by their wives—shuffled off the bus. Some leaned on walkers or canes, while others still had a spring in their step. I whispered to Rick, "There they are." From the pages of history, those unpretentious men were once vibrant young boys who willingly climbed into the B-17s for yet another mission or were the men of the dedicated ground crews who kept the bombers patched up and ready to fly.

The B-17 Flying Fortresses were referred to as the big bombers, the "heavies." According to the men who serviced them or the combat crews who flew in them, they were what the name implied—a Flying Fortress—and armed with thirteen .50 caliber machine guns.

The B-17 had the same guns as a B-24, but of course, everybody had a love for their airplane and thought it was the best. The 17 was a good, stable airplane to fly. It absorbed a lot of hits and unimaginable combat damage only to keep flying, returning her crews to their bases. Crews became attached to them because they offered protection and got them back home. The esteemed B-17 also acquired the name "Queen of the Skies." I don't know where the label came from—maybe from the book Queens Die Proudly *written by Colonel Kurtz, who started out early in the war in the South Pacific flying a B-17. Ultimately, Colonel Kurtz became Stan's group commander.*

By the same token, I saw one burst of flak take out three 17s. The flak burst hit under the right wing of one bomber, flipping it over, and it cut into the plane next to him at the waist, and then part of that plane fell into another, shearing off the rudder. In ten seconds, we'd flown out of sight and could not determine how many planes crashed or how many chutes blossomed. It was luck of the draw if and where you got hit. If nothing strategic was hit on the plane, the 17 didn't easily succumb. Nevertheless, one shell in the right spot spelled doomsday for many crews.

From his war experience in England, 34th Bomb Group veteran Angelo Grinaldo offered his insight. "Every time the crews loaded in the bombers, those young kids were facing death. Whether dropping bombs or not, the planes were merely a time bomb." He witnessed one bomber blowing up after it barely lifted off the runway.

"The crewmen all seemed to shuffle their feet and have the same tired look on their faces," Angelo remarked. "From gunners to pilots, it was no different. Those of us working on the ground took it to heart. We saw the crews going up, and a lot of them didn't come back. A lot of planes and men came back shot up. The first planes to land after a mission were the ones shooting off red flares, signaling injured crewmen on board. And when crews came back from a mission, they had the same look on their faces."

Yet young, "invincible" men hunkered down with no place to hide in those "flying bombs"—bomb bay racks stacked with bombs and fuel tanks topped off with over seventeen hundred gallons of fuel—and rumbled into the not-so-friendly skies of Nazi-ruled Europe. Following orders and not wanting to let their buddies down, the crews encountered perilous enemy flak and fierce fighter attacks on the long, treacherous, bitterly cold flight to, over, and coming off the target.

Once our duty for Uncle Sam was done, survival was on our minds. We aimed to get back "home" to the base and get the planes patched up and ready for the next day's mission. We depended on each other's skill and judgment for survival. And a lot of it boiled down to luck.

When I was in England during the war, there was something called the "Lucky Bastard Club." The only dues paid for membership in the club were completing the required number of missions. Originally, twenty-five was the required number of missions for crews in the Eighth Air Force in England. At first, the odds weren't very good for those crews flying into German territory without escorts. Maybe a fourth or so could expect to survive their twenty-five missions. Because of protection from our fighter escorts and because the threat from German fighters had tapered off somewhat, by the time I entered the war in early spring of 1945, I was to fly thirty-five missions. The war ended before my crew and I flew our tenth mission. We went from being boys to men quickly. We knew what the consequences might be but never really dwelled on it. When times got tough, you did what you did, and that's what you were there for. Some of us were lucky and came home, and a bunch weren't. Four hundred thousand or so American soldiers were lost in World War II. They're the heroes of that era. No matter how many missions we flew before the war's end, just coming home classified us as "lucky bastards." Many heroes are still over there.

Those veterans getting off the tour bus represented characters in books and stories on World War II, and every one of them had their own story, often a personal and private story. Some veterans had forgotten about the war. They'd returned home, assimilated back into society, and resumed their lives. Some didn't want to remember. However, if the mood was right, a story or two was shared, divulging a glimpse of history—the history that turned back the armies of fanatical dictators, leaders misguided by warped ideologies. Those graying veterans' service and sacrifice, along with the service and sacrifice of over four hundred thousand heroes, were part of an effort that altered the course of history and preserved freedom for millions. And yet, from what I've observed about Dad and fellow veterans, through their words and actions, they exhibit a brand of humbleness that's become rare to find.

Consequently, Dad's stories and experiences remained dormant for many years, but things happened that stirred up conversation. Some of it began with my three kids—actually, their high school teacher, Stan Meyer. The kids all knew that their grandpa had been a B-17 pilot, but they had never heard him talk about it. In 1998, about the same time our search for Stanley began, Stan Meyer, my oldest daughter, Sarah's, American history instructor, assigned his students to interview a World War II veteran. Two years later, my daughter Melissa had the same instructor and the same assignment … and ditto for my son, Nathan, two more years down the road. Each interview with Dad revealed snippets of his war experiences.

Besides the school interviews, the more Dad and I discussed Stanley and especially his military service, the more I gradually learned details about Dad's service and missions flown from England.

I turned eighteen in September of 1942, and as time went on and events unfolded, it became a reality that I was eligible for the draft into the armed services. At that time, the Draft Board, manned by local citizens, sent notices to all eligible men. You went before the board, and if physically able, your classification was 1-A. Deferments were issued to men involved with essential businesses, such as being the only person capable of running a farm.

So when it came time for me to join the service, the choice was easy. I enlisted in the Army Air Corps. I wanted to fly. I had always messed around with model airplanes and used to fly them all the time when we lived in Manhattan and Stan was in college. I've often wondered if that might have been the background for Stan's interest in the Army Air Corps.

When our search was underway, I didn't think I knew much about Stan's training, but the more we uncovered about Stan's life, I became aware that my training paralleled my brother's—only I was one year behind him. Stan graduated in the class of 43-G, and my class was 44-G. The number indicated the year, the letter the month. Stan earned his wings in July 1943, and I qualified exactly one year later. I also realized that we did about the same things in training. We flew the same kind of airplanes in primary and basic flying schools, different ones for advanced training, and then the same combat airplanes. We were both airplane commanders. He flew to Africa and eventually Italy via Brazil in February 1944, and I flew to England via Newfoundland in February of 1945. Stan flew his missions out of Italy with the Fifteenth Air Force, and mine were out of England with the Eighth Air Force.

When Stanley's furlough ended that October of 1942, he waved as he left Hastings on the Burlington Zephyr en route to his new home in Santa Ana, California. He had a fifteen-minute layover in North Platte, never mentioning the Canteen but taking advantage of the stop to call an old friend from his KGNF days in North Platte.

The first stop for Stan in the Army Air Corps was at Santa Ana, California. He arrived there in October 1942, classified as a cadet. Santa Ana Army Air Base was a classification center. When I entered the service on June 20, 1943, I made two stops before I went to Santa Ana. I boarded a train from Omaha to Kearns, Utah, to learn the army way of life at basic training. Stan already had his basic training from his previous military experience as a radio corpsman. From Kearns, I was transferred to Missoula, Montana, for CDT—College Detachment Training. It was a college program enacted for flying students, and it took about five months. Stan already had his college degree. At CDT, we brushed up on our math, along with other college courses, had some ground school instruction, became familiar with an airplane and the controls, and gained several hours of flying time to see if we adapted to flying. From CDT, I went to Santa Ana. So both my brother and I went through the classification center in Santa Ana, just at different times.

"We are still in the classification squadron here at Santa Ana," Stanley wrote. "We have taken our classification physical and mental exams and today were tested for ear, nasal, and sinus fitness in the pressure chamber. It was quite simple after having been instructed in the methods of equalizing inner- and outer-ear pressures."

We didn't do any flying at Santa Ana; it was preflight. We were run through all kinds of tests like aptitude tests and psychological tests to determine what we were best qualified for—pilot, navigator, or bombardier.

Stanley classified as a pilot, which was what he requested. He wrote home:

Dear folks:

Received your birthday telegram at 5:30 this afternoon, less than three hours later than the sending time on it. Started school today, just 26 years after I started my worldly schoolin'. We were really given a mental, physical, and psychological once-over. All men here in this group are previous servicemen, so I won't be pestered with the infantry drill that I had anticipated.

Am glad you folks got moved satisfactorily. If you mugs are settled down for a while, I will have the address changed on my dog tags. I might suggest, though, that you can name your job and your pay in Los Angeles. Pearl and Dusty are laying plenty away.

I'll have you know that I am considered and spoken of as "mister" and a "gentlemen." And we are allowed a buck a day here for meals instead of the infantry fifty cents. So we are being well taken care of.

Gotta put a mirror finish on a couple pairs of shoes yet tonite. Thanks for the telegram.

Oodles & gobs,
Stan

Dear Aileen and Bill:

This will be rather short, but it should beat nothing a little bit. Sunday, the day we have a little time to do letters and stuff, will be spent this time in the mess hall. KP, under the dignified name of mess management, is done on a big scale here. There will be sixty of our squadron on duty Sunday, all of us who were not on a couple of weeks ago. This will be my first hitch since Roberts. It lasts about sixteen hours, so it should be quite thrilling.

This week we have completed two 18-hour courses, and I wound them up with a 95 ½ percent average in one and 95 $^4/_7$ in the other. Another course, code practice, which I mastered at Roberts, will be a cinch for me. It's a 34-hour course, and I should get a hundred on it. I talk like a kid in grade school, don't I? I should have quite an education by the time I am one hundred twenty-six.

We've been confined to camp, so I haven't done a thing in the way of entertainment since I've been here. I still have within ten bucks of what I left Nebraska with. In another week, we will be free on weekends. We can go whenever we get off work, after 2:00 p.m.

Saturday, and have to be back by 3:00 p.m. Sunday, at which time we have a parade. I'll have to see Pearl and Dusty, and today I got a letter from the third girl that expects me to spend the evening with her. When women are so thick, one must be very choosy.

I got your newsy letter a couple of days ago. Sorta completes the news from home because I never hear about that side of home life from a direct source. Pop, in wanting Harold to get his Air Corps application in soon, is right. It takes a lot of time, and if Harold isn't careful, he might find himself in the infantry and even overseas before he can get an application through. If he applies now, he'll probably have more time at home than if he's drafted.

Gotta write the folks before I study. Write again soon.

Love,
Stan

Stanley remarked in a letter home:

Think it over, Harold and mom. And you won't be sorry. Fly over 'em while the many others exchange bayonet jabs with the Japs down on the ground. Few or no Air Corps men starved to death on Bataan.

Starving American and Filipino defenders surrendered to the Japanese on Bataan, and then the POWs were marched over sixty miles to their prison camp on the dusty, hot, tropical island. The atrocities of the Bataan Death March were a big deal when reported. Anybody who fell out of line was disposed of, often gruesomely. It was a tough deal. Tens of thousands suffered and died either on the march or at the disease-infested POW camp.

While I was working at a grain bin company in Hastings, I got my draft notice. At that time, the Air Corps was not accepting any more enlistees because they were full. Shortly after I received my draft notice, though, enlistments in the Air Corps opened again, briefly. My friend Floyd and I immediately drove his Model A to Omaha to enlist and stayed overnight at Floyd's sister's place. The first day, Floyd didn't pass his physical because he couldn't look cross-eyed—his mom had told him never to do that. That night, Floyd's sister and I taught him how to look cross-eyed. We exercised his eyes enough so that he could pass the test, and he went on to become a pilot in the Army Air Corps. It was a matter of timing, but I knew the Air Corps was my opportunity to fly. And just like Stan, there was a waiting period before I was called up. I left Omaha and went back home and was on standby until they were ready for me.

Dear folks:

The weekend is over, so I better do you a couple of lines so as you'll know your dear son got back from the big city safe and sound. I didn't do anything very exciting, just stopped here and there to visit friends.

Since cadets can't hitchhike, I got off the bus a couple of miles from Pearl and Dusty's. They came after me, and we had a rabbit dinner then talked until about 7:30. Pearl extended a Thanksgiving invitation. There was a slight possibility I could get off, until today, then we were confined to our area for five days because of a flu scare or something.

Reading between the lines of Lynne's letter, I gather he is headed for the tall and uncut, probably the South Pacific war theater. He said he had sent everything he owned home, that he's going to have a head start on me on the Japs.

We have our math final soon. Not much point to study it, though, because the only mistakes I've made in the course were kindergarten calculations. I was pretty rusty at first, after ten years without. However, I've been pretty much the barracks tutor when the going was tough. There was quite a joke one day when I was on fire guard and missed class. A couple of fellows were going to explain the day's lesson to me. They did tell me what the lesson was, but I had to show them how to work the problems.

We started a course in physics, that part of physics that is related to flying. It's going to be interesting but will require a little more time than most studies. We have at least five weeks for it, and I think it will be nearly Christmas before we go to primary. Christmas and New Year's Day are just two other days here. Probably won't have anything but a big meal.

The war news sounds pretty encouraging these days. Be a heck of a note if us guys didn't get through our Air Corps training, wouldn't it?

Going to hit the hay, so I better wash my teeth.

Love,
Stan

Dec. 30, 1942

Dear folks:

I had a very welcome Christmas letter waiting for me yesterday when I got off of KP duty. My first full day—and the last—at KP in the Air Corps.

During our three days off for Christmas, I spent part of the 24th, 25th, and a minute Saturday evening with Pearl and Dusty. They had a very nice gift exchange for me, including towels and a carton of cigarettes.

[Cousin] Beth wrote to me just before Christmas when she was feeling a bit emotionally unstrung in anticipation of spending a rather lonely Christmas, and as a result, it was one of the nicest letters she ever wrote. She's a credit to most women.

It's secret where and when we're moving, so I won't be able to let you know till we arrive.

Love,
Stan

In my phone conversation with Beth, she said, "Stanley was a wonderful, wonderful man. I loved him to pieces. He didn't want anything to happen to me, and like a big brother, he worried about the men I dated. We were close like a brother and sister. So many boys my age went missing and didn't come home. Stanley was someone very special."

Stan moved on to primary training at a camp near King City, California. When my time came, I did my primary training at Hemet, California. Stan never mentioned it, but for me there was a certain amount of hazing. For instance, while I was at primary, cadets had to wear their helmets around all the time until they flew their first solo flight.

In January 1943, Stan wrote home:

Here we are, all settled in our new home. And it's the nicest I've had since I've been in the service. We have a three-man room in stucco cottages, innerspring mattresses, Venetian blinds, etc.

Today we drew our flying equipment, and you'd never know your son when he has them on. Tomorrow we'll start to fly, so of course, we're all excited.

I'd like to tell you about the place, but I have an idea Uncle Sam wouldn't like it too well if I went into much detail.

There won't be much point to going out very much while we're here. King City isn't the best soldier town I've seen. Frankly, it stinks. There's nothing there but the USO, and it's just mediocre. King City is about like Tipton, only there isn't a woman in town. All social activity revolves around the USO. Anyway, this group of men has turned dead serious, and bedtime, et cetera, means something.

And the nickels I had saved (S'42) were as you suspected, the later no-good kind. Big help, aren't I?

Am going over to the flight line to watch the boys pick them up and set them down.

Primary was where we really learned how to fly and navigate. There were five cadets under one instructor. We rotated flying times. When we weren't flying, we spent our time in ground school classes and PT—physical training. It was a pretty rigorous regimen.

Dear folks,

I'm walking on clouds this evening after an hour in the air today, during which time the old belly stayed right with me and enjoyed stalls and spins as much as I. I am all through getting sick, but those first few trips were tough. They reminded me of the rough days at sea.

We are free to write letters or do whatever we like on the flight line while we're not busy. For a while, that time will be spent doing the brainwork of flying, but I should be able to get that down to a minimum before long.

I couldn't believe my eyes when I got a letter from Harold. Glad to hear he started to college; it was quite a surprise. Apparently, he's going into his schoolin' with a determination. I don't think they'd care much, Harold, if I told you a little about our planes. They're Ryan PT-22s. They're two place jobs, of course, with a low wing. The span is about thirty-five feet. They're darned nice ships and will take an awful beating. They have to around here. But the ground force keeps them in tip-top shape.

It sure would be tough if we didn't have to drill tonight, and maybe we won't. I wonder if I'll never get away from that stuff. I was an expert at it when I left Roberts but have to go on with it anyway. I'm sure I could use the hour to a much better advantage.

You can't hear anything but airplane talk around here. Each man has his own stories to tell, and there are more than enough for the odd moments we have.

That should bring things up to date.

Air pocketfuls of love,
Stan

"I'm beginning to wonder if I'll ever get to solo," Stanley informed his folks. "Flying was called off because of rain, and I haven't gotten but a couple of hours in since the first of last week. I have less than eleven hours time. These flying schools publish a class book for each group, and yesterday, at a meeting of the journalistic-minded members of our class, I was elected editor of the forthcoming edition. It will take a lot of work, but the staff is excused from drill and physical training during the publishing operations."

Stanley wrote home in February:

I'm about as proud these days as a new papa. The day I soloed I made two supervised trips and yesterday did three more. The number of supervised solos required is three, so whenever my instructor feels that he's tired of riding with me, I can check out a ship and be merrily on my way. I think he was right proud of me during my hops. He seldom says anything about how good one is doing for fear we'll get overconfident, but yesterday, there was happiness all over his face. He's probably one of the strictest instructors on the field, and a person must be on his toes at all times to please him. I'll probably learn much more from him than any other. He washed one of our five a couple of weeks ago and another is on the way now. The boys in our class are going pretty fast these days, and the wash rate is going to be rather high. Let it not be said that the army has relaxed its requirements.

Dear folks:

The editor's job is paying off. I have complete use of any of the dozen typewriters here in the army office during afterhours. And there's nothing that takes the grind out of writing letters than the touch and go method.

Starting yesterday and continuing until our lower class arrives the first of the week, we are now flying the whole day. The day yesterday was spent on one of the auxiliary fields shooting landings while my instructor watched from the ground with pencil and grade book in hand. It's a lot different when one is up there alone the first few times. When he has the instructor with him, he knows that the instructor's eagle eyes are open for other planes in the area. To make sure that there are no planes near, we clear the ship to each side before doing a maneuver. Today, I, like all the boys on their first trip up for maneuvers, spent most of the time clearing myself. As one of the boys put it well at the dinner table this evening, we spent the time "clearing ourselves to clear ourselves." In other words, if you're not familiar with our language, we made a turn to the left and to the right to see that the way was clear to make a turn to the left and to the right.

Last night turned out to be quite profitable for me. The physical training lieutenant, who is boss of the class book, asked me to be a table waiter at the upper class banquet. Besides having a good time and eating turkey until I was ready to bust, I made two and a half in tips.

So I shall hit the old innerspring. The two sheets, which were absent in the infantry, are mighty fine.

Happy landings,
Stan

Washout—the dreaded words of any cadet. It was probably the worst day of a cadet's life. In some cases, cadets chose to be reassigned because they didn't like it, but for most guys in training, they dreamed of flying. The training was an opportunity not readily available in civilian life. It was an education most young people didn't get unless a war was on. Each stage of training had its own hurdles and requirements, and it was pretty hard for some. For others, it was a breeze. Then there was pleasing the instructor. Sometimes personalities entered into it, although they weren't supposed to. The pressure was on. Some wanted it so badly.

But some guys just did not adapt to flying at all. Some were not mentally prepared; some did not have the coordination necessary, and some just plain screwed up. For example, "hot foot" was a form of entertainment for some of the guys. A fellow would fall asleep with his shoes or boots on, and another guy would stick a match between the shoe and sole and light it. It was a kick watching the fellow wake up and swat his foot. In one particular case, the fellow had walked through some gasoline, and when the guy lit the match, the whole sole caught fire. The victim acquired some burns, but for the prankster, it was so long pilot training and hello gunnery practice.

I saw several instances where guys were washed out because they had lied. They may have missed a formation or something and lied or gave a weak reason why they were gone. For me, the Army Air Corps made my life. If you made it, it was a lot of luck and a matter of timing.

Stanley wrote:

I'm getting so I feel quite at home in the airplane. The nervous strain that was apparent when we were learning has quite disappeared, and now the nervous reaction upon preparing to go up is pretty much like that of getting ready to take a ride in a car. Thanks to having an instructor who knows his onions, this old man is well up on the art of taking off and landing.

I have never seen a place where the usual conversation was as it is here. The gang not only flies half a day, but does hanger-flying the rest of the time. Tall stories about one's escapades in the sky are a dime a dozen. Like fish stories, they can be exaggerated to any extent. As someone said last night, this is the first place he ever saw where the main topic of conversation was anything other than women.

Feb. 21, 1943

Dear folks:

Last night a friend of mine and I took a 24-hour pass, came to town, and hit the hay. It's noon now, and we've been up an hour. We're at the USO now and plan to write here till our passes are up then go out to camp and continue until bedtime. I owe everyone I know, including my parents who probably think I have deserted.

It would be pretty hard for the powers that be to keep this kid from going on to basic. Day before yesterday I passed my final flying check. The checker told me the flight was very satisfactory, and later he told my instructor that I gave him a pretty good ride. And that's a pretty good compliment coming from those who have the dirty and thankless job. One of the things stressed greatly in flying is one's ability to pick out a landing field in an assimilated forced landing. I didn't take any chances on getting caught with my trousers at half-mast; I picked a pasture that composed the greatest part of a ranch out here, one so big that I could have gotten into it with my eyes closed.

I would like to take some of youse guys for a ride. I feel quite capable of showing you a pretty exciting time. At basic we'll be flying ships with about three times as much power. It will be at basic, I think, that it will be determined what type of ship we are destined to fly. Those of us who know each other know pretty much already. In the event that I finish, I'll probably fly a heavy bomber or transport ships. That would be my choice.

We're having a little trouble with the women here this afternoon. There are the two of us here typing, and that, in itself, is rather odd while on pass. And apparently our gum-chewing in cadence to our pecking is rather amusing.

Don't know when the class book will be back from the printer, probably in a week or so. We think our book will be quite nice. Our copy men were not up to par, and I didn't have time to go over the entire copy and rewrite it. But our cartoonists, layout department, and photography departments were exceptionally good. One of the layout men tried going over my head on the book policy, and after a verbal battle between he and myself, he walked out. He was a rather gruesome character, and everyone, including the lieutenant, was glad he left. So I better finish my milk shake and write to Aileen and Pearl.

Oodles,
Stan

The following week, he wrote more.

Here I sit again in my office—the King City USO. I seem to be becoming a figurehead in front of this typewriter. Just now, almost before I had started this letter, the program director saw me sitting here without gum in my mouth, so she dashed over and gave me a stick.

This one more step in my career as a hopeful pilot is rapidly coming to a close. We do finish flying Thursday but have a number of formalities, such as parades, banquets, balls, et cetera, that will last into next week. I have fifty-two of my sixty hours of required flying time, so the rest is just a breeze.

I thought about calling you folks, pap, when I passed my final check, and under ordinary circumstances, I would have done so, but my training under this instructor could hardly be considered ordinary. In the case of most of the gang, the hardest thing they have to do is to pass a check. When they have passed their final check, they're pretty well assured of going to basic training. But of course, I'd have to be different. In my case, a check is purely a formality. My greatest job is not to pass my check, but to pass in the opinion of my instructor. So I'm not through until I board the bus for basic. It's a strain, but undoubtedly, I will benefit throughout my piloting career for having been assigned to this instructor.

The ranks have thinned considerably since we arrived here. In basic, washouts are less frequent and in advanced training even less. As I have said before, it can hardly be said that requirements have been lowered in the Air Corps. The need for a greater number of pilots has not blinded the government to the fact that each man who successfully completes his training will have on his shoulders the responsibility of hundreds of thousands of dollars' worth of property.

After sixty hours of flying in primary and passing the other requirements, basic training was the next stop. Stan moved to Taft, California, and did his training at Gardner Field, which took about ten weeks. When my turn came, I was sent to Marana, Arizona, for basic training. For me, the rate of washout was still pretty high at some bases. I was the only one of five to make it through with my basic instructor. In advanced training, Paul Fort of Dallas and I were in a barracks room with four other guys. Of course, we had to stand inspection every morning. One day, Paul and I realized that we were the only two left to clean the whole thing up. We bitched and got some replacements.

In basic training, Stan and I both flew the BT-13, the Vultee. It was a low-wing, enclosed-cockpit, single-engine plane with fixed landing gear. It was faster and heavier than the Ryan PT-22. I knew a lot about the planes before I even entered the Air Corps.

When Stanley got to basic training, he commented in a letter home:

> Our BTs are Vultees as you surmised, Harold. That rather amused me because before I got in the Air Corps, I didn't know a Vultee from a bean hill. I can remember not so long ago, when we were making an attempt to master the Ryan, that the basic trainer looked awfully huge. It is large, tho I don't know just what the dimensions are. The fact, tho, that the tail assembly stands a couple of feet above one's head puts it at least one jump ahead of Harold's models. We're gradually getting it cut down to our size mentally. I crawled into one over at ground school this morning after breakfast. Can you imagine me piling out of bed voluntarily at 6:30 on a Sunday morning? And there are more gadgets in the cockpit than one can shake a stick at. However, thanks to the Ryan and a good engines course at primary, I have a pretty good idea what each is for and when to use it. It shouldn't be as hard as when I started out cold on the PT.

The folks thought it might be good before I got to the Army Air Corps if I had some flying experience. Along with the college math courses I was taking at Hastings College in the winter of 1943, I went to Mankato, Kansas, to learn to fly. I stayed with an aunt and uncle in Mankato. That's where I first soloed.

Thus, Stanley wrote his folks:

> I don't know that I can be of much more help on the private flying lessons. Trying to figure out the army in advance is hardly an easy matter. Some wise pfc with the only authority he ever had might

send a man with a thousand flying hours to a cooks and bakers school and might recommend a Colorado coal miner for the Air Corps. However, a few flying hours might, under another condition, turn the trick. Definitely Harold would find out whether or not he wants to fly, but having a pretty fair acquaintanceship with both Harold and flying, I would say that it would be pretty hard to get him back on terra firma once he got off. If the expense isn't too great, I would recommend it.

I guess the Air Corps has weened me as far as good times are concerned. And the old billfold shows the effects. Oh yes, speaking of the developing advantages of the Air Corps, I forgot to mention the most important. Enlisted men here on the post clean our latrines!

In primary training, we started aerobatics—hanging upside down in the airplane. We did more aerobatics in basic, flew cross-country flights, some formation flying and night flying, and started instrument flying. Basic training was still pretty regimented and entailed more advanced flying. Ground school work included meteorology, and we always had physical training.

Dear folks:

The main purpose of this note is to rescind what I wrote last night about having troubles with the BT.

'Tis a long story, so I shall begin at the beginning where all good things start. In arrival here, I was put in a flight under an instructor new at this field. At about three hours, the gang began to solo. And I figured that any day I would be cruising around in the crate by myself. But the days came and went, and the boss didn't crawl out of the cockpit. And my hours mounted till I began to wonder if he thought I couldn't fly the crate.

So, come the second weekend, I was still a rookie, and I wouldn't wonder if I sprouted a couple of gray hairs. It didn't help any when all the folks in town expressed the utmost confidence in my ability.

This week I knew something would break one way or another. It did, bright and early on the first half day of flight. I was scheduled for a routine upper-air flight with my instructor. But it didn't happen. While I was waiting, the squadron commander called me and asked if I was ready to solo. And I told him so in no uncertain terms. So I did.

I've noticed, and pa will verify, that the army doesn't make public to the ranks anything that is not necessary. Now, had they told me that an instructor new at the field cannot solo a cadet, I wouldn't have worried nearly so much. I had over nine hours when it happened, and I have an idea that the last few were for his instruction as much as mine.

So that's that. And I still wouldn't trade him for another. He's tops. It's a pleasure to ride with him after having spent some unpleasurable hours with my "chewing" instructor at King City. And it's my theory on flight training that his type of instruction is as permanent as the more harsh. One time he laughed heartily at me for rolling my flaps down instead of up. I haven't made the same error since and doubt that I shall in the future.

And he's the type of guy who congratulates with a firm handshake for an accomplishment, such as soloing, in spite of his commissioned rank.

Guess all that is just another chapter in the life of an eager kaydet.

Got a letter from Theron last night. He's happily married now, since February.

We were given two-day passes last weekend, and I had a date with Margaret Wells, remember her? I decided that I should drop around and make some kind of an attempt to apologize for not having even written after the abrupt break in relations when I started going with Bernie. They still cuss me for not having brought you folks out when you made the trip here. They're mighty nice folks.

I visited with Pearl and Dusty. Of course, they were glad to see their darling nephew. I went through the class book with them explaining some parts that only the cadets would enjoy.

And fourteen more letters await me, so

Much love,
Stan

Grandma and Granddad had packed a lot of stuff into Stanley's trunk. Together with everything else, there was a royal blue, hardbound book similar to a high school yearbook called *King's Log – King City, California – Class 43-G*. The staff of *King's Log* listed Stanley N. Dwyer as the editor, and like most yearbooks, it included photos of the organization's members and important people. Flipping through musty pages of commanding officers, staff and permanent personnel, photos of posed cadets dressed in flight gear, and collages of candid shots, I read, "Wide-eyed 'dodos', standing in semi-circle around the instructor, have been formally introduced to the primary trainer. Knee-deep in parachutes and instruction, the initial desire of the rookie is to rip the dodo tape from his helmet upon the successful completion of his first solo hop."

"You were right, dad, in your assumption that I wrote the articles," Stanley explained. "Would have written the whole thing had I had the time. However, in due regard to some of the fellows who worked hard and long on what they did write, it is better that they had a hand in it. The printer didn't do justice to the background of the dedication page, which is the price one pays for having a printer a jillion miles away."

The dedication page stated, "Class 43-G dedicates this issue of the *King's Log* to our wives, sweethearts, and mothers. It is their belief in us, their inspiration and understanding that is spurring us on to our sure and ultimate goal: complete and final victory!"

Stanley wrote more about the yearbook to his folks:

> Don't know whether you know what a Widget is. It is a baby gremlin. A gremlin is a little devil that, unseen and unheard, gives a pilot no end of trouble. He's the thing that causes creeping throttle or pulls a wing down in level flight, or pushes up the nose in a climb causing the ship to lose flying speed, et cetera. Anyhoo, that's who all the little devils are in the book. The illustration on the "from the ground up" page was the brainstorm of one of the cartoonists, and I didn't know he had given it thought until he had finished the thing. There are a few cartoons which can't be explained in mixed company. Gigs, pop, are demerits, as you expected. And the brown-nose cartoon and T.S. ticket cartoon will be explained out behind the barn.

Gigs, a way to discipline, were issued to cadets for things like not having your tie straight, not having your shoes shined, sleeping in class, unbuttoned uniform buttons, and other things like being late for formation. If a cadet goofed up, he walked an hour on the parade ground for every gig. Some infractions were worth more than one gig.

In a letter home in April, Stanley explained:

> Thought I'd have all evening to write and study, then after supper they posted a Link trainer schedule for tonight.
>
> If I haven't told you, the Link is a simulated airplane mounted firmly upon its base within a building. With it we get all the basic principles of instrument flying. Deception in instrument work is terrific. For one reason, there are forces in a plane so much greater than the pull of gravity that it's not impossible to be flying upside down or some other way without knowing it. That, of course, is when you can't see the horizon. Also, after turning in a certain direction for a while, you seem to be turning the opposite way when you straighten

out. You swear the instruments have gone haywire. The Link trainer is where it is proved that a man can fly straight and swear he's turning or vice versa. Course it's seldom as dark outside as it is in the trainer, but it could be, out in the jungles somewhere.

Today we took a 250-mile cross-country. Some fun. But it's so simple, it's pitiful. All you gotta do is look at your map and there you are.

Dear folks:

You guys come about as near to being orphans as anyone I know. This is the first time I've sat on my butt this week, except in a parachute. Even my bunk and I have become strangers. Sunday night we cruised around among the stars. Tuesday and Thursday night we did the same thing. Last night we ended our night flying by shooting blackout landings which are done only with smudge pots on each side of the runway. And surprisingly, they're as easy as falling off a log. I got pretty hot on formation flying, enough to stir up a bit of confidence that has been developing as I have progressed. I've had a mighty fine instructor here, one who would have liked very much to give credit where it was due and couldn't help but show it. A number of boys have gone the trip lately. Some that we thought were pretty good pilots.

I thought I had a prize birthday present for you, pop. I carried a nickel around for a week that I thought was the one you asked me to find for you an age ago. I've never seen one like it. Anyhoo, on closer scrutinization, I found it was from the Denver mint. And another one I found didn't have any mint letter on it. I've gotten in the habit of looking at all nickels I get in change and have probably looked at a million, but no soup.

I have a 40-hour and 60-hour check and an instrument check, then one is seated in a soft chair on the gravy train. Think I'll request the biggest they have. We are recommended for one type of craft or another before we are sent to advanced schools.

Oh yes, congratulations on the solo. I haven't heard from Harold, but there might be something in the box now. Hafta go,

Piles,

Stan

We were told we would get to choose which airplane we wanted to fly, but sometimes it chose you. The conversation I remember when asked what we wanted to fly went like this: "If you select a heavy bomber, you'll be a first pilot. If you select anything else, you'll be assigned copilot on something." That's how the choice went for me. I'm not sure how it was for Stan, but we both were pilots on a B-17 bomber. When I walked up to the bomber for the first time, I thought it was the biggest airplane I'd ever seen.

The B-17 had four engines, retractable gears, a tail dragger, a Plexiglas nose in the front, a top and bottom turret, and a defining dorsal tail. The G model was designed with the chin turret. Back then, there seemed to be a lot of room inside the plane, but now when I get inside one, I wonder how ten men could function in all their gear in such a small space. My first impression was the amazing amount of instruments. And when I sat in the pilot's seat and looked out at the left wing, it appeared like a road going to nowhere.

Stanley remarked:

Yesterday there was a B-17 in. What a beaut. In about thirty minutes, I take off on the night cross-country to Fresno. A week from next Saturday we have our graduation exercises and then the graduation party at a swanky place over at Bakersfield. Am going to try to get down to see Pearl and Dusty this weekend. It may be the last chance to see them.

We've been flying formation lately. It's quite a bit of fun. And it, like instrument flying, is quite an art.

My friend Ralph Lauper also put in for four-motor training. His folks have been coaxing him to go into a classification called "standard" so that he might get a job as instructor. But according to ussens who have been facing instructors for five months now, that doesn't look very exciting. Am hoping that advanced will take me inland a ways. And it might. If I were sent to New Mexico, that would put me quite close to home. We ought to know before long.

Stan went on to Marfa, Texas, to the Army Air Forces Advanced Flying School and flew the AT-17. I flew a UC-78 at advanced training in Ft. Sumner, New Mexico. They were both twin-engine trainers with a retractable gear.

Stanley wrote home:

In the hubbub of graduation, I haven't written even a card for two weeks, so I'll have to backtrack a bit. Graduation exercises were routine but very nice. I guess I told you about Harry Cuthbertson telling his family of my being there [Bakersfield]. I finally got out to see them the last night. They were swell, and incidentally, their daughter [Janice] is as nice as anything around there upon whom I showered my attentions. I should have met her sooner.

Damned if we didn't get a royal welcome [at Marfa, Texas], if it may be termed that. Here on the twenty-first day of May 1943, at a spot so near to the Mexican border that one can spit into the river when the wind is from the north, the ground is white! A while ago a huge green cloud breezed over, and when the bombardment ceased, there had been deposited on the ground two inches of hail, and twice as much had washed down the gutter with the accompanying rain. Some of the stones were an inch from head to tail.

Don't know what effect the aforementioned had on the planes. Probably none. Here we'll be flying AT-17s; they're two engine-jobs and pretty nice.

He continued another day as follows:

These are strange crates at first. Seems funny to have an engine tugging at you from each side instead of one in the middle. The instructors can ride with only one cadet at a time, and he must have both a pilot and copilot before he can send a ship up. We get 70 hours here but spend about 40 gratis as copilot. There's room for five in the cabin, two pilots and three in the back seat. Yesterday we started doing instrument work. It's much nicer in these ships because they're larger and heavier and rough air doesn't bump them around so much. This ship is definitely non-acrobatic. We don't even spin or stall in them. A couple of years ago when I took off from El Paso with Cousin Henry, I never thought I'd be piloting a plane over it.

And guess what we're doing today and tomorrow? Buying officer's uniforms. Uncle Sam dishes out $250 berries to each and every one of us for that purpose. It's funny how quickly time passes in this business, even when you are looking forward to something so big.

For men only: How can you keep flies from spreading disease? By keeping them buttoned.

That joke was probably the result of a lecture on VD. We had those lectures every once in a while. Stan and I went through the same training, one year apart, so at about the time he was in advanced training at Marfa, the Air Corps called me up. I reported on June 20, 1943.

"Reckon it seems pretty quiet around home by this hour," Stanley commented to his folks. "I have an idea your younger son will breeze through this training. And if so, you can feel pretty proud of yourselves. I'd like to tell you the percentages that don't make it, but I suppose it's a military secret. You'd be shocked at it."

He wrote more:

Just got back from a big trip. I'm all tired out, but it was fun. It was a four-hundred-mile cross-country five hundred feet off the ground. A man gets a pretty good view of mother earth from there, but if I didn't learn anything else, I found out in no uncertain terms that the air is much cooler on up.

Saturday wound up the ground school, so maybe we'll have time to turn around now and then. Three of us had a short pass and went to town and had huge steaks then took three Waco's to a dance. Wasn't that exciting?

I hit the jackpot today with a letter from home and a couple from feminine admirers. Got a letter and a package of candy and dates from Pearl and Dusty a couple of days ago. They requested that I send you some pictures that they enclosed in the letter. The picture of Ralph is p.poor. He's not at all bad looking. He's such a regular guy that you can't picture him doing missionary work in the past. Usually such people are a bit tetched in one respect or another. Wish we could have been stationed at the same advanced school.

June 29, 1943

Dear folks:

I expected a letter from thereabouts Monday, but durned if my imagination ran so rampant as to be expecting one of the size and scope of the one received. It was darned swell and digested with pleasure after I once got it in the old cud. Chewing it, though, was a bit harder. I got the first half page read before the ensuing whistle blew. Then, before that sweet sound again fell upon my ears, I was clear down to the last half of the second page. So after that hour was over, I called a halt to the proceedings and didn't budge until I had devoured the remaining contents. Then in the evening I sat down to find out what I had read during the afternoon. It is a masterpiece, to say the least, and I shall carry it with me to the far corners so that I may have a visit with the family most anytime I feel the urge. Fact is, that was probably my furlough. However, I'm going to keep hoping until the conductor yells "All Aboard" to those of us going on to transition school. And while we're on the subject, all of you raise your right hand who could be at Aileen's in Denver in the event that we should have three or four days between graduation and the touching welcome to the next school. If connections were just right, I could make it up there in not too many hours.

Love,
Stan

Harold Dwyer
Hastings
Nebr.

June 20, 1943

Dearest Aileen, Stanley, and Harold:

'Tis evening of Dad's Day in this year of our Lord nineteen hundred forty-three. It is not just another day. Nor just another Dad's Day, for it marks a complete change in status for this particular branch of the Dwyer tribe. Your Mother and I are alone tonight, and for the first time in almost thirty years, we know to a certainty that we shall be alone in the morning--that no child of ours will be coming in during the night and be on hand to gather round when the breakfast whistle blows.

This morning, the last of three swell youngsters stepped out into not only a world of his own, but also into his big adventure in the Air Corps of the Army of these United States, to do his part toward winning a war. It was this going which changed the status. Maybe it's the change, or maybe the fact that it comes on Dad's Day--or both--which has caused the day to stand out a little more than type-high so that the impression is greater and the imprint a little more bold than that of most of the preceding days.

All day I have been wandering back over the years and wishing all of us could spend the evening together and that I could tell you a lot of things which have gone unsaid as we went along--but knowing full well that if we were together I probably wouldn't say many--or any--of them. Just between us girls, the bird who invented the typewriter was on the right track. It is easy to talk to a machine. One can say things through his finger tips she probably couldn't or wouldn't any other way. By means of it, it is possible to gather round an 8½ x 11 sheet of bond stock and have a little visit in spite of the hundreds of miles in different directions which separate us.

Thirty years ago, the status here at home was the same. Ellen and I had no children around. But it can truthfully be said that certain women of the town--self-appointed lookers-after and inspectors of the family relations of the village were casting more than casual glances in the direction of your Mother, and wondering when or whether there would be anything to report at the next meeting

Twenty-five years ago, two of you were very much in evidence, and it was I who was going into the army--for the other war. I can still see most plainly , how you two were lying on your pillows the morning I slipped each of you a goodbye kiss without awakening you--and your Mother took me to the train to go into the service. Aileen was lying on her back, and Stanley about half on his side and tummy with one leg drawn up--the way he has slept most every night since.

Fifteen years ago, the whole crop was up, and the youngest sprout was three years old and had been able for years to throw stones through a windshield. In fact there were darn few places he couldn't or didn't throw rocks almost from birth.

Ten years ago, we had gathered in from the four corners and were

-2-

all together under the same roof and living as a family should. We were
working like beasts, but we all had our feet under the same table three
times a day, seven days a week, year in and year out. And there was plenty
on the table. I never have worked so hard nor long, but to me personally,
it was the happiest time of our family life. Verily, the ant has it over
the grasshopper in a lot of ways, even though the hopper does see a lot
more country and is on speaking terms with swarms of other kinds of insects.
The grind on the newspaper was so tough that I doubt the rest of you share
my feelings about that particular era. We went through some hard years,
but a depression was abroad in the land, and it is doubtful that we could
have weathered it any better elsewhere.

Nine years ago, the family had begun to come apart at the seams,
and we have been scattered from hell to heakfast ever since. Only Ellen
seems to be able to stay together. Each of you has gone your respective
way, and much of the time your dad, by comparison, would have made a dog
with a can full of pebbles tied to his wagger, look like a hitching post.
In those few years I have sat under the wheel a third of a million miles--
far enough to encircle the earth at the equator more than thirteen times.

One year ago, we were congregating at Pasedena for a grand good time
together with all hands present, and an enjoyable visit with Sergeant Stan
in the shade of California palms and cooled by ocean breezes. It was one
fine trip and I shall always be glad we made it.

The thirty years over which I have thought so much today, do not
seem long. Particularly the almost twenty-five since the close of the other
war. But one can't get around the calendar. The time has passed, and we
have seen a lot of things happen. Much water has gone under the bridge--
and some of it over.

In that time I watched Aileen grow from the tiny mite I carried as
far as from here to Mexico City the night she was three days old, to be a
sweet little kindergarten tot only a few days later. I can see her hippity-
hop from the curb to the schoolhouse when I let her out of the car that
first morning--so happy she could hardly wait to get inside. But the heart
she left in the car was anything but light. I had just come face to face
for the first time with what a road man is up against and the price he pays
for being away from his children. I was hardly acquainted with her--and she
was already in school. I saw her look out for Stanley when he started to
school, fighting his battles until he was able to do it himself, scattering
the larger boys--"darn'em"--when she had to. Saw her lead in the things
she undertook, take first in high jump and hundred-yard dash at track meets,
and become probably the only girl of her age who could "axe" a tree down.
I got glimpses of her as she grew and developed until she was fully capable
of walking, cold turkey, into a large city and making a right decent place
for herself therein, being quite able to tell any and all residents thereof
where to head in--and to see that they did it. One naturally thinks well
of his own children. But I have the satisfaction, in your case, Aileen, of
getting it straight from people who xxxxxxxxxxxxx are in position to know,
how you manage to have the time and inclination to look after others when
it is necessary, that you are "one real person." This has come straight
from more than one source, and after all, when that can be said of one,
then there isn't much more to be said.

In some less than thirty years I've seen Stanley grow from the little
tyke who beat his dad in the first race they ever had, arriving "out of the
Nowhere into the Here" some thirty minutes before I could make it from

-3-

Salina to Simpson and on out to the farm, to a lad who at four years old reported that he saw a bird flying backward, that he had seen a star but it went out--he 'spected "God stepped on it," and was sure when he and I were scuffling on the floor that one certain way I could be hurt was for "a iron house" to fall on me. I saw him learn to swim like a duck at ten years of age, and take to athletics like a duck to water even before then. Saw him retire the side unassisted in a school ball game in the fifth grade, making the three outs like a veteran. Saw him take things in his stride at college and get the job done without the aid of school politics or Greek letter affiliations. Saw him go on and become a man whose feet feel right at home on the deck of a ship on either ocean or either side of the equator and on the streets of cities of South America, Africa, Summatra, Borneo, China and those throughout the length and breadth of his own country, which feet, incidentally, have each morning for the past yearand a half, found their way down through the legs of the trouser part of a uniform of the United States Army, and who at this moment is probably piloting a twin-motored trainer plane of the Air Force of that army through the blackness over some god-forsaken area in the southern part of Texas, getting ready to play a full he-man's part in the he-man game of war. We have a Class Book published by his class when they graduated from Primary Flight school, which book is edited by him, as a bit of evidence that he doesn't exactly suck the hindermost teat as he goes along.

I have watched Harold only a little more than eighteen years. But have been with him, proportionately, more than you other two. The four years we were together on the newspaper was almost a fourth of his time, to date. Seems odd that he would grow as much, almost, in eighteen years as you other two have in twenty-six or eight, doesn't it? I happen to know he wasn't much larger than either at the start, and it isn't possible that throwing rocks would get him off to a better start as Stanley had thrown tons of them before Harold was born. It's probably Ellen's cooking. I've noticed in each case, that as soon as you leave home and get away from her chow you just practically quit growing. We all did a lot of watching of him as he went along. Babies were a bit out of the ordinary when he came along. We saw him at 17 months of age, make his get-away across the street and negotiate the slippery-slide and ladder on the school ground before a frantic Mother and swift-as-the-wind sister could head him off. We saw him refuse to go into Lake Michigan, and just raise particular Ned to get his Mother out on the beach because he "didn't want the water to shakle." We heard him read his First Reader lesson--"Lit-tul Fish, Lit-tul Fish, I have a wush, I have a wush." We saw him ride the spotted pony until he was almost a part of her. Then we saw him settle down to a lifetime of building airplanes--hundreds of them of all sizes, shapes, and colors--propelled at first by rubber bands, then by gas motors. We saw him bow his neck and sail into mathematics to help him along with that work. Then we saw him learn to fly civilian passenger planes. Then qualify for Aviation Cadet in the army air forces-- and today, leave to continue in that branch of the service the training of the last few years.

It is pleasant to sit here alone and dream back over those years-- thinking of the things all of you have said and done and the swell times we have had together. I used to look at you as you grew up, and wish I could run interference for each, taking all the knocks and the down's and the heartaches, so you'd have only the smooth sailing and the up's and the happiness that comes along in the coursemof a lifetime. Knowing it was im-possible, and that even if it were, it would be decidedly unfair to each

-4-

one of you. For the average person, that which makes life enjoyable and worth the effort is the knowledge of having been able to take the down's with the up's and the knocks along with the rest of it, having the feeling down within that, come what may, we will be able to keep the situation well in hand, and that we'll be in there pitching until the last out of the 9th, or in case of extra innings, till the game is called on account of Darkness.

It is the source of much genuine satisfaction to me to be able to look back over the way each of you has gone about this thing of living. As I have mentioned before, it is natural for one to think well of his own offspring, but I think all of you will agree that I have always been rather critical of mine, and with this in mind will know that it is not just another fond father sounding off when I say that all of you measure up. In the first place, you are all honest. And honesty is basic. With that as an inherent trait, one won't wander far off the course. You all tell the truth. If any one of you should tell me Sunday was Wednesday—I wouldn't go to church. I'd know it was And you all know what it is all about. None of you spend your time fretting about trivials, nor messing in other peoples' affairs. But I have noticed that in the things which really count, none of you are ever very far off the beam. You are all able, and have the happy knack of finding a way to accomplish most any thing you set out to do. Each of you is fully capable of taking care of yourself—and a few others if it becomes necessary. And it often does in this world.

I have enjoyed this little visit tonight a lot. There will be others, hundreds of them as I go on down the years, for pleasant memories have a way of coming on the screen most any time or place, but there of course will not be the time nor equipment to put any part of them on paper. My memories and I will just kinda go over things in our own way, and then go on up the road a little happier and more determined to do things ourselves. Perhaps after the war we can all gather round for a family get-together wherein the talking can be split five ways instead of one.

I have some regrets of course. If I could have it to do over again, I'd see to it that we all be together most of the time until time for you youngsters to take off for yourselves. I think the next time over I could make your childhood days a lot happier than they were. But the chief regret is that turn of fate which makes it necessary for my two sons to do a job for me of which I dreamed ever as a boy, and tried to keep myself in shape and position to do, for many years after—that of fighting a war. But after the other war, it seemed there could not be another in my time. I could not know that a Hitler was going to get his tail over the line and start a runaway, nor that when and if another did start, two grey hairs on each temple would disqualify a man for anything more strenuous than picking his teeth, regardless of previous training, ability, or inclination. It's a bitter pill —no foolin'.

As I finish tonight, please know that it has been a lot of fun to watch each of you start from scratch and grow and develop into what you are today. I am mighty proud to be the dad of three such, to have been privileged to take a hand in the proceedings now and then, and to have a good position on the sidelines where I can see what happens from here on out.

Heapses of love to each.

Dad

Granddad included his personal letter in *Uphill and Against the Wind*, the book that he wrote and published in 1963. A footnote added to the end of the letter read, "This family gathering did not come about—and never will. Both boys became pilots of B-17 bombers, and Stanley's went down over Wiener Neustadt, Austria, May 10, 1944. He is still missing, but is carried officially as killed in action."

In a letter home, Stanley commented:

> Don't know just what you meant by final tests but will make an attempt to explain the situation with the use of the six words that comprise my vocabulary. Finals in ground school, and the school itself, were finished last week. We are now men of leisure for half a day with the exception of extracurricular activities which include Link trainer, lectures, drill, calisthenics, and miscellaneous items too numerous to mention. As for the flying, the final check is every day, beginning with the first at primary. One flies as long as he can satisfy the powers that he can satisfactorily pilot the army way. At primary there were routine checks mostly for the purpose of offsetting any tendency of a cadet to relax. Here the instructor is a student's one critic. There's no time here for artificial stimulants. A cadet is considered a pilot when he arrives at advanced, and the time is spent preparing him for combat craft.
>
> Today I have been Officer of the Day. It is a long day, but the change makes for relaxation, so it has been pretty much like Sunday. And to be able to slip in to the next office and pound a typewriter during odd moments makes it a pleasure one is seldom fortunate to enjoy. But I must put my kiddies to bed. So, so long for now.

In another letter home, Stanley wrote:

> 'Tis Sunday again, and all through the cadet barracks, everyone has gone to the show except me. We had an overnight pass, but there wasn't much to do because Alpine—the only town of more than three population—is off-limits because of a case of infantile paralysis that broke out there last week. We went to a USO dance in Marfa but didn't do much except sit around.
>
> Got a huge letter from my mama this morning. The date of graduation is July 28, I think. Don't know what the program will be at the time, but we'll have a party with our instructors just before, I think. They give us stars for things we do wrong on the flight line,

then we have to pay off for them, or walk them off, and the proceeds are for the party. I donated about average. Most of the stars were received at the first of the training when we were learning our cockpit procedure. Then along about soloing time, we got about five apiece "on general principles."

Wrote Harold a short note a couple of days ago and will do him a letter when I finish this.

I thought pop would be in the harvest. Wish I were right alongside of him. Some soil and horse manure would smell pretty good for a change. One thing about airplanes though—you don't have to clean up after them. If they had those animal characteristics, everyone around here would wear the tin helmets cause the air is full.

"Two weeks from one hour ago, we will have graduated," Stan informed his folks. "And don't think we're not looking forward to it. In answer to your query, we'll probably be in transition school about three months, then, except in a case of emergency, we will go through other phases (I think with our permanent combat crews) before we will be sent across. If I can leave after graduation, I will be able to spend a few days in Denver."

The Marfa Army Air Forces Advanced Flying School held graduation exercises for Class 43-G pilots on Wednesday morning, July 28, 1943. On that date, Stanley became a commissioned officer—a lieutenant—and wore the silver wings of the Army Air Forces of the United States Army.

Stanley sent a telegram to his mother dated July 27, "Should arrive Denver late Friday."

Stanley received his commission and earned his wings in the Army Air Forces of the United States Army on July 28, 1943. Origin of photo unknown.

7

Combat Training

I think we're about ripe.
—*Stanley N. Dwyer in a letter dated January 27, 1944*

Simultaneously, while reading letters, digging through the trunk, and learning about Stanley, other aspects of our search evolved, as well, in baby steps. Before Mom and Dad's house fire, we had received some e-mails and information from Austria. And we continued to ponder that information. Many of our questions had been answered, but then those answers posed several more questions, and that cycle never seems to stop. It's disappointing; even now we must accept that it's impossible to know all the answers.

One question still was on my mind. If there were no remains or trace of my brother, how did the people in Austria know he was the pilot who perished in the crash? The answer to one question always triggered more questions.

So once more, we put together a list of questions, and Dave Hughes, Rick's cousin, acted as the middleman between us and Martin, his Austrian friend. Dave and his son, John, translated our letter and questions, written more specifically to the town historian of Vostenhof, who knew the location of Stanley's crash site. We knew from the MACR that the plane was carrying a full bomb load on impact and that it burned. Dad asked if there was any physical evidence of the pilot in the wreckage and if dog tags were found in the crash debris. If dog tags were found, where would they be? What happened to any remains of the wreckage, and was the crash documented in a local newspaper or museum? Was there information or copies that we could receive, and would it be possible to get a photograph of the crash site? And Rick and I still entertained thoughts of visiting Austria.

Dave eventually heard back from his Austrian friend. Dave e-mailed, "It's an interesting story. The village 'historian' is an old guy who lives a pretty remote life and has no e-mail himself. My Austrian friend [Martin] contacted his God-parents who live nearby, and they found the guy and talked with him. They are quite interested to help, and so I will have John translate the letter. They apparently have a reading knowledge of English but cannot write it very well. Their names are Udo and Inge Doerr." Dave enclosed their e-mail address. We appreciated John's offer to translate the letter. It took time.

After Stanley won his wings and briefly visited family in Denver, he was off to Roswell, New Mexico, for transitional flying. Then, from that desert location, he moved to other parts of the country for three additional phases of operational training, where skills were sharpened with simulated combat conditions, along with lessons and knowledge that only practical experience served.

Stanley spent two months in transitional training. From Roswell, New Mexico, he wrote, "The B-17 is a good ship, and we're doing everything in the books in the 17. We have already put in two hitches. We fly four hours at a stretch every other day. Flying and ground school and Link trainer is the size of our duty."

Furthermore, Stanley remarked, "Another week has rolled around, parleyvoo. Not much has happened since I wrote last. We have been shooting landings and doing instrument flying, which there isn't much to tell about. I have an instructor who is tops. I should know this buggy from stem to stern when he gets through. Flying formation isn't enough for a man to do for him, so he quizzes us on mechanics, et cetera, in the meantime."

Dear anyone home:

This weekend we are going on another cross-country. This time it is to Des Moines. I doubt that we shall pass so close that I can dip a wing at you as we go by, but we should go over some of the old stomping ground.

Nothing new has been added to our flying. Mostly because we were introduced to the whole works the first week or two. We're getting this instrument and radio work down pat. You couldn't get me lost in a fog over Podunk Center, Borneo. And I really greased the old crate onto the mat when we were shooting landings. Ground school is the same, and so is the village. Ought to be able to stir up something new in the city over the weekend.

Got a letter from Harold a couple of days ago. He says he will be in Santa Ana about birthday time. Pearl and Dusty will be glad to see him, and vice versa. One of these days I'm going to drop in on him out of the clear blue. Would be kinda nice if I could spend a weekend with Pearl and Dusty and Harold. Personally, I would just as soon he wouldn't have gotten the grades that boosted him up. There might be more chance of my being out that way later. But if they stay at Santa Ana as long as we did, then it won't make much difference anyhoo.

Will wind this up and give it a send-off.

Love,
Stan

I didn't remember exactly why, but right off the bat in my training, while I was at CDT in Missoula, I was moved up one class. I first was assigned the graduation class of 44-H but then was moved up to 44-G. That meant I shipped out two to three weeks earlier than the class behind. Years later, it was rumored from a buddy that the class behind—class 44-H, my original class—had too many pilots on line, so the whole class was washed out and put into infantry. That was only a rumor, but like I said before, if you made it, it was a lot of luck and a matter of timing.

Dear folks:

I shore enjoyed talking to you Sunday, mom. I was laying flat on my back in a nice room at the Ft. Des Moines Hotel. I had just awakened. I sent the call collect so I wouldn't have to dress and go downstairs. Is that alright?

And that was the climax of a swell time in the city. I had the room with a fellow whose fiancée was visiting in town. So it was decided that I should have a date with her friend. Both the girls were sweet. And though both of them had engagement rings on, I had a good time. Betty's boyfriend is in England. We went to a nightclub and had dinner and danced. During the floor show, a guy boasting mental telepathy asked for three servicemen to help him. He picked a sailor, an infantry lieutenant, and then said the third representative should be from the Air Corps, and they shined the spotlights on me and started playing the Air Corps song. So I was on the program.

We came back by way of Kansas City. But it was so cloudy we didn't see the ground until we were almost to Wichita. This old plane takes storms as easy as a rowboat on a swimming pool. And your uncle can fly instruments with the best of them.

Reckon the Roswell girls will think I have forgotten them. Was gone over the weekend and flew last night. Maybe I'd be more eager to go in if there were more girls of the quality of the two at Des Moines. But you don't find them so often around army towns. Most of them are looking for some brass to marry.

Will write letters tonight. I owe everyone as usual. And must get them all written soon so they won't think I've gone high-hat upon receiving the "comish."

So I better pick up my books and skip lightly off to school.

Love and kisses and all that there stuff,
Stan

Soon after, he wrote, "I reckon the biggest news these days is the fact that I soloed the 17. 'Twas really quite simple. Greased a couple of landings on the mat then went up for instrument work."

Transitional flying taught us new pilots how to fly the B-17 and to know its capabilities. The ship itself was a masterpiece of workmanship and design. Once you learned what a plane had and what it was used for, the rest was simple. Basically, you just crawled in the airplane and started flying it.

Dad and Stanley made it sound easy. For them, it probably was, but there were other perspectives. As I flipped through the pages of a coffee table book titled *The B-17 Remembered,* edited by Steven K. Harris, I read what Francis J. Killoran wrote. "Shooting landings with student pilots was never dull. Each class produced its share of very hard landings, bouncy landings, and just plain sloppy landings before attaining acceptable skill levels."

Aerial engineers like Francis J. Killoran monitored the pilot as well as the plane's performance while flying on board the B-17 during training flights. He wrote:

We followed a single B-17 in the landing pattern and, on the final approach, noticed the pilot take strong corrective action for crosswind. The next instant, the plane touched down, skidded sideways, and then took off. Now it was our turn. Likewise, we corrected for a very strong crosswind, and as we touched down our plane slid sideways. The pilot immediately shoved the throttles forward and took off.

After we were well into the air, I noticed skid marks on the left main landing wheel tire virtually at right angles to the tire tread. I tapped the pilot on the shoulder and pointed to the tire. I knew I had achieved perfect silent communication when he peeled out of the landing pattern and began navigational routines.

When an instructor felt a student pilot had enough basic takeoff skills in a B-17, he would confront him with a simulated "failed engine" on takeoff. As the airplane picked up takeoff speed and was just barely airborne, the instructor would pull one throttle back and shout, "Engine out!" It was up to the pilot to take corrective action promptly. Such action required fast, coordinated responses with both engine power application and flight control manipulation ...

The first-time reaction of student pilots to an "engine out" condition varied widely. A few student pilots would coolly take corrective action, skillfully turning a three-engine takeoff into one that was almost normal. More often, students faltered in their corrective action, allowing the plane to veer from side to side and to fishtail down the runway before achieving full control.

Worse were the students who took only marginally effective corrective action. In these instances, the plane would swerve sharply to the side with the failed engine. As the pilot attempted to bring the plane back on course, he would overcontrol and swing excessively in the opposite direction to the extent the barely airborne plane would drift off the runway. More than once, I watched in total fascination and increasing apprehension as flare pots at the edge of the runway slid under us—sideways—and we found ourselves crabbing at thirty to fifty feet over arid New Mexico grassland as three engines clawed their way into the air.

And formation flying, the engineer indicated, was not "effortless" flying. "In reality," he wrote, "formation flying demanded constant, intense concentration from the pilot to minimize the tendency of the plane to bob up and down and to weave from side to side like a piece of wood on fast, flowing water. On hot afternoons, formation flying in rough air was especially demanding."

Once when we were practicing formation flying in six-ship elements, I looked up, and all of a sudden, two six-ship elements—ours being one—were flying the same altitude and approaching each other on a collision course. We took evasive action and avoided disaster.

I never witnessed a midair collision, but they happened—and not just in the skies over England. Sometimes they happened during training exercises. In Missoula, a couple squadron mates weren't so fortunate when their Piper Cubs collided in midair. We marched from the school campus to the church for the funeral. The sound of the singing was loud and clear, and the hollow thump, thump, thump of perfect cadence when we crossed a bridge stands out in my mind.

There were training casualties as well as combat casualties. Takeoff collisions, getting lost, flying into mountains, and locking wings were things that happened when young men were mastering new equipment. It's the price of motion. Guys sometimes had to bail out of a burning aircraft. Some came out of it all right—

some didn't. It was rumored that one guy who bailed out landed near chow hall and said something like "That's one way to get into chow line."

Sept. 21, 1943

Dear folks:

Received a letter from each and every one of you during the last two days. In answer to yours, pop, the typewriter news sounds good. However, in the event that you get it, I would prefer that you keep it there at the house rather than sending it here. It probably wouldn't amount to much after having ridden the modern train for a couple of days. And besides, I have the best of intentions of spending a delay en route at the home fireside in a couple of weeks. As for you, ma, I received the pictures—thanx heaps—but can't say that I think too much of them. Guess all the photographers have gone to war.

Best news of the past few days is the fact that I passed an instrument check today for which I shall receive an instrument card entitling me to the right to take off from a closed-in station, fly in instrument weather, and land at closed-in stations should the need arise. And that about winds up the checks for this old man. We have to be checked out for night solo, but that will be only a formality. I almost feel like a pilot now.

Got a letter from Ralph Lauper the other day. He is down here at Hobbs. He has less time than I, and the time is getting short, so he may have to take cross-countries each week to get his time in. We may go to Carlsbad [Caverns] this weekend if he doesn't fly. I think I will go anyway.

So I better get back to the grind.

Love,
Stan

And Stanley wrote more the following week.

Dear folks:

Another month has rolled around, and the morrow will bring with it another paycheck of comparatively monstrous proportions. And they're not bad things to have around now and then. The clothiers will take a huge chunk of this one, especially if we are sent as far north as I am expecting. I'll need an overcoat, a raincoat, and a couple more sets of pinks or greens.

Not only that, but I'm still planning on spending a bit of the early part of the coming month on the loose. And that takes cash also, even though a part of the time is spent at home. The latest rumor is ten days, and rumors sound better as the transfer comes closer, but of course, it is still rumor. I advise, though, that the powers that be say nary a thing until the last day if there is no time off in store for us. And while we're waiting for official confirmation, you'd better be looking around for the best looking gal in your fair village, for I won't accept a substitute. I figger if a man is going to be within scrutinizing distance of a woman, she just as well be easy on the eyes since the matter of social engagements is basically one of pleasure.

Not quite as far along as we should be with our flying hours, we are flying—and ground schooling as usual—every day. I think we finish Sunday, but ground school may last a couple of days longer. My pardner and I flew solo today, half of it formation. Tomorrow we are going to do some instrument calibration, and Friday we'll be checked out solo for night flying.

I am toothless Jane again. The gum around my gold crown got a little sore, and I have wanted to get rid of the gold where it shows anyway. The dentist took the tooth out and will replace it.

Sent Harold a ten-dollar bill for his birthday but haven't heard yet whether or not he received it. Got pop's letter yesterday, and it looks like the typewriter deal is headed for a showdown just about the right time. Pearl is about as eager for Harold to get there [Santa Ana] as he is. She mentioned having saved gas coupons so they might have a better chance of seeing him.

Had thought a little about going to a formal dance in the village this evening but gave stronger thought to not going when we were rescheduled to fly at five thirty in the morning. Guess I have thrilled the Roswell women about as much as I will before leaving.

Will let you know of every little development concerning my toasting shins and shooting the breeze at home.

Love,
Stan

With transitional training behind him, Stanley transferred to other locations for the three phases of operational training, but not before stopping at home. A Western Union telegram placed Stanley in Hastings, Nebraska, the first week in October for about ten days. It would be his last visit home.

Operational training seemed to me to be a polite word for combat training, maybe disguised for the sake of mothers. Before Stanley went to Dyersburg, Tennessee, to begin the first phase of operational training, he was sent to Salt Lake City, where most of his crew was assigned. Salt Lake City was a brief stop—approximately three weeks—and Stanley wrote, "In their attempt to work out a new scheme, everything is in a mell of a hess. Ralph Lauper is here, and our names are so close together on the list that we may go out together."

Stanley spent most of the month of November 1943 in the first phase of operational training at Dyersburg. He wrote:

> The day started off quite normal with ground school this morn. Then we went to the flight line and had our first ride here. I greased a couple of landings for my instructor, then we had some tail wheel trouble, and while it was being fixed, a colonel decided he should ride with me instead of the instructor. And so, there being no one around to outrank him, he did.
>
> Don't know what he told my instructor, but the boss fairly beamed when I saw him later. And mention was made of my spot-check at a meeting this evening, and the squadron commanders seemed to be pleased with the results as well. So I reckon my name will stir pleasant associations in their minds in the weeks to come. And that doesn't hurt.
>
> We have our entire crews now, except the navigator. I have a good bunch of boys. Don't know how I'll get them all home to see their mamas though. They are from California, Texas, Missouri, Minnesota, New Jersey, and New York. A rare collection, huh?

During the first phase of operational training, combat crews flew together. Nine- or ten-man crews were made up of guys fresh out of gunnery school or other specialized training schools.

When my turn came in October 1944, my crew was assigned while I was in Rapid City, South Dakota. We all gathered for a big meeting, and then my name was called off. I went and stood over in a corner. Another eight names were called off, and those men joined me in the corner. That's when we met. We were all pretty young. I was barely twenty years old. Stan had a ten-man crew; mine was a nine-man crew. By the time I got in the war, the Germans were running short on fighter planes, pilots, and fuel, so one waist gunner could handle both sides of the plane.

The pilot was, of course, the "boss," and the copilot was second in command and took over if the pilot was incapacitated. We traded off at the controls so he could get his experience and the pilot could take a breather. In some instances, the copilot wished he was pilot, but my copilot and I got along fine. As far as that goes, our whole crew got along. Occasionally, a guy didn't "fit in" with a crew, and procedures were in place to make a replacement. Camaraderie took a while to develop. The military formality of saluting ended at the airplane. We knew who the officers were. We flew as a crew.

The navigator sat in a compartment about three feet below and in front of the pilot. He had a little desk down there, and his job was to know the position of the plane at all times. He navigated in different ways, sometimes using the stars or dead reckoning, and sometimes we flew off radio beams. A good navigator could always identify where we were. The navigator had two .50 caliber machine guns to command. We referred to them as the cheek guns—one on each side of the nose.

Also positioned below the pilot, on the same level and in front of the navigator, was the bombardier. He sat in the Plexiglas bubble—or the nose of the plane. His responsibility was the Norden bombsight, a top-secret weapon at that time, or it was supposed to be. Basically, it was a computer. The mechanism computed ground speed and wind drift to determine the exact release point of the bombs so they'd hit the target. When approaching the target, if the Norden bombsight was hooked into the autopilot system, the bombardier essentially flew the plane. When the two were hooked together, the plane responded to any correction the bombardier made on the Norden bombsight. The pilot's job then was to maintain altitude and airspeed. The bombardier had two .50 caliber machine guns to aim and shoot forward.

Standing behind the pilot on the flight deck was the flight engineer. He was the maintenance man of the plane and knew everything about the 17. Engineers were knowledgeable and mechanically inclined; they could fix any glitches that occurred. For example, the wastegates in later B-17 models were electronically controlled. It was so rigged that if the electronics failed, the wastegates would close, forcing exhaust gases out the supercharger turbine, which resulted in a terrific increase in manifold pressure within the engine. The copilot's job was to immediately retard the engine throttle before the engine or engines were ruined. As there were four engines on a B-17, we had four electronic devices to control. On takeoff for one mission from England, the electronic devices on our plane started to malfunction and caused a surge in the engines. Three of the four controllers malfunctioned. Hal Thorpe, my copilot, handled it well and retarded the throttles before the engines were damaged. Our flight engineer, Bill Brown, used one controller to reset all four engines, moving from one engine to another, and we proceeded on and completed the mission.

The flight engineer was valuable—as were all crew members—and he also manned the top turret gun. From his standing position behind the pilot, he turned and took one step up onto a platform. From his upright position, his head was sticking up basically between machine guns in the top turret with the gunsight right in front of him. Wherever he aimed the gun, the whole turret turned with him. Stops were placed on the guns to prevent the gunner from shooting off the plane's tail fin.

Behind the engineer was the bomb bay where bombs hung on racks on each side of the plane with a narrow catwalk between. The bombs were armed by the bombardier or flight engineer after we got in flight. Dressed in all your gear, including a parachute pack, the catwalk was a tight squeeze. Behind the bomb bay bulkhead was the radio compartment. The radio operator had a desk and a little window. His equipment amounted to long- and short-range radios, and some planes had a retractable machine gun above him that he manned.

The ball turret was the bubble that hung below the belly frame of the plane, behind the bomb bay. It took a pretty small guy to crawl into that confined space. Ralph Peterson, a ball turret gunner in my 34th Bomb Group, explained to Kay at one of our reunions, "I tell people the only training I had that prepared me for sitting in the ball for eight-hour missions, with my knees drawn up to my chest, was spending nine months in my mother's womb."

The gunner in the ball had a view like nobody else's. From his cramped space, he observed from the wings down and protected the underside of the plane. The top turret, manned by the engineer, had a view of everything above the plane. The ball turret rotated mechanically either by electricity or by hand and from either inside the turret or inside the plane. With the capability of rotating 360 degrees, the gunner inside the bubble aimed—from almost any position—his two machine guns at pursuing enemy fighters.

The turret had to be set a certain way for the hatch to open so the gunner could enter and exit the ball from inside the plane. The waist gunners helped the ball turret gunner get into position. If it happened that flak damaged the rotating mechanism, jamming the gears of the ball, and at the same time, if the landing gears were shot out, the ball turret would be the first thing to touch ground in a forced belly landing, whether anybody was in it or not.

The waist gunners, originally two of them, one on each side of the waist section of the plane, stood almost back to back, one gun placed slightly ahead of the other so the gunners could maneuver around a little. They were positioned in the middle of the plane, behind the ball turret. Their job was to protect each side of the bomber. The exit door on the plane's right side was about halfway between the waist gunner and the tail wheel. Another exit was through the bomb bay doors if they were open, and an exit hatch was located up front in the plane, behind the navigator and bombardier.

Protecting the plane from rear attack was the tail gunner. He had his own little spot back in the tail of the bomber—out of sight from the rest of the crew—and accessible from the waist of the plane. The tail gunner crawled back alongside the tail wheel to his position, and he manned his machine guns from a cramped, sitting position. He also had an escape hatch between the tail wheel and his position.

It was a coordinated effort by crews to fight off the enemy from inside their Flying Fortress, protecting not only their own plane but other planes in the formation. Once our mission duty for Uncle Sam was done, we hoped to get ourselves and the plane back home to our base.

Dear folks:

Just got back from a 48-hour pass to Memphis. Ralph and Dale, my copilot, and I went down. Didn't get too much accomplished since my prime purpose was to rest up and see if I couldn't break up my cold.

Most fun we have had recently has been dropping bombs. Can't say that I've helped my bombardier's average circular error, but until now, he has been flying with pilots who do nothing else. The second bomb we dropped hit thirty feet from the target (from 8,000 feet), and that's close enough to shake the old house even with a practice bomb.

The whole crew has been riding with us as of a couple of days ago. There's not a lot for the gunners to do just now, but most of them had never been in a 17 before, and it will be better for them to feel at home when we start gunnery.

Helped Ralph buy an engagement ring in Memphis. Don't you suppose he was grateful for my knowledge and judgment of diamonds?

Love,
Stan

For practice, we dropped one-hundred-pound bombs filled with sand, with black powder only in the nose. We practiced at night so that a camera from the plane could catch the explosion flash, and the accuracy of the bombardier was calculated. Our targets were lights on the ground that formed a "plus" or cross shape specifically placed for that purpose. Where I trained in South Dakota, many little towns had intersections lit in the same way as our "plus" targets. Well, some little towns complained of all the black powder and fragment lying in their streets. Therefore, standard procedure was changed for night-bombing practice. Pilots were required to sign the bombs—so then we knew who was screwing up. My bombardier, Ryan, sometimes shouted, "I got a 'shack!'" He'd hit the center line—bull's-eye.

The month of November 1943 drew to a close. Thanksgiving Day, yet another day for Stanley, revolved around ground school and flying and was topped off with a turkey dinner. He transferred to MacDill Field in Tampa, Florida, for the month of December and the next phase of operational training—in other words, combat training.

Dec. 5, 1943

Dear peoples:

How's the weather up your way? It's not that way here. When we got off the train the other morning, we thought the balmy weather was too good to last. But it's still here. Damn but this army life is rough—two winters in California and the next in Florida. Don't know whether I can stand it or not.

We're in our permanent organizations now, the one in which we will go across. Here's my address: 463rd Bomb Group, 775th Squadron, MacDill Field, Tampa, Florida. We may be here for both phases, but on the other hand, we may go north a little ways for third phase.

It is said that we will get our own planes for third phase since we have to have a hundred hours on them before going across. To the present, I haven't been struck by a good name for mine. Got any suggestions?

Am sending you $300. Keep forty of it for the typewriter and shoes, and dash down to the bank with the rest, will you pliz? Have you ever gotten any war bonds of mine?

I better do a note to Harold before class this aft.

As ever,

Stan

There was always schooling—survival techniques for bailing out and ditching— everything you might need to know. In the last phases of training, each guy on the crew had his own schedule, whether it was radio training, gunnery training, bombing and navigating practice, or maintaining a B-17. We also flew with our crews every day, and I remember a lot of formation flying. By the time I was sent across, I had logged about four hundred hours of flying time. It was more than the Germans had for training, but we were still pretty green. Nevertheless, our crews were the best prepared. We went from being boys to being men quickly.

Dec. 15, 1943

Dear folks:

'Tis eleven o'clock, and a man ought to be in the sack by now. But I otter let you know I'm still kicking. So here goes. One of these days I'm going to take inventory to see where each of the twenty-four hours goes. They surely slip by.

Just wrote to Pearl and Dusty. I don't know what I'm going to do for them for Christmas. I sent you and Aileen a little gift last time

I was in town. But when you see it, you will agree that it would not be an appropriate gift to send to someone in California. Should have sent one to the Clarks, too, but didn't think of it in time.

You go ahead and make definite plans to go to Wakeeney for Christmas. There's little chance that I will get off at Christmas for more than one day. And if I did, I could get to Kansas as easily as I could get home. That would be slaughtering half a dozen fowl with a single pebble anyhoo.

I sent Harold a ten-dollar bill this aft. Don't know that he will get it though. Mail here, at its best, is poor. Some wise guy sent himself a letter to see how it would do. It took six days.

And about the typewriter. If it is fixed by the twentieth, send it. Otherwise, hold it because I'll have another address to give you by the end of the month. That will probably be the last before a trip to England or thereabouts. It is said that we will have three months training after we get there. Guess we'll have to hurry to get in on the kill.

If this is the last letter to reach you before you go to Kansas, A Merry One, and we'll see if we can't stir up a merrier one next year.

Love,
Stan

A telegram sent to Wakeeney on December 26 read, "Wanted to be there no soap tried to call no soap my soul is full. Stan"

Dec. 27, 1943

Dear folks:

Just a note to let you know that the typewriter arrived right side up and in one piece. It is midnight now, so I better not peck on it. Thanks gobs for the time and trouble.

Am anxiously awaiting post-Christmas mail to find out if everything came and went as scheduled. I sent you folks and Aileen a similar gift. Sent Pearl and Dusty a nice box of candy and Harold the cash. Sent a dozen roses for the Wakeeney reunion. Hope they arrived. Were to be delivered Christmas Eve. Sent a telegram Sunday in place of an impossible call.

Between all that puttering around and a bit of fun here, I had a better Christmas than anticipated. Ralph and I went to a steak dinner served to us by the wife of one of the boys. They're Georgians by the name of Little. And swell people. The four of us helped a widowed neighbor lady fix her child's Christmas tree. We flew Christmas Day but had Sunday and half of today off.

And before I quit, let me thank you for the swell fruitcake. It's mighty good. Gotta hit the sack.

Love,
Stan

P.S. Looks like we'll be going over to Lakeland, Florida, for the third phase about the first of the year.

Operational training or combat training—it hardly mattered what it was called because it was obvious what would happen next. At home in Hastings, Nebraska, Grandma, as well as Granddad, undoubtedly read the headlines and, I'd guess, were distressed as they followed the war news. For months, news of bombing raids on Germany and other targets in occupied Europe frequently ran as front-page news in the *Hastings Daily Tribune*.

No war had been fought from the air on the scale of World War II. By the time World War II came around, there had been thinkers in the chain with ideas on air combat—ideas developed as a result of World War I where the forerunner of the American air force was introduced to air warfare. Essentially, World War II tested those ideas. With the right planes, equipment, trained crews, and so forth, air warfare went to a new level, a new frontier.

So then, coverage in the papers told the story, and in October 1943, news in the *Hastings Daily Tribune* read, "Will Rogers Jr. asserted today Nazi planes equipped with rockets have enabled Germany to gain temporary mastery of the skies over Western Europe. 'Germany is making our bombing raids from England very costly,' he said. 'Perhaps too costly. Initial successes such as those scored around Hamburg are not being repeated.'" [7]

And more news disclosed, "The American Eighth Air Force has grown by 450 percent since May 1, but still is less than two-thirds of the way toward the ultimate goal set for it." [8]

"The big American four-engined bombers, with an escort of Thunderbolts, equipped with belly tanks for the 800-mile round-trip, swept out across Western Europe only a few hours after a fleet of British night raiders dropped 1,000 or more tons of explosives on Kassel, another arms center 90 miles north of Frankfurt ... The Frankfurt raid was the deepest penetration into enemy territory yet made by the fast, heavily armored Thunderbolts as escorts for Fortresses." [9]

Information about the Ninth and Twelfth Air Force operations from North Africa also made the news. Aircrews, as pioneers of the new frontier, flew over the enemy—above the battlefield. Perhaps these crews would be immune from the grueling trench warfare of World War I. However, "flying over them" became its own dangerous and deadly proposition, but in the end, it was a triumphant proposition which infinitely contributed to—some say decided—the outcome of the war.

No single service won the war by itself. The air force did their part and was just one important cog in the whole war effort.

On the home front, plastered across pages of newsprint and broadcasted over airwaves, war news was inescapable.

The *Tribune* reported, "Thirty bombers were lost from the force of Flying Fortresses and Liberators which blasted the Stuka dive-bomber plant at Bremen and submarine installations at nearby Vegesack."[10]

"Fortresses and Liberators dropped 5,400 tons of high explosives on European targets during 11 missions on 10 operational days, an increase of 53 per cent over August, shot down 262 enemy planes, probably shot down 43 and damaged 115. Eighty-five Fortresses and Liberators were lost, well under 4 per cent of the total involved."[11]

I did the math—eighty-five Fortresses and Liberators times ten equals 850 crewmen, just like that, lost. Even though the losses for these eleven missions were only 4 percent of the total involved, it was still too many. The magnitude of the accruing death toll was alarming.

After the war, the death tolls revealed the grim reality of the entire aerial war. Statistics are debatable, but it has been widely quoted that percentagewise the Eighth Air Force lost more men in the war than the Marine Corps and navy combined. Overall, and figures vary, total airmen losses for World War II outnumbered losses for most branches of the military.

On a positive note, in 1943 the Allies had gained the upper hand on the waters of the Atlantic. So with dwindling interference from menacing German U-boats, the Battle of the Atlantic was one triumph for the Allies. But the war was not over.

Whether by air, by land, or by sea, all branches of the military fought on, facing diverse battle perils, challenges, uncertainties, and, unfortunately, casualties. On the ground, troops fought long, hard battles on more than one front, and casualties mounted. And once Allied troops finally defeated German forces in North Africa, they eventually launched their way into Axis Europe from the southern part of the continent. Allied forces gained a foothold in the lower boot of Italy and, battle after battle, slowly drove the Germans northward. As southern Italy fell into the hands of the Allies, the Fifteenth Air Force soon moved in and set up bases.

It seemed that Hitler had bitten off more than he could chew. News from the Eastern Front reported, "The Red Army is in motion along the entire 1,000-mile front from the Baltic to the Black Sea."[12] And nearly one month later, "Premier Josef Stalin proclaimed jubilantly—tonight the Allies have driven Germany to 'the verge of catastrophe,' and assured his people 'victory now is near, but to win it great exertions still are necessary ...' Stalin said the Red Army has killed at least 1,800,000 Germans in the last year, and by its victories at Stalingrad and in the Ukraine has 'decided the defeat of the German army.'"[13]

Nonetheless, the war on the Eastern Front entered its third harsh winter, and the carnage strewn on Russia's frozen landscape was incomprehensible. In contrast, barren beaches and malaria-infested jungle islands of the balmy South Pacific were strewn with their own gruesome carnage as the U.S. Navy, Marines, Army, and Allied troops fought one bloody battle after another against the fight-to-the-finish Japanese warriors.

Meanwhile, war news on December 7, 1943, in the *Hastings Daily Tribune* claimed, "The second anniversary of Pearl Harbor finds the American strategic position in the Pacific good, with our armed forces in place and set on a wide outer arc for the advance to Tokyo."[14]

The year 1943 drew to a close with these words, "General Dwight D. Eisenhower, commander of Allied armies massing for invasion of Western Europe, declared confidently today 'we will win the European war in 1944. The only thing needed for us to win the European war is for every man and woman all the way from the front lines to the remotest hamlet of our two countries to do his or her full duty.'" [15]

For Stanley, the New Year and the third phase of operational training coincided. Upon completion of the last phase of operational training, there would be no graduation ceremony, no pomp and circumstance marches—just marching orders. Someone higher in the chain of command gave the orders, sending crews to unknown parts of the world to face their greatest challenge of all—air warfare—and an education never to be equaled in any classroom.

"We have moved again," Stanley wrote, "just thirty or forty miles. It [Drane Field] is just a branch of MacDill Field. Haven't been to the village of Lakeland yet to see what it has to offer. They say it is a pretty good soldier's town but not as large as Tampa. There wasn't even a bowling alley in Tampa. About all a man could do was go to a picture show or to church. So our 12 o'clock curfew wasn't much of an imposition, and I didn't do much. Received your telegram on the first, mom. Think you're smart, don't you? I didn't know you could send messages of greetings. If you have asked any questions that I haven't answered, ask 'em again, will you?"

Jan. 12, 1944

Dear folks:

It's a good thing that some of these ships aren't in working order now and then or you might never hear from me. Right now we are having two ground school sessions a day, besides flying, so that we can complete a required number of hours in such things as chemical warfare before going over.

We're doing our last-minute preparation, but I don't know what the hurry is. I always figgered the last minute was the best time for that. I think that is a Dwyer characteristic. Yes, pop, the typewriter works fine. It's only errors are cockpit errors, either skull or thumbnail.

Ralph got married last night. He managed to get a pass till today noon for the occasion, so naturally, I was not present. The girl was from Utah. Her ma took her to Phoenix to catch a through train then at the last minute gave in to her curiosity and came along. She had never seen Ralph. He will be off again tonight till tomorrow noon. The Miss and Mrs. were in town seven hours before ever finding him and probably would be waiting yet if it hadn't been for your uncle Dudley. I happened to be in a telephone booth in the officers' club in town when she rang, trying every place she knew that he might be. Fact of the matter was, as usual, he was on the post, but no one here cared enough to help her find him when she called. All they had to do was call the BOQ [Bachelor Officer Quarters].

Just received another Christmas package. It was a billfold from Theron and his wife. Finally got Aileen's package after it had been on the road for three weeks. The cookies were rather dry. Will try not to wait so long to write next time. Harold probably beat me a little this time.

LovestaN

Letters continued regularly.

Dear folks:

'Tis a day off, and youns are number hut on my list. Dale, my copilot, and I got a room at a hotel here in town and brought the typewriter and equipment along. I have a powerful lot of writing to do, and if I don't get it done today, I probably won't before I go across. But the letters had to wait till I got some long sleeping in last night. I was really pooed out. Yesterday and the day before we did two simulated combat missions that stretched out longer than most of our training missions do. The first was nearly seven hours long, and the one yesterday was six. And if you think that's not a lot of formation, you're mistook. We take off at half-minute intervals, then after getting a ways in the air, we make a 180-degree turn so that the last ships can catch up with the first. And from there on, it's all formation till we peel off to land.

But these two trips were extra special and weren't nearly so hard on the constitution as they might have been. In the first place, it was your old man's private ship. Was assigned it the day before and was allowed to spend the afternoon playing around with it and getting it ready to fly. It's super and really a pleasure to fly since it hasn't had a bunch of punks flying it. And its conveniences are numberless. In the first place, it has a good heating system. And that is the battle, or a good share of it. The mission altitudes were twenty thousand, and it was great sport to be able to look at the outside temperature gauge reading twenty below then unzip my flight suit 'cause I was too darned warm. On the first mission, we were well back in the formation, and it's rather hard to fly good formation there. But yesterday, we were on our operation officer's left wing at the front of the formation, and flying there is really an art.

Still haven't decided definitely on a name yet, in spite of everybody's suggestions. I think I could get a lot of fine publicity up K-State way if I name it the Wildcat then let the powers that be up there know about it. My crew is as proud of it as a new baby and handles it just that way.

It still looks like we are going to England. Or close by. We won't know until we get there, and you will have my APO number before I know what it is. We filled out some change of address forms that will be sent to you before we arrive over there. And that time isn't so far away anymore. And now, at this unearthly hour of almost noon, I gotta go get some breakfast.

Love,
natS

The only place in the airplane that had heat, as I recall, was the cockpit. It was much like the old Model A Ford. In the 17, a cover was put over the exhaust pipes on the number two and number three engines, and the air that was ducted between the stack and the cover was piped into the cockpit. Worked sometimes. The rest of the crew had individual heated suits that they plugged into the electrical system at their station. I can't remember if every station had one or if some of the gunners just piled on more clothes. Some of both, probably. Anyhow, on one training flight at Rapid City, it was below zero when my crew took off on a night-training mission. In higher altitudes, the air temperature was always subzero. The folks had driven up to Rapid City to spend the weekend with me. It was around Christmas 1944. They'd gotten a hotel room, and I had their car so I could join them after we got down. During the flight, our ball turret gunner's heated suit shorted out. Needless to say, he was hot in one spot and getting real cold over the rest of his body. His crewmates cranked the ball into position and got him into the plane. He was so cold and shook so much that he couldn't hold a cup of coffee without shaking it all out. We had enough heat in the cockpit to get him thawed out, and we landed shortly after that. I jumped into the car and went into town and up to the folks' room. I think there was a roll-away bed in their room for me, but I told the folks to move over—I was going to crawl between them to get warm. Dad laughed about that years later when he called me the coldest human he'd ever felt.

In those days, we didn't have the luxury of pressurized planes. Each crewman had his own oxygen mask fitted to him specifically. They were quite uncomfortable and would ice up from condensation. The temperature at the altitudes we flew—between twenty thousand and thirty thousand feet—sometimes got anywhere from thirty to fifty below zero. It was quite a chore to keep everything working right. We assigned one crew member to have a crew check often in order to keep track of everybody and make sure they were okay. The check was done by intercom. More than once, somebody would not respond, and therefore another crewman would take the portable oxygen to whoever's station and revive the unresponsive crewman. Oxygen masks were put on around ten thousand feet and remained on for the duration of the flight, usually six or seven hours.

The following week, Stanley wrote:

> Just a word edgewise. We're about to wind up this training business and get on to bigger things. Don't know just when we're leaving, but probably the end of the week. We're going to staging in Georgia. Won't be there long, I guess. Staging, as I understand it, is a bunch of tests given to determine if a crew is ready to go to combat. No one seems to know about it to any extent. Don't know whether they make it tough on a guy or not. Don't think I have reason to worry anyhoo.
>
> Have been doing a lot of flying. Day before yesterday we had a wing formation of thirty-six planes. We went into Georgia to do camera bombings. Incidentally, your old man was out in front of the formation. I had a wing pilot, a captain; the wing navigator, a major; and the wing bombardier, another major with me. Tomorrow we are

going to have another big formation, but I don't know the details yet. My plane is now undergoing a hundred-hour inspection, and I'm not sure it will be ready by then.

A few days ago we took our long, overwater flight. We went to a small island off the coast of Yucatan, Mexico, and back. We were on the way almost nine hours. The automatic pilot really got a workout that day. And the day, in spite of the length, was rather easy on us.

Just got a letter from Pearl and Dusty. Guess he is trying to get out of his job. She wasn't sure what they were going to do if he succeeded. Maybe go home for a couple of months. Hope grandpappy is getting along alright. Tell Grace and Gayle I thank them a lot for the gift even though I haven't shown it since. Will try to write before I leave. Will keep you in touch.

Jan. 27, 1944

Dear folks:

The age of miracles is not past. Upon receiving this, you will agree with me on that. Sometimes I wonder if I'm not the world's worst as far as letter writing is concerned. Then I look at this stack before me, and I am assured that the assumption is correct.

I guess mom and pop are headed home now after their stay in Mankato. They undoubtedly had a good visit there, but mom probably didn't enjoy it as much as she might have at some other time. At the moment, she is worrying somewhat about her two wayward boys. Mamas always worry about one who is learning to fly, especially one as young as Harold. And the older son, having given her no end of worry during flight training, is getting ready to take off for parts unknown. We are scheduled to depart from these United States before very long. Of course, we don't know where we are going but assume that we will be in on the windup of the situation in Europe. We've been flying a lot of simulated combat missions lately, some with as many as thirty-six ships in the formation, and I think we're about ripe. We have our own ships now, the ones we will fly across, and have almost the required amount of time in them. I haven't named mine yet; guess it will have to be—shall I say—a bastard ship, since I can't think of a suitable name for it.

Still don't know if we are going to get a little time off before going across but doubt that we will. If we do, it won't be for any great length of time, perhaps not even long enough to be home for a few days. Had hopes, lately, we would get to fly home and stay for a couple of days, but someone at the top of the ladder decided we would be limited to landing at Third Air Force fields. And the closest one to home is Oklahoma City. And that would hardly do for the short time allotted to us.

Those in charge of the shipments at the port of embarkation are going to have to talk pretty fast if they are to convince me that I shouldn't take my typewriter along. Pop got it for me a couple of months ago, and I'm well attached to it now. Never go to town on our day off but what I take it with me. I'm hoping that I'll have more time to use it when we get over there.

Would like to have you keep me posted on the goings on in your part of the country when I get an APO number. Always like to hear from you. Till I see you again, the best of everything to you. And when I return I shall invite myself to see you and shall wear out my welcome.

Love,
Stan

Feb. 5, 1944

Dear folks:

Life is but a bowl of cherries, la-de-da. At least this one has
been for some three days now. We were given a four day leave. We
had hoped for half a dozen, during which I would have had time to dash
home for a couple. But four would have hardly been sufficient. Also
we were limited to a travel radius of five hundred miles. Most of the
gang dashed off for near-by resorts and cities, but my navigator and I
holed up here in the Terrace, saved ourselves the travel time, and have
had a mighty fine time doing nothing.

Of course during the stay I have spent no little amount of time
with a sweet little girl here. Have been going with her since the
first week we had time off. Have grown quite attached to her, and will
miss her when I'm gone. And I might add that she is rather fond of
the old man. To the extent that she would have liked to have spent
these few days honeymooning. She's got an awfully nice family, all of
which thought about as much of me as she did. The mother got out of bed
last night to tell me good-bye just in case she didn't see me again
before I left. And the older daughter requested that she be wakened
when we came home so that she could. She lost her husband in the war
about six months ago.

Now xfor the requested statistics. I can't off-hand give you the
addresses of my entire crew, so will limit that part of it to the home
state. Co-pilot, who has been through the same training as I since
Santa Ana and who is a rated first pilot, Manley H. Dale, S. Dakota.
Navigator, graduate of Dartmouth, and a mighty fine guy, Walter R. Swan,
Beverly, near Boston, Mass. Bombardier, one of the best in the group,
and a small scale manufacturer in civilian life, Allan A. Klute of
St. Louis. Engineer, to be master-sergeant when we get across, John J.
Boros of New York. Assistant Engineer, Gail Popplewell, from the sticks
of Missouri, and naturally a good gunner. Third engineer and assistant
radio operator, jack of all trades and probably the most valuable man on
the crew because of it, Donald O. Pratt, Iowa. Radio operator, George
Mitchell, also a student at Dartmouth, and a good kid, from N. Jersey.
Armorer and tail gunner, a fine boy of I think Arabian decent from
xFresno Calif., John J. Papazian. Ball Turret Gunner, as eager and as
easy to get along with as any, Darris Oldfather. That, I think, counts
nine--nine men who form as good a crew as could be picked out of the
group by concentrated study and test.

Perhaps nothing so valuable will be gained from having been in the
air corps as the associations I have made during these months. The
officers are of the best, and the enlisted men better than average by
far. It has been a pleasure, expecially to one who was in the service
prior to air corps training and is acquainted with army life in other
phases. My better friends for some odd reason are almost all married.
You have heard of course of Ralph. And that he was married recently.
He as a lovely wife, and one who when he is gone will return home to ma
and pa and wait patiently for him to return. There aren't many like
her any more. Another couple with which I have spent no little amount
of time are Rosser Little, and wife Cora, of Atlanta Georgia. Both are
graduates of Georgia U. He was in building and loan business before the
war, a practical, shrewd business man, a fine guy, and once Georgia State
golf champion. She was from quite a wealthy family, was a debutant, and
I might say in spite of that, one of the grandest personalities I have
met, a girl without an enemy in the world. The Rossers have been married
five years, and still are on their honeymoon.

I doubt that I can xname half a dozen acquaintences during my life time that compare with these. At the moment I recall these few. Gerv Keogh, tops in young manhood. H. B. Summers, whom you are acquainted with, Ralph Lashbrook; whom you know; and some of my college chums. This list of cou se includes the relatives, all of them swell people, and a constant reminder that of my heritage I can be justly proud. Oh yes, I cannot omit Harry Cuthbertson from this list, the fellow whom I went through basic training with, went to the 35th Division Headquarters with, and who followed me into cadet training some two weeks later. He xgraduated from Stuttgart Ark. and since has been kept there as instructor. He, as is the entire family, whom you remember I visited while in Garder field, is literally inclined, and a master of the language, and it is a great pleasure to correspond with him. To this list I add his sister, Janice, the only girl on this list incidentally, and the type I hope to fall in love with someday. She is real America, as I want it, clean and real clear through, and lovely.

Now for a small detail that as a result of my friendships needs be taken care of. It has been requested by Theron Newell, that in the event that youns in the future are recipient of a telegram from the powers that begins like this "We regret to inform you" that he be notified of such. That, I would say, is a superfluous request, if requests can be superfluous; besides I don't think that is spelled correctly. Anyhoo, to carry out his request, is address is 1704 F. St., Vancouver Wash. Incidentally, he has now been re-classified as 1-A, in spite of his asthma. But he has not been idle in the mean time. He has been making some hundred dollars a week since the outbreak of the war, has married, and has picked out and is able to buy an acreage near Vancouver overlooking the bay and that part of the picturesque state, on which he intends to build his permanent home. Chances are that his request has been thought of by otheres, but by those whom not knowing my family hesitated to say. Included are these: the Cuthbertsons in Taft, Doc Summers, 57 E. 88th St. N. Y.; Margaret Wells, 2165 N. Highland Ave., Hollywood; R. R. Lashbrook, K.S.C.; of course the Davidsons; Dorothea Stratton, 1844 E. 76th St. Kansas City, Mo.; Cora Little, 205 Lawrence St., Marietta, Ga. I could go on like that for some paragraphs, but as I said before, think it is a waste of good paper and ink. In the meantime, just worry your heads about how you can possibly feed me as I shall request on the leave after the required number of missions, or after Germany folds. Remember, my plans are to wear out my welcome.

Have a lot of letters to do this aft. And doubt that I can be spared tonight. So I shall be on. If we can send mail from the port of embarkation, then I shall. If I don't then you will know that it is not permitted, but that you will hear from me as soon as I reach a destination, which incidentally might be a week or a month.

It was fun talking to you last night. I will be look'ng forward to the next one. Till then I don't want a gray hair shed, unless its caused by worrying about those victuals.

Greatest of Love,

Stan

P.S. I have neglected, though I intented each letter to tell you, that our commanding officer is one Colonel Kurtz, whose capers in the "Swoose" was the subject of the great book "Queens die Proudly". If you haven't read it, then to do so will much better describe to you the organization in which I shall go across. Yesterday the girls and I attended the christening of Swoose II, which will lead us to battle.

8

⸿

Italy

The natives are working overtime keeping life and limb together.
—*Stanley N. Dwyer in a letter dated March 15, 1944*

Once we were issued flight plans, we knew where we would be stationed "over there." Orders were "top secret," often issued in a sealed envelope to be opened en route. My brother and his crew staged out of Georgia; we staged out of Lincoln, Nebraska. Everybody met in a big room or hangar, and then six or eight crews, mine included, were called out and given keys to a brand-new B-17 to fly over to our base in England as part of the Eighth Air Force. The rest of the crews, probably a couple hundred, went by boat. As it turned out, they beat us there.

From Lincoln, we flew to Bangor, Maine, and then to Newfoundland, where we were detained for several days while we searched for one of the crews that didn't land. We never did find the airplane. On the way from Newfoundland to Prestwick, Scotland, we sprung a leak in the fuel system. Jack Noe, my radioman, called me back to the radio room and raised up the floorboards to show me where all the radio stuff sat in gasoline. Needless to say, we turned off all electrical, and when it was time to land in Scotland, we put the landing gears down manually. It was quite a job. As I recall, it took about five hundred turns of the crank while straddling the bomb bay. We dropped the ship off in Scotland and took a train to London, or close to it, and we were trucked out to our assigned bomb group.

Stan, on the other hand, assigned to the 463rd Bomb Group of the Fifteenth Air Force, had a similar trip, only he went south through Brazil and then across the Atlantic to Africa on his way to Celone Field near Foggia, Italy.

Feb. 19, 1944

Dear folks:

Somewhere in Brazil—and I might add, it is rather warm here. I never thought when I was in the southern hemisphere before that I'd be there again so soon.

My boys are getting a big kick out of the trip. None of them have been out of the States before. Now they have seen the Amazon, the dense South American jungles, and have crossed the equator. I have an idea we all have seen more clouds in the past couple of days than the rest of our lives. It is quite obvious to us why the Amazon is so huge. At times we have wondered whether we were in the air or in the ocean.

The ship has been performing very nicely. We have had no trouble, and the captain who is riding with me in place of my copilot says it's probably one of the best in the group.

Don't know whether or not I have mentioned it before, but I'd like for you to keep the letters I write on this trip as on the other. They ought to make good reading sometime.

Will write you from hither and thither.

Love,
Stan

On February 24, 1944, Stanley wrote home:

This time it's North Africa, and it is cold enough to be Iceland. We've been in sandstorms and rainstorms since we got here. I'll be glad when we get where we're going and get settled down. And I can dig out the typewriter.

We have been here long enough to get fairly well acquainted with Arabian life. The boys, who didn't believe all that stuff in books, find it quite true. And they're having a lot of fun. We get off the post in the afternoon.

And Stanley wrote more from Africa during the first week of March 1944.

This is to advise you that your wandering boy is still, well, ornery as ever, getting fat, not doing much in particular other than taking in the sights in the city. We were supposed to fly a practice mission this afternoon, but the weather looked like it was going to act up, so it was called off.

You should see my "den." I am sitting on a cot with my typewriter on an ammunition box. I have one bag full of junk heaped around me that I had to unpack to get at the machine. In front of me our homemade gas stove is burning merrily. Beyond that my bombardier just turned over to get his afternoon shut-eye. The light to see by comes down through the hole through which the stovepipe sticks.

Only a few miles from us are age-old ruins that we used to study about in ancient history. We walked over there the first afternoon. People have paid thousands of dollars to view the ruins that we saw for free. From atop the structure we could view the construction of ancient man and the destruction of modern man. There are a number of wrecked English and German planes around.

The city is typical. Filth and poverty, even worse than that of the seemingly uncivilized Arabs during peacetime, is very noticeable. An American here, like I have found in other parts of the world, is a lord. The American soldier is pretty much a sucker as far as bartering is concerned, but I suppose that is good in that it keeps us from having native starvation on our hands in the areas we have taken from the enemy. We find the natives friendly to the Allied cause, also to Americans in particular because, basically, they are honest, pay for what they get, and like to give to those in need.

I suppose Beth is semi-settled down to married life by now. And Pearl and Dusty are settled. And Aileen is growing. Sent her a birthday greeting from down the line. Would like to know how Harold is getting along but don't expect mail for a couple of weeks yet. If he's still in there pitching, then he should be over the biggest hump by now.

The Fifteenth Air Force, comprised of bomber groups of B-17s and B-24s—the heavies—and fighter groups, moved into southern Italy after the Allies battled and pushed the retreating Germans farther north. Thus, most missions flown from Italy targeted southern and southeastern Europe, targets out of range of the Eighth Air Force and RAF bombers in England.

Stan flew with the 775th Bomb Squadron, one of the four squadrons within the 463rd Bomb Group of the Fifteenth Air Force. The 463rd Bomb Group was made up of the 772nd, 773rd, 774th, and the 775th squadrons. There were roughly ten to twelve planes per squadron, four squadrons in a bomb group, and one bomb group, about fifty planes—approximately six hundred men, including ground crews—assigned to one airfield.

Lieutenant Colonel Frank Kurtz commanded Stan's 463rd Bomb Group. Colonel Kurtz started out early in the war in the South Pacific, right after Pearl

Harbor, when our scanty forces battled the Japanese as the prepared Japanese made their move to control the Philippines and conquer the rest of the South Pacific area. During that time, Colonel Kurtz flew the famous B-17, "The Swoose," and ultimately, Stan's bomb group acquired the name, the "Swoose Group."

Down the road in our search, we learned that Stanley's bomb squadron, the 775th, was commanded by a man of Irish ancestry, Captain Robert H. Allyn. It seems, however, that the squadron was nicknamed "Allyn's Irish Orphans," due to the lack of any other Irishmen in the group.

March 15, 1944

Dear folks:

Somewhere in Italy, and I think I can safely say that my letters for some time in the future will bear that statement or same may be assumed. We have set up housekeeping and are pretty well fixed up for comfortable living. This is the second time I have had the typewriter out. This time it will stay awhile. We brought the stove along that we made at the base where I wrote last. It was a wise move since there was a shortage here. It is a little colder here, but the weather in general is much more pleasant. Today seemed like the first day of spring, and I hope it is. Weather has held up operations in this theater quite a bit recently.

We started ground school today; in fact, we have another class at eight tonight. Hope we can get into gear right soon. There's nothing here for recreation other than what the army provides. The natives are working overtime keeping life and limb together; they are war-starved and hardly present a cheery spectacle to a visitor.

So, let me ask you a couple of questions. Is candy rationed to you? If not, can you get it in any amount? It is said that with a request from a serviceman overseas that requested articles may be purchased and sent over. If the answer to the first question is no and the second is yes, then I would like for you to send me a box of preferably almond Hershey's. Our candy purchases are rationed, and more for that reason than any other, we have created quite a sweet tooth.

We still don't have our mail. It is in the countryside, someplace, and the Colonel is making an effort of finding where. But up to now, we don't know whether ma still loves us or not.

One of the old heads here came in a while ago and started spinning yarns. And when there is conversation of bomber and fighter nature, there's nothing one can do but listen. My first impression of this business is that it is darned interesting. And we're all eager.

I reckon I better dash over to class. Can't say much but will try to write oftener from now on.

Love,
Stan

Sometimes, crews fresh from the States flew with combat veteran crews for a mission or two to get experience. It was possible that Stan did just that, and in the beginning of our search, we weren't sure when he flew his first mission.

Usually, something turned up that helped fill in the blanks and put Stanley's letters into context. Grandma had received a letter from the War Department in 1945 awarding one of Stanley's Oak Leaf Clusters. The citation read:

"Oak-Leaf Cluster to Air Medal—'For meritorious achievement in aerial flight while participating in sustained operational activities against the enemy from 19 March 1944 to 6 April 1944.'"

Also in Stanley's trunk, I found *The Fighting 463rd*, a book, we presumed, Granddad got his hands on after the war in their quest for answers. Only after the war, with declassified records and personal accounts, did the heretofore little-known mission details offer a more complete war story.

The Fighting 463rd described, "The Group's introduction to war was a sudden and drastic one. On March 18th the 775th lost a crew that was flying with the 2nd Bombardment Group on a mission to Villa Orba, Italy. A large force of German fighters had attacked the formation, downing one of our ships. The next day while accompanying the 97th Bombardment Group on a mission to Klagenfurt, Austria, the plane piloted by Maj. George Burges, commanding officer of the 772nd, was rammed by another bomber. Both crashed into the sea. The loss of its entire operational staff dealt a hard blow to the squadron. On the same day the 775th lost another ship."[16]

Reading between the lines, by the time Stanley wrote letters on March 21, 1944, we assumed he'd flown at least one mission.

March 21, 1944

Dear folks:
Mail and more mail, and then a bit of mail for a change. A few days ago we received the first batch of letters in which was included fourteen for me, no two of which were from the same person. The latest I have now was mailed on the 24th, if I can read it correctly.

You mentioned that Harold should be flying P-38s by now. That rather surprised me. However, I hereby voice my approval of his choice. There once was a time when they were just another airplane to me. But them days are gone forever. No man who ever flew in this theater failed to fall in love with it on their first mission, or shortly thereafter.

Just a word about some of the details involved in the operation of a combat organization. When a man is missing from his organization, he is, for the purpose of records, "missing in action." The report of that, sent to relatives shortly thereafter, creates absolutely no reason for worry. There are umpty-ump stumps upon which a man might sit his pimply butt other than those around his tent. Men downed in enemy territory, of course, are interned, and in this theater they are taken care of better than might be expected. In neutral countries they are interned, and of course, in friendly territory sent back to their organization. So let's have a cease to the anxiety back there on the home front. Those persons whom I find worrying will be subject to sound paddling by me and thereafter will be forced to bake an angel food cake with an even dozen eggs.

Beth's letter was very nice. But she failed to say much about the marriage, which I was under the impression was a subject that was dwelled upon to great lengths by newly married girls. Aileen's letter contained a thanx for a birthday gram I sent while on the journey. Harold's letter was not recent but was the first I had received from him since shortly after he had soloed.

Keep the way from your house to the bank clear for you are to be making trips there right regularly. There isn't place one to spend money here except the PX. And one spends very little there. Gotta get on.

> Loads of love,
> Stan

Cousin Beth, who thought of Stanley as an older brother, had saved one of his letters.

> March 21, 1944

Dearest Beth:

First of all, a belated congratulations to you, the both of you, and a wish that your marriage will bring you nothing but happiness.

True, it has been a long time since you and I talked face to face. And it is strange that we should have such a complete understanding.

But it has been that way. And many times I have wished that our paths might cross. Someday they will, and I'm looking forward to it. Also to meeting one of the luckiest guys in the world.

I don't know where to begin on a brief resumé of my activities in weeks past. Guess the beginning is as a good place as any. We packed up bag and baggage, took off in the middle of the night for faraway destinations. Dawn found us well beyond the borders of God's country. Two of the three continents we have been on since, I had visited before, and no doubt I failed to feel the thrill that was apparent in the rest of my crew. But it was fun for me to watch the reactions of the boys. They were somewhat bewildered at finding the English language useless but soon picked up sign and symbol that enabled them to communicate with the natives. They have been disappointed in those natives, but said reaction has made them very much aware that their own is a great nation and that they are really fighting for a cause.

The natives live only from one day to the next and are fortunate being able, under the circumstances, to keep life and limb together. Theirs is only an existence until the war and its aftereffects are written in history books. For some that will be never in their lifetime, for there are some wounds that only death will heal. Be thankful that the war is not within the bounds of the great U.S.A.

We have gotten our feet wet, so to speak, since arrival here. We know for what has been the intense training for a year and a half. And we know now that every bit of that training is needed for success here.

Gotta go fly. Write to me often, will you? Your letters are a source of much pleasure, and I look forward to receiving them. Best of everything to you.

Love,
Stan

March 21, 1944

Dear Aileen and Bill:

Received two most welcome letters from you last night and will answer the both of them with one stone today. The first day we got mail, about a week ago, I got fourteen and have gotten eleven since. So my hands are full, and I guess they will have to call a halt in the war until I can get caught up. Just in case they don't, though, I shall use every spare minute thru out the day and night. At the moment,

I am burning a candle (only at one end) rather than the lamp that is too far away from the sack, the softest spot in the tent.

Don't assume from the preceding paragraph that I dislike the task ahead. I don't know how one in overseas duty could be more content than in mail knee-deep to a camel. Dusty says he may have to rename his kitten Harry instead of Sally. That may be excusable in his case, but you watch your step. I insist on knowing from the start whether I'm an uncle or an uncless. Was surprised to hear that Harold is probably flying P-38s by now. He has my approval. There is no one in this theater who has less than adoration for that ship. Guns are blazing away, then a couple of 38s pass by, and that's all. Firing ceases. I'm going to marry one.

I gather that mom is worrying herself overtime. Wish there were some way to prevent it, but I doubt that such would be possible. If she should some bright day receive a notice from unc to the "missing in action" effect, she will have pups. I have explained to her that such gives no appreciable cause to worry, that no matter where one is other than his organization he is considered missing, that there are a jillion places one might land a plane or bail out. But I have an idea that my explanation has been to no avail. So I shall have to complete my share of this job, I guess, and dash on home so that she can get a night's rest.

I doubt that a description of our trip would be of particular interest to you. You have gotten many such descriptions before, and once one is out of the States, his descriptions are about the same. Note—I am practicing writing the word description. Just got word that I'm due at a meeting in ten minutes, so I better hit the road. Will write again as soon as I can, tho time does not lay heavy upon our hands.

Love, and that's for the three of you,
Stan

I found a letter Stanley wrote to Lou and Gertie, Grandma's sister. Bits and pieces of his letter told more.

Dear Lou and Gertie:

Received your most welcome letter, not at the time or place that you had hoped, but perhaps where and when it was even more welcome. I am using every free moment to dig out via typewriter. The machine was picked up by the pa, and I was able to bring it along. Don't know what I would do without it.

Yes, I'm sure that you are right in that ma is doing a good bit of overtime worrying. Have tried every verbal means of convincing her that such need not be, but I'm sure that my words have been to no avail. It's Mother Nature, I guess, and I doubt that she will cease till I again park my big feet under the family table.

Life here is not at its best. It would be impossible for unk Sam to provide American standard living conditions in every faraway outpost. Realizing that, we have no complaint to make in regard to conditions. We feed well, have comparatively nice quarters, and are provided with such necessities as capable medical aid. There is little recreation here, only that which is provided by the army. We have an officers' club on the post and one in town. The native people offer no form of recreation other than English-speaking pictures. The life of the native of a nation that has been invaded and reinvaded is one of keeping life and limb together through unceasing effort. Theirs is a country that will take years to rebuild, and we may be thankful that the war has not taken place within the boundaries of our homeland.

Other than that, there is little that I can tell. A book could be written about each day's activities, but that book would be more valuable to an enemy who might intercept the news than it would be to folks back home. So we shall all get together after it is over and have a huge session. In the meantime, it is great to receive mail from you.

Best,
Stan

"Each day's activities"—it was no secret what was happening. War news was plentiful—and censored and stingy on specific details and virtually void of stories from behind-the-scenes. Maybe Grandma and Granddad were better off not knowing everything. As long as they received letters from both of their sons, it gave some reassurance that everything was okay. The anticipation that built between letters must have been nerve racking.

March 27, 1944

Dear folks:

Have been getting mail recently, as regularly as a human being. Of course, some of it has failed to arrive in the proper sequence, but little by little I can piece it together and make a semblance of a train of thought.

But in all the letters, I have not found the one that told what is going wrong with my ma. I have read a number of times that she isn't feeling up to par and have failed to mention it thinking that I would hear what the trouble is. Young lady, you are hereby receiving a verbal paddling. I would postpone the event except for the fact that one letter indicated that you were back in the saddle again, or at least you had one foot in the stirrup.

Seems to me that you folks should be headed right into some warm weather by now. I hope our weather here is no indication. Spring seems to be way over the snow-capped mountain. And from your letters, I gather that there might have been an addition to the family by now. I was under the impression that it was not due yet, but perhaps I have allowed a couple of months to slip by unnoticed. Time is really fleeing, and here it is nearly payday again. Will send practically the two months' return to you, including the extra remunerations.

Activity has been rather slow recently. Most of our time has been occupied with training. Seems the army never believes in calling a halt to training, and I reckon they're pretty much right.

Have a bit of straightening around to do tonight so better get at it. Otherwise I'll be in the midst when the rest of the gang is trying to sleep. Is it possible that you folks aren't helping Harold recover from homesickness by reminding him of it?

Love,
Stan

Back in the air March 30, 1944, B-17s from the 463rd Bomb Group—including planes from Stanley's 775th Squadron, Allyn's Irish Orphans—flew and bombed the Imotski Airdrome in Yugoslavia—a milk run. Twice, the 775th was part of a contingent that bombed the marshalling yards in Brod, Yugoslavia. On the first raid, April 2, antiaircraft flak found targets, and crewmen were severely wounded; however, the mission on April 3 was tabbed another "milk run."[17]

"Milk run" or not, I can't imagine any mission for those "fly boys" amounting to just another day at the office.

From my experience in England, in the dark, wee hours of the morning the day of a mission, the orderly woke us. He shined a flashlight in your face and said, "Sign here!" That cleared his tail if you didn't show up. I didn't know anyone ever not to show, but it was awful hard for some people—they were apprehensive about going.

B-17 Flying Fortresses of the Fifteenth Air Force. The tail marking—the *Y* on the slice of pie background—designates Stanley's 463rd Bomb Group. The origin of this photo is unknown. I found it in the pages of Granddad's newspapers.

Stanley asked in a letter home on April 3:

> Am wondering if I am an uncle yet? And of what? Word in your letter received today indicated that Harold would graduate in a week. I assume that since the letter was so aged that it was from primary. I have an idea he is a hot pilot by now—signified as H.P. in the corps.
>
> Little has happened since I wrote the other day, other than the fact that we have been hard at work during off-hours expanding our tent. Had visions of laying a floor, but material is so scarce that we used what lumber we had to make the extension. Put up a good clothes rack and tomorrow will shovel out a path to my bunk. I think, probably, this will be our last move-about, and we'll start living like kings as soon as we get straightened around. I hope, too, to find my hat tomorrow, even if it is at the bottom of the heap. It has taken a terrible beating since Dyersburg where first it was sat upon. Will keep the letters flowing, but material for same is as scarce as hen's teeth. Hope your reception is better than on this end. If not, then don't be surprised at long durations of voidness.

"'Allyn's Irish Orphans,' headed by Major Allyn and crew, led the 'Swoose Group' on a very successful mission against the Nis, Yugoslavia, marshalling yards, 5 April 1944."[18] "Takeoff was at 1152. Our planes were over the target at 1449 and dropped 112½ tons of bombs from 23,000 feet. Twenty-eight enemy planes were sighted, but none attacked the formation. Bombing was reported to be very good. All planes back safely."[19]

On the same day, other crews from the Fifteenth Air Force bombed targets near Ploesti, Romania, and several bombers were lost. "The 451st Group's 34 Liberators were intercepted by waves totaling 85 enemy aircraft and had to bomb through a maelstrom of intense and accurate flak. They lost five bombers ... The mission thereby launched the Fifteenth on a campaign against German oil and also began the battle to destroy Ploesti, the enemy's largest oil and refinery center."[20]

Operational on April 6, Stanley's 463rd group took off from Celone Field and targeted Zagreb, Yugoslavia. "Heavy cloud cover made bombing unfeasible. Thirty to forty Me 109s and Fw 190s attacked the Group from the rear and level in a line abreast formation, firing rockets and machine guns. Two of our ships went down, one was lost to flak, the other to fighters. Seven chutes were reported from one of the planes."[21] The very next day—under heavy, accurate, and intense antiaircraft fire—the 463rd and other bomb groups attacked marshalling yards at Treviso, Italy.

Bomber crews took off from Celone Field, but there were no guarantees of landing there. For Sargeant Raymond Crouch of the 463rd, one particular mission went like this: "Our ship was burning. The aluminum skin was melting away from the ribs. My pilot came running back to the waist section, kicked me in the pants, and yelled, 'This is too hot for comfort. Better get out.' I started to bail out when I remembered I didn't have my gloves. I ran back into the fire, put on my gloves, and jumped. About five seconds later the ship blew up."[22]

I reread Stanley's April 8 V-Mail. "This won't be a letter, just a tracer," he wrote.

> Business is so good here that we seldom get to town to take a shower. Well, maybe it's not that bad, but we have a day off today and are going in right away. So this will be brief. When we are there, I will try to find some place to send a cable or Mother's Day flowers in the hopes that you can have something from me that is somewhat recent ... Had a letter from Harold yesterday, but the squirt sent it free and was sent from primary. First thing I know, he'll be an ace, and I won't have him to basic yet. Your unc is now eligible for the air medal having done the required number of missions. 'Twas a breeze though ... Everything here is lovely. Have no complaints to make. Am looking forward to coming back to the States before too long a time. You'd better begin saving up those points.

According to the book *Allyn's Irish Orphans,* a copy once in Granddad's possession, Easter services on Sunday, April 9, were conducted by the group chaplain on the base. Some men attended Easter services in Foggia.

Stanley corresponded with Aileen:

> Letters keep right on coming. One from California made the trip in eleven days. I have gotten eight in the last three days. And that's mighty good for a guy over here who doesn't have much else to look forward to. I even dislike going to town over here and spend practically all my time in a tent or an airplane. And don't mind it as much as I thought I might. Also, it makes for good financial security. I sent quite a bit home this month.
>
> Here's a suggestion. Though I cannot tell for sure, there might be a little difference in the length of time required for airmail and V-mail to get here. If so, the V-mail gets to the destination a little

ahead. So if you have super exciting mail, and you should about this time, send it that way.

You should see our home. It's made of canvas and doesn't have the latest conveniences of an American home. But we have done a lot of work on it, have handmade about everything in it, and are as proud of it as a mother cat. We built the stove, the tent sides, the door, the windows, the tables, everything except a bathroom. That room, I think, would take a little extra work and equipment, both of which we are short of, so we probably will continue to use the outside one.

Reckon the folks have visited Harold by now. Wouldn't be surprised if they weren't a little disappointed in that cadets can't knock off work most any time they feel like it. But it probably did the brother a lot of good. Guess he's going to be a hot pilot and fly fighters. Which is alright with me. So drop me a line now and then, and keep the home fires warm.

On April 12, a bomber formation, including Fortresses from the 463rd, invaded Austrian airspace and bombed an aircraft factory near Vienna. Despite the piercing flak and attacks from enemy fighters, all planes in Stanley's group returned to Celone Field. Meanwhile, the same day, wave after wave of heavies from other bomb groups in the Fifteenth Air Force attacked other aircraft component and assembly factories in Austria, including a factory at heavily defended Wiener Neustadt. Antiaircraft guns put up a thick barrage of deadly fire, and enemy fighters relentlessly pursued—and more bombers tumbled from the sky. But enemy fighters were eliminated too—they were either knocked out of production or knocked out of the sky.

On the home front, the *Hastings Daily Tribune* reported on April 13, 1944, "Simultaneously the 15th Air Force sent its Fortresses and Liberators against Hungary, a few hours after British bombers had pounded Budapest, the capital, by night. They hit aircraft factories at Gyor, 65 miles west of Budapest, Tokol, 10 miles south of Budapest, and other objectives."[23] In reality, those raids were the largest Fifteenth Air Force mission yet, with over five hundred bombers being put in the air. More specifically, Stanley's group bombed an aircraft factory at Gyor while other groups raided factories and two airdromes near Budapest—and "eighteen heavy bombers and three escort fighters were lost to enemy action."[24]

Stanley wrote Cousin Beth:

And I have a new love now. You have seen her often. You, and everyone else who has seen her, have admired her. She, tho, is much faster than one whom you have assumed I would become attached.

But I adore her. They call her Lightning, but because of possible inferences, I prefer the name "P-38." One cannot appreciate her to the fullest until the time comes when, with German fighters on a fortress's tail, the pilot sees a group of thirty-eights pass by, then a few seconds later, all firing ceases. I repeat, I adore her.

During World War II, the Fifteenth Air Force was comprised of around twenty-one bomber groups and about seven fighter groups. Years later, sitting around the breakfast table at one Eighth Air Force reunion, Mom, Dad, Rick, myself, and others in our group visited with guest speaker Alexander Jefferson. Mr. Jefferson, a Tuskegee Airman stationed in Italy in late 1944, had flown a single-seat P-51 fighter with the 332nd fighter group of the Fifteenth Air Force. I asked Mr. Jefferson if he ever flew missions to Wiener Neustadt, Austria. He shook his head and said, "Ugh, Wiener Neustadt—flak alley." He continued, "We flew about 220 miles per hour, back and forth above the slower B-17s flying at 160 miles per hour. At 160 miles per hour, I would have stalled out." Mr. Jefferson relates his story as a fighter pilot and POW in his book *Red Tail Captured, Red Tail Free*. As he said to us and elaborated in his book:

> My most unforgettable mission was flying cover over the Ploesti oil fields. After we picked up our bombers at the border of Hungary and Romania, we encountered only sporadic anti-aircraft fire on the way to the target. Then some fifteen or twenty miles ahead, I saw a huge black cloud, shaped like a hockey puck, from 20,000 feet to about 26,000 feet. I could see a series of fires and lots of smoke rising from the ground underneath it, which appeared to be an oil refinery complex. The B-17s flew out on a sixty-degree angle and then aimed directly for that black cloud. We pulled off to the left and orbited while they disappeared into the black cloud. Then, we saw four or five B-17s falling out of the bottom of the clouds, spinning down lazily, trailing smoke and flames. Unconsciously, I yelled, 'Bail out, damn it! Get out of there!' Out of one of the planes I counted one, two, three chutes opening up. Then there was a big whoosh. The B-17 had exploded in a huge red ball of flames. Realism set in: three chutes had opened; that meant seven men had died, right there in front of my eyes. Seven men no longer existed. I threw up into my oxygen mask—at 31,000 feet. That experience—including my crew chief's refusing to clean my oxygen mask after I returned to base—burned itself into my mind.[25]

"Aileen," Stanley commented in a V-Mail, "a letter the other day indicated a soon arrival. Bet there are some proud people around that neighborhood, including a ma and pa, and gramps and gramma, to say nothing about the uncles. Would like to be in on your reunions but don't expect to make it quite that soon. And when I do get home you will probably be spread from hither to thither. But I'll hunt you all down and use up more of your ration points than you can shake a board at."

The missions added up for Stanley's crew and others—their "ticket home." His group targeted a marshalling yard in Belgrade on two different days, but due to bad weather, their mission to bomb a communications target in Italy was aborted. And then, hundreds of bombers in the largest raid yet returned to flak alley—Wiener Neustadt—on the twenty-third of April, where thick flak and the fierce pursuit of enemy fighters upheld the target's reputation. "[The] Group lead bombardier was struck by flak just on the bombing run against the Wiener Neustadt aircraft factory causing most of the bombs to overshoot the target and hit a neighboring airfield ... The number one engine of Plane 770 ... was hit by flak and burst into flames. [The pilot] ordered the crew to abandon the plane. However, the windmilling propeller suddenly flew off, extinguishing the fire." Five men bailed out, and the other five returned with the plane to base. "The tale is told that 'Salvo,' the dog belonging to T/Sgt. Donald E. Bolen, engineer on 770, refused to leave the hardstand all day, evidently having a premonition that all was not well with his master and plane.'"[26]

Once more, Stanley's group flew back to the oil fields of Ploesti. Because of heavy cloud cover over Ploesti on a previous mission—the April 15 mission—no bombs were delivered, and no crews were shot down. The April 24 mission was a different story when over one hundred tons of bombs pummeled that target in Romania. After bombs away, crews in shot-up planes limped back to Italy. Some—including Stanley's crew, we learned later—barely cleared the mountain peaks. Lieutenant Anthony Namiotka of the 463rd relived his version. "My wing tanks caught fire and we started down in flames. We bailed out and were captured after landing ... A Me 109 took a few shots at me [after bailing out]. I played dead and that must have satisfied him."[27]

April 26, 1944

Dear folks:

The last letter I wrote to you was to Denver. That should catch some of you on the way back. And some of the dozens that I have written while on this continent should get to home before another age. I sent a letter to you folks in care of Pearl and Dusty at Tucson after hearing of the reunion there then got a letter the next day telling that they had moved on toward Kansas.

Today is real April weather. Just like back in the homeland. Hope it doesn't last long though. It sorta puts a crimp in business. And I like good business. Not much except the typewriter to do when we're unbusy. I rather like the sack though.

Have gotten a little mail recently but nothing very recent. Got a letter from Doc Summers. It had been forwarded from Lakeland. Got some "Industrialists" from Ralph Lashbrook. They contained a lot of news of the K-State gang that I knew. Got word from Aileen of her youngster the same day I heard the news from you.

You wouldn't know me with this beard, but I think I will let it grow until tomorrow. It feels good now and then to let it grow and let the rash on my neck heal from shaving every day. And my hair is still short since I found the barber cutting it off the top and myself unable to speak his language to tell him to stop. Could have told him by way of finger gyrations but didn't figure it worth the effort.

Have been reading some good books lately, a couple that I have seen shows based upon but found myself unable to connect the two since the shows were so long ago. Better get myself in the sack. Don't really need it, but it's time.

Love,
Stan

April 27, 1944

Dear Aileen & Bill & C.J.:

Was going to write to you last night but am glad now that I didn't. Got your V-mail of the 15th this morning, and that brings me quite a bit more up to date. I got your letter written in the hospital about ten days ago and hadn't heard anything more from any source. Don't know why, but it takes me about seven or eight weeks for a round of correspondence with the folks. Once in a while their mail gets through in fair time, but not often. And it doesn't seem to make much difference whether they use V- or ordinary airmail. Got two letters from the folks this morning and one from Harold. It was practically a family reunion.

April has come in with a splash. It was rather late getting here but finally arrived. Am wondering whether to don the swimming suit to go to chow or to stay in the tent and eat boxed rations.

Had mention in two of the letters this morning that the youngster had gained a whole ounce. Pa 'lowed that if she gained that much for a hundred years that she would be quite a sizable lass. I haven't figured it out on paper but think he's not far wrong in his calculations. On the tother hand, I think you should hold her down to a certain extent for two reasons. One is that I don't want her to be too big before I get to see her the first time, and the other is that I dislike fat women.

And her coming starts me off on another milestone. Until her arrival, my best girlfriends were someone else's wife. I correspond with half a dozen married couples and have very little exchange with single ones. Which makes me wonder if it is not true that most of the good ones are already taken and if I'll be able to find one when I get back. I have not found a woman during my army career that I could play golf with and feel lucky if I find a bowling partner. And never realized there was such a voidness of humor among present-day women. Their only abilities seem to be graceful sitting at a picture show or at a bar.

We seem to be winding this affair up over here in pretty good shape. I think we have the Germans looking at their hole card. They still seem to be continuing the fight, but I don't know what on. Reckon their best weapon now is the fear of the coming invasion.

Will write again before long. In the meantime keep all three noses clean.

Love,
Stan

For days I was immersed in thought as I read Stanley's letters. Then one morning I awoke, lay in bed, stretched, and rubbed my eyes while the fog in my mind cleared. A dream from the night before replayed in my head. Stanley, in his olive drab officer's jacket with gold buttons, had appeared, stood by me, and we conversed. A few nights later, in another dream, both Dad and I talked to Stanley. He was dressed in his fleece-lined, brown leather flying jacket. Exact words from both conversations escaped me, yet Stanley was "right there." He was almost tangible; the closest I would come to physically meeting him. I wanted to go back to sleep and keep dreaming.

Three more bombing raids, two to Italy and one to France, rounded out the dreary, rainy month of April for the 775th Squadron and the 463rd Bomb Group.

Extra, extra, read all about it. The *Hastings Daily Tribune* ran headline news on May 1, 1944, from London. "'Hour of Liberation Is Near,' Chained Peoples of Europe Told; Air Giants Roar on—May Air Attacks to Outstrip April's and Shatter Nazi Force—Allied plans call for air attacks from now on which will overshadow the April record by a wide margin and which, with good weather and good luck, might reduce the German air force to a skeleton before the great land campaign gets under way … Some enthusiasts compare the role of American air striking force with the invention of gunpowder, the first use of the British long bow against the knights of the Middle Ages, and the birth of the modern battleship in the clash between the Merrimac and Monitor. All agree that if hopes are fulfilled and the German air force is reduced to a minor factor in the coming campaign, air power will have made its greatest single contribution to the war."[28]

Increased air attacks had consequences, good and bad. The book *The Fighting 463rd*—after the war, after the missions were flown and all the losses added up—referred to May 1944 as the "Black Month." Seventeen crews were lost in May 1944. That month the countryside was also described as follows: "Italian fields were blood-red with poppies and wheat fields a bright green. Dust whipped up by frequent winds penetrated the tents. Rain hardly laid the dust, it seemed."[29]

After a four-day lull, missions resumed on May 5.

Not just during lulls, but around the clock and through the nights, ground crews labored long hours to keep the planes and equipment working. Those guys were always patching up planes, getting them ready as soon as possible for another mission. A ground crew chief was assigned for each plane, and he had assistants, depending on the battle damage he was required to fix, if the plane was determined to be fixable. The ground chief worked closely with the airborne crew chief and knew the airplane inside and out. Missions could not have been flown without the ground crews. They didn't rotate out after so many missions. They served for the duration of the war. Ground crews are unsung heroes of the war. There were thousands in all branches of the service.

On May 5, it was back to the all-too-familiar smoke-filled skies obscuring the oil refineries of Ploesti. "Curtains of flak raised over this target are visible from fifty miles. Making the target approach and bomb run is a slow and tortuous process ... Sgt. Donald McDowell, gunner ... was busy throwing lead at a flock of attacking fighters when the plane exploded. The tail section broke off from the rest of the fuselage. Trapped in the falling tail section, McDowell fought to get free. 'While struggling to get out, I pulled my ripcord. The chute spilled out. At about 2,000 feet I forced the hatch open, grabbed the silk in my arms and jumped. I landed with an awful jar.' Later he figured he had fallen more than 20,000 feet in the tail section before working himself free ... On this day [May 5] 35 planes [of the 463rd] waded into the flak and 32 staggered out. Two of the planes were seen to blow up. The third one was last sighted lagging behind the formation with a feathered prop. Smoke was rising to 23,000 feet as the planes turned off the target."[30] The mission took its toll on the Fifteenth Air Force as nineteen bombers were shot down.

For each bomber shot down, ten crewmen scrambled to bail out or went down with the ship. Casualty and missing in action numbers added up quickly—too quickly. There was one bright note though. Some crews previously listed as missing in action ventured out of occupied territory and trickled back to their bases in Italy. Some crewmen evaded capture with the help of partisans, and others, eventually, after the Russians ran the Germans out of Romania, were released from POW camps. Lieutenant Victor Marak from Stanley's 463rd Bomb Group related:

> I landed near a small town, and I made a run for the woods. They spotted me and marched me to the town of Fornuculesti, which is about 50 miles southwest of Bucharest. A mob followed behind me, gaping at the stranger from America.
>
> A few of them spoke English. They asked whether we bombed their homes intentionally, or if it was an accident. I told [one man] that we bombed only military targets, but that it was almost impossible to keep a few bombs from going astray. When he repeated this to his friends, they warmed up a lot.
>
> I was taken to a police station where I found two other members of my crew. A Rumanian doctor there spoke good English. While he was dressing my wounds he asked if it were true that New York and San Francisco had been bombed. I told him those were German lies.
>
> German propaganda had made a strong impression on these people. They had been told that American flyers get $1000 a raid, that all crewmen were criminals who would be pardoned only if they joined the air force. They also believed that we were all from Chicago, and asked me if Al Capone was a flyer too.
>
> They were pitifully ignorant about the true war situation. I told the doctor that Germany was in full retreat on every front. And I told them they could be expecting the Russians any day. The doctor translated what I had said to the farmers. They shook their heads as though they didn't believe me ... [31]

Replacement crews arrived and filled vacancies left by MIAs and KIAs. Lieutenant Kilmark, 463rd pilot, had limped back from a mission to Czechoslovakia with a B-17 "too proud to die, but it was a sad sight. A gaping hole showed in its belly where the bottom turret should have been; the wings were frayed and streaked with oil, and all hatches had been salvoed. He made a smooth landing, but at the far end of the runway the plane reared up on its nose, teetered there with the props chewing into the steel mat, then flopped ungracefully into a normal position."[32]

Lieutenant Kilmark then related stories to the questioning replacements.

[Later] the nightly bull session was underway, and the conversation soon got around to the usual groove ... I'll skip the days when I came back on three engines. Most of those times weren't so bad. The trouble started gradually. On my first trip to the oil refineries near Munich, we were at 26,000 feet for two hours. Temperature was minus 48 Fahrenheit. My heater wasn't working, and my souvenir from that ride was a case of frostbite.

Then, a few days later, we waded through flak alley over Rumania and emerged with an engine out, a punctured wing tank that was throwing gasoline like a fire hose, and other minor damages. I did a little praying and we got back without catching fire ...

Approaching the target [oil refineries at Vienna] I saw a solid black cloud ahead. I called my navigator and asked him where all that flak was coming from. "It's coming from where we're going," he said. So I pulled my helmet down around my ears and waited for the fireworks to begin. The ship jumped, and it felt like a kick in the pants. Both right engines were out of commission. Then another 88 shell broke under the nose and knocked the bombardier unconscious.

My navigator was on the ball and salvoed the bombs on the target. We couldn't get enough power from the two remaining engines to stay with the formation, but we trailed the others as long as we could. Then we made a turn and headed straight west to avoid some German fighter fields. We were at 14,000 feet, dropping 1,000 feet a minute. Up ahead was a 12,000 foot range that lay between us and the Adriatic.

Out of nowhere a flak battery opened up on us and blew off four feet of one wing tip and set the wing tanks afire. Another chunk of flak came through the cockpit, knocked the helmet from my head, slit my cap, and tore off my oxygen mask. On the way through the ship it almost cut the control column in two, and slightly wounded my copilot and I about the hands. Luckily we had drained the wing tanks earlier, and the wing fire burned itself out.

Still dropping fast, we were a long way from that 12,000 foot range. One of my gunners chopped the ball turret loose, and we dropped it. We threw everything out of the plane but the bombsight and our parachutes.

After we got rid of that weight we gained a little altitude and just skimmed over that mountain range. We sighted the Adriatic when the No. 2 engine began to throw oil and caught fire. The flames swept clear back to the tail. I called the boys and told them to listen for the bail-out signal. A connecting rod broke loose from the burning engine, cut through the fuselage, tore my rudder control cables, and wrecked the automatic pilot.

By this time I figured the situation called for outside help. I did some concentrated praying while we fought the fire. I rescinded the bail-out warning then radioed the Air-Sea rescue boys to be expecting some visitors. We chopped a hole in the top of the cockpit, and kept in touch with the rescue team until we hit the water. It was a nice landing, and we were all out of the plane in 35 seconds.

The left raft popped open easily, but we had to chop the right one out with our trench knives and pump it up by hand while we were swimming around. The old bird floated for about three minutes then slid down to the bottom of the Adriatic. We climbed aboard the dinghies, tied them together, and opened two parachutes for sea anchors. Two hours later a seaplane taxied up and took us aboard.

Those Canadian Air-Sea rescue fellows were really a great bunch. Gave us a good supper, some dry clothes, and put us to bed. Four days later we were back at Celone and flying again ...

My copilot and I call the cockpit our chapel. A few prayers go a long way up there.[33]

In Cousin Beth's letter, Stanley commented:

I wish I could say that when it is over I will be able to bring them all back to receive the reward of their fighting. I cannot. But I will do everything in my power to see that they return. They are a grand group of boys, and the fact that I censor their mail keeps reminding me that ten mothers are counting on me. One more thing tho. "Missing in action" does not constitute a source of worry. It is rather common among our ranks but seldom means no more than internment for the duration, and not often that.

Brasov, Romania, was the target on May 6, 1944, from which all planes of the 463rd returned "without incident." Allyn's Irish Orphans led the way to bomb the marshalling yards at Bucharest, Romania, on May 7, 1944. However, it appeared Stanley sat out that particular raid. He used the day off to write his last letter home.

Stanley's last letter. I had randomly picked his last letter out of the stack before and read it. But when I reread it in sequence with all three hundred others, I was overwhelmed with unexpected emotions. For days, I was engrossed in rereading Stanley's correspondence—his "diary"—and with the letter of May 7, 1944, it all ended. I wanted more. I now knew my uncle, and I didn't want it to end. Imagine Grandma and Granddad's sorrow when they realized there would be no more letters from Stanley.

May 7, 1944

Dear folks:

Oh happy day, I have the entire one off. So I shall write a couple of letters, clean up this junk heap, and dash into the village for my rations. Reckon I should write all day, since if I remember correctly this is the first I've written this month. And day before yesterday I received the measly sum of eight, including two from you written almost two weeks apart. The second one dashed across the pond in an even ten days. Also had one from Gertie and Lou that made it in ten. That is pretty fresh news, and as welcome as clear skies over a target.

Those clear skies are a bit of a rarity these days, but we keep plugging away and the missions are piling up. It is said that clouds over Europe are quite common all through summer but maybe they won't be so bad as previously.

The old buggy is doing mighty nicely up to now. She was in the hospital for a cuple of weeks a while back thanks to some rookie who apparently didn't know how to correct for a cross wind and landed at an angle to the runway. A new tail wheel had to be installed. We are painting the flak holes white to make them show up better--we're proud of them. However because of that period of convalescence she isn't very pimply.

Think I shall invert the typewriter ribbon as soon as I finish this. From the looks of this side of it, it would seem that the letters I have written, should they be placed end to end would bridge the Atlantic. However the tent mates have helped a bit.

Had the picture of my crew taken the other day for the Special Service office. Hope to get some prints of it before too long. Don't have any idea when it will be though, because material for developing is rather scarce.

P-38s give us no end of buzzing here in the area. But we do not frown upon it. We kinda like 'em. Am wondering about Harold, since the last I heard he was the only one left out of five. That's cutting it down pretty fine. Guess that the air corps is about full up as far as personnel is concerned.

And unk wonders how the youngin is these days. Reckon gramma had a mighty fine visit when she was there. I gathered from her letter that she would like to take up house keeping there but probably is home by now. By the time this arrives, you should have the last two months hundred dollar allottments, 350 that I send a month ago, and another hundred sent a week ago. Let me know huh?

Love
Stan

(over)

P.S. Stupid for me to write then go check the mail, wasn't it?
Got three V-mails from you this morning, of the 19th, 23rd and 26th.
And had a total of eight all together, which has happened twice
in the last three days. Such popularity. Will answer them in a
couple of days, and it will be as you requested, by V-mail.

Weather scrubbed the May 9 mission to Wiener Neustadt, but it was reassigned on May 10, 1944. Stan's last mission flown to Wiener Neustadt on May 10 was, by my initial calculations, probably his sixteenth or seventeenth mission, somewhere in there. He probably hadn't flown every one recorded for his group, but almost. We would learn that the required mission count was different for the Fifteenth Air Force, and some crewmen flew fifty. It came to my attention as we progressed through our search that some missions flown by crewmen out of Italy were counted as two. The mission count was based on the distance flown. For instance, we learned that crewmen received credit for two missions when they flew longer distances to targets in Austria or Hungary or to Ploesti (and other targets in Romania). In that case, Stan could have been approaching twenty-five missions of his required fifty. Having flown in the left seat of a bomber just like my brother, I can imagine what he went through.

Like Stan had done many times before, his last mission might have started the night before, maybe at the officers' club. In England, we'd stop at the club for a toddy, but we left early if and when there was a sign hung on the back of the bar that said, "There's a giant on the beach," meaning there was a mission planned for the next day and the bar was closed. In other words, quit drinking—go home and go to bed.

So in the early morning, after signing the orderly's paper, I rolled out of the sack and was trucked first to chow at the mess hall and then to briefing. In England, on the day of a mission, we were served two fresh eggs instead of the usual powdered eggs. At the briefing room, we filed in, checked in, and sat in unassigned seats. When the commanding officer walked to the front of the room, the small talk with your buddy sitting next to you stopped. We stood up. At the podium, the officer said, "At ease." Chairs scooted on the floor as we sat down, and then the briefing for the day's mission began. The curtain was pulled back, exposing the maps, and if it was a tough mission, you heard a big groan from everybody in the room.

Religious services were offered. I heard that one guy went to all three—Protestant, Catholic, and Jewish services.

After thirty minutes or more of briefing, it was to the equipment shack, and then crews were trucked to their respective plane's hardstand. The ground crews had the planes ready, even if it took all night. We did a walk-around check on the plane, checked the bombs, and worked with the ground crew chief. Some of the .50 caliber guns had to be installed and all others checked for ammo and to see if they worked. Each crewman had his own procedure and was responsible for his own flight gear.

For me, first I put on long johns and then a shirt and pants. Some guys had heated flying suits. As I recall, we wore heavy flying jackets, a Mae West vest, parachute harness, and over everything else, we wore a flak jacket. We had our flak jackets with us and only wore them when needed because they were so heavy. If there was an extra flak jacket lying around, we'd grab it to sit on for extra protection.

On your head, you wore a leather helmet, goggles, your personally fitted oxygen mask, headsets and throat mike, and a steel helmet over all of that. Footwear was heavy socks and fleece-lined boots. I strapped my regular GI boots to my parachute harness so I would have walking shoes if I had to bail out. On my hands, I wore three layers: silk gloves, wool gloves, and leather flying gloves, in that order. It was all pretty bulky.

About ten minutes before takeoff, most everyone lined up out back of the airplane to relieve themselves. We had a relief tube in the back of the plane, but it seemed like every time someone went back there, we hit rough air. Turbulence moved the tail around quite a bit, so I'd hold it for an entire ten- or twelve-hour mission.

After throwing my stuff through the nose hatch, I chinned myself and pulled up into the plane.

If Stan's starting procedure was the way we did it, it went something like this:

We wore government-issue watches that could be set to the second—they called it "time hack." So at about fifteen seconds before 5:00 a.m., starting time, you heard about thirty-six starters whine. At five o'clock sharp, thirty-six starter engagers kicked in, and then thirty-six twelve-hundred-horsepower engines fired up. It was quite a sound. Radials belched out a lot of smoke, and ground crews were on standby with extinguishers. Then we followed the same sequence for the other three engines.

I called for the tail wheel to be unlocked and taxied out to the strip. Approximately thirty-six B-17s, lined up nose to tail, waited their turn to take off—about one plane every thirty seconds. The tower shot off a green flare, signaling a go for takeoff.

After one last check, I released the brakes, pushed the throttle handles forward, and our approximately sixty-five-thousand-pound bomber accelerated down the runway. You could tell when your airspeed was 110 to 120 miles per hour, and she was ready to fly. The plane gradually lifted off the runway, and Katy bar the door if you lost an engine on takeoff. A really good pilot might survive it. It took muscles to handle the plane; there was no hydraulic help. But we got used to it. It seemed like we threw it around like a kiddy car.

Once airborne, we banked off the same direction as our squadron leader, and in order to catch up, we banked a little steeper. Each squadron leader fired a certain colored flare. In that way, the ten to twelve planes of the different squadrons identified the leader they needed to tag up with. All planes were under strict radio silence. The only contact with the tower was if you needed to abort.

Squadron leaders had a certain place to be at a certain time to fall in with the group leader. Group leaders knew their sequence to get all planes from bases in England—in Stan's case, Italy—into the vast bomber stream. In tight formation, planes were ideally spaced sixty to seventy feet apart, wing tip to wing tip, at staggered altitudes, maybe one hundred feet above or below between planes. If you weren't a squadron leader, your job was to follow the guy in front of you.

Oftentimes over England, we climbed through clouds. When you felt the bomber lurch when flying through clouds, you knew you'd flown through another plane's prop wash and were close to a midair collision.

It was all coordinated. The bomber groups converged with the combat wings and then converged with divisions, and when our entire Eighth Air Force bomber stream was formed—maybe twenty to thirty minutes or longer after takeoff—hundreds of planes loaded with crews, ammo, fuel, and bombs flew the designated course to the IP point and then on to the target.

Prior to reaching the IP—initial point—the lead pilots of the group could take evasive action in response to antiaircraft fire. Our courses were plotted to fly around known antiaircraft batteries. Some German antiaircraft guns were on train cars, mobile, and moved to different areas. However, once over the IP, you just had to hang on and take it and hold the plane steady so the bombardier could get his sights lined up for an accurate bomb run. The ten- to twenty-mile course line drawn from the IP to the target had to be followed exactly.

So that gave us an idea how May 10 started for my brother as he took off and proceeded from Celone Field, out over the Adriatic Sea and on toward Wiener Neustadt, Austria. And the way it ended—on May 10, 1944, Stan and his crew were part of a contingent of approximately six hundred planes that comprised one of the largest air raids at that point in the war. From his 463rd Bomb Group's contingent of thirty-five bombers sent on the raid, seven of those bombers would not return and land at Celone Field in Italy. Stan's plane was one of those unlucky seven.

9

c-y

Hope

Write to me.
—*Stanley N. Dwyer in a letter dated March 24, 1944*

I had read all of Stanley's letters from his trunk—but there were still other letters. Meanwhile, our twenty-first-century search progressed. Dave Hughes had volunteered as middleman for correspondence to and from Austria, and even though it took some time, he produced a translation of the letter I had received from Austria. Dave's e-mail response began with the following message:

Attached is the original German and following is our translation.

Dear Family Hughes, warmest greetings to you in America!

We are glad to answer your questions to the best of our ability. We have our information from the following gentleman:

Mr. Augustin Stranz
Pottschach (This is the name of the town he lives in)
Austria

Now, to your questions:

1. *Herr* Stranz told us that no remains of the pilot were ever discovered, also no dog tags. The plane had bombs on board which exploded on impact. We're sorry we don't have better news.

2. *Herr* Stranz has a book which has a photo of the crash site as well as the motor of the plane.

3. We only know of the documentation of *Herr* Stranz. (I asked them if they could get a picture of the crash site, etc.)

4. There is a photo of the crash site in the book of *Herr* Stranz. (Not clear why they mention this a second time—most likely the book is an old record and difficult to copy, etc. Probably not something they can send electronically).

If you come to Austria, we would be glad to take you to meet *Herr* Stranz. He can show you the crash site.

We are very glad to get to know you, and we are glad to offer any further assistance.
With very warm greetings we remain: Inge and Udo Doerr

[Dave wrote] Hope this helps in some small way. My guess is *Herr* Stranz lives in the area—it might be interesting to find his town and see how close it is to the first village you found. He apparently does not have Internet access.

That e-mail named the heretofore anonymous town historian, Augustin Stranz. Inge and Udo Doerr were Martin's godparents.

I also received a personal letter from Inge and Udo Doerr postmarked in Bad Fischau, Austria, and written in German. Included with the letter was a copy of a page from a book with photos, the text in German, and three separate snapshots of the crash site at Vostenhof—one vintage photo from 1944 and two photos taken in 2001. Dave came to our rescue and translated the page from the book. (The title of the book written by Augustin Stranz is *Vergessene Vergangenheit Band 2*, V.M.M. Verlagservice Gesmbh, Pottschach 1996).

On the [tenth] of May 1944 there were air raid warnings from 11:00 a.m. to 1:00 p.m. During the return flights an American airplane was hit by a shell near Wiener Neustadt. The pilot kept losing altitude. Probably he was looking for a landing place. He flew a loop over Burg-Gasteil-Transach (location names) and then crashed into Saubachgraben (probably the name of a mountain) in the woods of the Auer family at Burg number 16 (address). Three soldiers died in the crash, the others were able to parachute safely. One soldier jumped from the plane just before it hit the mountain, but his chute did not open. He hit like a rock in the Mohr meadow, on the way from Burg to Thann, and died on impact. The two other American soldiers died in the crash. The airplane still had several bombs on board, one of which exploded on impact and started a forest fire. The three dead soldiers were buried on the tenth of May 1944 in the cemetery in Pottschach. After the end of the war their bodies were exhumed and sent to America. The names of the dead: F. Gilhooley, P. Precott, F. Olfenius [some misspellings].

[Caption under photo of half a tree in a forested area] – At the crash site the airplane ripped the upper part of a giant spruce in half. The tree had a circumference of approximately five meters (fifteen feet!).

The personal letter translated:

Dear family Hughes-Dwyer,
    We received three more photos of the crash site of your uncle's plane from *Herr* Stranz today, and we are happy to send them on to you. So that it is easier to read the text from the photos, I've typed them here for you:
    Photo 1 taken by Kurt Eisner (sp?) and Augustin Stranz in 1944
    The general area of the accident where on the tenth of May 1944, the B-17 piloted by Lt. Stanley Dwyer crashed and cost the pilot his life when one of the bombs the plane was carrying exploded. To the left of the crater you can see the shattered trunk of the giant spruce that the already low-flying plane hit and which caused it to crash.
    Photo 2 taken by Augustin Stranz in 2001
    The still visible crash site of the American Bomber B-17 that crashed on May 10, 1944, in Vostenhof of the Neunkirchen region. The pilot of the plane, Lt. Stanley Dwyer, was killed by an exploding bomb.
    Photo 3 taken by Augustin Stranz
    The still recognizable crash site of an American bomber that crashed on the tenth of May 1944 in Vostenhof, Neunkirchen region. Picture taken in 2001.

Dear family Hughes,
    We're sorry that we don't have better news to share with you. I have to tell you that I sympathize with your feelings since my family was bombed by American bombers in the war on the first of October,

1943. My younger brother who was six years old at the time was killed. My family had nothing left except the clothes on our backs. My parents had to begin all over again. I have not overcome the shock of that time even now, many decades later. I guess we must always see how brutal and inhuman war is.

It is for me no accident that we are writing to each other. The war brought sadness to all of us.

So we wish you a very peaceful Christmas and God's blessings for the coming year 2002. Perhaps we will see each other in Austria and get to know each other (become friends).

Kindest greetings and we wish you all the best.

Inge and Udo Doerr

Casualty numbers from World War II approached fifty million, or more. Behind those casualty numbers were intimate, personal stories. With almost tunnel vision, I focused mostly on American military losses; however, Inge opened my eyes even more to up-close, firsthand, real suffering experienced by millions, civilians as well as military. Udo and Inge had an e-mail address and an understanding of English, and I thanked them for their help, the information and photos, and Mr. Stranz's help. We sympathized with Inge's family's loss. I expressed a hope that someday we could travel to Austria and meet them and see the crash site. Many times, Rick and I discussed going to Austria, yet Dad and Mom were, at the most, lukewarm to that idea.

On May 10, 1944, in Hastings, Nebraska, tender, green sprouts wormed out of the earth and pushed skyward in backyard victory gardens planted across town. The perfumelike smell of lilacs saturated my grandparents' yard, and the sweet fragrance of roses filled their home. Unaware of the details of the May 10 mission to Wiener Neustadt, daily life continued.

Attached to the flowers, the bouquet of roses delivered to Grandma in honor of Mother's Day on Sunday, May 14, was a greeting card signed, "Lt. Stanley N. Dwyer," the same small Mother's Day greeting card that had been packed away in Stanley's trunk. Granddad was on the road on that Sunday, so Grandma wrote letters. Again, I reread one of Grandma's letters. She thanked Stanley for the "scrumptious roses" and wrote, "I'm alone today, so I get quite a lift out of first looking at them and then at your picture." It was one of the letters he never received, one in the stack saved in his trunk bound with a crusty rubber band and stamped "Returned to Writer."

In his May 15 letter to Stanley, another letter Stanley never received, Granddad wrote, "I talked to Ellen yesterday from Beloit. Your Mother's Day gift arrived Johnny-at-the-rathole, and she was plenty pleased. She had a card from each of the others. I will talk to her again tonight and see what came in the way of mail from you folks. We kind of figger on something Mondays as there is the two-day accumulation. Harold will leave for advanced about a week from today."

A photo of crewmen "hitting the silk" over Wiener Neustadt on May 10, 1944, was front-page news in the *Hastings Daily Tribune,* along with continued rumors of the invasion of Western Europe. The headlines didn't go unnoticed by Grandma. She commented to Stanley in another returned letter, "They have really begun to stir up things in Italy, haven't they? I hope they do all over the line before too long so this thing will be finished up. And all you boys return home."

Stanley's letter dated May 7 arrived on the twentieth, and Granddad, back in Hastings, commented in his response, "It must have had a tail wind practically all the way." He wrote, "With two boys in the service and a brand-new shaver in the lineup, the principle indoor sport is looking for the postman. Sometimes he does all right, but other times I think we should have a new one." Grandma and Granddad continued to receive letters from Dad and Aunt Aileen, but, unknowingly, they had received the last one from Stanley.

The preface of *The Fighting 463rd,* the book from Stanley's trunk, read:

This book was written for the men who were part of the 463rd Bombardment Group and for the parents and families of the men who will not return. To all others, it will be merely a collection of events, anecdotes and pictures having no particular significance.

The "Foggia Era" will mean different things to different men: it will be memories of the boat or plane ride on the way to war— the first sight of a foreign land—a bomb run of several minutes which seemed to last forever—bailing out of a burning plane, of being flung bodily into space like a big-league speedball—cold, wet H-hours and the Intelligence officer saying that the target for today is Ploesti—watching the flak slide closer and the groups up ahead catching Hell—throwing lead like mad at attacking German fighters and remembering what they said at Gunnery school about short bursts only—an old man and woman pushing a wheelbarrow through an Army convoy amidst the ruins of Cassino [Italy], and on the wheelbarrow a small white coffin covered with wildflowers— miserable wet nights and warm sunny days—walking down Via Roma in Napoli—strolling along Via Tragara on Capri—eating a good dinner and drinking sweet wine in France—chewing the fat with some of the boys—writing letters and awaiting replies—sweating out the long months in the POW camps and the 1,000-mile Black March out of Poland and Pomerania—drinking artificial lemonade and eating cold donuts after a mission, courtesy of the American Red Cross—crap and poker games when purple and green 1,000 lire notes were tossed around like streetcar transfers—Italian kids yelling: "Hey Joe, you wanta eat. Hey Joe, my seester she multo buono"—watching the planes limping home so lacerated they must have been held up by a prayer—drinking ulcerous cognac and vino and waking up with a head as big as a barrage balloon—these are some of the memories.

For the parents and families of the men, the memories are different. They sweated out the days too. Lt. Stanley Dwyer's father expressed it when he said: "We were afraid every time the phone rang or somebody pushed the doorbell, thinking that now we would hear the news we dreaded." And too often, these fears were confirmed.[34]

Granddad was back on the road by the twenty-fifth. When the Western Union boy showed up at Grandma's doorstep on the evening of May 27 with the dreaded telegram, she was alone again. And her world, their world, was turned upside down. Yesterday's worries were now reality. Their lives would never be the same; yet life went on.

It must have been a long, agonizing drive home for Granddad.

When the folks got the MIA telegram from the War Department, I was in advanced training at Fort Sumner, New Mexico. My dad called and said, "Stanley may be a prisoner of war." I asked him if he wanted me to come home, and he said, "No, you'd better stay with your class and graduate." I concurred, as I was getting along really well with my instructors and the flying involved. In fact, while I was still in the underclass, I had passed my instrument check ride. Most of the senior class had not done that yet. Anyway, I got the call about five o'clock in the evening, and the next morning, my instructor and I were airborne, and I didn't do something just the way he wanted. The instructor sucked in his breath to say something not too complimentary, and I said, "Sir, I don't feel like having my butt chewed out today." Whether he had heard about my phone call or not, I'll never know. Anyhow, he accepted it, and we had a good flight.

Nonetheless, the sun came up, and Granddad's Western Union telegram to his daughter, Aileen, in Denver stated, "Stanley may be prisoner of war. Missing in action over Austria since May 10th. Much love, Dad."

Official responses arrived next, within days after the original telegram. Government letters were always addressed to Mrs. Ellen J. Dwyer, designated as "emergency addressee." War Department correspondence dated May 29, 1944, read:

I know that added distress is caused by failure to receive more information or details. Therefore, I wish to assure you that at any time additional information is received, it will be transmitted to you without delay, and if in the meantime no additional information is received, I will also communicate with you at the expiration of three months ...

The term "missing in action" is used only to indicate that the whereabouts or status of an individual is not immediately known. It is not intended to convey the impression that the case is closed. I wish to emphasize that every effort is exerted continuously to clear up the status of our personnel. Under war conditions, this is a difficult task as you must readily realize. Experience has shown that many persons reported missing in action are subsequently reported as prisoners of war, but as this information is furnished by countries with which we are at war, the War Department is helpless to expedite such reports. However, in order to relieve financial worry, Congress has enacted legislation which continues in force the pay, allowances, and allotments to dependents of personnel being carried in a missing status.

Permit me to extend to you my heartfelt sympathy during this period of uncertainty.

And then I read a letter addressed to Grandma from the Fifteenth Air Force Commander, General N. F. Twining.

I am sorry I cannot give you any assurance of Stanley's safety. The Flying Fortress on which he was the pilot was hit by antiaircraft fire while over the target. Soon thereafter, it went into a steep glide. What happened after that is not known because all of the other crews were busily engaged warding off the enemy fighters. I sincerely hope that we will eventually be able to inform you that he is a prisoner or otherwise safe ...

Stanley's record speaks very credibly of his services to his Country. For his meritorious achievements while on operational flights, he was awarded the Air Medal and one Oak Leaf Cluster. His many friends wish me to extend our most sincere sympathy to his family.

The original telegram said we'd be informed of more information as it became available. It seemed that after those first few official letters, there wasn't much more to go on. My dad did a lot of research. I remember one time he saw a picture of a bunch of soldiers. It might have been an Irish regiment someplace, and there was a guy standing there with an image of my brother—the curly hair, everything. Dad snooped that photograph down somehow, through the Associated Press or whoever, and he received a letter from the company commander assuring him that the guy wasn't Stan.

In the early years, we—my folks especially—didn't know where to go or who to talk to. Of course, Dad was a writer, and he was always on the typewriter, so he sent out many letters informing friends of their news and trying to figure out what happened on May 10.

Dad did everything he could. Right away, he corresponded with Stan's crewmen's next of kin to get more information. I knew those letters were somewhere.

In fact, those letters were mixed in with all the other ones. I sorted them into piles: Stanley's letters, government letters, the letters from friends and acquaintances, correspondence from family, the crewmen's next of kin, and even Stan's crewmen themselves. A letter from Grandma's friend Mary Davidson of Manhattan, Kansas, read:

Mr. Dwyer's letter came yesterday, and it was an awful shock to us. We had started to town and picked up the mail; we just had to pull off the road and stop until we could get hold of ourselves. Next to our own boys, Stanley was next. We will always have pleasant memories of the many, many times Stanley and Lynne came across our yard together and the times Lynne called me, "Mom, I'm over to Stanley's." I had such a nice letter from Stanley since he went overseas … Always remember you are not alone in your sorrow. Mr. Davidson and I feel the loss so much. I sent Mr. Dwyer's letter on to Lynne.

Lynne Davidson responded:

Mom's letter came today written on the back of yours. I never hated to read anything so bad in my life. It seems to me that I have lost more than a brother, and things won't seem right without him, so let's all hope that he is a prisoner of war until definite word comes that it can possibly be anything else. Somehow I feel pretty confident that he will be all right. I can realize how hard it must be on you folks not knowing and hoping for the best.

Dozens of friends responded. A sampling follows.

Dear Harold and Ellen: It was indeed with deep regret that we heard the news about Stanley, and while it is hard to put it in words, we offer you our sincere condolence and sympathy in this hour of sorrow. However, let us not forget that the star of hope still shines brightly, and we sincerely hope and trust that all will yet be well and that you will hear shortly as to just where he is. Keep up your courage, and we feel that there is far better than a 50-50 chance that Stanley will yet return all OK.

**

Naturally, my thoughts turn to you and yours, more particularly since you have an anxiety to bear. I assure you that we share this with you as much as it is possible for friends to do. I hope that you will receive better news from Stanley and that wherever he is all will be well with him. I suffer whenever I hear of losses on land or sea or in the air, and I take no pleasure even in the losses of the "enemy."

**

I saw in the *Glasco Sun* that Stanley is reported missing ... However, there is one thing to hope for and that is that he might have landed somewhere and is safe and will return in time. I sure hope so.

**

All anyone can do is hope for the best, and we'll remember him with a prayer.

**

Maybe he is a prisoner of war. Not a very comforting thought, either, but more hopeful.

**

No one but a parent of the boys has any idea of the terrible mental suffering this war is causing.

**

Dear friends Harold and Ellen, I was so sorry to read the sad news. Words, and anything we can do, seem helpless in the face of such as this. I do know this: our American boys cause our hearts to almost burst with pride, and everything that we have, or will have, the privilege of enjoying has the blessing of their sacrifices upon it. And we are ever humbled. Blessings to you and yours. Myrtle Griffith (and family)

***

With so many letters to read, it was hard to keep the names straight. One name, Janice Cuthbertson, sister of Stanley's friend Harry Cuthbertson, rang a bell. She wrote from Gardner Field in Taft, California, where Stanley had trained.

Dear Mr. and Mrs. Dwyer,

I have purposely put off writing this letter, since I received yours last Monday, for one reason. That is, that I thought I could get you a picture of Stan when he was in cadet training at this field, so waited until I got the picture before writing. I am enclosing it under separate cover. [I believe this is the cover photo taken by the AAF Training Command.]

Of course I was not happy to receive your letter, although I want to thank you for writing me. I heard from Stan last, shortly after Easter—he had written Easter morning—and since I answered right away, I had wondered why I had not heard since. However, like you, I feel that there is an even chance he may be a prisoner of war.

Your letter came as quite a shock even though I knew as soon as I saw the return address on the envelope what the contents would be. With three older brothers, numerous acquaintances, and many good friends all in one branch or another of the armed forces, I have been bracing myself, as it were, for such messages, but your letter, being the first of its kind I've received and concerning so fine a boy as Stan, it hit pretty deep. Please know that I feel for you, his parents.

You may be interested in knowing how I met Stan. He was Harry's friend first—I believe they were in the Infantry together—and it was through him that we became acquainted. Unfortunately, it was on his last day at this field, so we hardly had time to really know one another. However, since that time, we have kept up a rather irregular correspondence which has led me to consider him one of my closest friends. The one night we had a chance to have him in to dinner my mother took such an instant liking to him, she has followed our correspondence with an almost too eager eye ...

Rather than trying to offer consolation—a thing at which I am so poor—may I congratulate you on having such a real person for a son ...

244

I shall hope to hear from you again, and I shall pray that you receive further news—further good news!

> Sincerely,
> Janice Cuthbertson

Names on some letters I recognized—like Stanley's old girlfriend Margaret Wells, Dorothea Stratton, and college professor Ralph Lashbrook—but not others. As we focused on one aspect or another of the search, some things, names included, were inadvertently overlooked or didn't register. It took a while to figure things out. Letters didn't come out of the trunk chronologically, and as we moved in and out of the trunk, we sometimes didn't pick up where we left off. Over the course of nearly ten years, though, the parts of the whole picture merged and came full circle. Initially, we couldn't place the name Huretta Wright, a different and pretty name, but in time, after reading and rereading letters, I eventually put two and two together.

Dear Mr. Dwyer,

I hope you will forgive my forwardness in writing you, but as I am writing about Stan, I thought it would be all right.

I met Stan when he was based at Drane Field, here in Lakeland, and became quite fond of him. While he was here I went with him, and since he has been overseas, we have corresponded quite frequently.

In the last three weeks, I have failed to receive an answer from any of my letters and naturally have been rather worried. I would appreciate it if you would let me know if you have heard from him or had any word of him recently.

> Sincerely yours,
> Retta

Huretta Wright ... so she's the one! Stanley described her in a letter home as the "sweet little girl here [Lakeland] ... she would have liked to have spent these few days honeymooning."

And Granddad's letter-writing campaign included a letter written to Colonel Kurtz, Stanley's group commander, dated June 1, 1944, mere days before the official D-Day, June 6, 1944. A copy of the letter was in the trunk.

Dear Colonel Kurtz:

This is a small matter with which to bother a busy man, but I have thought that through you it could possibly be placed in the hands of someone who doesn't have so much on his mind.

My son, 2nd Lieutenant Stanley Dwyer, was pilot of a ship in Squadron 775. We have received word from the Department that he is reported missing in action over Austria since May 10.

In our last letter from him written May 7, he stated that the crew had been photographed for the Special Service office. Also that he would try to send us one of the pictures after they were finished. I'm wondering if it would still be possible for us to have one of them.

It is understood, of course, that to you this lad was just another pilot, which are expendable, and that others will be issued to take his place in the outfit, and that it can be no other way in time of war, but to us he is fifty per cent of the boys we ever raised, and the other fifty gets his wings August 4.

We have also understood all along that the boys play pretty rough in the game you're in and knew that he didn't train a year and a half and go over there to pick daisies, but when it comes, it's a jolt anyway. He may, of course, be a prisoner of war, but in either case, it would mean much to us to have one of the pictures, and any effort on the part of anyone to bring it about will be more than appreciated.

Sincerely,
Harold W. Dwyer

"I received your letter dated 1 June 1944 concerning your son Lt. Stanley Dwyer," Colonel Kurtz responded. "I feel deeply for you at this time." Because of "official procedure" Colonel Kurtz was not allowed to give any details or the requested photo for ninety days after official notification of missing in action.

I picked up on a small detail, years into our search, while reading various accounts of Stanley's 775th Squadron missions. It was one of those tidbits that added interest to the puzzle but really led nowhere. Colonel Kurtz flew copilot with Lieutenant Dwight Hanson on the fateful May 10 mission. From my understanding, Hanson and Kurtz flew lead in the 775th Squadron, with Stanley's plane positioned in the same element only a few hundred yards behind—until Stanley's shot-up bomber became a straggler. "A shell went through the right wing of Lt. Hanson's plane and entered the radio compartment, breaking control cables, destroying the radio, and severely wounding the radio operator."[35] Even so, pilot Dwight Hanson was awarded the Silver Star for his gallant efforts when "he pulled his squadron out of formation to cover four bombers which had been crippled during the bombing run. Two of the crippled aircraft were forced down, but the other two were given protective cover by Lt. Hanson's squadron on the return flight, when attacked by 30-40 enemy fighters, and brought safely home."[36] Several questions came to mind. First, was the lead squadron plane protecting Stanley's bomber? And what might any surviving crew recall?

From my best estimation, Edward Rohrbach, who probably flew as a waist gunner on that lead squadron plane, was one of maybe two crewmen living that might remember something. To contact him required a cold phone call. I reasoned it was always worth a try, still procrastinated, and then dialed his number. Ed flew on May 10 but did not remember details. A nineteen-year-old, drafted just out of high school, Ed served as a waist gunner and flew forty-nine missions. We had a nice visit, and I concluded our conversation with, "Thank you for your service, Ed."

By the end of June 1944, Army Air Forces Headquarters updated Grandma. "Further information has been received indicating that Lieutenant Dwyer was a crew member of a B-17 (Flying Fortress) which departed from southern Italy on a bombardment mission to Wiener Neustadt, Germany [Austria], on May 10. Full details are not available, but the report indicates that during this action our planes encountered enemy antiaircraft fire, and in the ensuing battle, your son's Fortress was seen to sustain damage and leave the formation. This occurred about 11:00 a.m. in the vicinity of the target. The crew members of returning planes were unable to furnish any additional information concerning the disappearance of this aircraft."

So the agenda for years of searching had been set in motion. The questions—what happened on May 10 and what happened to Stanley—seemed to haunt Grandma and Granddad and the family for the rest of their lives. And decades afterward, those age-old, recurring questions resurfaced and ran through our minds too. Furthermore, it had become obvious that those questions nagged more than I ever knew. For years, they'd percolated in Dad's mind.

It's always been in the back of my mind a little. Decades after the fact, the folks had passed on, but about the time the Missing Air Crew Reports were released in the late '80s or early '90s, and before that day in Kay's kitchen, I'd read in Air Force Magazine that Stan's 463rd Bomb Group was having a reunion. The article listed a contact name if you were interested in finding out more reunion information. So, one day I called the contact person and said I was trying to find out if any of the survivors of my brother's crew might still be around or signed up for that reunion. If so, I'd like to talk to some of them. The man I had called asked, "What was your brother's name?" I told him, "Stan Dwyer." There was a short pause, and then the man responded something like, "You're talking to one of his crewmen right now." His name was Eugene Parker, and he had been Stan's ball turret gunner on May 10, 1944. I choked up and don't remember much more of the conversation.

The time was right. It was years after that day in my kitchen and even more years after Dad's fluke phone conversation with Eugene Parker. Something had been on my mind. Maybe I'd been going through letters in the trunk or questioning Dad, trying to put some pieces of the puzzle together. Anyway, filed away in my memory was Dad's long-ago phone call with Eugene Parker. I wanted to call Eugene; I had a lot of questions, so I telephoned him.

Eugene, one of the founders and active member of the 463rd Bomb Group Historical Society, was happy to talk. He told me, "On May 10, I flew with Stanley on the mission to Wiener Neustadt. Our plane was tail-end Charlie. I saw fire in the left wing. I got out of the ball turret, preparing to bail out. The left waist gunner told me the fire was out. So, to protect the airplane, I went back to the ball turret. But as I was preparing to close the turret door, a 20 mm shell exploded where I was standing. I received wounds in the head, across my shoulders, and in my left arm. As I was preparing to operate the turret, I noticed both wings on fire. It was then I got out of the turret, and all damaged connections from under my seat that were attached to my oxygen mask—my oxygen and intercom and electric outlet—came out with me. I bailed out the bomb bay, between the radio room bulkhead and the bombs that were still in the bomb bay. I was wounded in over fifteen places."

Eugene explained that he was not one of Stanley's original crewmen. Some crews were split up that day. Losses were heavy. They had replacement crews.

"Stanley, Dale, Boros, and Mitchell were the four regulars flying on May 10," Eugene said. "Five of us were from my crew, and Milewski came from yet another crew."

Many names swirled around in my head. It was hard to keep track of everyone, so Rick started a spreadsheet.

Original Crew	May 10, 1944 Crew
Pilot—Stanley Dwyer	Pilot—Stanley Dwyer
Copilot—Pete Dale	Copilot—Pete Dale
Navigator—Walt Swan	Navigator—Francis Gilhooley
Bombardier—Allan Klute	Bombardier—Prescott Piper
Flight Engineer—John Boros	Flight Engineer—John Boros
Radioman—George Mitchell	Radioman—George Mitchell
Ball Turret—Darris Oldfather	Ball Turret—Eugene Parker

Waist Gunner—Don Pratt	Waist Gunner—John Boyett
Waist Gunner—Gail Popplewell	Waist Gunner—Stephen Milewski
Tail Gunner—John Papazian	Tail Gunner—William Olfenius

Through their own tireless letter-writing crusade in 1944, Granddad and Grandma eventually figured out that some of the crew members flying with Stanley on May 10 were not the fellows—the crewmen—Stanley had listed in a previous letter to his folks. In that particular letter, Stanley mentioned his crewmen's home states and that the navigator, Swan, and radioman, Mitchell, were Dartmouth graduates. For reasons of "military security," Headquarters strictly withheld, until a "later date," my grandparents' request for a list of crew names and addresses. Well, there was no waiting around. Instead, Granddad did his homework.

A letter in the trunk from Dartmouth College in Hanover, New Hampshire, alluded to Granddad and Grandma's determined efforts. It stated, "We have no report that either of the Dartmouth boys [Mitchell and Swan] are missing in action, but it is often some time before such news reaches us." The letter included the requested names and addresses of those two boys' parents.

So, with that information, Grandma and Granddad's search moved into high gear.

> Dear Mr. Dwyer – Your letter reached me today. I am George's [Mitchell] mother. The boys were on the same ship until misfortune overtook them over "Wiener Neustadt" in Austria. Like yourself, we received a telegram on May 27 from the War Department and later a letter confirming the previous message ... I had sent the boys a St. Christopher medal for their plane which they hadn't named up to the last letter we had ... Mr. Mitchell has been very ill and was in the hospital recovering from an operation ... Naturally, he couldn't be told at that time. Have told him since his return home. He was always looking for letters from George ... Any information I may be able to get, I shall tell you or any family members of other men. [It] takes time. All we can do is hope and pray, God willing, that our "dearly beloved" will in time return to us, unhurt.

Mr. Mitchell's letter soon followed, stating, "George repeatedly spoke of the fine qualities of your son. He was our only child; we are desolate." This was followed by a telegram on June 27. "War Department wire states International Red Cross reports George prisoner. What news Stanley?"

Still not aware of the change in crews, Granddad received a letter from Walter Swan's mother, the other Dartmouth boy, weeks before the "official" crew list was released. She wrote:

> I received your letter yesterday morning. I can sympathize with you in the news you have received about your son. Walter could not have been navigator on his ship at that time as he was reported missing in action March 18. I received the telegram April 12, and May 3 I received a telegram saying he was a prisoner of war of the German government ... I sincerely hope you will hear good news soon. I have been told that it often takes ninety days before word is received.

Yet even without the Internet and high-tech networking, Granddad managed to connect with an old friend and then editor of the *St. Louis Globe-Democrat* who, in turn, tracked down the address of Allan Klute's folks from St. Louis. Klute's fate was the same as Swan's—MIA March 18 and reported as POW May 3.

Through a friend, Granddad located yet another crewman's family in California, crewman Johnny Papazian. Lucille Papazian wrote:

> Dear Mr. and Mrs. Dwyer;
>
> This afternoon we rec'd a letter from your friend ... telling us about Stanley. We've heard lots of nice things about Stanley, and a few weeks ago we rec'd a picture of Johnny's crew, and your son was in the picture. Johnny is my twin brother and is a tail gunner and armorer, as you probably know. I'm very, very sorry to say that Johnny hasn't mentioned a thing about Stanley. He never mentions anything like that so as not to worry us. Reading some of Johnny's old letters, we found out that between May 6-14 Johnny was at rest camp ... As far as we know, Johnny is safe as we've been receiving letters from him all along ... My parents and myself send you and yours our deepest sympathies and prayers ... I guess the best we can all do is to pray that this war may cease very soon and that God will watch over Stanley and all the others like him ... Did Stanley send you his crew picture? If not, we can have one made for you.

Grandma and Granddad received letters at a steady pace, even more so after the government released the official list of crewmen. One letter from Peter Milewski of Delaware read:

Dear Mr. Dwyer:

We were very glad to receive your recent letter and sincerely hope by this time you have had more news about your son ... May 28 we received a telegram that Steve was missing in action; shortly after that, we learned of the German shortwave broadcast every night at ten during which time the Nazis read the names and often messages from their prisoners. We listened faithfully, every night. But on June 14 the static was so bad that, try as we may, we couldn't get the program at all. It seems that was the night that Stephen's name was mentioned as being a prisoner of war. For the next day we received cards and letters from all over the U.S. and Canada. On the thirtieth of June, we were notified officially that Steve was a POW ...

As you probably know, Stephen was not the usual gunner on this Fortress. He was just scheduled for that flight on May 10. So far as we can learn, this is the only time when he did not fly with his regular crew in their plane, "Club 105."

Soon after Stephen was reported missing, we received a letter from one of the boys in the crew of Stephen's plane, the "Club 105." He said their plane was not scheduled to fly that day, but for some reason unknown to them, Stephen had been scheduled to fly in another plane, but just for that one day. When they learned the plane did not come back, they tried to learn all they could, and one of the boys wrote us. He said that all he could learn was that the plane had been hit and fell out of formation. The men in the other ships watched as long as they possibly could and reported seeing either five or six parachutes bailing out before they had to continue on with the formation.

I pray God that the entire crew got out in time, and since you have not heard any further news from your son, is it not possible that he may be in the hands of the underground who are trying to smuggle him back to our lines?

I shall be very interested in hearing anything you may wish to forward about your own son or any of the others.

Best wishes,
Peter Milewski

Eugene Parker's mother, Mabel, wrote that she, too, knew her son was a POW. Mrs. Boyett "wondered if our sons are together" in a letter to Granddad telling about her son John's status as a German war prisoner.

The copilot's mother, Mrs. Manley H. Dale, informed Granddad that "we received notice that Manley Jr. was a prisoner on June 26 ... Your son

Stan was the only person Manley Jr. ever wrote about when they were all together ... We heard thru Ralph Lauper, a member of the squadron but in another plane, that the right wing of our boys' plane was shot away. Also that they were so busy themselves that they couldn't watch the other planes ... When we hear from Manley Jr., I imagine it will contain only what they want him to write ... I do hope and pray your son is safe and well some place."

It seems the crew photo in Stanley's trunk was included in a letter Lucille Papazian sent to Granddad. Each crewman was identified on the back of the enlarged photo.

Stanley's B-17 crew. Photo presumably provided by Lucille Papazian in 1944.
Back row, left to right: George Mitchell, radio operator; John Boros, engineer
and upper gun; Darris Oldfather, ball turret gunner; John Papazian, tail gunner.
Front row, left to right: Don Pratt, waist gunner; Stanley Dwyer,
pilot; Manley Dale Jr., copilot; Gail Popplewell, waist gunner.
Two crewmen, navigator Walt Swan and bombardier Allan Klute,
are not pictured. They were shot down on March 18, 1944, flying
a mission with another crew, and both became POWs.

"[My brother] Johnny wrote," Lucille penned, "and said that he had completed his missions and expected to be home by our niece's birthday which is August 17 ... I promise to show him your letter, and if he has any information whatsoever regarding your son or any clue at all, we'll see to it that you get the information. I imagine he will know a little about it. I hope he will ... Mother and Dad send you and Mrs. Dwyer their regards also. Mother told me to tell you that she prays for Stanley and the rest of the crew every nite, and so do Dad and I."

Johnny Papazian's letter was written on August 11, 1944.

Dear Mr. Dwyer,

I'm Johnny, the tail gunner on Stan's crew. With the grace of God, I successfully finished my fifty missions without a scratch and am now at home where I wish the other nine men on our crew could be also. Immediately after my arrival at home last night, Lucille, my sister, brought out your two letters for me to read and supplement more facts to you, if possible. As you already know, Donald Pratt (our left waist gunner) and I were at the rest camp at Bari at the present time. Gail Popplewell, our right waist gunner, was grounded on that particular day (May 10). We didn't hear about the boys until the sixteenth of May, the day we reported back to camp from Bari. The story I then painfully received from Darris Oldfather, our ball gunner who had flown as tail gunner May 10 for another crew (Darris later was shot down at Ploesti, Rumania, on May 18. I was flying in the ship next to him and saw his chute blossom). Darris told us that the "Asunder" got hit by flak in one of its engines, and so Lt. Dwyer had to stop the engine consequently putting them at the mercy of the many enemy fighters (Me 109s and Fw 190s) following the formation and waiting for stragglers. The boys put up a fierce fight, and when Lt. Dwyer saw that the fight was impossible, gave the order to abandon ship. Darris then states that six chutes appeared, and by that time, the "Asunder" was out of sight, still under control, and not on fire. From that I gather that Lt. Dwyer was probably trying to make it to Turkey. If things got too rough, he could have abandoned the ship. That's all I know about the tragedy, sir; wish I knew more. Their target for that day was Wiener Neustadt in Austria, one of the roughest targets we've ever had. Lt. Dwyer had, I believe, around twenty-six missions in when he went down.

Lt. Klute and Swan went down on the eighteenth of March as you state. They were flying alongside of us that day when the Jerry fighters started lobbing rockets at us. I believe parts of their controls were shot away for their plane went in a sharp dive as they peeled off. Luckily, they left it in time. You may be wondering why they didn't fly us as a group the first few missions. The reason was that they wanted to break us in with more experienced crews.

That's about all I know, Mr. Dwyer, and in closing, I want you to know that we all thought a heck of a lot about Stan and the other boys. We were truly a great team. Thanks for the invitation, and I'll certainly try to make it if circumstances permit.

My warmest regards to Mrs. Dwyer. Here's hoping for good news soon.

Sincerely,
Johnny

Every now and then, I'd pick up the phone and call Eugene Parker. He explained, "There were ten crewmen in all. On May 10, five bailed out and were POWs until the end of the war. Of those five, John Boyett and I are still alive. We still stay in contact and see each other at 463rd reunions. Plus I think George Mitchell is still living, too, but I don't know about Milewski. Copilot Dale has passed away. Some of Stanley's original crew members that weren't flying together on May 10 are still alive too. I think Papazian lives in California, and I'm pretty sure Don Pratt is alive. Oldfather died on a mission to Ploesti on May 18. I'm not sure about Klute, but I think both Swan and Popplewell are gone."

From that conversation, I had a list of five probable contacts. The mood "hit" one day, and I finally convinced myself to call Mr. Papazian. Would he want to talk about the war? Would a phone call dredge up bad memories? Would he remember any details of his August 1944 interview with a *Los Angeles Times* reporter when the gunner stated, "My first mission was to Udine, Italy, and although the Germans used rockets, we were not hit and about the only damage was when a waist gunner drilled a bunch of holes in our stabilizer in his eagerness to hit a fighter. After the first five missions, however, each succeeding assignment becomes a 'scarier and scarier deal.' You see planes and men going down all around you, and you realize it could happen to you too."

So I sat at my desk and dialed his number in California. My heart thumped in my chest, which, I doubt, is much of a dilemma for most telemarketers. Whenever I made a cold call, I assured whoever answered that I was not a telemarketer. Before putting Johnny Papazian on the phone, his wife mentioned that his memory had slipped. Indeed, Mr. Papazian had forgotten about Stanley and details of May 10. What did I expect? Even under "normal" circumstances, would he have remembered any more than what he'd written in his letter to Granddad back in 1944? My heart went out to Mr. Papazian. Just talking to someone who trained with and knew Stanley seemed to bring Stanley closer and make him more real.

There were more letters in Stanley's trunk dated 1944.

Dear Mr. Dwyer:

Thanks so much for your immediate reply to my inquiries concerning Stan.

At the time I wrote you, I knew that his copilot was missing. However, they sometimes fill in on other crews, so I was in hopes that Stan had just neglected writing and that he wasn't along on that particular mission.

I have written Lt. Lauper, one of the fellows in his squadron, asking for any information he could give on what has taken place since we have heard from Stan. When I hear from him, I shall let you know any news that I receive.

In the meantime, I would greatly appreciate your writing me if you receive any further information.

Gratefully,
Huretta

Dear Mr. Dwyer,

Sorry to bother you again, but as I have heard news of Stan's copilot, I was wondering if perhaps you have had additional news of Stan?

From a letter I recently received, I learned Pete Dale, copilot, is now a prisoner of war.

Have you had any such news of Stan? If so, please let me know. Any suggestions as to how I might write to Stan, if such is possible, would truly be appreciated.

Thanking you for your trouble, I remain.

Sincerely,
Retta

Theron Newell reminisced about Stanley in a letter written to Granddad on, of all days, Father's Day 1944.

Really, it doesn't seem like five years ago that we took off together. When two people take out together like that, one doesn't measure its worth in time, but experience. Facing and battling the world together brought us closer than living every day life at home for a longer time ... Because of a slight physical handicap, I could never keep up with him on the last series of adventures. I really felt so envious of his learning to fly that I put my thoughts down in poetry, dedicated to him. Enclosed is a copy of it, dated and dedicated. It has been read over a local radio station here with the dedication some time in March ... (see Appendix E) There is nothing that I could say that could ease your anxious parental hearts. It is a blow that time alone can ease, but never heal. Stan lived a lifetime in a few short years. He lived fully, completely, unafraid, without regrets. I'm sure he met life's last great adventure the same as I had seen him meet others. However, we can both hope that he is still alive.

And between the pages of letters from parents whose sons were reported as POWs were letters from families whose loved ones were not so fortunate.

Tech Sergeant Prescott Piper's brother-in-law, Milton Newberg, thanked Granddad for his letter. "T/Sgt Piper was reported missing first and then later reported killed in action. Sometime later Mrs. Piper, his mother, received the Purple Heart for Prescott ... I am glad for you that your news is better to date than ours. Let us pray for the early return of our boys and a speedy end to the war."

Francis Gilhooley, father of Francis Gilhooley, wrote:

The intelligence contained in your letter of August 16 was the most complete information and in more detail than any communication we have yet received, either from the War Department or any other source.

After the initial telegram stating that my son, Lt. Francis Gilhooley, was missing, we received on June 27 an additional telegram to the effect that he had been killed in action on May 10. The letter from the War Department that followed this second communication was wholly devoid of detail ...

And so you see, our information is extremely meager. I wish for all our sakes that this was not so. May I, however, say that in your case, since you have received no second telegram, that there is every cause for hope. May I also say that we here hope that when you do hear, the news will be of the best and that your son will come back to you when it's over on the continent. May God grant that!

In another letter, Helen Olfenius stated:

[I was]very grateful for the information you passed on to me ... On June 26, I received a telegram reporting my son as killed in action, and I telephoned Mr. Gilhooley, and he told me his son was reported the same.

Any information you receive from any of the crew will be appreciated as I am very eager to know if my son really has been killed. Am hoping and praying to God to bring him and his crew back safe to their loved ones. I won't give up hope, but this waiting is almost driving me insane. Bill was a tail gunner on the plane …

I do hope your boy is safe and well and you hear good news of him in the near future. I can sympathize with you in your anxious waiting as I have been going through the same thing since May 28 when I got the first report of Bill.

Mrs. Mitchell corresponded somewhat regularly with Granddad, passing on information she had gathered from her contact with other crew families.

Mrs. Olfenius is frightfully upset, cannot believe it is true. Feels as long as some of the crew are reported prisoners of the German government, Bill may also turn up sometime. Who knows, he may. Her son was eighteen years old when he enlisted in the Air Corps. He gave up fourteen months of high school. Enlisted on his birthday. He was a tail gunner. May 12 his mother received a beautiful plant, not knowing her Bill was in trouble, like the other folks too … Mrs. Boros, wife of the engineer called on us. She received the same kind of report as you did but is convinced her husband, John, is safe. She has no further word than the first telegram. Boros's wife picked out Johnny [in the crew photo Granddad sent] the nite she was here. He is next to George. They were married seven years; he was thirty-two years old, a good engineer, no doubt … Mrs. Gilhooley accepted the word she received and is now a grandmother to her son's child. They also have a son in the navy.

Meanwhile, a few years into our search, my friend Susan Biba handed me a *Journal Star* newspaper article telling about Jerry Penry of Milford, Nebraska, who was searching for a friend's brother, a missing pilot of a downed B-17 over Belgium in May 1944. Jerry's helpful suggestions on what information to gather and his assistance posting my message on a heavy bomber website forum opened the door for more cyberspace exposure and produced some feedback. Jerry forwarded several responses only after he found my "lost" phone number and address. One e-mail mentioned contacting Eugene Parker. Someone else passed on information about requesting an Individual Deceased Personnel File (IDPF), and several people responded that the serial number on Stanley's plane was #42-31685, "Pete's Playhouse." However, one particular e-mail response had conflicting information.

Dear Sir,

I read your message on the heavy bombers webpage. I am a cadet in the Austrian Military Academy. I am working on a report about the USAAF bombing raids against Wiener Neustadt (Austria) in the years 1943–1945. Maybe I can help you. Please tell me what you are looking for. I know about the plane and his crash place at Vostenhof Pottschach Austria. The serial No. was 42-31804. I am looking, also, for any information concerning these raids.

Yours sincerely,

Markus Reisner, Cadet

Markus Reisner, from Austria, responded to my personal e-mail, and he thought I was a male.

Dear Sir,

First of all, I have to apologize for my long silence. A lot of things for me to do in the army. On 10 May 1944, thirty-one heavy bombers and three fighters were shot down over Wiener Neustadt. The 463rd lost seven planes at this day over Wiener Neustadt. One plane was the plane of 2 Lt. Gerald Gowen (42-31685) which crashed at Lichtenworth in the northeast of Wiener Neustadt. Another one was the plane of your father's brother, the plane of 2 Lt. Stanley Dwyer (42-31804). His plane crashed at Vostenhof Pottschach in the south of Wiener Neustadt. I am in contact with Joseph C. Meyers, his uncle was 2 Lt. Gerald Gowen. He also told me about the different serial numbers. The cause is that the German air force made a mistake with the numbers of the planes. Is the local historian Mr. Stranz (I hope this is the right spelling)? I heard about him. He knows a lot about the crash place at Pottschach and about what exactly happened. I heard about him from another person Mr. Rameder (also an historian). Mr. Rameder told me about him after I told him about your e-mail. The plane of Lt. Dwyer was badly damaged and was going down. Some men of the crew managed to bail out. Lt. Dwyer was fighting with the piloting of the plane, but suddenly the plane crashed in a wall of rock and killed him and the rest of the crew. One man who bailed out landed very close to the plane in a tree. He was screaming for help. Some of the local farmers heard this, but they were not able to get closer to him because of the burning parts of the plane. Suddenly, some remaining bombs or fuel exploded and killed the man who was hanging in the tree. Five dead bodies were recovered from the crash place. Five persons got POW. Mr. Rameder told me that today there is a memorial existing there and that one of the crew (he thought it was a gunner) visited the place some years ago. Okay, hope this will help first.

Yours sincerely,

Markus Reisner

For Grandma and Granddad, the days slipped by, weeks came and went, and by early fall of 1944, they had made a round-trip to Ft. Sumner to attend Dad's graduation.

The folks went down to New Mexico in August when I completed advanced training and earned my wings. I had two weeks off before going to transitional training, and the friend that I had enlisted with some fourteen months before, Floyd Marion, rode back to Nebraska with the folks and me.

Grandma wrote her sister Gertie:

We had a big time while Harold was home, but the time was so short it seemed as tho he was no more here than it was time for him to leave again. It would have been better for him if he could have stayed another week. He had such a big time with Carol Jean, as we all did. I felt sorry for him the morning he left. He didn't want to go a bit. However, he didn't know that anyone guessed that. We went to Mankato Saturday where we had a good time, including a plane ride for his pop, mom, Aileen and Gayle. We were the only ones out there who would go up ... He did a few stunts with Gayle, but I took mine just straight. It was quite thrilling to us, more so with Harold as the pilot ...

Well, little by little, since the government released the names of his crew members, we are able to sort out and piece together the things that happened to Stanley on the day he went down. That is, I mean, up to a certain point. We still don't know his and his engineer's fate, but we do know about the rest of them ... We know now that five of them are prisoners ... We don't know, of course, when they [the other crewmen] were killed, but it was probably over the target, and Stanley might have wanted to land the plane knowing they were gone rather than to bail out and let it crash. It looks like if they had been killed in the crash of the plane, we would have been notified the same as the others ...

Then we also had a letter from Stanley's girlfriend in Florida. She had had a letter from Stanley's friend's wife who said she had a letter from him in Italy. He told her the favorable opinion around there was that Stanley was in friendly hands. They didn't explain why they thought this, so it may be just wishful thinking. But on the other hand, they may have a little to go on. A few airmen that were shot down the same day have returned to their base in Italy ... We also have learned that the plane had a wing shot away. We feel confident that Stanley wasn't hurt, at least not seriously, as long as the ship was still under control when last seen as the copilot was one of those that bailed out ...

I may go down to Mankato for a while. I thought when all our company was gone I would feel like staying alone again, but my nerves went haywire again yesterday, so guess I won't try it for a while …

For my grandparents, correspondence slowed to a trickle. The only information the government had to offer was "no further report in his case." About the time Stanley's birthday approached, notification was sent of "some personal property belonging to your son" being forwarded—Stanley's dark brown leather trunk.

Mrs. Dale stated in her last letter:

> We received Manley Jr.'s clothing and effects from Kansas City last week, too, and know how hard it was for you and Mrs. Dwyer to sort and store them … Harold, I take it, is another son? Do hope all goes well with him. It certainly must be hard to see him go, too, after the heartache and uncertainty over Stanley.
>
> Manley Jr. thought a great deal of Stan, so we are hoping somehow he can get some word to us about him, and we'll certainly let you know as soon as I hear anything from any source … Anyway, don't give up hoping … We are praying with you for his safe return.

So Granddad and Grandma were able to sort things out and piece together what they could. And, as for the ten-man crew, it stood that five crewmen were POWs, three were reported KIA, and Stanley and John Boros were carried as MIAs.

I tried to put myself in my grandparents' shoes. Did they toss and turn all night long? Did they stare off into space during the day wondering where Stanley was, waiting for the postman or the next telegram? With no second telegram and nothing conclusive to go on, was no news good news? And just what did Grandma think about my dad going off to war?

I can answer that by saying she wasn't very happy. When I finally shipped to England in February 1945, I remember purposely not telling Mom when I started flying combat missions. She found out, anyway, and she wrote me in a letter that I could "come clean." She'd read in the newspaper what I'd been up to, about my "baptism of fire during an attack on German railroad yards in the Ruhr Valley."

When the folks received word about Stan, I was in intense training at the time. Though it was a dreaded message to get, we had a sliver of hope in that he was missing in action. The government usually waited a year before declaring the person dead if no more information became available. By December, I was in the final phases of training at Rapid City, South Dakota, and the folks came and stayed a few days around Christmastime. Kay has asked me if we ever talked about Stan missing the few times the folks and I were together during that time period. Maybe it was mentioned a time or two, but it's been many, many years, and I just don't remember anything specific.

After thinking a bit, though, I did remember the last letter my brother wrote to me. I had carefully saved it in a file with some other papers. So I went to my file drawer and pulled out the file to show Kay his letter. Stan's last letter to me had been filed away with many of my letters I'd written the folks during the war years.

Somewhere in Italy
March 24, 1944

Dear Harold:

Yes, ma, you may read before sending this on. Reckon Harold is moving from place to place too rapidly for me to use an address of his. However I doubt that there will be contained here-in anything that I haven't said before. The last letter I got from you Harold was from primary, written about the first of February. Had word from the folks the other day that you area about to transfer from the training planes to fighters. If so, then I have lost all track of time, or else the cade's are being sent through much faster than when I was there. The folks mentioned the 38, and if that is it then all the boys over here will extend their hearty approval. The 38 is popular here, and if there are any ugly rumors still floating around about her then they are unfounded and untrue.

Life here is much different than in training in the states. You of course have assumed as much. However, don't harbor the idea that 'his is paradise. The army can hardly be expected to furnish the nice quarters on foreign posts that it does in the states, which at the moment you aren't taking time to appreciate. But considering the distance, the difficulty of transportation, and the lack of native facilities, we are living quite comfortably. We have tents, with electric lights, an officers' club that is nice, comfortable sleeping and good food. When one's day is all business, then there is not much more that a man could ask for.

Of course you are far from being ready to come across. But here are a few suggestions. These are some things that I would try to bring if I were making the trip the second time. Most of them though I would plan to get after you are staged, because their is a limit to what you may start the trip with and to stock up might be in vain. I have found that lighting facilities are not the best in all places. We have electricity here, but there have been times when a small kerocene lamp would have been handy. Some places where there is electricity there is a shortage of bulbs. An extra razor is useful, and blades, longer-than-ordinary woolen sox, an extra fountain pen, even though it is a cheap one, and ink. Candles, flash-lights and batteries and bulbs. Plenty of underclothing, and some beaten-up clothes to knock around in. You will have very little use for your good clothes, and the natives have poor facilities from for dry cleaning. You probably will have less baggage space when you come, for ours is a big ship and will hold much junk. In which case such things as condles would be better than a bulky lamp.

I think that list will apply in whatever theater you are sent. And that is about all the advice your weather-beaten brother can give you. Other than to keep your head out of the cock-pit. Of course you have heard that before. There are other places you have been accused of having your head, also. And it is little good there.

I hear you have been spending a lot o' time with the Schoutens. And Beth. It is good that they have been there. Also that you could help break up the monotony of theirs that might be present if they were there alone. Found the names of some Manhattan and some Glasco men in the officers' directory here. I doubt that you might have known any of them tho. One I think was the son of Ahearn director of athletics at Kansas State. Write to me.

Love
Stan

261

In the last line of that letter, Stan said, "write to me." And that's the last conversation, or communication, I had with him.

Time marched on. The year 1945 approached.

Dear Mr. and Mrs. Dwyer:

And I want you to know that at least part of this time has been spent in thinking of you folks—hoping your Christmas was a pleasant one—but hoping far more that the New Year will bring you good news of Stan!

I expect so much of this new year. I hope for the return of several intimate friends; I hope for a deeper thinking home front; I hope for a more united, more sincere peace policy embracing all peoples of all nations, and I even dare to hope for the ultimate—Peace. Facing the facts, it is hard to believe that I might realize any one of these, but thank God, it is still not impossible to hope. And I still take refuge in the fact that during World War I, right up until the Armistice, many military experts were still predicting the end in terms of years rather than days. Can we not hope then, too, that as in so many cases, history repeats itself in this one? Call it the hope of an optimist, not an escapist; for I think I've seen and indirectly felt my measure of heartbreak and sorrow in these past three years enough to acquaint me with that broad term, realism, and I still profess it to be as broad as it is wide, as it were. And miracles, as such, only seem impossible to those who are too lazy to wonder about them; hence, fail to see why they happen. All of which is really too deep for my 24-year-old mind to grasp completely, so I will stop boring you. If ever I master the art of self-expression, I will certainly be considered either a philosopher or a fool, but for fear of being prematurely considered the latter, I will stop. Cannot explain my urge to write in this manner to someone I so little know, unless it was in this vein that I felt so much in common with Stan. And I treasure so much the answers I got to such mental outpourings. Only his rich sense of humor kept me from going off the deep end, at times ...

We hear from [my brother] Harry in India about once a week, and we are counting the days until his fiftieth mission has been completed ... He had written asking for your address, and I think he intended writing you about some news he had received indirectly from friends of fellows "missing in action" whose situations, more or less, paralleled that of yours. I know that it was no direct news of Stan or of any of his crew, but just one of those quirks of fate which just go to show that one should not lose hope too rapidly … A Happy New Year to you.

Sincerely,
Janice Cuthbertson

Another letter from Lakeland, Florida, written by Huretta, read:

Dear Mrs. Dwyer,

Thank you so much for the Christmas card and your nice letter. I hope you enjoyed a pleasant holiday season.

I wish I could write that I have had good news of Stan, but I have heard nothing. I keep waiting and hoping, but as yet my prayers have not been answered … I do remember, though, that it was this time last year that I first met Stan. Oh, I wish someone would hear something, and soon …

You were very fortunate in getting back Stan's clothing and effects. Was his typewriter among the things returned? When he was here, he wouldn't come in town on his day off unless he brought his typewriter with him.

Has Harold Jr. left the States yet? Or am I getting ahead of him? From your letter I take it that he has graduated and been assigned to a crew. What type of plane is he on?

I shall be waiting to hear from you.

Sincerely,
Retta

There still was hope, and we waited. We all waited for the end of the war, hoping and thinking Stan may come out of a prisoner camp. In the meantime, in February of 1945, I was sent across to England.

10

c-o-fc-o

Life Goes On

Damned if they don't fight a harder battle than we.
—Stanley N. Dwyer in a letter dated April 14, 1944

Unlike Grandma and Granddad's search, our search included information directly from people in Austria. I continued to sort and read letters, and other vital information accumulated; however, as of yet, there was no strategic plan on our part, and it didn't occur to us that we were being led on a journey. What occurred to us, though, was what to do with the collection of information.

In the pile of information was an article I'd saved. The article, from the *Parade* section of one Sunday paper and written by Dianne Hales, told of Dr. Patrick Scannon searching for missing planes from World War II—more particularly in the South Pacific—and then locating the crews. Scannon, compared to Indiana Jones, was quoted as saying, "I'm filling in a page of history, not just for the sake of what happened on some little coral island 50-odd years ago but to make sure we don't forget any of the people who sacrificed their blood and sometimes their lives. Not everyone fought on famous battlefields in the war, but they fought and died no less bravely—and they should not be forgotten any sooner."

It seemed like a far-fetched idea to undertake personally, but my secret desire was to be like Dr. Scannon and search for missing planes—one plane in particular, only in Europe, not the South Pacific. But, I'd set that article aside.

I had a buddy I went through high school with—Russ Kime. He had been in the service and was aware that my brother had been shot down and no remains were ever found. Russ had moved to California, and, out of the blue one day, Russ sent me the November 2, 2002, front page of the Los Angeles Times. *An article, which I passed on to Kay, told about CILHI excavating a crash site in Germany.*

After skimming that article, the newspaper landed on my desk with accumulating papers, because there were schedules to juggle and ... plug in here whatever excuse fits.

Information and leads came in many ways and often when we least expected it. Dad's article, though, put answers right in front of us—just follow the lead. Hindsight proved the article would be a turning point in our journey, only something needed to happen. It did, finally. It must have been a divine nudge—more like a push. One day, I found the article on the desk and carefully read it. It was a moving story about a daughter's attempt to find her dad, Lieutenant Bill Lewis, a missing American fighter pilot, downed September 11, 1944, over what became East Germany after the war. The six-decade mystery unraveled, and I recognized some similarities to our search. Subsequently, CILHI, the Central Identification Laboratory, Hawaii, sent a U.S. Army excavation team to the site in Germany to dig and screen for remains.

The article stated, "The team was from an Army unit in Hawaii, half a world away. Created after the Vietnam War primarily to find and recover Americans missing in action in Southeast Asia ... CILHI ... is relatively new to the task of bringing home American servicemen who died in the Second World War."

So, I just picked up the phone, called Information, and contacted Esther Schrader, the *Times* staff writer who'd written the article.

"How do I get in touch with CILHI?" I asked her.

"CILHI is located at Hickam Air Force Base in Hawaii," she replied.

I dialed the number she gave me for CILHI and was connected to Johnie Webb's extension. Ignorance, sometimes, is bliss. Little did I know I had just circumvented the whole chain of command and gone nearly to the top. Johnie E. Webb Jr., a Vietnam veteran himself and currently serving in a civilian capacity as deputy commander, listened to me ramble in my excitement about Stanley and many aspects of our search. I made the point. We knew of a World War II crash site near Vostenhof, Austria, with possibly two sets of remains, those of Stanley Dwyer and John Boros.

"We'll take information any way we can get it," Johnie Webb assured me.

"My original involvement with CIL began in July of 1975," Johnie told me. "CIL was formed in March of 1973. I went to Thailand in 1975 because, at that time, it was set up in Thailand to do identifications and recoveries as a result of those killed in the Vietnam War. There's a military tradition in all the services—never leave your buddy behind. During the Vietnam War, we had thousands of U.S. forces in Thailand. After the war, the Thais wanted to reduce the U.S. military footprint in their country, so they came up with a number. It turned out we were part of that drawdown of U.S. forces, so I had the responsibility of moving the operation. I moved it to Hawaii in May 1976."

Thus the name changed to CILHI, the Central Identification Laboratory, Hawaii. It's Johnie's "baby."

Okay. Now it started to register. Too many coincidences made it obvious. We were being led on this journey—and sometimes, it seemed, almost prodded down the path. Looking back, we recounted our tracks in the sand; we anticipated what lay ahead. In the meantime, there was more to learn.

Letters, letters, and more letters. I was practically up to my knees in letters, and then Dad's file of letters written home during the war—some in a familiar type, other pages handwritten—was added to the stack. Good old-fashioned letter writing. The modern-day rival, electronic mail, is at the mercy of the delete button. The Internet played an indispensable role in our search by putting information and the world, especially Austria, at our fingertips. However, unless printed first, electronic mail easily disappears. There's just no comparison between an e-mail and curling up in a chair to read a pile of letters written by your dad on authentic United States Army Air Forces letterhead. I reentered what seemed like a time machine and dialed up 1945.

In the early months of 1945, a path of death and destruction lay between the D-Day beaches of Normandy and Berlin. The Allies "secured" Normandy, France, in August of 1944 and pushed to Berlin from the west while Russia breathed down Hitler's neck from the east. In the Pacific in February of 1945, U.S. troops raised the American flag on Mount Suribachi on Iwo Jima. The horrific island-hopping campaign favored the Allies as they closed in on Japan. And operating from islands overtaken from the enemy, U.S. forces bombed mainland Japan.

Still in training, Dad wrote home:

> My bombardier's brother showed up the other day after spending so many days in Holland. He has been reported missing since 17 Sept. Now all we have to do is have one more show up and we will all be happy.

Then Dad wrote:

> The Ryans have heard their other son is a prisoner of war. Wish we could hear some good news along that line.

Dad wrote his folks from England starting in February 1945. A sampling follows.

We are all fine over here and should remain so in the future. Write soon and don't worry.

***

There is no need to worry as this group hasn't lost anybody for quite a while.

***

Will you folks mail me Stanley's last address. Believe I shall get the Red Cross on his tail over here.

***

Most all runs are now classified as 'milk runs.'

***

Gen. Patton is having quite a time in Germany tonight, I'll bet. He is really moving along, and we don't care if he doesn't ever stop. Of course, we are all expecting to go to the CBI [theater] in the future, but then this part of the war will be over, and that is what we are waiting for, to have Stan come back.

***

Don't worry as there is nothing to worry about. Take it from me firsthand.

***

I see where the Russians have liberated a lot of prisoners in Austria the last couple of days. We can stand some news anytime now, can't we?

***

I could use some fudge.

***

It should not be too long before this thing is over, over here. The news about Stan should come before long now.

Before the end of the war in Europe, a couple of weeks before Germany surrendered, it happened that thousands of Dutch people were starving. During the invasion of Europe, the Dutch helped the Allies instead of Germany, so the Germans cut off even more of their already dwindling food supply. Some higher-ups worked out a plan with the Germans, allowing the Americans and British to

267

drop food over Holland. We called it Operation Chowhound. We loaded a couple of tons of food in the bomb bays and flew across the English Channel, two to three hundred planes at a time. One time, I led two planes over the channel. When we made a turn, I looked back. Our planes were so low that they were dishing water out from the prop wash, stirring up a wake in the water like a motorboat.

We came across the drop zone about fifty to one hundred feet above the runway, basically a legalized buzz job. On one drop, I hit the salvo switch to drop the food, and nothing happened. It was determined that one of the ground crew had failed to cock the manual set bomb release mechanism. We decided to make more passes while the crew unloaded the food out of the bomb bay while balancing on the narrow catwalk. Some of the rations were unloaded forward, and some were unloaded backward in order to keep balance in the plane. The engineer got down and cocked the bomb shackles, and the crew reloaded the food back in the bomb bay.

On the very first "manna drop," the thought crossed more than one mind as we wondered whether or not the Germans would shoot at us. The Germans had agreed on a corridor in and out of Holland and a set time frame to get the job done. Red flares would be fired as a warning if we were out-of-bounds or took too long. Antiaircraft fire would follow. Well, on that particular drop when nothing released, after several passes, we finally dropped the rations, and then the whole sky lit up in front of us with red flares. I started an immediate 180-degree turn. Navigator Menafee got a fix, and we headed for England.

On the first food drop mission, the Dutch didn't know what to expect. The next time, it was different. Dutch flags were flying, and some of the people wrote on the ground, with white cloth or something, "Thanks Yank" or a big V. I thought of home at that particular moment. It reminded me of when we were still in the States and had been transported to Lincoln, Nebraska, for staging. While in Lincoln, my crew was assigned a new airplane to fly across, so we had to put so many hours on the plane to make sure it was okay. One of the chores was to "swing the compass," which meant picking a known spot on the ground and flying radials off that spot every thirty degrees while the navigator plotted it on a map to check for compass accuracy. I chose my hometown, Hastings, Nebraska, as my "spot on the ground," the folks' house in particular. I called the folks to tell them I would use their house for the hub of the procedure we were to follow. As we flew over, we saw where my dad had taken Mom's wash off the line and wrote the words "Hi boy" on the lawn. The crew got a kick out of that, and I remarked in a letter home, "I bet Mother is a weary woman about now. We were over there three hours, and every time I saw her she was waving to beat four of a kind. It was easy to pick up the old joint."

My radioman, Jack Noe, kept a diary. His May 5, 1945, entry mentioned the "spam mission."

"It took seven runs over the target before Brown, Dad, and I got them all out," Jack wrote. "Came back an hour and a half late, everyone thought we had gone down." And Jack's May 10, 1945, diary entry noted, "Dwyer's brother went down in Italy one year ago today—B-17."

The one-year anniversary always caused a stir for families with someone missing in action because that was when the government "officially" declared a missing person dead.

The War Department, promptly on May 11, 1945, sent Grandma an official letter. In addition to the statement that "your son was promoted from Second Lieutenant to First Lieutenant with rank from 27 May 1944," the letter informed Grandma, "In view of the fact that twelve months have now expired without the receipt of evidence to support a continued presumption of survival, the War Department must terminate such absence by a presumptive finding of death ... The finding does not establish an actual or probable date of death; however, as required by law it includes a presumptive date of death for the termination of pay and allowances, settlement of accounts and payment of death gratuities. In the case of your son this date has been set as 11 May 1945, the day following the expiration of twelve months' absence."

In a letter home, Dad reassured Grandma:

As for the letter from the War Department, Mother, I wouldn't pay any attention about it for it does not mean a thing. If he is in hiding in Austria today, then he will still be there tomorrow after you get the thing. Have gone back several times to get prisoners, but there have been no Americans there though. You are undoubtedly keeping in close contact with Lt. Dale's folks, and that is the thing to do. If anything happened before they left the formation, then he would be the one to get the inside poop from. If you think that he might be a little reluctant about telling you folks, then send me his address, and I'll see what I can do.

Right after the war—V-E Day was May 8, 1945—all we knew was that Stan was MIA. Some of our Eighth Air Force missions were to fly down to Linz, Austria, and pick up an airplane load of French POWs. My crew wasn't assigned for one trip, so I asked a buddy if I could fly copilot on his trip down. Sure, no problem. So I rode down on that mission and landed in Linz with hopes that Stan would come walking out of the mist. Patton's tanks were still running around the airfield because the area had just been liberated a couple of days before. My letter home dated May 17, 1945, indicated that I'd made some inquiries and talked to one major that ran the field. He indicated that four airmen came in days before. They had been hiding in the country for a couple of years. We felt Stan had a chance. Nothing transpired then, of course, and the next day or so, my crew was scheduled, and we flew back to Austria for more prisoners.

Jack Noe wrote in his diary, "May 18, 1945 – nine hours and thirty-five minutes. Got up at 0315, briefed at 0445, took off at 0715 in very dense fog. First landed in Austria after looking over some German ships. We loaded 30 French POWs and headed for Paris. Some had been POWs for five years. On the way ran into awful electrical storm, so we landed in Belgium and waited for storm to pass. Finally made it to Paris and were these boys happy. The women and kids were going crazy. We got back here at 2100. A pretty long day."

One of the things that struck me when we looked the airport over in Linz was the Norden bombsight. It was pretty secret stuff, or so we thought. We'd been instructed to destroy the bombsight, if possible, if a crash landing was imminent. I walked over to a hangar, and along the entire east end of the building was a pile of Norden bombsights, probably three or four hundred in the pile. I don't think they were too secret at that point.

Dad's letter home read, in part:

Was looking over the Christmas cards last night along with the pictures of Stan and his crew. Have any of the boys written home yet, that is the ones on his crew? Something is sure to come out before long, and I have a sneaking hunch that it will be good too.

Still I found more letters in Stanley's trunk, written near the war's end from Francis Gilhooley, father of Stanley's navigator, Francis Gilhooley, who was reported as KIA. "As I sit here I wonder whether you have had good news of your son," Mr. Gilhooley wrote. "I hope so from the bottom of my heart, because I'm hoping that through him we may be able to get some idea of how our boy died. Not that it matters much, but still we'd like to hear some details.

"Do you have any idea how boys killed over enemy territory (like our son was) are buried? My wife worries so much about it that I fear for her health."

May 13, 1945

Dear Mrs. Dwyer,

I have hesitated in writing hoping that the good news from Europe would also bring good news from Stan.

Of course, I realize that it will take weeks to notify the families of all the men who have been liberated, so again, one must wait for news.

I suppose you read in the paper of the carefully kept records the Germans had of all men who went down over Germany or German-held territory. From that the government should be able to give you some idea of what has happened to Stan.

Lt. Dale's wife arrived last week in Lakeland. She is quite eagerly awaiting his return to the States. In one of his last letters to her, she hasn't heard from him since December, he wrote that Lt. Swan (navigator) had recently been transferred to the camp where he was being held. A reunion for part of the crew ...

I hope by the time this reaches you, you will have had good news of Stan. Please let me know if you hear anything.

Sincerely,
Retta

May 14, 1945

Dear Mr. and Mrs. Dwyer,

I was just wondering if you had any news about your son as my husband, John Boros, was declared dead. Your son and my husband were the only two that were reported missing. Somehow I can't believe that Johnny is dead and am still hoping that it is a mistake.

I spoke to Mrs. Mitchell, and she told me that her son was liberated. Mrs. Mitchell also told me that as soon as he comes home, she will let me know so that I could speak to him in person.

Will you be kind enough to let me know what you have heard concerning your son?

With God's help I hope it is a mistake about my husband.

I would appreciate any news that you could let me have.

I thank you very much.

Stella Boros

And Granddad wrote the following letter to Aileen on May 15, 1945:

Precious Aileen Girl:

Yist a word between jumps this morning to tell you that the letter from the War Department, which we knew had to be along shortly after May 10, arrived yesterday.

But, if Stanley were alive day before yesterday, he is still alive today after we have received the letter. It doesn't change the facts any but just lets us know that officially he is presumed to have been killed in action May 10, 1944. The letter states some things in connection, therewith, which we have every reason to doubt.

It states that reports indicate that Stanley's ship was hit and set afire by flak and that it exploded in the waist section and no parachutes were seen to emerge from the falling aircraft.

Even if Papazian's letter were made from whole cloth and written only to up our morale, we still have the knowledge that five of the men are prisoners of war. Under the circumstances set forth in the letter, none of them could have escaped. If part of it is cockeyed, we have every reason to assume that they know nothing of it at all. Sixty bombers went down that day, and the report on which they base their findings could have been made of any other ship that was lost. When they are falling at that rate, and everyone else in the group is trying to save their own bacon or looking for a place to light, no one is going to sit around with his legs crossed and take the numbers and positions of the ships as they go down.

So, we're still looking and hoping and expecting. It may be a hell of a while before we have any word, though. The rag this morning carried a story from over there to the effect that a request for a meeting with the Russians to work out means of flying out some three hundred thousand British and American prisoners of war known to be in the territory held by them has not even been answered. That doesn't look like they were going to break any legs getting word out to the folks at home. And down where Stanley probably is, they are still fighting ...

Heaps to all,
Dad

A letter from the mother of fill-in crewman John Boyett explained:

Yes, he [John] is at home. He was liberated May 2 and has been home a month the 28th. He was in good health ... and is hungry all the time. I am sorry my son can give you no information other than what we already know. He said the plane was burning heavily, and the boys parachuted out, but through the excitement and smoke, he never knew how many or who parachuted out, and just as he heard of them, as we have, is all he knew.

Dear Mr. Dwyer,

This is Eugene Parker writing now. I feel very bad about not writing sooner, but honest, I just couldn't sit myself down to do it. I know this isn't good news, but you want to know.

As far as I know, Stan is dead. The last time I saw him was in the plane. To me he looked alright because he was at the controls. I will admit that we had a very rough time of it. There was only one boy on the crew that wasn't wounded. That was George Mitchell.

Stan was really a swell fellow. I was never afraid to fly with him. There are some fellows that the boys are afraid to fly with. You couldn't meet a nicer fellow.

Sincerely,
Eugene Parker

Granddad and Grandma received more letters from crewmen, undoubtedly highly anticipated letters. One from Stanley's original crewman and radioman, George Mitchell, read:

Dear Mr. and Mrs. Dwyer,

Can you ever forgive me for not writing sooner? If I could do (or have done) anything to really help you, I would be in Hastings in nothing flat, but as it is, I'm home, and Stan isn't, and I've been afraid to write. Not afraid of you but for you.

To me, Stan was the salt of the earth. The others used to say I was prejudiced because I was his "pet," but that wasn't true at all. He had no pets and treated us all the same. But I did get along well with him right from the first.

It was way back in October nineteen hundred and forty-three when we first met. John Papazian and I had walked all over the Salt Lake City Air Base looking for our newly acquired officers. Klute and Dale were out, but Lt. Dwyer was there in the barracks spending a quiet evening "at home" with two wonderful guys and great buddies of his Lts. Lauper and Little. Pappy and I spent about an hour in there talking to them and after saying good night did a snake dance all the way back to our quarters because we were so happy about him.

Later on, when we had started to fly, we found out what a good pilot he was and then had something else to shout about.

No need to tell you how very thorough he was about everything he did. Stan wanted us to be the best combat crew *ever*. But he wasn't a martinet about it. We were his boys. He knew what was best for us but consulted us about it. My own dad couldn't have been more thoughtful.

You know, he and I went on our first mission together, same plane, same day. He was flying copilot in our "baptism by fire," and I can remember how he called me on the interphone every once in a while to see how I was way back there in the lonely radio room.

I could go on all night remembering things about him, and me, and us. About the night (or should I say morning) we all had a wee bit too much to drink and got in after two and had to get up at four to fly; about the way we used to kid him about that typewriter he carried with him; about the night be helped me get a pass to my cousins' in Florida for Christmas.

I believe Stan liked what he was doing and was happy, as happy as any of us can be in the middle of a war. I haven't said the things I have just as idle praise but because I want you to know that I appreciated him too.

I do wish we could get together tête-à-tête. Right now that's something to look forward to. Anytime that you care to write, I'd like to hear from you and will do my best to answer any questions you might care to ask.

After having Stan for an "air daddy" and after reading all of your letters, I find it hard to believe that we have never met, and now that I've begun, writing you seems most natural. I hope you're both well and have some good news of Harold to pass on to us. My folks send their best. Until later then.

Sincerely,
George

As letters came out of the trunk and described the 1940s' scenario, our search expanded. We were like attentive students eager to learn, and Eugene Parker fed us information. Eugene shared combat reports and books, along with other information he'd gathered, including a copy of a declassified report concerning the May 10 mission—more specifically, a request for a unit citation for the 463rd's performance on that day. Grandma and Granddad probably never read the report. The original statement, written by C. W. Lawrence, brigadier general, was released from Headquarters Fifth Wing.

On 10 May 1944, the 463rd Bombardment Group (H) USAAF was given the assignment of destroying specific units of the aircraft factory at Wiener Neustadt, Austria ... one of the most heavily defended spots in Europe.

Since Germany embarked on its rearmament program, Wiener Neustadt, Austria, located thirty miles from the capital city of Vienna, has been the chief production center of Nazi fighter plane component parts, especially vital as a final assemblage center of Messerschmitt 109 fighter planes, pride of the German fighter force ... Allied air strategy commanders, having learned that it was more feasible to knock out German fighters at the ground assembly points than to blast them from the sky in aerial combat, had drawn up their plans on that premise ...

In accordance with its selection as one of the prime targets on the Fifteenth Air Force high priority list, heavy bombers had all but blasted it out of existence, and the overall strategy called for the 10 May mission to complete the destruction ... The entire Fifteenth Air Force was going over the target in an all-out effort to finish the job they had been methodically hammering at in the past, and all groups were assigned special objectives to bomb, which fit into a master pattern. The 463rd Bombardment Group had been assigned Building No. 16 of Werke No. 2, one of the more strategic installations of a unit which was described as the greatest assembly center in Europe of German Me 109 fighter planes ...

Although many aircraft had been seriously damaged during the twelve long missions of the previous fortnight, ground crews worked unceasingly to make certain that thirty-five planes were ready for the scheduled take-off ...

On the morning of May 10, thirty-five B-17s were in excellent condition ... Take-off was at 0730 ... At briefing, the crews had learned that heavy flak could be expected en route to the target, and that over the target area itself, a wall of flak surrounded their objective. Seventy-five fighter planes of the Me 109, Ju 88, and Fw 190 types were located in the vicinity of the target and were expected to offer a savage resistance. All this the combat crews well know. They had been to Wiener Neustadt before.

Rendezvous was made with other wings of the Fifteenth Air Force, and hundreds of heavy bombers began this mission deep into enemy territory while from other fields, fighter escorts formed to protect the bombers to their target ...

Fighter escort had not yet arrived, and at the initial point, German antiaircraft ground defenses began putting a tremendous barrage of flak into the sky. As the bombers rocked with each burst, enemy fighters appeared from nowhere and peeled off at the group. With several planes already badly damaged by flak, the 463rd Bomb Group was attacked by sixty German fighters ... Deployed four and five abreast, the enemy turned a deadly continuous fire on the bombers which sustained great damage before reaching their objective. And the enemy fighters did not relent in their round-the-clock attacks.

Despite the overwhelming enemy opposition from flak and fighters, the group continued on; there had been no early returns despite the damage sustained en route. The usual curtain of flak covered Wiener Neustadt on that day. Heavier than ever in some spots, it forced enemy fighter planes to break off their engagement immediately over the target. Direct flak hits badly damaged the lead ship's two wingmen, and they quickly broke into flames which fanned backward to the tail and completely enveloped them. Then as a team, they plummeted downward. Other flak bursts knocked down an enemy fighter, a member of a formation which persisted in attacking our ships over the target, and as a result, the enemy airmen completely broke off the engagement until bomb bursts on the target signaled completion of the bomb run.

The remaining members of the 463rd Bomb Group, most of them severely damaged, swung over the target at 1101, dropped their load of one hundred and five tons of high explosives from an altitude of twenty-three thousand feet, and turned for home. At this time, two more of the big bombers exploded in flight, their destruction caused by direct hits from the accurate flak barrages, then the enemy fighters which had been trailing just outside the formation resumed their attack as the bombers passed from the inner flak defenses.

Below, bright glowing flames were distinguishable through a smoke cloud rising to five thousand feet. Clear weather at the target enabled crew members to watch bomb strikes which landed on the target area with exceptional accuracy, destroying the assigned objective as well as blowing up a locomotive works not designated at briefing ...

Flak was still exceptionally heavy and accurate, repeatedly piercing the damaged bombers, while superior numbers of enemy fighters now concentrated on the crippled B-17s trailing the formation. For thirty minutes the skies were filled with racing fighter planes pouring continuous bursts at the big bombers whose crews returned the fire from twin fifty caliber guns with cool and unusual accuracy. Four more Fortresses were shot down so fierce and persistent were the fighter attacks, but their own losses were mounting steadily as the battle progressed.

About the time when it began to appear that the enemy knew that it had more than met its match in the effective cross fire of the Group gunners, an aggressive band of P-38s arrived on the scene to engage the enemy. Immediately assuming a vigorous offensive, the friendly fighters joined the bombers to put the enemy into a rout ... the enemy fighters lost all desire for combat and soon broke off the engagement ...

The loss of seven bombers and the serious damaging of thirteen more was more than offset by the destruction of sixteen enemy fighters and the probable number of five others. In addition to the losses inflicted on Germany's Luftwaffe in the air ... the 463rd Bomb Group had completely destroyed their portion of the target while other groups had achieved such successes that the aircraft factory at Wiener Neustadt no longer presented a formidable menace as a vital production center of German aircraft ... Possession of those unborn planes would have provided the enemy with means for stiffened opposition to our forces, but now Allied bombers could blast important targets almost at will ...

The loading lists in that declassified information showed Stan and his crew flying plane 685. Other reports we have listed him flying plane 804. It goes back and forth. And as I looked through the list of missions flown by the 463rd, it came to mind that if Stan could've finished the mission to Wiener Neustadt, he might just have had a chance to complete all fifty missions.

With that comment, of course, I wanted to rewrite history again. And Eugene Parker insisted he flew on plane 685.

So Grandma and Granddad turned the pages of their calendar. It was well into the summer of 1945. George Mitchell sent a second letter.

Dear Mr. and Mrs. Dwyer,
Your last two letters were waiting here for us when we returned from a two-week holiday in upstate New York ...
I've been writing to "Pete" Dale but still don't know if he visited you in Hastings or not. That was what he intended to do before he left St. Valery, but maybe something came up. I couldn't help but think how grand it would be for you to be able to talk to someone who was with Stan on May 10 face to face, and Dale was the nearest.
I feel much easier about talking to you now, and do forgive me if I repeat facts that you already know. Letters just aren't the *right* things for occasions of this sort.

Mother tells me that you all understand about our being farmed out to fly with experienced crews when we hit Italy. That was when we lost Klute and Swan, and we never flew a mission as a complete crew ... The squadron didn't hear a thing about either of them for ages. I thought they were both dead, and then what a grand surprise when I saw "Pete" at St. Valery, and he told me how our two "truants" welcomed him to his POW camp ...

And now about *that* day over Wiener Neustadt. I suppose it must have begun like any other while we were on operations.

Stan lived in a tent some ways away from the tent we slept in. He shared a tent with the officers of another crew, he and "Pete," but we enlisted men had one all for ourselves. He used to come up and make sure we were awake and getting up on his way to breakfast. It was always still dark, and I can see him now with his flashlight shining in my face and tickling my feet (you see, I was right next to the entrance of the tent, and being about the laziest, I was attacked first).

There was never any question about our *not* coming back from a mission. And we weren't arrogant about it. If you had fears (and I suppose subconsciously we did), we never admitted them. Our crew had had close calls before. Once in Dyersburg [Tennessee] we had to land *without* any brakes. And that was the first day we had ever flown together. We had pieces of flak on our person for souvenirs, pieces of flak that had ripped holes in us on other missions.

I can remember what a grand day it was all the way in to the target. The particular raid was one of the first really large raids of the Fifteenth Air Force. I could see planes all over the sky as we headed out over the Adriatic. We had been to Wiener before and muffed the show (that sort of thing happened more than we'd like to admit) and knew that next to Ploesti, it was really the roughest of our targets.

Just before we got to the IP, I put on my flak suit and helmet. I always waited until the last minute because they were so damn heavy. As we made our turn (it was a very long bomb run), I could see the puffs of smoke from the flak that was being thrown up at the planes going over before us. Harold has probably heard, or said so himself, that some of the flak was so heavy you could get right out and walk on it. Well, this was one of those times. And some of the puffs were *red*, which was a new one to me. Right away I got that old tingle up and down my spine, and before I could think, things began to happen!

The inboard engine on the left side (facing the nose) was hit first but didn't burst into flames right away. I believe this same blast must have gotten Piper and Gilhooley, or at least their interphone, for I never remember hearing them speak again. This same blast got at the flare box in back of Stan's seat and set off all those multicolored signal flares. It looked like the Fourth of July, and the weirdest looking red smoke filled the plane. Boros put out this fire with the extinguisher and signaled to me from across the bomb bay that everything was OK. Just then I heard Stan say to Dale over the interphone that Little and Lauper were having trouble (they were in our formation), then he said, "My God," and I looked out and saw their ship *without* a tail section. How lucky they were to get back!

Then we were hit in one of the engines on the right side, and it broke into flames. And the engine first hit on the other side started to flame too. Right away we started to lose altitude and fell away from the formation. That was what the Hun had been waiting for. He came in and sent rockets and twenty millimeters at us. The tail caught on fire. One of the radio sets blew up, and then the interphone went out. Stan had *always* told us that if the plane caught on fire badly, never to stay in. This looked like the time. I could see the flames creeping up around the edge of the bomb bay. We still had our bombs, our tanks were half full of gas. Talk about sitting on top of a volcano! I looked over at Boros and pointed thumbs down, and he shrugged and turned to talk to Stan and "Pete," I suppose. The door into the waist seemed to be jammed, and I could see the three boys there getting ready to come up and go out the bomb bay. I was just in the way, so with Parker right behind me, I stepped on to the catwalk and then rolled out.

I can't remember seeing any other chutes at all around me. I don't know how long I spun around in space, but I do remember seeing a plane (our plane?) seemingly under perfect control but aflame from end to end going off behind me.

And that's the way I recall what happened. Of course, it didn't take any time at all. That first blast hit the bomb release mechanism, the door controls, everything. We couldn't even salvo them.

Dale told me that when Stan told him to go, it appeared as though Stan was going to follow right away. Whatever happened must have taken place in the split second between Dale's turning his back and slipping down to the navigator's hatch to make his leap. But what did happen?

And about Boros? Dale and Stanley would both had to have gone *past* him to get out, but obviously, he wasn't in their way, so where was he?

After I was captured and taken to a wee town for questioning, some wardens or something brought in Piper's holster for his revolver,

Gilhooley's swap case, and Olfenius's charred parachute (it hadn't opened all the way) and wallet. That led me to believe our plane was in the area. Then the schoolteacher, the only one able to speak English at this place, told me that *our* ship had started a forest fire when it hit the ground. That made me believe that the ship didn't explode *in* the air. Never did I see anything of Stan's or Boros's or talk to anyone who had seen them.

And that's about all I have to say. That's all I know from my end. It's not very pleasant, but I believe you're entitled to know. Just don't think about it. I'm trying to forget the bad parts. I spoke to the folks about it once, and that was enough. I don't know if I've cleared anything up or not. I certainly hope it does some *good*.

I must stop now, my arm is howling in protest. I should have the Dwyer typewriter! Do write again, and remember that if any of you are ever near us in Newark, do come in and see us. Until later then—

Sincerely,
George

Fill-in crew member and waist gunner Stephen Milewski wrote Grandma and Granddad explaining:

As they [engines number 2 and 3] burst into flames, the left waist gunner and I bailed out. As far as I know, your son kept trying vainly to regain control so that the rest of the crew might bail out. As much as I hate to say it, your son knew that he had no chance for he had to be the last to leave. Five men were lost while the other five got out alive. It was through your son's heroism that we escaped with our skins. Although I can't give you exact details, I am almost positive that he went down with the ship. Nevertheless, I would not give up hope, for the strangest things happen in wartime.

Furthermore, copilot Manley Dale Jr. wrote Granddad and Grandma a letter, noting, "Your son may have spoken of me as Pete, but that is only my nickname." His letter stated:

I must admit I have put off this letter for so long I am quite embarrassed over it. As you know, your son and myself flew together for a long time. We went all through cadet training together and ended up getting our final training together before going overseas and flew together in combat. We were also together on the day we were shot down out of the skies.

Your son and I ran around together for quite a while, and I always thought he was such a grand guy, so I know something of your loss, and I am at a loss as to what to say except that I am very sorry. I think you would like to know the circumstances as to how we were shot down and what happened as I remember it all. If you don't feel like reading it, I suggest you throw away the second page to this letter.

I am sending a couple of pictures that were taken of us while we were in Lakeland ...

As to my treatment in prison camp. We had a few hard times and were hungry for a spell, but it wasn't too bad considering everything. The Red Cross was the one that actually took care of us. We were liberated by General Patton's Third Army on April 29, and I arrived back in the United States on June 4 ...

The second page of copilot Dale's letter read:

Since I left the airplane I have heard nothing of your son, the only thing I can do is to go back over and give you my impression of what happened. I believe you would like to know what I saw. On the raid over Weiner Neustadt we were first hit by flak. The airplane was set on fire in numerous places; a fire in number 2 engine, in the bombay, the flares went off inside of the airplane, and the oxygen was shot out. We actually should of jumped then but we decided to stay with it and see what we could do. We got all those fires out and started home on auto-pilot as some of the controls were also shot away. It was then that the German fighters jumped us. Four of them came down and riddled us and sta rted fires in No. 2 & 3 engines. It was then that a twin engine fighter came up real close to us and threw a rocket into our tail and set it ablazing. Radio contact throughout the plane was almost out and I tried to tell the crew to bail out. They started to leave and your son told me to go. I asked him if he was alright by a motion of my hands and he was O.K.. I reached for my parachute and it had opened up. I put it on and gathered up the parachute in my arms and started for the escape hatch. It is then that my memory is blotted out as I believe I passed out from lack of oxygen as we were still very high up in the air. I hazily remember a face in front of me coming from the navigators hatch and I believe either the bombardier or the navigator threw me out of the airplane. I am the only one accounted for out of the nose of the airplane. It was in this section of the airplane that the oxygen was shot out so I believe the rest of the cre w passed out from the lack of air and so were unable to get out of the airplane. Out of the rear of the plane the tail gunner was the only one missing, the rest of the boys back there except one were shot up by 20 mm shells from the four fighters, but they were all able to get out of the airplane.

For my grandparents, the crew letters spelled out, from each of their perspectives, what had happened in the skies over Austria. It was fairly evident what happened on May 10, but still, where was Stanley? What exactly happened to him? The head alludes to the facts, but could the heart accept it? What happens to the mind when there are no remains, no funeral, and no closure, truly nothing finite? Were Grandma and Granddad ever 100 percent convinced that their son was dead? Granddad appeared to draw his conclusion in a letter to Aileen, dated August 1, 1945, when he summarized the many details of the May 10 mission they'd gathered. In that letter, he also stated:

> You're first on the list this morning. It is my job to tell a lot of folks what we've hoped wouldn't be necessary but what we've known for a long time just about had to be the case. It seems Stanley was killed May 10, '44. I have felt from the first that this was the case but had hoped that his usual luck would possibly pull them through this one. And for that matter, I guess the luck was all right. They were set afire in several places and No. 2 engine put out by flak. But they decided to take her home and put out the fires. Then four German fighters came in and riddled them. Only one man on the ship wasn't wounded—George Mitchell, the radioman. The copilot thinks the rest of the men who didn't get out were put out by lack of oxygen before they could make it. However, Stanley signaled to him that he was OK after he told him to bail out. It was one of those things, but I have an idea the condition of some of the men wounded by flak caused Stanley to decide to try to take the ship back. Anyway, five of them didn't make it, and five did ...
>
> She [Ellen] is looking better all the time. When Harold came home, she had to stand twice in a place to cast a shadow. But having him here—she was with him every day from the time he landed in Beloit—and getting a change of food and something else to think about, and getting to see you and Carol, is just what the doctor ordered. I doubt she will get run down that way again. The uncertainty about Stanley and sweating Harold through the European war was about too much. The stay out at the farm was good for her. She ate as much as any of us ...
>
> It's been a long hard grind for us, but I guess we can take it. And do it while we're sweating out the next chapter.

At the end of July 1945, Dad finally returned to the States from England; however, the war with Japan still raged on. Therefore, the next chapter.

I was sent to Sioux Falls, South Dakota, where we sat around waiting—waiting to see if we'd be put in the pipeline for duty in the Pacific theater or CBI theater. Over in the China-Burma-India theater, it was almost a whole different war. A lot of it was airlifting supplies over the Himalayas to supply the Chinese that were fighting the Japanese. It was called "flying the hump." There was nothing for us to do in Sioux Falls. I was making model airplanes and writing letters on V-J Day, August 15, 1945. Japan finally surrendered after atomic bombs were dropped on Hiroshima and Nagasaki. World War II was over. But I wasn't discharged from the army until October 1945, after I spent two months in Boca Raton, Florida.

I'd learned you never knew what to expect from the army. In Boca Raton, it was more sitting around and doing some flying to get our pay in. We were assigned B-26s and B-24s, which I considered "crates." I did buy me a car—a 1940, cream-colored Nash convertible—which helped pass time. It got me to the beach and back, and I drove it home after my discharge. While in Florida, the thought crossed my mind to contact Stan's copilot, Pete Dale, but nothing materialized.

While reading through Dad's file of letters, I came across one that Granddad had written to Dad on his twenty-first birthday. It wasn't the first time I'd read that particular letter. I'd seen it once before in a newspaper-sized scrapbook of Granddad's and was confused. In the letter, Granddad mentioned seeing Dad in Oklahoma City. Somehow, there was a connection between Boca Raton and Oklahoma City.

While I was at Boca Raton, there was a hurricane warning for south Florida, so we had to ferry the airplanes out. Tinker Field in Oklahoma City was chosen. I flew a B-17, and on the way, one engine froze up. I feathered the prop, of course, and when we landed at Oklahoma City, the line guy came out and asked what was wrong.

"The engine froze up," I told him. Well, he reached up, grabbed a prop blade, did a couple pull-ups, and said, "Yeah, you're right. It'll need a new engine."

"How long will that take?" I asked.

"How long would you like it to take?" he questioned.

"About a month," I replied.

"Come back in about a week, and it'll be ready," he said.

So I got a leave out of it, started on a bus to Nebraska, and stopped in Beloit, Kansas, to see Pearl and Dusty. I missed the connection in Salina, so then I hitchhiked. It was about 2:00 a.m., and I was standing at the junction of highways 81 and 24, west of Manhattan, Kansas. The first car that picked me up asked where I was going.

"Beloit," I told him.

"Who do you know from Beloit?" he asked.

"George Schouten."

"Well, I live right next door to George!"

He took me right to Pearl and Dusty's house. I made it to Hastings, and then the folks drove me back to Oklahoma City.

Dad returned to Boca Raton a couple of days before his twenty-first birthday and was there until his discharge.

Harold Dwyer, 906 West Sixth, Hastings, Nebraska

September 23, 1945

Dearest Harold Boy:

Well, Son, the Dwyer tribe has this day reached another milestone. This is being done on the 23rd day of September in the year 1945. At about four per clock this afternoon, you became twenty-one years of age. It's the first time that ever happened to you. And it will be a long time before it does again.

And it's the firstest time since February 17, 1915, that your mother and I have not been able to say we had a child in the family. That night, Aileen stepped "out of the Nowhere, into the Here" and the family has carried the name of at least one youngster on the roster ever since--until this afternoon. But it can't be said that we are right back where we started. We have stored up a wealth of sweet memories in that time, most of them happy, some sad. We can look back over thirty years of pleasant association with three fine youngsters of the kind which makes the heart of a parent glow with pride, and to thank the powers-that-be that he was chosen to be that particular parent.

I've thought of these things since we left you--or rather, you left us--at the airport at Oklahoma City the other day, and while we wer on the way back here to celebrate your birthday today without you. Incidentally, that was one grand trip. It was enough that we get to be with you a couple of days, but to be able to go through the bomber, and then stand by while you warmed her up, then take off and circle the field and dip your wings at us as you flew into the bright glue yonder in the directions of Florida, was much more than could have been hoped for. That was one of our red letter days.

You will never know how I appreciated a chance to explore the inside of that bomber. To you of course it was just another old crate which has about served its usefulness, but ot me the interior was sort of a holy of holies. It was the inside of a B-17 like the ones in which you and Stanley had spent hundreds of hours of grueling training, the same kind of a pilot's seat in which he and you went into action time and time again against the enemy and weather and lack of oxygen and intense cold, the same kind of a cockpit in which Stanley spent the last few hours on this Earth, the same kind of a ship he flew across the Atlantic once, and you twice. To me the flight deck of that crate or any other of its kind, is hallowed ground.

As you sat up there warming up those engines and looking about the size of a minute atop that hulk of a ship, I thought of other ships you had flown. I thought of the night I came home at Manhattan and you took me out to show me how a model propelled with rubber bands could do its stuff, down the alley in the glow of a street light. You were a little shaver then, but the ship flew, and did a good job of it. It was built right. As you got No.1 engine of the bomber going, then the others in succession, just by making the right contacts, there came

to my mind the everlasting "cranking" of the gas model engines to get
them to function. It is a far cry from the little red ship you had,
the one with the 30-inch wingspread and pulled with an Atom motor
having a transparent fuel tank about the size of a thimble, to this
B-17 capable of lifting many thousands of pounds of load to thirty
thousand feet and carrying them hundreds of miles. After what you
have done and been through, it is hard to realize that three years
ago you were building and flying the little ships.

I was glad when you circled the field after the take-off
and banked so I knew you could see us there on the runway from where
you sat. It brought memories of another day, when you circled Hastings
in the ship you flew to England. It was a proud dad who stood on
the ground that day and watched that sleek silver bomber circle
overhead, knowing his boy was in the pilot's seat and that he cared
enough to come a hundred miles out of the way to take a good-bye
turn over the old home.

That pride was mixed with a feeling akin to happiness, although I knew that this was it--that after that turn you would be on
your way into that hell in the midst of which Stanley had been
missing for nine months. I was as nearly happy as one could be under
the circumstances--happy with you and for you in that you had accomplished a good measure of what you had set out to do when you enlisted
in the Cadet training program a year and a half before. Much of what
you had been through in those eighteen months I could not know, but
I did know enough about it that I would have been selfish indeed had
I not shared your feelings at having attained the goal.

After the Fortress headed back for the base at Lincoln that
day, I wondered how you felt up there above the old burg, of what
you thought of, and what spots you noticed particularly. I wondered
if you flew out over the area near the airport where you boys went
to fly your gas models back in the high school "Areo Nut Club" days.
And if you compared in your mind the size of the bomber with that of
the balsa wood and paper ships you had flown out there.

It was with different feelings that I watched you take off from
Tinker Field the other day. I was the same proud dad, but it was good
to know that you didn't have to make any more bombing missions over
Germany and France, and that V-J Day came along before you had to go
into action in the Pacific. We're mighty glad it is over Over There.
We're glad you are where you can pick up the loose ends and go on with
your knitting in a world at peace, after you get out of the service.

And we're glad you are 21 years old. Not that we wouldn't like to
have you our little boy forever, 'cause we would. But that would deny
you the thrill of doing the things you want to do, of growing in strength
and ability by making your own decisions out ways and means
of bringing about the ends you desire. It's great to be able to do things
for one's self in a country where one has that privilege, so long as it
does not interfere with the rights of others. And from what you've seen,
I think you agree that there can be no greater privilege than to be
born under the Stars and Stripes--and as nearly the middle of these
United States as possible.

All of which leads up--or rather, down--to the point of wishing
you at least a hundred more happy birthday anniversaries. We'd like to
stick around and help you celebrate all of them, but that would be asking
a bit too much. But we'll try and help you enjoy the next few, anyway.

Heaps of love.   Dad

Fall turned to winter, the seasons cycled, and the new life and freshness of another spring cast off winter's varied shades of brown. And with spring came the second anniversary of that fateful day, May 10. Aunt Aileen, mother of a second daughter—nine-month-old Mary Ellen—noted in her diary on May 10, 1946, "We lost Stanley two years ago today."

Another year passed, followed by 365 more days. As the fourth anniversary of May 10 approached, Dad and Mom married, and Theron Newell wrote to Granddad, offering to finish Stanley's novel. "My mind agrees with all that you have written," Theron said. "I don't see how there can be any doubt. Yet perhaps that ungovernable part of my heart is wrong. It still seems impossible that it is that way. I know it, yet even now I refuse to entirely believe it or give up hope."

When, if ever, does one "let it go?" After a funeral, there still may be sadness, but there is a sense of relief, a sense of closure, and a sense that it's time to move forward. Without that closure, when Stanley's fate was inconclusive, does one ever give up hope and let go?

As I reflected back over the years, my dad did mention two or three times that he was hoping to see Stan get off the train and come walking up the street.

Time passed. Then in August 1949 Granddad received a letter from Stanley's old friend from the California infantry days, Harry Cuthbertson, Janice Cuthbertson's brother.

Dear Mr. Dwyer:

Today, on my vacation, I thumbed through some of my wartime letters and pictures and remembered how ashamed I should be for letting so many first-person-singular things crowd out, year after year, other things really more important. I have always wanted to write you, at least, and if possible, meet your family—but I got married a month after returning from overseas, separated and divorced in short order, and had a pretty damned rough time readjusting in general. Not an excuse, but a reason.

I have two letters from Stan, one of January 18, 1944, and another of April 14, 1944, which I prize very highly. But I cannot escape the thought that your family might well treasure them more, if you had them. Anyway, when I read them over, it only makes me so enraged and frustrated at the whole memory and portent of war; it is possibly better I forget them. I have lost more than one close friend in combat, but none more admired than Stan ...

Neither my sister nor I (she married a marine pilot, has a three-year-old girl, and lives in Southern California) ever met you or the other members of your family; through Stan we both feel we know you well ... You and I have something in common, except that you carried your journalism talent into print whereas I have been sidetracked, due to the old familiar expediency of how-much-do-I-get, into other endeavors ...

Harry enclosed two of Stanley's letters; I only found one in the trunk. Stanley's letter to his friend read:

Somewhere in Italy – April 14, 1944

Dear Cuth,

We came, we saw, we have gotten our butt shot at. But it is still intact, and if the knowledge I have gained thus far is as helpful as was beginner's luck on those first few missions, then I should be able to complete the required number without undue loss of ham.

It's a big game, old fellow, interesting as the devil but quite heartless at times. Having previously separated the men from the boys, now and then it separates the men from the men. It would be a bitter pill, sometimes, if a man should enter combat without first having prepared himself mentally. One becomes attached to those around him in the time required to train a group and would hoe a hard row if life meant as much to him as it once did.

However, it is not as dark a picture as I have painted. The invaders have had the upper hand, with possibly a few exceptions, and as time passes, we find the enemy less able to offer maximum resistance. Fighter escort—I love those P-38s—gives a security the value of which cannot be estimated, and it hurts more to see one of them go down knowing that he risked his to save yours. But those pilots seldom find themselves with inferior training or equipment and are unquestioned kings of the sky.

But perhaps I am talking to a veteran. Your sis, in a recent letter, stated that you might be coming over to join the fray soon. And speaking of letters, yours has been conspicuous in its absence. However, it would be unjust to slap one's wrist, even so slightly, because a feller who moves so often and so far as have I hasn't received mail. So, instead of punishment, I shall give my APO number.

I suggest, if you haven't already pulled stakes, that you begin a propaganda campaign on the folks back home that might cause the pain of worry to be lessened. Brother, those folks worry, no end, especially those who think as much of their boy as yours. Damned if they don't fight a harder battle than we.

The home is of canvas, modern conveniences are lacking, the natives in their war-weary state can offer no entertainment, and I long for a bottle of beer. I stay pretty close to the tent and the typewriter and am much more contented without those necessities of a few months ago than I had expected. Am sending all of my cash home, and it adds up fast.

And business is good. We're flying more than I had expected, and a man can look forward to a rest in the States without having to use too much imagination. Come on in; the air's fine. Let no man in the staging area shortchange you on flying equipment under the assumption that it's already here. It isn't.

As ever,
Stan

Granddad wrote the following to Harry:

Stan had told us about you, and about Janice. She took it upon herself to see that we got the only good picture of him [Stan] in the service ... You have no idea how I appreciate the fact that you took time to write and that you enclosed the two letters of Stan's. I know something of comradeship in the service. I know how he felt toward you particularly, and I'm returning one of the letters. It would be out of place in the files of anyone else. The other I shall keep to remind me now and then of the kind of men he had among his friends and of the thoughtfulness and consideration of one of them for the parents of a buddy who "stepped out for a cup of coffee ..."

Incidentally, the typewriter which wrote the letters you received from Stan is doing the same by the one you are about to get from his dad. In the autumn of '44, when his clothing and other effects came, the machine was among them. Harold used it during his last three phases of training and flew it to Scotland when he went across. But when he came back, Germany had folded, and he had to haul ten extra men. That took all the room in the B-17, and the footlockers had to come by boat. When his arrived two or three months later, the old Remington was back from the wars again. It has been around some. Both boys flew it across, and even tho only a bit of machinery, it is close to our hearts ...

I'm glad to know that you have a son—and Janice a daughter. People are inclined to think they live before they have children of their own. But after the first-born arrives, they know they haven't. It was a lot of fun to be with our three and to love them and watch them grow and develop and do things. But times flies so swiftly ... Only the other day, Stan was six years old and went down to the armory where I trained a troop of National Guard Cavalry. He sized up the horses and rifles and pistols and troopers in uniform, and said, "Dad, I'd sure like to belong to your troop."

As to that old urge to put thoughts down on paper. Stan had told me of yours and that you had what it took. I think I can tell you something about it that may help. It won't ever be cured. If you have it—you have it. And it will be well not to try to rid yourself of it. The only way to satisfy it is to square yourself away in front of a typewriter and begin to paw. I have not accomplished anything at it, as success of big name writers is measured. Maybe I don't wear the size. That, I'll in all probability never know, as I've never made any effort to write along lines that produce big names and big returns ...

But I have owned small weekly newspapers and worked on others and county seat dailies ... The country is kind to folks. Country people can feel and say what they think of you and what you do without waiting to see what the crowd and the critics have to say. I liked it. And kept getting into it deeper ... I became aware that if one is going to write, he never has wasted a minute since he was born. No matter what he has done or where he has been or what he has been thru, if he's going to hammer out stuff for people to read, little bits of all of it are filed away for use when the time comes. The hells he's been thru and the heartaches he's had, along with the rest. The greater the variety of what he's been thru, the greater the number of humans who will read between the lines and sense that he has traveled the same road they have and will enjoy his stuff that much more.

When one is doing what he likes to do, he works twenty-four hours a day, and he wishes there were more of them. If he awakens at night, he starts thinking of his work and doesn't care whether or not he goes back to sleep. He lets slumber take care of itself. Ever since I started at that kind of work, I have thrilled inside like a youngster. The book of livestock verse—I think I sent you folks one—was done on the side between jumps. I printed them myself, which is also unorthodox. But I've sold a few hundred of them, without effort. If you had written it, I could sell thousands of them. I'm too cussed thin-skinned to peddle my own wares. It boils down to this: One can scarcely sell anything unless he says something good about it. If I say anything good about that book, I'm bragging. And I'm a poor bragger ... Last winter I finished another small book of verse—from an entirely different world—sort of a "picture of life's other side," as it were. It's from the racetracks, where gambling is as much a part of things as is the air they breathe ... I'm enclosing one. If you don't like it, chuck 'er in the waste basket ...

I know a few thousand people. I've observed and read of many thousands more. I've concluded that what ails this old world is that people are so damned much like human beings. And that such a large percent of them are so much like cattle—so content and satisfied with a full belly and a chance to lie in the shade—that they permit themselves to be led or driven into any kind of a situation by anyone who will promise the fullest belly and the most dense shade, without any thought of what may happen farther up the creek. Universal peace is a beautiful dream. But there will always be those who want war, and those who are decent and don't want it must either fight to protect themselves or be exterminated. And a war is a war, whether it was planned that way or bungled into. It is not a pretty picture, but I believe it's better to look at it now and then than to turn it to the wall ...

By hell, I had no idea of writing a true confession short when I started this, but if I've said anything that may help you see that you're not wasting any time at whatever you're doing, perhaps you will overlook some of the cap I's ...

But to things more pleasant. This tribe would most surely like to come to Oakland ... and visit the Cuthbertsons ... And if any or all of the Cuthbertsons should ever get to this part of the country, we want you to come and stay until you tire of our company—or the cooking.

Again, I sat at the computer and clicked around the Internet, and from the best I could determine, Harry Cuthbertson was deceased. Searches involving maiden names, such as Janice Cuthbertson, Beatrice King, as well as Huretta Wright, were nearly impossible.

On May 10, 1957, Granddad wrote to Ralph Lashbrook, one of Stanley's journalism professors at his alma mater, Kansas State College. By 1957, the Korean War was recorded as history, and I would have been three-and-a-half years old.

Friend Lashbrook:

It has taken a long time, but we have had to come to it and conclude that Stanley isn't to be that one-in-a-million who might show up sometime.

Though no one has seen him since his ship went down over Wiener Neustadt, Austria, thirteen years ago this morning, the last communication from the Department advised that he is carried officially as killed in action.

It stated further that captured German records showed the B-17 to have gone down at that point that day. Also that the copilot's statement was to the effect that Stan kept the ship in a flying attitude so the others could bail out, and to the best of his knowledge and belief, went down with the ship. The bombs which they could not release were detonated when the ship came down. The copilot and four others did bail out and were in the German prison camps a year before they were liberated by United States troops.

My check for a hundred dollars for the Kedzie Memorial Fund is enclosed herewith. You may expect more.

I just don't remember exact details, but Dad and I attended, back in the '50s, some sort of dedication at the college in Manhattan, Kansas, to honor the students who lost their lives in World War II. A memorial fund awarding scholarships had, at one time, been established.

"Every time I looked over the list of eight boys who lost their lives in World War II or glanced at the bronze plaque which hangs in our main hallway," Ralph Lashbrook responded, "I always wondered if you had received any further information. I am indeed sorry you have had to conclude that Stanley will never return."

Spring, summer, fall, winter. Time passed, years added up, and lives moved on. War-torn countries rebuilt, and years turned into decades, until, well, there we were, looking back to the past, piecing together the lives of those who came before. During those passing decades, Dad, instead of building model planes, built homes, but he still flew planes.

After the war, I went to work, which took my mind off of things. We had holiday family get-togethers, but I don't recall ever really talking about Stan.

Even my older sister, Jan, and my younger sisters, Sue and Lori, do not remember either Grandma or Granddad ever talking about their son Stanley—the uncle we never knew. Mom and Dad wanted four boys, but surprise, they were blessed with four girls. Mom once said the boy's name she and Dad had agreed on was "Craig Stanley."

I can still see the oval-framed photograph hanging on my grandparents' bedroom wall—the black-and-white, sepia-toned picture of a good-looking man in uniform who resembled Dad. Yet, as a child and then a teenager, I never seemed curious enough to ask who it was.

My cousin Carol, Aunt Aileen's oldest daughter, died in 1989; however, Mary Ellen recalled, "I liked snooping through Grandma Ellen's dresser in the bedroom. I found a brooch—a picture bauble—of both Uncle Harold and Stanley, and I didn't understand why there was a guy who looked like my Uncle Harold, but not exactly. Grandma would be trying to rest, but I wanted details. Understandably, she never talked about Stanley much. Neither did my mother."

For me it was always fun going to Grandma and Granddad's house. Granddad was usually in his den on the second floor, typing and humming. He liked to hum and sometimes pulled a harmonica out of his jacket pocket and played a tune. One day, as I hung around his upstairs den, he pointed to a nest on the tree branch right outside the window. Together, we watched for a long time. The featherless babies in the nest strained their wrinkled necks and opened their tiny, yellowish beaks while the mama robin stuffed a gooey worm inside.

"Carol and I played in his office, or den, next to the attic where olive drab uniforms and other things were stored," Mary Ellen said. "Grandma would give Carol and me fly swatters to swat the moths. And once, Granddad showed me a sealed manila envelope he had among his papers and said that it was for Stanley should 'he come walking in the door.'"

Granddad left a pleasant odor trail of Old Spice, and especially when he leaned down for the requested peck on the cheek, you got a good whiff of his aftershave. He shared his cashew nuts, and he'd stand at the kitchen counter eating sticky dates or pouring a glass of tomato juice, both of which I thought were yucky at that time.

Grandma mostly wore a belted dress and stylish, clunky, thick, high-heeled shoes. When we walked four blocks to the Safeway grocery store, the aroma of freshly baked bread from the nearby Debus Baking Company smelled delicious—Grandma thought it was fake. At the store, she'd let me pick out one treat. Almost always, I chose a big Tootsie Roll. I slowly chewed one sectioned chunk at a time on the walk home. Grandma carried the brown grocery bag in one arm, her matching handbag in her other hand, while I skipped along, careful not to "step on a crack and break my mother's back," but I was forced to walk on the grass next to the stretch of sidewalk made from bricks laid out in perfect herringbone design.

Grandma and I played cards and made up all sorts of marble games, aiming and rolling our shooters across the nubby carpet, trying to hit the other's line of marbles. Sometimes, I'd sit on the back of their sofa, straddling Grandma leaning into the cushion in front of me. I'd twist and curl her grayish blue, dyed hair with a brush, pretending to be a hairdresser.

One Sunday evening, we gathered in Grandma and Granddad's living room around their big, new, black-and-white console television to see what the screaming was all about. Ed Sullivan, in his distinctive, nasally twang, announced, "Ladies and gentlemen, the Beatles." The Beatles debuted on *The Ed Sullivan Show* wearing black suits, white shirts, and ties, long sideburns, and their hair flopped around when they sang "I Want to Hold Your Hand."

As shocking as the Beatles might have seemed, Grandma and Granddad had experienced other significant changes in their lifetime … from horse and buggy to Henry Ford's Model T to vehicles equipped with automatic transmissions and air-conditioning … from Orville and Wilbur Wright at Kitty Hawk to Neil Armstrong and Buzz Aldrin at the Sea of Tranquility … from the peaceful prairie landscape near Woodston, Kansas, to the ruckus at the Woodstock Festival … from women's suffrage to women's lib … from treatment for the 1918 "flusies" to heart bypass surgeries. The list goes on and on. But they lived a good share of twentieth-century history, the history we read in books.

So life went on. In their "golden years," Grandma and Granddad moved to their Ninth Street home, the house Dad built for them, where my sisters and I spent hours playing pool with Grandma. The oval-framed photo hung on the bedroom wall there too. The undetectable heartache must have been woven into the fabric of their everyday lives.

Then Grandma passed on in 1969 of heart failure. She was seventy-four, and it seemed her heart was broken.

In 1962, before Mom died, my dad made a career change. When he was seventy-five, the feed company he worked for thought he should get off the road, so he was out of a job. Fred Seaton, owner of the Hastings Daily Tribune, *asked him if he would like to write a column for the paper. Dad thought that would be okay, so Fred sent him to see the paper's business manager, one Bert James. Bert was a little skeptical and asked Dad just how many hours a week he thought he could work. Dad said, "Oh, about twelve or fourteen hours a day would be about right." He was hired on the spot and worked until he was almost ninety years old.*

On another May 10 anniversary—the year was 1976—Granddad wrote the following:

Dear, Dear Aileen and Harold. This may be it. I fell one night a week ago and landed with the old fan wedged in between the stool and the tub. More fun than a few. Haven't said anything as Bill needs Aileen more than I do, and Harold never has time to urinate. I dreamt one night that I was dying, but that one didn't come true. It was a vivid one tho. The fall left me with a cracked rib. Plenty sharp! But I'm long past-due, and it will come as no surprise. I'm taking no more breaths than necessary. They're too sharp. Please know that it has been a lot of fun being the dad of two such as you two—and with one like Stanley tossed in between. Lucky me!

> A bushel and a peck of love,
> Dad

My dad passed away in 1980. He specifically wrote one last column for the Hastings Daily Tribune, *which was printed on March 10, 1980, after he died. In the column, Dad stated, "As I approach the time of death, there is no feeling of sadness. It does find me not entirely ready to go, as I've always wanted to take a horseback ride on an ostrich." He also offered readers some fatherly advice. "Never ever leave home without a ladder. One never knows when he may be invited to have a drink on the house."*

Grandma and Granddad were like walking history books, but for them, one chapter in their family history was incomplete. They both left this earth never knowing exactly what happened to their son Stanley or where he was. Closure was an illusion, and their invisible wound never seemed to heal. In fact, as we would discover, they yearned to bring their son's remains home to the United States for burial.

I can imagine Mom suffered a lot more than she let on. Yet everything the folks did, all their original efforts, laid the groundwork for what we've done and helped us continue the search. Really, the whole search—including our search—has been a cumulative effort for over sixty-plus years.

11

c﹏ﬡ﹏

The Search Goes On

... the cost to America of recreating civilization will be great.
—Stanley N. Dwyer in a letter dated April 22, 1944

Letters in Stanley's trunk helped us understand Grandma and Granddad's gallant efforts in their search for their son. Unwavering, they exhausted all known resources, but unanswered questions remained. And then after decades of "silence," our journey became a rekindled effort to resume the search and pick up where they left off. It was all part of the sixty-year, cumulative effort. But in sixty years, the world had become smaller, enabling our search to broaden beyond borders.

Our unmapped journey charted new terrain. The unsolicited *Los Angeles Times* article led us to CILHI, the Central Identification Laboratory, Hawaii, and set our journey on an unforeseen course. Engaged, we followed along and, in time, closed the incomplete chapter of family history.

CILHI's website stated:

> CILHI's primary mission is to search for, recover, and identify remains of American military personnel and certain American civilian personnel, and certain allied personnel unaccounted for from World War II, the Korean War, the Cold War, and the Vietnam War.
>
> The CILHI maintains eighteen search and recovery teams. A typical ten- to fourteen-person search and recovery team consists of members with specialized duties and skills including anthropology, photography, explosive ordnance disposal, medicine (medics), mortuary affairs, linguistics (interpreters), and radio communications. The CILHI mission is worldwide in scope.

CILHI shoulders a worldwide mission, and the number of unaccounted-for soldiers from this country's previous wars are staggering. According to their statistics, approximately seventy-eight thousand American soldiers are still missing from World War II, and of those, about thirty-five thousand are considered recoverable. It's estimated that eighty-one hundred are missing from the Korean War, approximately eighteen hundred from the Vietnam War, 120 from the Cold War, and one is missing from the Gulf War.‡

CILHI's Deputy Commander Johnie Webb stated, "We've learned valuable lessons in every war we have fought. Just look at the number of unaccounted-for individuals as you go from war to war and see how those numbers are reduced after every war."

A loss is a loss. One isn't considered more or less than the other, but the seventy-eight thousand number jumped out at me.

Seventy-eight thousand? I compared it to Memorial Stadium in Lincoln, Nebraska. The University of Nebraska Cornhusker football team has done their part and contributed to Nebraska's identity. Home games are played at Memorial Stadium in front of the Husker nation's red-clad, faithful fans. Before stadium skybox additions, a sellout crowd ran close to seventy-eight thousand. Squeezed in the "sea of red," I scanned the crowd of approximately seventy-eight thousand fans. That translated to a lot of missing heroes, to families without closure, and thousands and thousands of unanswered questions.

Stanley and John Boros were part of that statistic. However, to get the ball rolling, Johnie Webb asked, "Do you have Stanley's IDPF?"

"His what?" I asked.

"His Individual Deceased Personnel File," Johnie answered.

Military acronyms. Contact with CMAOC, the Casualty and Memorial Affairs Operation Center in Virginia, part of the government's link to families, pointed me in the right direction.

A couple of months after my request, I received Stanley's eighty-two-page IDPF, a compilation of papers pertaining to Stanley's incident. The papers, pulled from all sorts of files in the archives, gave a relatively complete overview of the status of his case.

Some information in Stan's IDPF we already knew, but there was quite a bit of information in it that we had never seen. There was a page from the MACR 4660 like the one I had, only legible, there were copies of dental charts, a list of Stan's crew, correspondence with my folks, the serial number of the plane (which was was listed as 804 rather than 685), and there were synopses of the case. One summary stated that only three bodies were recovered from the crash and that no

---

‡   In 2009, the Gulf War missing soldier was identified by the Armed Forces Medical Examiner.

additional remains were discovered when wreckage was removed by the German military. One thing that impressed me was the follow-up that had taken place in the years after the war. It seems that the American Graves Registration Command, AGRC (now AGRS, American Graves Registration Service), had sent a team to Pottschach, Austria, in May of 1948 to pursue an investigation of the crash and interview eyewitnesses.

Information from the narrative of that investigation stated:

About ten minutes after the crash, a Mr. Josef Wagner and a Gendarme named Exner approached the scene of the crash and observed two bodies lying on the ground near the wreckage. Later a third body was found on the other side of the mountain. According to witnesses, the Gendarme Exner, who is not available for questioning, examined all three bodies and removed all identification tags and personal effects. Their present whereabouts are unknown.

Two days after the crash, the local undertaker, Franz Pogacnik, was ordered to remove the remains and bury them in the local cemetery. He put three caskets in a horse cart and went to the scene of the crash with the Gendarme Exner. In the presence of the undertaker, the Gendarme copied the name of each flier from the identification tags and inscribed this information on each casket as the particular remains concerned were placed in the casket. The undertaker then personally escorted the caskets to the cemetery and supervised the burial. He personally observed the transfer of the information from the caskets to the crosses, which were placed above the grave, and certifies that the information on the crosses is identical with the information taken from the identification tags in each individual case.

The names of the buried crewmen matched with the names of the deceased men from Stanley's crew. The report continued:

The whereabouts of the remains of the remaining missing two crew members, Lt. Stanley N. Dwyer, 0-751540, and T/Sgt John J. Boros, 32869413, could not be ascertained. No parachutists were seen during the entire time that the local townspeople observed the flight of the plane. No trace of additional remains could be found on the scene of the crash. The two strongest possibilities are that these two remains have been among the many unknowns disinterred from Wiener Neustadt, or they are buried in some location which has not yet been visited. The Soviets do not permit area searching in their zone, so the case will have to be held in abeyance until additional information is received.

As a result of the AGRS investigation, the two missing crew members were classified as "non-recoverable." That designation was made in November 1949, but only after disinterred remains and unknowns recovered from Austria were compared for a match with either Stan or John Boros with negative results. In 1953, Stan's name was deleted from a deferred search case list. And one other thing the government did was to go back a second time and question Stan's surviving crew members.

Manley Dale Jr., the copilot, wrote in his 1949 report in a Casualty Questionnaire:

> I stepped down out of c.p. seat and reached for my parachute. It spilled and I gathered it up in my arms. It was then that I saw S/Sgt Boros. I turned around and saw T/Sgt Piper. I then passed out from lack of oxygen and awoke during the parachute descent.
>
> Bomb – Piper, Prescott - T/Sgt – last seen in doorway to navigator-bomb compartment. I believe this was the man that pushed me out when I passed out from lack of oxygen. No actual information known.
>
> Pilot – Dwyer, Stanley N. - 1st Lt. – Last seen still in pilot's seat.
>
> Eng – Boros, John T/Sgt – Last seen putting on parachute & working toward bomb bay to bail out.

Eugene Parker's report in the IDPF stated, "I was out of contact with the rest of the plane in the last minutes of flight. My intercom was knocked out of commission."

Stephen Milewski wrote:

> I don't know too much about what happened in the front since I was in the waist of the plane … After helping the ball turret operator with his chute, I went back to my position and called the pilot, but I didn't receive any answer. It's possible that I may not have made my interphone connection because I heard neither my voice nor anyone else speaking over the interphone. There is a possibility that the interphone was shot out … Two weeks later, after spending some time in a hospital, I met some of my crew members, and I got the following

story: The controlling mechanism of the plane was shattered, and Lt. Dwyer tried to keep the plane under control while T/Sgt Boros was trying to shoot some flares to notify our escort of our trouble. As the story goes, Boros forgot to secure the flare gun, and when he squeezed the trigger, the gun bucked and the shell exploded in the ship, setting off the box of flares which he had around the turret.

Excerpts of George Mitchell's 1949 letter to the government read:

Dear Colonel Metz,

As vivid as the memory of the day of our tragedy still is, I doubt that I can add anymore to what I have said previously to certain Air Force investigators and to Mr. Dwyer, Stan's father.

We were on our bomb run that morning of May 10, 1944. After things became more than hot and the plane began burning furiously, Lt. Dwyer gave the signal to "abandon ship."

I was in the radio room and parachuted out through the bomb bay.

Just before I jumped, I looked across the bay and saw Sgt. Boros in the process of getting ready to get out, too, through the bomb bay. I never saw him again. I don't know if he continued on out after me or not.

I didn't see Lt. Dwyer after we took off on the mission that morning. I do have a recollection of Lt. Dale (the copilot) telling me (after we had been captured and when we were together for a short time) that Lt. Dwyer was making preparations to leave the flight deck as he (Lt. Dale) made his way out through the belly hatch nearest them ...

I never knew the name of the town I was captured near, and near where the plane finally hit. I imagine it is in the Russian Zone as is Wiener Neustadt at present. I very much wanted to go there when I was over this summer. But we have so very little to go on. I have always felt that the boys we never heard of were still in the plane when she hit and perished in the fire. But what happened to keep them from jumping when both Lt. Dwyer and Sgt. Boros were apparently on their way out? I know we were still pretty high up after catching fire, and *it seems* as though there was plenty of time ...

I know the Dwyers have always been hopeful of at least finding out where Stan was buried, but I just don't know anymore.

Glad to help you anytime I can.

Sincerely yours,
George D. Mitchell

It appeared, from the IDPF and from letters in Stanley's trunk, that the last correspondence the government had with Granddad and Grandma was in 1947. In October 1947, Grandma had received an updated copy of the Battle Casualty Report, signed a form in December 1947 acknowledging receipt of Stanley's posthumous advancement to first lieutenant, *and* Grandma had advised the government of their address change. However, I don't believe they knew about any follow-up information gathered by AGRS after 1947 or what we learned from Stanley's IDPF.

One yellowed newspaper clipping saved in Stanley's trunk listed 127 individuals, including Stanley Dwyer, as "The County's World War II Gold Star Roll." Another clipping read, "How to Bail Out of a Flying Fortress," and I found a February 12, 1947, *Kansas City Star* article written by Maureen Murphy and sent to Granddad by someone. From this information, especially the *Star* article, I thought I understood my grandparents' train of thought. They seemed to be on the right track in their search.

The article stated:

> More than 800 R.A.F. men are combing Europe in search of thousands of British and American airmen listed during the war as "missing, presumed killed." This quest is the R.A.F.'s last operation of World War II, and the task set them is gigantic: discover exactly where each man fell, how he died, and where he was buried.
>
> The total number of American airmen reported "missing in action" over Europe was 23,287. Of that number, approximately 10,000 turned up alive in German concentration camps and at hospitals at the end of the war ...
>
> Some 38,000 British airmen were also missing; about 10,000 have been accounted for. Those lost in air action number 79,281— just sixteen more than the number of American fliers killed ...

Johnie Webb told me, "After the war, teams, including AGRS, had the responsibility of cleaning up battlefields all over world.

"Even though parts of Austria were under Russian control at that time, teams were given access to some areas. Eyewitness accounts were generated, and an effort was made to identify remains and come to some conclusion, even if it was 'non-recoverable.'

"Information from unknown remains was compared to known losses to see if they had a match. If no matches were made, the remains were buried in American cemeteries as unknown. In the 1950s, depending on the conclusion, information began to be released. But considering the magnitude of information, families probably had to make a request."

As I read through the pages of my brother's IDPF, I looked over a list of his personal effects that were returned to the folks. A watch was listed. When Stan's personal belongings were shipped home in the fall of 1944, I was in training in Lincoln, Nebraska. I remember standing with the folks at home in Hastings going through his things. I picked up the watch. It had stopped running. When I looked at the time on Stan's watch, it was the exact time of day as I stood there in Hastings, Nebraska.

And another coincidence. Grandson Nate, Rick and Kay's son, for his Eagle Scout project, buried flagpole sleeves in the ground around the Fillmore County Courthouse in Geneva, Nebraska. The sleeves are used to fly flags of deceased veterans from their county. The veterans' names and branch of service were stamped along the edge of the flag—the border edge with the eyelets. Rick suggested that we bring Stan's flag, from my county, down to Geneva and fly it on Flag Day.

Well, I talked to the men at the VFW in Hastings, and it wasn't a problem— if only they could locate Stan's flag. It seems Adams County, my county, has over three hundred veterans' flags, and not every one of them can be flown at the same time in our cemetery on Memorial Day. So, if they ran across Stan's flag, they'd let me know. Besides, I knew Stan had a flag because one previous Memorial Day in Hastings, years ago, Darlene and I had gone to the cemetery for the service and to see the flag display—maybe only a hundred or so were displayed. I proceeded to check out the names on the flags. The first one I walked up to was my brother's.

The VFW called me about a week after my request, and they told me that as they were putting folded flags away, one flopped open, exposing the name— Stanley N. Dwyer, USAF. Stan's flag flew on the courthouse square in Geneva on Flag Day.

With this information plus these "signs," our pursuit seemed justifiable. I had the feeling we were on the right track in our search for Stanley and was compelled to continue.

For CILHI's purposes, Stanley's IDPF was a starting point. And next, following instructions, I mailed Johnie Webb copies of the research we'd accumulated, especially the information from our Austrian contacts and Eugene Parker.

I can only imagine that the papers we sent to CILHI helped put us ahead in the line.

"It will be several months before you hear anything back," Johnie had said. "Our own research, just in the beginning stages, will take a long time."

Nonetheless, we had our foot in the door, and we waited. The arduous process began with CILHI's historians and analysts thoroughly researching the incident, meticulously combing through historical data and the archives in order to establish a case. Their task seemed complicated and the workload unending. Yet CILHI, as part of an entire network, was like the tip of an iceberg.

While we waited, we attended the St. Louis family update sponsored by the DPMO, Defense POW/Missing Personnel Office. Family updates, scheduled about eight times a year in strategically located cities around the country, are the government's attempt to reach out to families of the missing and to let them know they haven't forgotten the missing—that efforts are being made to help them get answers and achieve closure.

The week of the update, Mom said to me, "Your dad is thinking about staying home to take care of some minor business matters."

"Well, okay," I said. I paused and responded, "I guess Rick and I will go."

I don't know what Mom said to Dad, but the four of us drove to St. Louis and learned about the unimaginable extent of our government's humanitarian efforts to recover soldiers and ultimately account for the missing. DPMO carries their torch, "Keeping the Promise," the promise of bringing servicemen and women home with honor. As part of the Department of Defense (DOD), DPMO has the job of coordinating policy and overseeing all efforts to achieve their mission—the fullest possible accounting of our country's missing servicemen and servicewomen. In addition to the updates, briefings are held once a year for Vietnam War families and for families with missing persons from the Korean War and Cold War.

And just when we about memorized the words to one acronym, CILHI, it was replaced with the acronym JPAC. Attendees at the St. Louis family update learned that, in order to operate more efficiently, on October 1, 2003, the CILHI would merge with JTF-FA, Joint Task Force-Full Accounting, the unit responsible for the Vietnam War missing, and become the JPAC, the Joint POW/MIA Accounting Command.

Nevertheless, JPAC's mission, as stated in their handouts, remained the same—to "conduct global research, investigation, excavation, and identification operations in order to achieve the fullest possible accounting of Americans unaccounted for as a result of past conflicts."

The CIL—Central Identification Lab—remained part of JPAC, and JPAC became a household word for us. Their motto is "Until they are home."

JPAC excavations are one component of DPMO's mission. In order to account for the missing, crash sites must first be located. And most former enemy countries cooperate, some on a limited basis, with our government's attempted accounting efforts.

At the St. Louis family update, approximately one hundred family members of missing servicemen listened as government officials explained their coordinated roles for DPMO's mission. Officials negotiate with other countries—the former Soviet Union, China, North Korea, Vietnam, Cambodia, and Laos, to name a few—for access to archives. They also seek cooperation and opportunities to interview witnesses, bilaterally as well as trilaterally, in an effort to locate, recover, and bring home missing soldiers.

Local eyewitnesses are crucial in locating remote crash sites. In some countries, documentation, as well as memories, is sometimes sketchy. However, if a site is located and then selected for excavation, a JPAC team conducts the scientific field recovery, where soil is typically sifted through one-quarter-inch mesh screens. Pertinent materials recovered at the site are transported to the Central Identification Lab in Hawaii.

And the lab, an accredited crime lab and the largest forensic anthropology lab in the world, is under the direction of Scientific Director Dr. Thomas D. Holland.

"The identification process," Dr. Holland said, "is a long process which begins with a field recovery carried out by one of the recovery teams from the JPAC. The site is treated like a crime area, using archeological principles. Recovery sites range in size from a small burial plot to sites one-quarter to one-half mile in diameter, some even thirty feet deep.

"Multiple lines of evidence are factored into an identification, including circumstantial evidence, archaeological findings, material evidence analysis, forensic anthropological analysis, forensic odontological analysis, and mtDNA analysis. Dog tags and parts of a uniform help to identify but are not the only way.

"In Southeast Asia, we're racing against the clock. Acidic jungle soils dissolve the calcium in bones. Bones with a lot of surface area deteriorate first; however, teeth, protected with a hard enamel coating, are the last part to disappear. Teeth are almost as good as a fingerprint, if the corresponding dental records or X-rays for a soldier are on file.

"Matching is important in making an identification, but exclusion is equally important in leading to an accurate identification. In the words of Sherlock Holmes, 'Eliminate all other factors, and the one which remains must be the truth.'"

DNA is sometimes used to confirm an identity. CIL provides DNA samples for processing at AFDIL, the Armed Forces DNA Identification Laboratory, located in Maryland. Playing a valuable, supportive role, AFDIL has established an extensive DNA database from which recovered remains could possibly be compared with collected specimens.

Nuclear DNA, found in the nucleus of each human cell, identifies us all as unique individuals but deteriorates over time. Losses prior to 1992 have no nuclear DNA references on file. Mitochondrial DNA (mtDNA), on the other hand, is made up of many strands found in the cytoplasm of a cell, giving the cell energy—and mtDNA is inherited maternally. Male mtDNA is in the tail of the sperm. At conception, the tail falls off when the head of the sperm penetrates the egg, giving way to the inheritance of only maternal mtDNA.

But even in harsh conditions, mtDNA resists deterioration. A mother passes her mtDNA on to her male and female offspring, and then only the female offspring pass the mtDNA to her offspring and on down the line. A simple swab collected from the mouth of qualifying family members provides AFDIL with vital reference samples for comparisons. Similar mtDNA sequences may exist across the population. Therefore, mtDNA alone cannot provide exact proof of identity but is another valuable tool, possibly the key link, to confirming an identification.

Since Dad and Stanley inherited the same mtDNA from their mother, Dad donated his DNA which is on file at AFDIL; however, a reference sample from a qualifying member of the Boros family is critical.

Furthermore, attendees were told about the Life Sciences Equipment Laboratory in Texas and its ability to analyze artifacts, aircraft and military equipment, and other material evidence recovered at crash sites to also support an identification.

Another thing we learned was just how little we knew about our government's relentless efforts to account for the missing. We tried to absorb bits and pieces about the vast archival research sources available to families, along with other information topics.

And working as liaison between the government and families, the Service Casualty Offices' personnel are willing to meet one-on-one with families to answer questions. They regard their POW/MIA accounting work as a mission, not a job.

When I heard and read that some of the bombs on Stan's plane had exploded on impact, I didn't believe there would be much to find. A five-hundred-pound bomb is very powerful, and Stan and John Boros, in the cockpit, were practically sitting right on top of them.

JPAC representatives emphasized that recovery teams could find a needle in a haystack.

Dr. Holland answered more of our personal questions. "Dog tags are made of monel, a material similar to stainless steel. It is very durable, resists corrosion, and can withstand very high temperatures—higher than the fire that presumably ensued at Stanley's crash site in Vostenhof, Austria."

And Dr. Holland indicated that the fire at the site was not hot enough to completely destroy all bones. Sometimes, fire preserves bone. Even after a cremation, chunks of bone are often mixed in with the ashes. It was an arcane little fact that had never entered my mind, but now I knew.

Leaving the hotel ballroom for a break, I walked past the round tables and noted name tags other attendees wore. Ours tags included the words "1st Lt. Stanley N. Dwyer, World War II," and we were the only World War II family represented. The majority of families represented the Korean War, with a smaller number of Vietnam War families. Yet, back in the 1970s, the families of loved ones missing from the Vietnam War had brought attention to the MIA issue and demanded answers from our government.

During another session, from table to table, one family member for each group stood and made introductions. It was irrelevant which war the families represented because everyone at the update shared a common mission. Everyone had a story. Families like ours were on a quest, searching for answers about the fate of their missing loved ones, almost driven to fill in the missing pieces. Whether it was a father, mother, aunt, uncle, sister, brother, niece, nephew, cousin, or wife, someone spoke, exposing the cost of war. Sometimes, a voice cracked or lips quivered, or maybe they spoke softly and wiped a tear, but the missing soldiers were remembered.

Yet, despite our government's steadfast, around-the-clock investigative and accounting efforts in Southeast Asia, the Korean Peninsula, and all over the world for that matter, it occurred to me as I listened to the introductions that the Korean War families still seemed to be holding out that, miraculously, their loved ones were alive. The Vietnam War families have many, many unanswered questions—some have little information to go on. I realized that circumstantial evidence for some MIAs is minimal, maybe nonexistent. We at least knew where Stanley's bomber crashed, and we had some answers and a relatively good idea of what happened to him.

It was explained to me that World War II–generation families had seemed to accept things—it was the way things were. They took it in stride—or at least it appeared that way—and got on with life.

"My position is the grief never lessens from generation to generation," Johnie Webb once told me. "Everywhere I go, as I go to family updates, I see the very raw emotions that still exist as family members, who never knew this individual, still get very emotional because, again, they've never had that closure. They saw the grief that their mother or father or whoever lived with for many, many years, and many of them made promises that they will continue to carry the torch to bring that individual back home."

"That is true," I remarked. "That is the role you assume. But I never saw my grandparents' grief because they never talked about it, except I see it in what Granddad wrote." I thought a minute, back to the house fire cleanup, and said, "Dad once commented, 'I don't know why it wasn't me instead of Stan. He was the talented one.'"

"Even though the families didn't talk about it," Johnie continued, "those close saw the toll it had taken on the first generation of that loss. From the time of the incident, from when they got that telegram, as time passed with that first generation, the grief did deepen."

"You don't want to ever forget them," I said.

"You can't let them be forgotten," Johnie replied.

So we patiently waited for JPAC to do its historical analysis of "our" incident to see where it would lead. The direction of our journey had become obvious, but things seemed out of our control.

My understanding was that of the eighteen recovery teams, approximately ten were assigned to Southeast Asia, five to Korea, and about three, more or less, were designated for World War II recoveries for both the European and Pacific theaters. Three for seventy-eight thousand World War II missing were not very good odds and was a monumental task.

I reminded Dad that of the seventy-eight thousand missing, thirty-five thousand or so were believed recoverable.

Dad said, "Okay, three into thirty-five thousand."

"That's a little better," I added.

It would be like winning the lottery. But we'd done some footwork and had gotten on JPAC's list early, when they were still reactive to World War II cases rather than proactive.

One thing in the back of my mind was the discrepancy in Stan's plane number in many of the reports we'd read, including the synopsis from the St. Louis family update. Was the plane number 685 or 804, and had we located the correct crash site?

Undoubtedly, JPAC had done their homework thoroughly, but to clear up our questions, I scoured through our records. Without a doubt in my mind—and Dad concluded the same—regardless of the plane number discrepancy, Stanley's plane crashed at the site near Vostenhof because (a) the sheared spruce tree was a defining landmark for the locals who (b) went to every effort to properly identify and bury Stanley's dead crewmen found at the scene.

I faxed more pages to JPAC, including letters from another Austrian historian, Felix Rameder. In one e-mail, Markus Reisner, the cadet at the Austrian Military Academy, mentioned Mr. Rameder. And come to find out, Mr. Rameder corresponded with Eugene Parker, sent him a small piece of the crashed plane, and analyzed, "Only the broken spruce tree is on this place (the place your plane crashed)," and he summarized, "Plane 804 is crashed Lichtenworth, Plane 685, your plane, is crashed Vostenhof. I think the mistake about the two crashed planes was made in Dulag Luft 1944."

Soon after the sixtieth anniversary of May 10, 1944, and over a year after we had contacted JPAC, we received notification that a JPAC investigative team had been assigned to deploy to Stanley's crash site in Austria. We'd made it to step two of their process—the investigation. After JPAC thoroughly analyzes records and establishes a "loss incident case file for each unaccounted-for individual,"[37] an investigative team is sent to potential recovery sites. Beyond that, two crucial steps remain—excavation and identification.

The DRI, Detailed Report of Investigation, raised our hopes. In Austria, the seven-member investigative team, accompanied by Udo and Inge Doerr, interviewed Augustin Stranz, the local historian, as well as the landowner of the crash site, Mr. Auer.

Information collected for the report corresponded with historical records. The report read:

> He [Mr. Auer] was in the German army at the time of the incident but visited the site while on leave a few months after the crash. Some wreckage was cleared away, but the crash scene consisted of a crater and a burned section of the wooded slope ... Mr. Auer pointed out the location of the one individual who attempted to bail out and was found at the top of the slope ... The elderly landowner expressed his opinion that, as the site is the resting place of the missing aircrew, it should remain undisturbed. The landowner only agreed with reluctance to allow a surface survey using a metal detector.

According to the report, "The team encountered material evidence consistent with an American air loss at the loss location and in the possession of Mr. Stranz." An American loss was crucial criteria in determining whether a site would be recommended for excavation. A survey of the crash site turned up "a significant concentration of surface aircraft wreckage," and the report continued, "incident-related materials are scattered at least thirty meters in all directions and will have been subject to significant downslope transport."

Because of the wide area of scattered debris, an excavation, as the report noted, could require "several Joint Field Activities." And the report went on, "As the site appears to be relatively undisturbed, the highest probability of recovering remains is in excavation of the immediate impact crater area and the area downslope ... Recovery of the crash location could collect evidence for the two remaining unaccounted-for personnel believed to be aboard the aircraft upon impact."

Investigative teams doing work in advance consider many factors before recommending a site for excavation. Besides establishing a U.S. loss and the possible presence of remains, other factors include site accessibility, water sources, terrain and vegetation, wildlife, weather conditions, safety for the recovery team, and coordination and cooperation with the host country. Flagging tape at the Vostenhof crash site marked an ongoing ecological study, which would require extra and careful coordination with involved parties.

"Recommend this site for excavation," the team leader concluded in the report.

Never in our wildest dreams could we have imagined our journey at that point, the possibility of bringing Stanley's remains home. But we weren't there yet; only step two was completed.

"Looks like we will try to excavate the site next year [2005], if possible," Johnie Webb wrote. "At this time we cannot say when next year we might be able to do the excavation."

More waiting. So, in order to turn every stone, another road trip was in the works. The morning we—Dad, Mom, Rick, and I—were to leave for our final destination of Ohio to visit Eugene Parker, it had snowed. Well, it had snowed just a little—a dusting—and the forecast was for more. But it was just enough that Mom and Dad reassessed the fifty-mile drive from Hastings to Geneva where we were planning to load up and depart. After several phone calls back and forth, Dad proposed postponing the trip for a few months. It was one option and their decision. That's the dad that had taught his four daughters how to drive in all kinds of weather, especially snowstorms. Maybe with age, or rather, as birthdays add up, wisdom and caution go hand in hand. Finally, Dad decided, "We'll try the roads and see what they're like." Fifty miles and fifty minutes later, their van pulled into our driveway, and the clear roads continued for the rest of our trip.

Rick drove most of the way, and our first stop was Don Pratt's house in Iowa. Eugene Parker helped us locate Don.

"On May 10, 1944, I was at rest camp at the Isle of Capris," Don said. "Those were my orders. I'd say it [May 10 mission] probably was Dwyer's twenty-third mission or so. Every one of those I was on, but because I flew two missions with the 2nd Bomb Group when we first went over, I had twenty-five missions and was sent to a rest camp that day.

**Don Pratt was a waist gunner on Stanley's crew, but
Don was at rest camp on May 10, 1944.**

"Stanley was a hell of a nice guy. He was quiet and a very good person, concerned about everyone. We'd go up to fly, and when we'd get back, he'd come around and want to know how we all were—if anyone was having a problem or anything. He cared about the crew just like family. He kept us going.

"Popplewell, Darris Oldfather, the ball turret gunner, and Pappy (Papazian), the tail gunner, we were all from the original crew but weren't on the May 10 mission. I don't know why the crew was split that day. Oldfather got shot down with another crew later on. I heard two stories on him. I don't know which is true. Darris and I were buddy-buddy all through gunnery school and on the same crew. His nickname was Danny. My son, Darris, was named after him.

"I made fifty missions and came home in August 1944. I made two missions in one day; I spent sixteen hours in the air that day. We went up, dropped bombs, came back and reloaded, and went back again. I got injured on my fortieth mission. I got a piece of shrapnel the size of my finger in my shoulder. Not too many made fifty. I was lucky. Our losses were high."

Dad said, "When you do the math, it doesn't come out too good. What was the base like?"

Don continued, "When we were in Africa, we slept under nets to keep the insects off—mosquitoes carried malaria. A wooden frame [held the net] at the top, and we tucked the lower end under us.

"[In Foggia, Italy] we lived in tents. It wasn't bad. You soon learned when it was raining you didn't touch that tent. You touch that tent and it started leaking.

"I think I had about thirty missions in when we built this clubhouse. We went around on midnight requisitions picking up stones and stuff to build a nice clubhouse. Then we had showers, and we rigged up hot water. But up until then, your helmet was your shower. You wore it when you went over the target and then kept it—that was your bathtub. We had dinner plates and cups—a lot of K-rations.

"The runways were metal or steel mats, made from sixteen-by-ten-foot-long pieces of ribbed, interlocked mesh steel hooked together for a runway that was about five thousand feet long by sixty or seventy feet wide and about one-quarter to one-half-inch thick."

"As the number of missions added up for a crew, did it have anything to do with where you were placed in the formation?" Rick asked.

"It didn't make any difference," Don said. "They just moved you around.

"Dwyer was business; he flew in tight formation. In tight formation, you get stacked in pretty close to the plane next to you. Stanley would stick that wing in so close you thought you were going to hit. He could stick that wing in there.

"And it made a difference with the [enemy] fighters. If they saw a group in tight formation, they'd leave you alone and take one in loose formation. The tighter your formation, the better the firepower from all the machine guns. As a waist gunner, I could go full range or up and down with our .50 caliber guns. If you went up and down, you had to make sure you didn't hit the plane next to yours. You had to make sure you went under and above him.

"And Lieutenant Dwyer had a rule. When we hit twelve thousand feet, he'd tell us, and we'd have to put our oxygen masks on. We saw Mt. Vesuvius erupt; we flew right by it. The lava was flowing.

"One thing Stanley did that no other pilot I flew with did—and I probably flew with ten different pilots after that [May 10]—when we lined up for the bomb run and went into flak alley, Stanley came on the intercom and said, 'We're going in. Find a hole, crawl in it, and hang on.'

"The first 'bump' of the day was always scary. You'd worry, and you could hear it [flak] hitting the plane. Sometimes it was pieces of it, and sometimes it wasn't. When a plane started going down, you sat there and started thinking, 'Bail out, bail out!' Sometimes they did, and sometimes they didn't.

"It was always a good feeling when you heard someone say, 'Bombs away.' You knew when you came off the target because the antiaircraft fire wasn't there. Then we went back to our positions. After the bomb run, when we came off the target, you'd hear the pilot-to-crew report, and that meant the tail gunner all the way forward had to report to Stanley what their condition was and what the condition of the plane was in their area. He wanted to know, and he was a darn good pilot.

"I went on six or seven missions to Ploesti, Romania—two times with Dwyer—one on April 14 or 15, and we made another one in April … April 24. I'll tell you about the one mission, and that's the only one I'll talk about. The number four engine was completely out, and we could only get half power out of the number two. We had to get over the Alps to get home, and Lieutenant Dwyer told us over the intercom, 'I don't know if we can clear the mountains or not because we're losing altitude. Anyone who wants to bail out, do so.' I asked Stanley, 'What are you going to do?' and he said, 'Stay with the plane.'

"I didn't see a parachute open, and we made it over the mountains, barely, but we made it. Dwyer and Dale were both fighting the controls, both controlling that plane to keep it in the air. As far as I knew, we were crippled that day. We were out of formation, fell behind, and when you fall out of formation, the Jerry fighters are there. We had quite a battle, but we held them off until all of a sudden, a P-38 showed up. Those Jerrys left. They didn't like those P-38s. Anyway, we got down—two of the 38s stayed with us and protected us. The rest went on.

"When we got back and got on the ground, we counted over two hundred holes in that plane from fighters and shrapnel. They [ground crew] patched the holes, and old 685 was back in the air.

"The plane, 685, was never named—685 was the one that got shot down.

"I had a lot of pictures. In 1963, we had a flood here. We lived close to the river, and I lost everything I had—all my pictures, including wedding pictures."

Dad told Don, "Since I never knew Stan as a man, I wanted to talk to somebody that knew him."

"I was surprised you called me. You caught me off guard," Don said. "I don't talk about it much. Well, what can you say? Nothing. The heroes are the ones not here to talk about it.

"I tell you, every day when you got in that plane, you looked around, and you knew someone wasn't coming back. It might be you, or it might be someone else. You just got, well, I might say, you got so you didn't give a damn. I think that's what carried me through. I didn't care whether I made it or not. I didn't care. And I made it, but every time you'd be lining up, you'd say, 'Someone isn't coming back,' and that was about true. You knew you had to do it, and you just went and did it."

Usually you'd chum up with one or two guys. But everybody else you just kind of knew. You didn't want to get too close because you knew some of them were only going to be around for a while.

"I didn't know about it [the crew being shot down] until I walked into the camp, and there was only three in there instead of six," Don said. "I wanted to know what happened, and they told me. It kind of hurt because we were family." Don looked at Dad and said, "I'll tell you, Harold, you remind me of Stanley, through the eyes. Like I say, he was a hell of a good guy."

There were so many stories about the service and sacrifice of unpretentious men—along with the invisible remnants of war. Soon, we'd know more.

Our road trip continued to Marietta, Ohio, where we met our good friend Eugene Parker, crewman on Stanley's plane May 10, 1944.

Eugene Parker, ball turret gunner on Stanley's crew on May 10, 1944.
He became a POW. Photo courtesy of Eugene Parker.

Eugene was probably one of the last guys to see Stan alive, when they got on the plane that morning for the mission.

"Boros, Mitchell, 'Pete' Dale, and Stanley were regular crew," Eugene said. "I knew Stanley and thought he was a real good pilot. I didn't have any problems flying with him. I filled in that day and knew I wasn't coming back. Even though I was planning to come back, I had that feeling."

Dad said, "I had the same kind of feeling the last time I saw Stan, when he left Hastings on the train. I knew I'd never see him again."

Eugene said, "I brought my New Testament along on each mission, and I said, 'Lord, I want to turn this plane around because I feel like I'm not coming back.' Still, a small voice said to me, 'Be still. I'll take care of you.'

"The navigator, Gilhooley, from my crew, didn't see his daughter. His daughter was born probably after he was shot down [on May 10].

"My part as being a ball turret gunner was to protect the belly and see what was going on underneath. One engine was on fire, and I was going to bail out, but John Boyett said, 'Get back down in the turret. The fire's out.' So I got back in the turret. I didn't get the door shut, and we were hit again. Then both wings were on fire, and I said good-bye.

"One of the things I looked at all the time, from the bottom in the turret, was to see if the bombs were out. I followed George Mitchell out through the bomb bay, and the bombs were still in it. John Boyett went out the back door. The heat on the door in the waist section seemed to keep it shut. John Boyett was burned in the face from the fire."

One of the things mentioned in some reports were the flares that flight engineer John Boros had accidentally set aflame in the cockpit area. Eugene had no recollection of the flare incident, possibly because of his position in the plane. Things happened pretty fast up there.

"We got hit before and after the bomb run, and something happened so we couldn't salvo the bombs," Eugene continued. "After we got off the bomb run, Ju 88s, flying out of range, started lobbing rockets into our formation. We were hit with a blast from Ju 88s. The fighters wouldn't follow you over the target because of the concentration of flak. Sometimes, the flak was so concentrated it looked like you could just step from one to the other all the way down. We got blamed for a lot of things that the Germans did to themselves with antiaircraft fire."

Dad remarked, "Everything that goes up has to come down."

"We didn't have to worry so much about the fighters and antiaircraft guns at Ploesti," Eugene said. "It was terrible at Ploesti. The Germans burned smoke pots there so you couldn't see the target.

"Ploesti was counted as two missions. It was the length of the mission, so some counted as double. And that's the reason Don Pratt had to do fifty."

As he had mentioned in one of our previous phone conversations, Eugene repeated, "Pete Dale told me at a reunion that Stanley and Boros were killed in the plane before it crashed—Stanley slumped over the wheel, and Boros slumped over the belt by the top turret."

Dad replied, "More unanswered questions and nobody alive to ask."

"Well, the outcome of May 10, 1944, remains unchanged," I commented.

"We lost seven planes that day out of about thirty-five in our group," Eugene said. "Our plane flew in the tail-end Charlie position."

I was surprised that Stan, with as many missions as he'd flown, wasn't positioned farther up in the formation. Orders ... luck of the draw. Tail-end Charlies were vulnerable, being the last one in the formation, and naturally, the first ones the German fighters shot at in a pursuit.

"I was a prisoner of war for one year and three days," Eugene told us. "I probably bailed out at over twenty thousand feet and went into a free fall for quite a while. When I got lower, I knew I was wounded—I was wounded in fifteen places. I saw a Me 110 coming after me. I thought, 'Oh no, don't tell me I'm gonna get killed in this parachute.' I landed in a tree, and I dropped on one foot because my left foot was wounded. When I slipped down the mountainside on my buttocks to get to a stream, I must have passed out or something because the next thing I remember was somebody shaking me. He was dressed up in the full Austrian garb—hat, feather, suspenders, the short pants, and knee-high socks. He shook me and had that gun pointed at me. I put my hands up and actually said, 'Don't shoot, Mister. I'll marry your daughter!' Thank goodness he didn't understand English.

"He took me across this little stream, put me in a two-wheeled cart, and took me to a little town where they gathered everybody. They took me up to the hospital and sewed my foot up. He started sewing up my foot before I was completely out. In front of the hospital, there was a line of five-hundred-pound bombs, three high. I couldn't understand why they were stacked there. After about a week in the hospital, I got on a train and went to Vienna. Then from there, I hobbled on one foot, on cobblestones, from one train station to another, about a mile apart. I didn't have any crutches or cane and hopped on one foot most of the way.

"We were put in the boxcars, forty-by-eights, with about fifty-five men and two German guards—locked in without toilet facilities except for two buckets. We weren't allowed off the train. In the case of an air raid, the guards were to get out of the boxcar to take cover.

"While on the train going to a permanent camp, my life was taking a turn for the worse. There were red streaks beginning to run up my left leg from the wound in my left foot. There was a medic, an American Air Corps sergeant, on the train. All he had was aspirin and no penicillin. So he crushed two aspirin tablets in the palm of his hand to make it a powder. He put it in the wound of the left foot, and it took all that infection down out of it. I couldn't even imagine that.

"At a prison—Stalag Luft IV—John Boyett, one of my crew, looked at me and said, 'Parker, that you? Oh, hell, Parker, I thought you were dead. I saw your helmet, and it was full of blood.' We learned some of our enlisted men lost their lives on the mission. I was trying to justify my thoughts that I was alive and others lost their lives. I was on a guilt trip and still am at times today.

"When the Russians were coming at the end of the war, I was shipped over to Stalag Luft I, an officers' camp. We were eight days in crowded boxcars to go about seventy-five miles. John Boyett ended up on the Death March where the Germans marched the prisoners back and forth across Germany [in the fierce winter months], until the war ended. I don't know how they survived.

"The sad part about being a POW is you're up there, and there's just nothing you can do except play cards, read books, walk around the compound to see what's going on, and then get back and play some more cards. There wasn't much food to eat, and I only got one package from home through the Red Cross.

"Roll calls were trying times, as we knew how long we would be out there. Also, the guards in the towers would test-fire their machine guns over our heads every so often. Big Stoop, one of the guards, was a mean man. This guard would walk up behind a man and with his huge hands and bring them both over the ears of a POW. Then there were rumors of what he did in other barracks.

"We were just air jockeys getting those bombs to the target. I always try to impress upon people that the ground crew was just as important as the aircrew. And it helps to talk about it, to get it off your mind and off your chest. But I still have reoccurrences of PTSD, Post-Traumatic Stress Disorder. Loud noises like firecrackers remind me of antiaircraft guns and flak and make me jumpy."

Eugene's small frame would still fit in a ball turret. He drove us around the countryside in Ohio and pointed out the church where he preached. We traded letters and notes, shared details about JPAC and crew reports from Stanley's IDPF, and then he showed us the piece of the crashed plane that historian Felix Rameder from Austria had sent him. The world continued to get even smaller.

Eugene furnished photos and more documents for our files, including a diagram of the planes in formation on the May 10 mission. And we returned home with a list of possible contacts. Don Pratt had written down Allan Klute's address in Missouri and confirmed that copilot Pete Dale was deceased, but neither Don nor Eugene could come up with anything on the original crewman and radioman, George Mitchell.

Also, Don Pratt said something that triggered my memory, and the name Ralph Lauper came to mind. Ralph was one of Stan's good friends in the Army Air Corps. Don didn't know him, and Eugene couldn't find his address.

315

At first, we came up empty-handed in our search for George and Ralph. Therefore, online, I posted a request on the Fifteenth Air Force forum and, by mistake, the Eighth Air Force forum—did anyone know the whereabouts of George D. Mitchell and/or Ralph Lauper, both from the 463rd Bomb Group, 775th Squadron?

Ralph Lauper, along with many other acquaintances, was mentioned in some of Stanley's letters, only I didn't catch on right away. Maybe I'd hit a lull going through the trunk. Maybe I hadn't even read those particular letters, or perhaps I had skimmed them at first and the name didn't register. But Dad remembered. In the end, it all fit together.

I persisted in sorting through more letters in the trunk. Still in Italy in the months after May 10, 1944, Ralph had corresponded with Granddad and Grandma. Ralph's letters were optimistic. He wrote:

> This letter isn't so difficult 'cause Stan would want me to write it and because I'm not much worried about him, tho he is the closest friend I've had in this army of ten million ever since we met one night at Sq. 12 (first day, Oct. 9, 1942) in Santa Ana, California ...
>
> The reason I'm not worried about my best friend too much is that I was on that mission and was flying about one hundred yards away from him. We had one H_ _ _ of a time that day, and I had some trouble myself. Things were happening so fast we didn't get a chance to look around much, but if his ship had exploded or caught fire, almost all of us would have seen it.
>
> After we landed, I frantically questioned everyone on the mission and am convinced ... that Stan had the superchargers on one or two or more engines shot out by flak and couldn't keep up with the formation, so he dropped down and bailed out ...
>
> Now Stan was and is a "smart" flyer. He wasn't trying to be a hero over here and trying to bring home ships that had lost all their chances. He had stated definitely in our discussions that he'd get his crew and himself out of his ship, if he ever got so much flak it didn't seem he could avoid fire or explosion, "in about ten seconds."
>
> I'm sure I can understand, in part at least, your concern for your boy, but my guess is that his condition is more secure than mine right now 'cause he's either walking out somewhere or is sitting in a prisoner of war camp grousing about his tough luck—we're not worried much about him.
>
> Sooo, when we finish this mess over here, your kid will be waltzing home to you and those three or four dozen girls who are trying to

make headway with him. I've seen them try it from California to Florida and all points between.

We had lots of fun together. My wife says he's a really unusual and refreshing personality ... We understood each other perfectly, and I'm looking forward to some more of those six-hour "bull sessions" and some more "evenings out" with that boy ...

I made certain that all of his important papers were placed in the proper custody.

Lauper and Little, copilot and pilot respectively, flew plane 770 on May 10. A photo in *Allyn's Irish Orphans* showed their shot-up plane—a damaged rudder, one damaged engine, and no tail turret. Apparently, after weaving in and out of clouds and dodging enemy fighters, 770 barely landed back at Foggia from the May 10 Wiener Neustadt mission.

Cora, pilot Rosser Little's wife, had also written to Granddad from Lakeland, Florida, in June 1944:

"Mr. Dwyer – Stan was to my husband and myself as close as any friend could be, and we love him very deeply ... Rosser and Stan fly in the same squadron ... and their leisure time was the same, and we were constantly in search of the other's company ... Let me hear from you just as soon as you all hear from Stan." Rosser Little's son told me in a phone call that his father had passed away in 1969.

Ralph flew fifty-one missions, and the May 10 mission was noted in his diary, which we eventually acquired. Ralph wrote:

Whitey Kurowski, one of the waist gunners, cuts in [on the radio] and reported, "Louie [tail gunner] ain't here no more!"

"Go back and look at the damage," you [Ralph] tell him in a calm voice.

He straps on his little emergency, walk-around oxygen bottle, good for about fifteen minutes. He will report to you, "The tail is shot off. Some cables and lines are flying around. Everything's all twisted up back here. Louie's gone and you can crawl right out the back end ..."

Just imagine. A bomber with no tail guns! All shot up, on three engines and flying below normal speed! What a picnic [for enemy fighters].

Stanley's crew member George Mitchell had written about plane 770 "that day" in a letter to Granddad. "Just then I heard Stan say to Dale over the interphone that Little and Lauper were having trouble (they were in our formation), then he [Stan] said, 'My God,' and I looked out and saw their ship *without* a tail section."

Ralph's last letters to Granddad in May and September 1945 stated:

> Your last letter brought me up to date on the May 10th fiasco. I hate to say it, but I believe the story ends right there ... God Bless my dear friend's parents who have given so much to a harsh and bloody quarrel ... They just don't make medals heavy enough to fit men like my friend Stan. I came to learn that personal honor and integrity were to him as valuable as life itself. He proved that to me one day in a bomber over Austria. He could have cleared the ship if he had been content to give his crew less of a chance, but he knew why he took over command of those men and that ship, and by heaven, he lived up to the trust. What more can a man do? I feel plenty little when I think how his last thoughts were of my welfare in another ship. Thanks for telling me. I'd fly one hundred more missions over Wiener Neustadt if only it would bring that boy back. He was a man's man, and I'll always think fondly of our many happy hours together and the fun we had.

But was Ralph Lauper still alive? At that point in our search, we weren't shocked when information from who-knew-where landed in our laps. Edouard Reniere, from Belgium of all places, responded to my erroneous posting on the Eighth Air Force forum with information summarizing Stanley's service. Ed wrote, "[Stanley] is memorialized at the Florence American Cemetery in Via Cassia, Italy." We had been aware of this information, and my sister Jan had visited the cemetery. Ed also referred me to more websites.

In my opinion, if there is such a thing as "King of World War II Internet Research," Ed deserves the crown. Ed, however, simply refers to himself as an "Allied aviation buff," doing his best to help others utilize sources that someone has made available on the Internet. He had checked the NARA—National Archives Records Administration—database and the white pages for George D. Mitchell with no further contact information.

In addition, Ed directed me to the Lauper family website where there was a story written by Ralph, who mentions his good friend Stan Dwyer. Ed continued:

> I was saddened to find at ssdi [Social Security Death Index] that Ralph passed away on September 25, 1993, in Vacaville, CA. Hope

this helps somewhat. I was born right before the war, and it's thanks to people like your uncle, his fellow crew members and many, many others, from many countries that I live in a free country. They are not forgotten, and they deserve our deepest respect and gratitude.

Over our years of searching, Ed's directions paid off more than once.

So, I logged on to the Lauper family website, read about the family's history and their reunions, and e-mailed the contact person, who was more than surprised to receive my odd request. In his response, he attached a few pages of Ralph's history of war stories. He also forwarded my request to Ralph's daughter and to his son David. The contact person's e-mail stated, "If you do not hear from them in the near future, please let me know, and I will follow up."

When I thanked the contact person, the words "I will let you know if I hear from them" came off my fingertips at the same time the phone rang. It was none other than David Lauper. Good timing. After our conversation, he called Dad.

It was another coincidence and a connection to Stan. Less than a year after our phone conversation, we had dinner with David, Ralph's son, when he was in Nebraska on business. Ralph's wife and David's mother, Jane, was still alive but struggled with memory loss. Jane knew Stan, especially from the Lakeland, Florida, training days, when Jane, accompanied by her mom, arrived in Florida from Utah to marry Ralph just before he shipped out.

"I was conceived before Dad was sent across," David Lauper said, laughing.

Stanley and Ralph had trained together and had flown in the same squadron on the May 10 mission. Excerpts from Ralph's diary disclosed more.

Stan was a man about a year younger than I and, having been born of goodly parents, was possessed of many strong moral and spiritual convictions, much like my own. Although I was never able to convert him [to Mormonism], we still had much in common, and he became my closest friend in the army ...

Stan and I liked the same kind of women. There were always plenty of them around, and we double-dated a lot. There were lots of places to go, especially around Los Angeles ... I can remember Lawrence Welk at the Aragon on the Pier in Santa Monica, Woody Herman and his Woodchoppers Ball at the Palladium in Hollywood, and Count Basie and his Big Band at the Trianon Ballroom ... out in South Gate. I recall we even went by boat to Catalina Island, twenty-two miles off the coast, and danced to the music of Jan Garber in the Avalon Ballroom there. We had fun times and spent lots of time just talking.

May 10, 1944, ended all of that ... As I entered the Briefing Room on May 10, I spotted Stan Dwyer ... We sat next to each other and engaged in small talk ... neither one of us had any inkling we were having our last visit together ...

When I was stationed at Sioux City, Iowa [after returning from Italy], Harold [Stan's dad] dropped by and took me to dinner at the Warrior Hotel. Stan looked like him, talked like him, and acted like him ... Harold wanted to bring his son home and bury him in the Kansas heartland of America. He was never successful in his search for Stan's remains or even the exact circumstances of his death. I couldn't help him much, except that Stan had often written of our friendship, and that dinner provided for him both a welcome and sad link to the past.

Again, subtle confirmation that our search was on the right path.

12

"Keep the Flame Burning"

And tomorrow is another day.
—*Stanley N. Dwyer in a letter dated April 22, 1944*

Johnie Webb called in early 2005 and broke the news. Stanley's crash site in Austria was not on JPAC's operational schedule for 2005. Two sites in Germany and two in Hungary were on the list, and two separate teams would be in New Guinea. Then factor in funding limitations ...

On the one hand, it was disappointing for selfish reasons. Aunt Aileen was almost ninety years old, and Dad was eighty. Time worked against us, just as it did for other families. On the other hand, however, some family, somewhere, would hopefully have their loved one returned to them. There are thousands of stories similar to ours. Maybe our turn would be next year. More patience.

When you're dealing with the army, things happen when they happen. I knew that from my own military experience. To me, the excavation was a remote possibility.

Rick boosted my optimism and said, "We've come this far. See where it goes."

Sometimes, in anticipation of something important happening and not wanting to be let down, I have a tendency to be pessimistic in order to soften the blow. Not then. I continued to go through the stuff in Stanley's trunk, we scheduled day trips to Kansas, and I followed up with some of our contacts. Almost four years had slipped by since we'd updated our Austrian friends, Inge and Udo Doerr and Augustin Stranz. In fact, I tried to establish contact with the other Austrian historian, Felix Rameder.

Also, I wondered if we had retrieved all archival records relating to Stanley. His military records had burned in the 1973 fire at the St. Louis archives, the National Personnel Records Center. I knew I could request, through the Freedom of Information Act, the IDPFs of Stanley's four other deceased crewmen. Eventually I made the request and waited several months for their files. Trying to locate Huretta Wright still bugged me. Ralph Lauper had mentioned Huretta in one letter, referring to her as, "the young lady who thinks a lot of him [Stanley] ... a good girl." Again, my search efforts for Huretta were futile. Still, I was energized to learn more about Stanley. We marked our calendars for the DPMO family update in Omaha, Nebraska.

Before it was all said and done with, we contacted two others who'd flown with Stan—Allan Klute and John Boyett—just curious to get more of the story and learn about Stan. Fill-in crew member Milewski had passed away. Bombardier Klute, one of Stan's original crew and someone he "buddied around" with in training, never had flown an actual mission with Stan since Klute was shot down in March 1944 while getting experience with a veteran crew.

When Dad talked to Allan Klute, Allan said, "I'm close to ninety. It's been so long."

John Boyett, waist gunner on Stanley's crew on May 10, 1944.
He became a POW.

Initially, I made a phone call to John Boyett. A couple of years later, the four of us visited him at his home in Texas. John was on Eugene Parker's crew and flew as waist gunner on Stan's plane May 10. He remembered giving the orders to "bail out." Years after the war, he attended some reunions and didn't talk about his experiences much until the 1980s. He remembered someone telling him "that the pilot got hit in the head, and it blew his head off."

"Flak was as thick as a cloud and sounded like gravel hitting a tin building," John said. "The flames from the wings trailed back to the tail. Fire had melted the doors in the waist section, as I could not open the door. I jumped and hit the door with both feet; the door flew off, and I went out the hole with the door, right into the fire. My face was burned. I held my breath as long as possible as I hung in the air beside the plane for a while before I dropped clear. My left forearm had a big chunk of flak in it, and my left leg and back had flak scattered in them. My face was also bleeding until I could hardly see.

"As I was floating down, a German fighter plane whizzed by and shot at me. He missed, but I was out of range by the time he turned around and came back for me. I also missed an electric high line by maneuvering the lines on my parachute. I was not able to miss a tall pine tree and landed in the top of it.

"I was captured by an old man with a rusty rifle and a barking dog and taken to a farmhouse, where I ate my last good meal for a year. Two SS men came and took me away on a motorcycle with a sidecar where I rode. By that time, it was dark. They stopped and had an argument about what to do with me. One wanted to shoot me, and the other didn't. I was glad he won the argument.

"They took me to SS headquarters. I was interrogated but would only tell them my name, rank, and serial number. I had left my dog tags on my bunk back at the camp, so they accused me of being a spy. Finally, a German officer brought a big book and turned to a place in it and read me a biography of where I lived—in Hollis, Oklahoma—when I was born, and where I took all my training after being drafted.

"The prison camp was called Kriegsgefangenenpost. I was first sent to Stalag Luft III then to IV where I ran into Eugene Parker. In early February 1945, the Russians got close, and the Germans didn't want the Russians taking the prisoners out, so the prisoners were taken on a five-hundred-mile, several-month march, now known as the Death March. Some wounded were taken out on the train. Eugene Parker was taken out on the train.

"They walked us to get away from the east part of the country [Germany]. We stopped at night to rest. It was one of the coldest winters. We lay down in grass in ditches to sleep. I had a GI overcoat, which I wrapped up in. It was freezing cold. I had a couple of letters from my wife in my pocket, so I set them afire to warm my hands. One of the guards saw the fire and stomped it out and chewed me out. I was pretty sad. I had no letters and no fire for warmth.

"We were strafed by planes on the road. We didn't know if they were German or American planes. We finished walking one day and stopped in a park area, not a settlement, out in the open, and we were attacked by airplanes again that day. I don't remember anyone being hit that day. I remember hiding behind a two- to three-inch-tall piece of curbing.

"We were marched through Berlin twice. Once in Berlin, the civilians lined the way and hollered at us. The guards had to keep civilians away from prisoners. When we were freed, an English officer and private came up in a jeep to near where we were. The soldier guards threw down their weapons and ran away, so we knew we were free. It was about May 2, 1945. I had lost about sixty-five pounds."

Then in July 2005, over two years after I first had talked to him on the phone, we met Johnie Webb at the family update in Omaha, Nebraska. A tall Texan with a slight hint of a drawl, he explained, "Our top priority is last-known-alive cases, especially from the Vietnam War. If we think we're going to lose a site, it gets priority. If a site is in imminent danger, if something is going to cause that site to be lost, whether it be construction or land reclamation of some type, it gets chosen. We were going to lose the crash site in Germany, so I had to send a team there this year. We're planning to go to Austria in 2006."

My fingers were crossed.

And in previous conversations, I'd expressed to Johnie our own long-standing desire to go to the crash site in Austria. So again, we double-checked with him about the likelihood of our family being on site during an excavation.

"As deputy commander," Johnie explained, "my responsibility is to deal with all external relations—veterans, family members, Congress, anything external to the operation. Normally, we don't recommend that families go to crash sites due to liability. If you show up, you will be allowed to go and visit with the understanding that JPAC offers no support to the family."

Family members crowded the hotel ballroom. Officials explained their determined efforts to account for the missing. Everyone listened intently for any information that might provide a lead to answers that would heal a family's wound.

Typically, a family knows nothing about the government or JPAC's efforts to solve their loved one's MIA status, let alone excavate remains. Considered humanitarian work, JPAC operates on a worldwide scope, but in 2005, knowledge of JPAC's existence itself was rare. Since then, the word has spread, but not enough. Since we personally had contacted JPAC about the two missing servicemen who had perished at the site in Austria, we had the inside track and followed the progress of our case. However, we represented the minority.

During the one-on-one sessions at the Omaha family update, Johnie joined the group at our table to personally address questions posed to him earlier by one lady. She was one of her group of three family members attending their first update, hoping to get some information—*anything*—on their uncle Walter Knudsen missing from World War II.

"Those three gals happened to read about the update scheduled for Omaha," Mom remembered, "and living next door in Iowa, they signed up for the meeting."

"I was aware they were signed up," Johnie told me later.

"Johnie is a very patient man," Rick observed. "He's willing to answer all questions. Those ladies asked him question after question about what he knew about their uncle, basically beating all around the bush. Finally, one of them came out and asked, 'Do you have his remains?'"

"Yes, we do," Johnie quietly said.

Walter Knudsen was one of nine crewmen who had crashed on a B-24 training flight in Papua New Guinea. A local villager had tipped off authorities when he turned over Walter's dog tags retrieved from the remote, overgrown tropical crash location. JPAC became involved and subsequently identified eight of the crewmen, Walter included—eight more to add to their list of nearly 250 sets of American World War II remains recovered in Papua New Guinea.

"It seemed like Johnie wanted them to be mentally ready for the big news rather than drop the bomb on them," Rick said. "And it was a moment to remember."

Walter Knudsen was coming home—testimony to our government's tireless efforts to achieve the fullest possible accounting of missing service personnel. Walter's remains would be returned to his family for burial, and then the family could rest with his fate resolved.

In the words of Brigadier General Michael Flowers, JPAC commander at that time, "JPAC will continue to fulfill our country's promise to those American heroes and the families waiting for their return."[38]

Every family in the room at the update had a story. Considering the big picture—the total number of missing service personnel—JPAC's task is overwhelming. However, each recovery and each identification must be gratifying and rewarding. We felt fortunate that Stanley's crash site was even considered for excavation.

JPAC welcomes visitors to their headquarters on the Hawaiian island of Oahu—a long flight from Nebraska. The final approach to Honolulu International Airport skirts the mouth of Pearl Harbor. I strained to peer behind the wing. Features within Pearl Harbor are symbolic of a beginning and an end. The white *Arizona* Memorial stood out in the bluish green water, and it depicts the beginning of America's involvement in World War II. Like a long covered bridge surrounded by water, the memorial spans the sunken hull of the USS *Arizona* and has seven windowlike openings on each of its two long sides and seven identical openings on the top of the white structure. There are twenty-one in all—a twenty-one-gun salute for the over one thousand servicemen who succumbed on December 7, 1941, and who are entombed in the sunken USS *Arizona*.

Imagine the frenzied island population on the chaotic Sunday morning, December 7, 1941, running in a panic, scattering for cover as ships exploded in the harbor, black smoke thickening around them, and Japanese planes zooming above them, fast and low, the *tat-tat-tat-tat-tat* of machine guns strafing, bullets ripping apart anything in their paths. Jagged, shot-out hangar windows on Ford Island still are a visible reminder.

Adjacent to the *Arizona* Memorial, accessible from Ford Island, the retired USS *Missouri* battleship, representing the end of World War II, exhibits her massive sixteen-inch guns. The end of World War II culminated on the deck of the USS *Missouri* in Tokyo Bay in September 1945, when Japan signed surrender documents and eyes looked upward as hundreds of B-29s thundered overhead.

Farther inland on Oahu, a lush, green, extinct crater serves as the final resting place for thousands who honorably served their country. At this place, the National Memorial Cemetery of the Pacific, also known as the Punchbowl National Cemetery, unknowns rest alongside their known comrades in arms.

Furthermore, those missing in action from the Pacific region of World War II, the Korean War, and the Vietnam War are honored at the Honolulu Memorial in the cemetery. One inscription reads, "In these gardens are recorded the names of Americans who gave their lives in the service of their country and whose earthly resting place is known only to God." The missing are not forgotten.

Also on the island of Oahu, JPAC headquarters are located at Hickam Air Force Base. On the base, streets dotted with palm trees lead past buildings pitted with December 7, 1941, Japanese strafings and past vast tarmacs. It is upon these tarmacs that recovered remains of fallen servicemen are returned to American soil. During a repatriation ceremony, a flag-draped transfer case containing the unidentified remains is carried off a military transport plane by an honor guard. Military personnel, veterans, and sometimes family members solemnly stand to honor a repatriated soldier.

After the ceremony, the remains are transported to the Central Identification Lab for possible identification and answers—an "ending," a resolution for families of missing servicemen. JPAC firmly stands behind the government's steadfast promise to bring home the missing.

At JPAC headquarters, we observed, behind a wall of glass windows, scientists, forensic anthropologists, and forensic odontologists in white lab coats examining evidence in the restricted-access Central Identification Lab, the largest accredited crime lab in the world.

A forensic anthropologist examines recovered remains in order to build a "biological profile." Bones can reveal an individual's age, race, sex, stature, and other unique physical clues; however, the identification process entails a thorough and meticulous examination of many factors. Previously, at one family update, we had heard Dr. Thomas Holland explain how "multiple lines of evidence are factored into an identification, including circumstantial evidence, archaeological findings, material evidence analysis, forensic anthropological analysis, forensic odontological analysis, and mtDNA analysis.

Dr. Holland had also said, "The field of forensic anthropology is pretty low tech, and in many respects, the tools haven't changed in fifty years. It's still pattern recognition. It's still getting a good analyst with a good eye and good hands who can recognize these disparate parts and realize that they all go together. What has changed from a technological standpoint is that, very often, anthropology may get us 80 percent there, but sometimes we can't pull the trigger and bring a case to resolution.

"And that's where DNA has changed how we do business. A small fragment of bone can provide the final piece of the puzzle. We're getting DNA now from small fragments the size of a thumbnail. Teeth are also a good source of DNA because it's encapsulated—it's the inside. But once the integrity of a tooth becomes compromised, it's not good for DNA, but it is good for traditional dental identifications which are as good as a fingerprint."

"An identification takes anywhere from thirty days to ten years," Johnie Webb stated. "It's a big range, but we average about seventy-five identifications a year."

Dr. Holland commented, "The work in the lab is done blind, and each case is unique. We are trying to resolve fifty- to sixty-year-old puzzles. The intellectual challenge draws you in, and then the mission takes hold and becomes part of you. When you think about how difficult it is to make identifications under the best of circumstances and then you add twenty-five, thirty, fifty, and sixty years to that, it's amazing that we can do what we do. I've never had an average case, and some keep you awake at night. The emotional satisfaction we gain from our work makes it the greatest job in the world.

"Obviously, our mission is the recovery of and identification of U.S. war dead. We're still looking, and we're still finding them. We have identified one serviceman from World War I.

"This country does not close the book on anyone. We're not writing any last chapters."

"Ultimately," he said, "the reason you do this is one brother to another, one father to another, one son to another, because I think that's the debt one generation has to another."[39]

The people associated with JPAC take pride in their work and their organization. Even though their main role is recovering and identifying the war dead, Dr. Holland explained, "We view ourselves as a national forensic resource. We feel an obligation to return to the community and to return to the society. We make the results of our analyses available to the law enforcement community, to the archeological community, and to the medical examiner community. We also feel the need to give back in terms of assisting in mass disasters. We were the first people from the U.S. to respond to the tsunami that hit Thailand and essentially headed up the U.S. recovery efforts for the next couple months. We assisted in identifying the victims from the 9/11 attack on the Pentagon, and we've done aircraft crashes. We feel a broader mission because there's nobody else out there standing by on a daily basis with the resources we have, doing what we do."

Johnie Webb stated, "Our mission is considered humanitarian. We think it allows us to have greater access to countries. This organization does get used as a means to open the doors to certain countries that we haven't had real good relations with."

While at JPAC headquarters, we met historian Christopher McDermott and anthropologist Dr. Mark Leney, two of JPAC's more than four hundred civilian and military employees. They were members of the 2004 investigative team to Stanley's crash site in Austria. Chris and Dr. Leney briefed Dad, Mom, Rick, and me on their findings in Austria and reiterated the landowner's reluctance in allowing an excavation. Photos of the crash site in their investigative report put it "just out of reach."

Johnie, following through on his statement made at the Omaha family update, confirmed that Stanley's crash site was on JPAC's short list for 2006—in fact, number two.

"And if you visit the crash site," Johnie said, "just behave yourself."

Nothing was in stone. However, in the early months of 2006, Johnie wrote, "I am currently in D.C. working on our budget issues. The good news is that your case is still on our list for this year even though others have been cut."

"Families are pressing us to do more," Johnie commented. "So we have to maximize what we do with the assets we have."

By spring, Johnie wrote, "I have good news to report. Our [investigative] team returned from Europe. They were able to meet with the landowner at Vostenhof while there. He is agreeable to allowing our recovery team to excavate the site this fall. At this time I see no obstacles in being able to conduct the recovery this year."

Things were falling into place, but we weren't there yet.

Locating George Mitchell took extra effort. I went to my friend Steve Einsel's office. His computer setup was a little more sophisticated than our home versions. Compared to the ocean, most home-system people searches cover the top depth, about a foot, whereas a sophisticated system takes your search to the bottom. Steve pulled up a list of men named George Mitchell—quite a few, maybe a hundred. The last name on the list was the one we were looking for, George D. Mitchell. Soon after, I called George. When I mentioned the name Stan Dwyer, there was a pause, and then George replied, "Stan Dwyer, he was my pilot in Italy. He was my kind of guy; a fine young man. I had camaraderie and a rapport with Stanley."

George said the phone call was "a wonderful present."

Even though we'd talked on the phone, George happened to be the last one alive from Stan's original crew that flew on the May 10 mission. A personal visit was in order. George lived in Hanover, New Hampshire.

George Mitchell, Stanley's radio operator on May 10, 1944.
He became a POW.

Yet weather reports of flooding with more rain forecasted for the Northeast almost scared off Mom and Dad and nearly squelched that trip too. But we pulled it off and discovered that either the waters receded quickly or weren't as widespread as reported on the news. By the time we checked in at our hotel a few miles downriver from Hanover, New Hampshire, George had left several messages. "Waiting for you at the Hanover Inn."

George stood up from his chair next to the fireplace in the Hanover Inn's lobby and shuffled toward us with his walker. Sensing a common bond, we greeted each other like old friends. Across the street from the Hanover Inn is the campus of Dartmouth College, George's alma mater. Almost a permanent fixture in the inn's lobby, George was on a first-name basis with the entire staff.

George relished being our personal guide for the next few days as we toured his neck of the woods and dined at some of his favorite restaurants. Over dinner, George said, "I taught English and history for twenty years at Collegiate in New York City, considered one of the finest independent boys' schools. The parents of my students weren't your ordinary parents. They were the likes of Lauren Bacall, Leonard Bernstein, and Jacqueline Kennedy Onassis."

George had attended Dartmouth two years before the war and then graduated from the college after the war.

"When I didn't come back [to college] at the end of the sophomore year," George told us, "I tried to get into the Naval Air Corps. I have a deviated septum in my nose, which made me ineligible to fly ... though, being ineligible to fly, here I am, taking the oath to join the Army Air Corps, but I didn't get to wear the 'gold crown hat.'"

The army operated on quotas. Early on, they had more pilots than airplanes, but when I went through, they needed pilots. It just depended when you went through the program.

"Fate is a funny thing, just being in the right place at the right time," George said. "Stanley and I talked about books a little," George told us. "We 'went over' a beautiful way, with Stanley at the controls. The B-17 was a gorgeous plane, and Stanley knew how to fly it. We flew from West Palm Beach to the Port of Spain in Trinidad. We stopped in Belem, Brazil, on the Amazon River. From Natal, Brazil, on the end of the dog's nose, [we flew] to French West Africa, near Dakar, where the French had scuttled their fleet. It was an eight-hour flight.

"I was in the radio room, and the intercom buzzed. Stanley said, 'George, look out the right side of the plane. The speck down there is Saint Helena where Napoleon was imprisoned.'

"We continued across the Sahara, Tunis, across the tip of Sicily, and the boot of Italy. That was a holiday that we had together—the way over—and after that, war was real.

"We were a very close fraternity. It was funny—the concept of flying a B-17 or a B-24 was acting as a unit. It was strange that they separated us [in crew quarters] according to rank when the higher-ups wanted unification, and there's nothing better than sharing sleeping quarters.

"I didn't like being farmed out to other crews. I flew two or three missions with other crews, and Stanley wasn't the pilot. There was no pilot in the Fifteenth like Stanley Dwyer. Anybody that tried to assume that position, forget it. That's how confident we were. A mission to Ploesti, just before we were shot down on May 10, decimated our group. But we needed replacements, which broke up crews. It was sad for us. [My] faith was in Stanley. I flew twenty-three missions with him, and we were looking forward to getting some rest in Cairo or Capri."

Dad asked George, "Did you have a tube in your radio compartment to drop chaff out of?

Chaff, or chopped-up pieces of tin foil, floated out below the planes in an attempt to jam the Germans' radar signals.

"Yes, and they say it worked," George said. "I also checked out in the ball turret," he continued. "It was another place I hated—claustrophobic, spinning around—and outside the whole world was sky."

Dad commented to George, "I was in the eighth or ninth grade when Stan left home, and then I only saw him about three or four times after that. George, you probably knew Stan more as a man than I did."

"Stanley was very proud of his father," George said. Even though George had never met Granddad, he had talked with him on the phone. George had talked to crewman Johnny Papazian over the years but never attended any reunions. "Everyone moved on with their own lives," George said.

Almost like his adoptive family, George's close friends, veteran Tony and his wife, Kitt, joined us for dinner. George sat at the head of the table. With his white hair and matching beard, he looked different from the young man standing behind Stanley in their crew picture. Stanley remained the same as in his photo, a twenty-seven-year-old young man.

Dad proposed the dinner toast. "To the guy we wish were here after sixty-two years."

George spent most of his days at the Hanover Inn, but he showed us around his classy assisted living facility. Using his walker for balance, he rolled it down the hall. Looking into residents' rooms, he remarked, "The turnover rate here is pretty high."

And like many veterans, George hadn't talked much about the war. I gave him copies of the letters he had written to Grandma and Granddad after the war, as well as George's mother's correspondence. George recalled, "The May 10 mission was approximately a six-hundred-plane raid. We rendezvoused over the Adriatic. We went around and around until the complement for the raid was all in the air, in formation, and flying off to the north. We were hit before we got to the target. There was a certain disappointment in all the crews' minds that we hadn't hit the target and that it was a depressing thought that the mission, as it would end up, hadn't been worthwhile."

Dad told George, "We have the official report of the mission, and the bombing was excellent after they got there. The group had a certain building to hit, a plant making parts for Messerschmitt fighter planes, and they hit it."

"We were on oxygen, and when we went out, we were pretty high," George said. "I saw Boros, the engineer, doing something with his outfit, his parachute, and I sensed John and Stanley were talking. When I stepped out of the radio room on the bomb bay walk, it got hazy. Should I jump or not jump? In the back of my head, I'm thinking, 'I should have to jump. We're on fire.'"

Dad asked him, "Was it close quarters going out the bomb bay with a rack of bombs?"

"I believe we dropped some of the bombs," George recalled.

Dad replied, "Oh, you did?"

"Between the time I jumped out and pulled the rip cord, I always thought I had blacked out," George continued. "It could've been—it was a very, very few minutes—and when I came to, that's when I pulled the cord. I subconsciously was afraid of the parachute not opening. We took it for granted that it would open. I didn't behave myself when we went to parachute training because we never thought we were going to have to use it! I pulled the little handle and everything went up. I wouldn't have had time to read any notes from a beautiful lady packer.

"My shoes were ripped off by my parachute belt when I jumped out—the backflow. A German farmer picked me up in a dairy truck and took me to the back of his bakery. They didn't offer us one thing to eat. The man who interrogated me asked if I was related to Billy Mitchell [the early pioneer of air warfare]. If I was not related to Billy, he asked if I was related to Margaret Mitchell, author of *Gone with the Wind*. I called Margaret when I was back to Dartmouth, and she said she hoped her name helped me.

"We [prisoners] were put on a train, which took us to Gross Tychow, where the POW camp was—Stalag Luft IV. I was a prisoner from around May 10, 1944, to April 18 or 20, 1945. We were liberated on the road walking from a camp in Poland on the Polish-German border to a camp in Germany near the French border. All the villages we went through—they weren't so happy to see us, and the guards didn't let them get very close to us."

We were told if we got shot down to get to the military if we could.

"It was ridiculous," George continued. "We were in the way of the Germans, their wheeled vehicles and tanks. There must have been close to eight hundred or nine hundred on our march. They should have left us in the camp and left us to the Russians, but they were terrified. Every German soldier, every Nazi, was terrified of what the Russians would do to them. I hadn't lost a lot of weight, but I'd lost some. My stomach was all mixed up. My feet were in terrible condition from walking on the march. There was a shortage of socks, and my [substitute] shoes didn't fit. When they got wet, they were rotten.

"It was bad, and we could have done without it in our lives, but it was nothing like the hell the Japanese prisoners went through. I used to say a prayer every night that I wouldn't get reassigned [to the war in the Pacific].

"It all comes down to the fact that your loss was final, and my capture and life in the camp wasn't. It wasn't meant that we should die. That's the way I feel. It wasn't meant to be."

Dad said, "We're the lucky ones. The ones that didn't come home are the heroes."

"Sherman said, 'War is hell,'" George commented.

On our last night with George, we dined in the main restaurant at the Hanover Inn which overlooked the lobby below through glass windows. Young couples, arm in arm or holding hands, walked through the lobby, men sporting tuxedos or suits, the ladies dressed for their formal affair in long gowns—backless and strapless and some low cut. As we ate, George leaned across the table and commented, "Rick, this is a bumper night for bosoms."

The mood tempered when we hugged George's frail body and said so long. George intended to regain his strength so he could travel to Nebraska and visit.

Meanwhile, George planted a thought that stuck in my memory. He told me, "Keep the flame burning."

13

◇◇◇

Hallowed Ground

Having previously separated the men from the boys,
now and then it separates the men from the men.
—Stanley N. Dwyer in a letter dated April 14, 1944

It was well into June 2006, and everything was falling into place, more or less. I'd always hoped JPAC would excavate the crash site and possibly identify Stanley's remains while Dad and Aileen still walked this earth. Aunt Aileen passed away on June 1, 2006. Mary Ellen tried to explain JPAC's work and the scheduled excavation in Austria to her mom.

"Mom didn't understand the fuss," Mary Ellen said. "My friend told me how Mom once talked to her about Stanley. Stanley was on her mind more than we knew, but she never said much to us."

As far as we knew, a recovery team from JPAC would excavate the crash site in Austria that summer, not fall. Dad, of course, cautioned, "When you work with the military, schedules can change." Yet, if we were going to Austria, flight and hotel reservations needed to be made. We had a couple of hurdles.

Mom cornered me one day at their home in Hastings. "You might want to talk to your dad. I've heard him say he doesn't know if he wants to go to Austria."

I found Dad sitting on the sofa and reading the newspaper. I stated my case, "Whether or not you and Mom go to Austria is entirely up to you. Rick and I have been looking forward to something like this for a long time. I've never traveled to Europe; I do not speak the language, and I am not familiar with the culture. I'm outside my comfort zone. But the more we can learn and understand before we go, the more comfortable we'll be. We do have contact with people in Austria, and I'm sure they could help us, if needed."

Dad surprised me. He put the paper down and without hesitating said, "Okay, we'll go."

Without knowing JPAC's official time frame, we guessed, and I went ahead and made reservations. Yet for Mom and me, there was something about wanting to see the crash site before the JPAC team started digging, which meant we had to coordinate with them, being careful not to interfere.

Even though our request wasn't customary, Johnie Webb worked with us. Via e-mail, he introduced us to Major Michael Legler.

"Welcome to the team," Major Legler wrote.

To start, let me introduce myself and the rest of the team. I am Major Mike Legler and will lead the team in Austria during the upcoming mission in August. Dr. Jay Silverstein is our anthropologist and is the recovery leader in charge of the site. SFC Bunnell is our team sergeant, and we have fourteen more team members with expertise in the Medical, Explosive Ordnance, Communication, and Recovery fields.

We are honored to have the opportunity to perform this mission and look forward to meeting you and your family. We are scheduled to arrive in Austria on 1 August and will go to the site on 2 August. We are still finalizing some of our plans, such as our lodging. The Embassy is arranging our hotel, and tonight or tomorrow I should have confirmation on where we are staying.

Please feel free to correspond with me and ask any questions you may have. I will do my best to answer them.

Thanks to the Mileage Plus rewards program through United Airlines, I changed our original flight reservations with ease, and we flew as far as Munich. Three generations of the Dwyer family arrived jet lagged in Austria via Germany on August 1, 2006, for another leg of our journey—the journey that had begun eight years before.

Mom and Dad had been to Europe before on group tours. Our version started out as a five-person, personally funded group tour including Mom, Dad, my daughter Melissa, my son Nate, and myself.

"We're following you, Kay," Mom said.

It seemed I was the designated leader—everybody's "Mom." Thankfully, the kids stepped it up and helped carry the load.

As we exited our United Airlines flight in Munich, Germany, I walked away from the last bit of familiar "America" and transitioned into the foreign terminal. It resembled other modern terminals, but I remarked to Melissa, "Do you know how it is when we hear somebody speaking a foreign language in America, how they stand out? Well, we're now the foreigners speaking the foreign language."

And we probably stood out—five of us speaking English, hauling a total of twelve pieces of luggage, carrying travel guides and a *German at a Glance* dictionary, and wearing passport necklaces as well as looks of confusion. We rode the train—make that *trains*—from Munich to Vienna. What better way to see the countryside? Only I overlooked the logistics involved. We quickly figured out a system for getting on and off the trains with our luggage once we determined which train to board. Melissa and I each carried bags and helped Mom on the train first, and then Nate and Dad heaved the rest of the luggage up to us—that way everything and everybody was aboard when the train lurched into motion.

While riding the trains, patchwork fields, green countrysides, homes with red-tiled roofs, and window boxes overflowing with flowers of every color flickered past our windows. Then the motion of the train lulled us to sleep until the rhythmic movement slowed and sometimes stopped. It started to shower. The gray skies, the train stations, and the eerie shrill of the train whistle reminded me of World War II scenes when trains moved displaced persons to camps and unknown fates.

Most tourists are lured to the grandeur of Vienna with its renowned museums, architectural wonders, theaters, up-scale restaurants, and cultural affairs. Bypassing the hustle and bustle of that city, we boarded yet another train for our final destination—Wiener Neustadt, the small city located about thirty miles south of the capital city and the target of the Fifteenth Air Force bombers and Stanley's bomb group on May 10, 1944.

And another logistical discovery—it appeared nothing is handicap accessible in Germany and Austria. Often, getting from one side of the train tracks to the other side to catch the next train required going down a flight of twenty or so steps, through a tunnel under the tracks, and then up another flight of stairs back to the main deck. Mom nursed a gimpy leg—the result of some arthritis along with the beginning stages of a deteriorating hip joint. She slowly descended the first flight of stairs while we hauled the luggage down the steps. Then, with Mom positioned at the top of the next flight of stairs, we lugged our bags up to her.

At last, we made it. What a relief to be at our final destination and not mistakenly in the Czech Republic. In Wiener Neustadt, a one-block walk from the train station put us at our hotel's doorstep. We wheeled our luggage that remaining block and rejoiced knowing we would not be moving luggage for weeks. On the train ride from Vienna to Wiener Neustadt, a gentleman asked me, "Why are you staying in Wiener Neustadt? *What* will you do there for thirty days?"

Our journey had led us to Austria. We were on a mission. The long-anticipated excavation was almost a reality. We were grateful JPAC had chosen

Stanley's crash site, and of course, hopeful that the team would find the remains of Stanley and the missing flight engineer, John Boros.

In an earlier phone conversation, Johnie Webb had made a prophetic statement about the excavation. "It'll be an experience you will never forget. You can't even imagine and will be absolutely amazed."

Not knowing quite what to expect, I reminded myself to take one day at a time.

My thoughts were to expect nothing—and anything more would be great. I was pleased to be in Austria and appreciated everything JPAC was doing.

Hotel choices in Wiener Neustadt were slim, and Rick had encouraged us to stay at the same place as the team. So the five of us settled at Hotel Corvinus, and Rick would join Mom, Dad, and me later, about the time Melissa and Nate would be returning to Nebraska for college.

The day after our arrival, a car, stretch van, and a moving vanlike truck pulled up in front of the Hotel Corvinus. The eighteen-member JPAC team unloaded all their gear, about one ton's worth, according to Dr. Jay Silverstein, the team anthropologist, recovery leader, and the only civilian on the team. The rest of the team members served in the military. Most of them served in the army, three were in the air force, and there was one marine. Team leader Major Mike Legler and mortuary affairs specialist Sergeant Jennifer Sweet introduced themselves. In her earlier e-mail to me, Sergeant Sweet noted that she would be in country, providing logistical support prior to the team's arrival. However, due to a scheduling conflict, Sergeant Sweet's offer to meet us when we transferred through Vienna fell through.

"People have no idea what goes into just planning one of these [excavations]," Johnie Webb had stated. "Just the logistical support that is required to support those teams while they are on site … it's enormous. In some countries, we ask, 'Where do we get water?' The teams have to be well taken care of. In Germany, for example, we've got a forward base warehouse where we maintain supplies. So, if we can get supplies out of the warehouse, we'll get supplies there. If not, we take a look and see about buying from the local economy. Many times, it's cheaper simply buying from the local economy than it is to ship."

And, for us, there was the matter of transportation. While the team moved equipment to the crash site, we rented a car. Since taxis in Wiener Neustadt didn't accommodate five passengers, we decided to walk to the rental agency. But nobody could direct us to Europcar Rental, not even the English-speaking clerk at the police station. But, somehow, we figured it out. After a two-mile stroll, we became mobile—with a sleek, black, stick-shift VW Diesel Jetta.

The car rental agency employee helped me as I fiddled to find the lever to move the driver's seat forward. Then Mom commented, "I think he is wondering if you can even drive a stick shift."

Feeling like a fish out of water, I did get us back to the hotel—without getting lost and without so much as jerking the car once—in time for the planned rendezvous with the team.

Dr. Silverstein had invited us to the team's daily meeting, where everyone was introduced. I offered some background on how we'd reached that point—that Stan had taken a typewriter with him to war, and the letters he wrote practically filled up his trunk. I told the team my folks never knew exactly what happened to Stan. Stan was always my big brother. I never knew him as a man. Our family grew up in Kansas, and maybe I included the story about waking up one Halloween morning in Tipton, Kansas, when every farm machine within ten miles was parked right in the middle of town. It was a big, tangled mess that plugged Main Street. I don't know if Stan was involved in it or not, but he probably was.

"We're moving from the deployment phase to the execution phase," Dr. Silverstein summarized. "The site is approximately seventy meters across, and the crater is in the center where the bomb or bombs went off. Fragments may be small when screening. We may not be looking for much. A metal detector will be used to determine the edge of the scatter field, and we'll flag where the concentration of debris is located and work outward. The soils are good for screening. It is a big grid and may take up to forty-five days."

As we left the team meeting, Bill "Danny" Frye shook Dad's hand, personally introduced himself, and welcomed the family.

Now there was work to do. The next day, the team led the way to the crash site, a thirty-minute drive. Good thing they knew the way. Well, they did stop for directions once, but they had the linguist, Frederick Smith. Some of the route would not have been on a typical sightseer's "things to do and see" list. Out there, well off the beaten path, is a rare historical site. It's a sacred site. It's the burial ground for a couple of war heroes thousands of miles from home, far from Nebraska and Kansas. It's not listed in any tour books.

Farther off the beaten path, the road narrowed. The European countryside resembled the picture pages of a fairy-tale book. The crooked street, comparable to an alleyway just wide enough for one car, edged right up next to the buildings and stucco homes. Vibrantly colored flowers cascaded from even more window boxes. Nothing separated the street from the buildings until the crooked street curved and eased into a two-lane road that gently wound through the green countryside. We drove through what seemed like a tunnel of trees, and then the road broke out into an area with open fields. We passed a few stucco farmhouses along the way, more tree thickets, Vostenhof road signs, and then the landmark castle came into view.

The first stop was Mr. Auer's home, the landowner.

Mr. Auer, a small man and hunched over probably from years of farming, carried a small hatchet. While we were in Austria, he spent many days clearing trees from his land and cutting them into firewood. He didn't speak English, but we shook hands, and I handed him a letter written in German. Kay's friend Sue Rickert did some translating before we left home. The letter introduced me, and I thanked him for allowing JPAC to excavate my brother's crash site on his property. Major Legler had given me a JPAC ball cap to present to Mr. Auer.

And while standing in a small field of wheat stubble where Mr. Auer allowed us to park our vehicles, team members pointed to the adjoining unobstructed, sloped field, maybe a third of a mile long and one thousand feet wide. At the opposite end of that area—on the hillside below in the thick trees—was the crash site. Distant peaks and wooded, rolling hills faded into the hazy overcast. The shortcut to the crash site was across the open field. However, Dr. Silverstein walked with us through the forest for about a half mile or more.

First, we hiked an overgrown trail that followed a trickling stream. It was cool under the canopy of trees, and the smell of pine made me think of Colorado. The thought of Colorado and the Rocky Mountains reminded me of something Stanley wrote: "I don't know where I'm going to settle down, but the Rockies are getting their share of thought."

After hiking farther down that trail, Dr. Silverstein turned right onto a narrow and muddy road that we followed through the woods to the crash site. Stately pines swayed in the gentle breeze. The stream meandered through the valley, parallel to but beyond the narrow road, hidden by a tangle of shrubs. The crash site, on a forested hillside in a small, narrow valley and hidden from the distant mountains, was serene—a peaceful resting place.

Then team members spread out on the sloped area of the crash site. We followed. Team Sergeant Chris Bunnell pointed to metal debris, rubber, Plexiglas, and .50 caliber cartridge casings scattered on the surface over the area. A distinct and slightly sunken, leafy green area—the impact or bomb crater—contrasted with the brown ground.

Usually, an excavation team consisted of ten or eleven people. We had a beefed-up team with eighteen members. It was a big crash site. Gunnery Sergeant Kris Donald, "Gunny," the EOD tech (Explosive Ordnance Disposal technician), along with recovery specialist Eric Ahlstrand, ran a metal detector over the area, flagging the debris field. They grabbed Nate, and he followed along.

"I'm looking for a Christmas present—a five-hundred-pound bomb," Gunny commented.

I was really surprised at the amount of stuff that was scattered, but I've never been close to a five-hundred-pound bomb explosion, so I had no idea what trajectory of the projectiles or whatever was close to it would be. It's a pretty steep slope, so over the years, everything started to wash downhill.

"A metal detector search would identify the scatter limit of the wreckage and the areas of highest concentration," Dr. Silverstein explained. "My plan will consider the best approach, and we'll begin gridding off areas to begin digging."

And one by one, we learned the names of the team members—recovery specialists Brad Thompson and Dave Hansen talked with us. Dave picked a four-leaf clover at the site and gave it to Mom.

As we explored the crash site, Major Legler asked me, "Are you looking for dog tags?"

He read my mind.

"Teams are more likely to find dog tags at a World War II recovery than at a Vietnam recovery," someone commented. "One difference is that World War II aircraft were bigger and 'slow movers,' and more wreckage stayed on the surface. With Vietnam-era, fast-moving aircraft, debris was buried in the ground. Sometimes, the roots of a tree have pushed pieces down in the ground."

Except for the physical remnants of war, the crash area appeared the same as the rest of the hillside. We continued to search for wreckage for part of the day. But before returning to Hotel Corvinus, Dr. Silverstein wanted to interview Mr. Auer. Dad, Melissa, and I joined Dr. Silverstein, Major Legler, Frederick Smith, and Derrick Goode around Mr. Auer's kitchen table. Mrs. Auer, ill, lay on a bed in the gloomy but warm kitchen.

Translated, Mr. Auer said, "I am eighty-four years old. I was in the German army at the time of the crash. I spent one year in a prison camp in Brussels and returned home in 1946. After returning home, I heard about the crash from my mother. She said the plane was coming in, crashed, and the explosion broke all the windows. There were people in the area that saw the crash, but they are not alive."

Mr. Auer left the warm room and returned with photos from 1944, including one graphic photo of a deceased crewman from the crash. He remembered being told, "One crewman lay on the ground, and one hung from a tree. Maybe the explosion killed him. It was a long time ago."

I almost had to pinch myself. We were in Vostenhof, Austria, the location deciphered years ago from the squished letters on MACR 4660, Stanley's crash site—unknown to Grandma and Granddad. And we hoped to carry out Granddad and Grandma's wish of bringing home their son's remains. Our search for Stanley had moved from my kitchen, where, unknowingly, we picked up where Grandma and Granddad's search left off, to standing at the place where Stanley Dwyer, John Boros, Francis Gilhooley, Prescott Piper, and William Olfenius became heroes.

It's hallowed ground for us.
I can see Stan. I go back to the image where he's standing in front of his training plane with his harness on, only I see him without his hat—his reddish curly hair and his smile … a little bit of gold in his teeth … about the same build as me. That's what I see coming out of the mist … him just walking toward me with his hand out, getting ready to say "hello." I return the handshake, and I expect we'd hug a little. That's a fantasy.

So for about thirty days, we spent our time in Wiener Neustadt, driving twenty-some miles one way, back and forth to the crash site.
"Every day was an adventure," Mom recalled.

The excavation was very thorough. JPAC team members marked off the area to be excavated with string in five-by-five-meter grids. The team's work was like an archeological dig, its integrity controlled by Dr. Silverstein, who calculated the starting point to be the grid next to the bomb crater. Said starting point was determined by taking into consideration the concentration of debris and the area most likely to have remains. The top layer of a grid contained leaves, pine needles, rocks, and twigs mixed in with loose dirt.

Usually when we arrived at the crash site, four or five team members stood in a grid, the "pit," digging and shoveling dirt into five-gallon buckets that were then passed along a human line—the bucket brigade—to a screening area. The screener dumped the bucket of dirt into a quarter-inch mesh screen tray. Larger rocks were sorted out and tossed away, and sticks and twigs were examined closely, for they resemble bone. Finer dirt was sifted through the screen. Then the screener methodically inspected the rest of the debris, looking for bone, teeth, and other material evidence—life-support materials and personal effects. Some pieces of aircraft wreckage were a little more obvious.

One day, in addition to the JPAC team, five or six others "huddled" on the wooded hillside, and Frederick, the team linguist, stood in the middle of the group. I saw another man and heard and recognized the name Markus Reisner. He was speaking in English, and I finally made the connection. Years before, while a cadet at the Austrian Military Academy, researching a report on the bombing raids against Wiener Neustadt, Markus responded to our e-mail posting. His report turned into a 1,128-page book, *Bomben auf Wiener Neustadt*, hot off the press just two days before our arrival. The Vostenhof crash and Stanley's crew were documented on page 568, written in German.

And now we were here together, meeting at the crash site. Markus, an expert on the air war in Austria, had brought some of his books. He autographed one for us, "Crash place Vostenhof 04.08.06. If you think about them, they are not forgotten!"

In addition to Markus, museum curator and historian Mr. Friedrich Brettner was on site with the *buergermeister,* or mayor, and reporter Wilhelm Theuretsbacher from the *Kurier.* Interested in lost soldiers, the reporter talked to us and said, "JPAC is the best worldwide operation and a good example for Austria. We have the same history—your family history and part of Austrian history. They are not forgotten—members of the family never forget. Old Austrian women are still weeping and waiting for their husbands to come home [from war]. The younger generations are now searching for information."

Also mingling with the others on the hillside was a distinguished-looking gentleman wearing a felt fedora. He had a 35 mm camera hanging from a strap around his neck. He reminded me of someone I'd seen in a recent photo. We shook hands with historian Augustin Stranz, and I handed him another translated letter brought from home introducing Dad and myself and thanking him for his information that helped us locate the crash site. Dad gave Mr. Stranz a JPAC cap. Frederick and the reporter helped translate our conversation.

"On May 10, 1944, I was in school when the air raid alarm sounded," Mr. Stranz said. "After school, I was free to go home. My brothers and I went to the [crash] place, already blocked off by the police. The plane was blown into many little bits, which were scattered over a large area. Because of the force of the explosion, nothing was found of the two missing men."

As he pointed up to the sky, motioning in a counterclockwise direction, he continued, "The pilot circled back, probably trying to bring it down in a flat area, but the plane sheared the giant spruce tree at midheight. You could hear the engines trying to rev up; several times, they tried to restart. The engines just whined, and the plane lost so much altitude they could not fly over the mountains."

Mr. Stranz walked me to where the spruce tree had once stood, west of the bomb crater.

I always wondered how long after the crash it was before the locals knew the identification of Stan and John Boros, the missing crewmen. Mr. Stranz indicated that he had learned that information about forty years after the crash, probably from some of our government's official reports.

Reporter Wilhelm was curious to know about our connection to Mr. Stranz, and I began to realize that two sides of a story were merging. I attempted to explain to Mr. Wilhelm parts of our version, starting with the Dave Hughes, Martin, and Udo and Inge connection that led to Mr. Stranz's involvement. Mr. Wilhelm then translated to Mr. Stranz. And I passed out photos of Stanley and his crew.

"I didn't think we would ever meet in person," Mr. Stranz said to me. "I hope your family finds something, but if not, that you will get satisfaction from being here."

The daily adventures had begun. Standing and leaning into the uphill slope, like walking into a strong wind, we observed the excavation. The pit crew broke up the earth with their shovels and scooped it into buckets. The heavy black buckets, filled with dirt, were handed off down a human line to the screeners. Every day we watched the process. From the first day of excavating, screenings were productive. The team recovered scraps of metal from machine guns, ammo clips, bomb pieces, bullets, Plexiglas, and many two-by-two-inch metal armor plates from flak jackets. One big find was an eyelet and a piece of leather, possibly from a boot.

Dr. Silverstein alerted the screeners, "Be on the lookout for possible bone fragments and teeth since life-support material, the flak plates, and also a possible boot piece, have been uncovered in this area." Dr. Silverstein packaged and labeled some items in ziplock baggies, noting their location in the grid system. When the team returned to Hawaii, he would personally transport them to the Central Identification Lab.

At the end of a day's work, everyone returned to the hotel—our home away from home. The lobby setup was ideal for hanging out. Entering the lobby through the main doors, the front desk was located off to the left, next to a small seating area situated front and center. The bar was arranged at the back of the quaint lobby, complete with counter stools and more tables and chairs off to one side—next to the door leading to the restaurant. Diners looked through restaurant windows to the outdoor patio area. The elevator opened directly into the lobby where, after showering and cleaning up, some team members would congregate. Almost every night, impromptu groups formed to go out to eat while others relaxed and socialized.

Hotel Corvinus bordered a park and was situated on the edge of Wiener Neustadt's approximately eight-square-block main square, replete with

343

The photo shows the crash site near Vostenhof, Austria, in May 1944. The sheared tree appears on the left side of the photo. Augustin Stranz provided this photo in 2001. It was probably taken by Kurt Exner.

boutiques, cafés, bars, and a variety of shops. Down the one-way street in front of the hotel, past the church where the bells chimed every quarter hour and at the far end of the main square, was the rebuilt military academy. The academy, once commanded by Erwin Rommel, was destroyed during the war.

One evening, Jennifer Sweet and Frederick joined us for dinner. A short walk from the hotel and right in the middle of the main square on the central *platz* was Café Siegl, a favorite. They served good food and had English menus, which eliminated the usual guesswork. We also liked the outdoor seating— tables with umbrellas—where we watched the world go by. Farmers' market vendors displayed their wares, including bright yellow sunflowers beneath protective green and yellow awnings. People pedaled bikes—young boys with backpacks, mothers with infant seats, men in suits holding briefcases, elderly ladies in dresses, and young ladies with "doggie" baskets. Nobody wore helmets. Occasionally, a car drove through the *platz*, which seemed like driving on the sidewalk. We noticed that Austrians conversed for two to three hours while dining, so we followed their example and suppressed the urge to hurry and get on to the next thing on the list.

Frederick, an American, lived in Germany. As I remember the story, word came one day from Vienna that JPAC needed a linguist. I presumed he worked in a cubical at Ramstein Air Base recording history. Frederick signed on, thinking he'd be working out of Vienna. He was a linguist, all right, but he also sweat a lot digging dirt. Not ideal working conditions by his standards, but he helped us tremendously and was a good sport when some of the team ribbed him.

"It's nice to have family here at the site, and you are not an imposition," Jennifer said. "It personalizes the people we are looking for. It puts a face with the name."

In fact, the Vostenhof field recovery claimed a couple "firsts"—the first JPAC excavation in Austria and the first time ever for a family to be on site during an excavation.

Meanwhile, many evenings my son, Nate, went out to eat and to the bars with recovery specialists Kili Bald Eagle, Tuni Amani, and Tony San Luis. Nineteen-year-old Nate adopted the motto, "When you're in Rome, do as the Romans do" under the watchful eye and usually the accompaniment of his older sister. Melissa told me, "The team is looking out for us."

Evening PT, pub training, meant something different from morning PT, physical training. One was optional, one mandatory. Melissa and Nate couldn't seem to roll out of bed early enough to accept the team's standing invitation to morning PT. However, after one evening of PT, Nate said, "I met a man from the Austrian army. He was thankful that Stanley and other Americans sacrificed so his country could be free."

But despite these recreational interludes, the real work continued. Sometimes Dad and I walked the shortcut to the crash site, along the edge of Mr. Auer's flat, sloped field. At the top of the ridge, we surveyed our route downhill. Approximately fifty yards below, the excavation was barely visible in the trees. We zigzagged down the steep slope as if we were skiing down a mountain and leaned against sticky pine tree trunks to keep from sliding down the hill. We huffed and puffed, trudging up the slope, but going down was easier, as long as we didn't slip on the loose ground cover and roll to the bottom of the hill or hit a tree or boulder first. Aircraft debris littered the hillside. As we got closer to the excavation, we could see team members working side by side—digging and filling buckets and moving buckets and screening dirt. They repeated the process again and again, all day long—digging, filling buckets, moving buckets, and screening dirt.

One day I arrived where the team worked before Dad did.

Dr. Silverstein handed me something and said, "Look what we found."

I rubbed a United States of America silver dime between my thumb and pointer finger. Then I flipped it over and turned it back to the front. On the front was a lady's head. She wore a leafy wreath "crown"—different from most dimes in circulation. The date was a little faded but readable. The mint date was 1916. By then, Dad stood next to me.

I handed Dad the coin.

Then it dawned on me, and I said, "Nineteen sixteen—that's the year Stanley was born."

Dr. Silverstein glanced up from his work; his questioning eyes peered from under the brim on his Indiana Jones-style hat. The leather chin strap dangled. I can still see his solemn facial expression.

Dad examined the dime, put two and two together, and added, "My dad was a coin collector. Hmmm." Dad thought for a few seconds and then said what everyone was thinking, "There's a good chance Stan carried this coin as his good luck piece."

Even though Mom and Dad questioned me about Stanley's birth year, I was certain. His birth date was one day after my October 25 birthday. Stanley was born October twenty-*six*th, nineteen *six*teen. Stanley was the only one of his crew born in 1916. Missing crewman John Boros was five years older.

Making our idea even more credible, someone from the team explained, "Studies show that most coins found at World War II crash sites are usually minted in the 1930s."

1916 dime excavated at the crash site.
JPAC photo—Derrick Goode, photographer.

What a morale booster. Right off the bat, there was a lot of hope. I was ready to start digging right then and there.

But, orders for family from someone higher in the chain were no digging or screening due to liability. In Southeast Asia, hundreds of locals are hired to screen, but not in Europe.

So I made my way uphill to Doc's "station," his desk. One screen had been tied between two pine trees spaced about three feet apart. Whatever materials the screeners collected, the anthropologist examined everything, bit by bit. Being a pilot, I never really did any mechanical work on the B-17. But it was surprising how much debris Dr. Silverstein and I could identify. We figured out where pieces came from or what part of the airplane the pieces were on. Jagged scraps of metal, bomb frag, metal flak plates, and bits of Plexiglas were showing up in the screens.

Before departing Nebraska for Austria, Melissa and Nate had agreed to spend the first few days at the crash site before they started touring Europe. However, the excavation was magnetic, and opposite their intentions, they spent many days at the Vostenhof crash site.

And when Melissa and Nate went with us to Vostenhof, they, of course, took turns driving. Mom said, "Nate, you'll have culture shock when you get back to Nebraska. The legal speed limit there is slower than driving on the Autobahn, and you have to stay out of bars until you're twenty-one."

Once we worked out the kinks, the Autobahn was the fastest and most direct route from Wiener Neustadt to Vostenhof. One time, we overshot, missed our exit, and ended up in Gloggnitz via beautiful countryside with a vista of distant mountains and a glimpse of grand castles shadowed by trees and veiled by a haze.

Aircraft wreckage unearthed at the crash site near Vostenhof, Austria.
Photo taken by Christian Feigl.

Driving through Wimpassing on another day, Melissa commented, "We've been this way before." Driving in circles, we'd been that way at least four times. But through trial and error, we stumbled on a shortcut through town to the crash site; then we drove past the pretty-as-a-postcard roundabout, impeccably manicured with flowers blooming in masses of red and white and accented with clumps of yellow blossoms.

At the site, there was no loafing. The team always worked hard—no doubt about that—and the leaders led by example. Now I've dug a few ditches in my life, and standing around without a shovel in my hand while everyone else worked didn't seem right. For Nate, who grew up on a farm, it was second nature for him to grab an idle shovel and get to work. So Nate and I scavenged along the ridge, the area away from JPAC's flagged debris fields, and found scraps of aircraft wreckage. Dr. Silverstein needed to keep track of the size of the debris field and be alerted about any life-support materials we located. I found a piece of rubber off the tire from a landing gear, the tread still visible, and all over there were chunks of black rubber from the bladder lining the inside of the wing fuel tanks, some larger pieces half buried in the ground. The area was good mushroom country, so any obvious wreckage would have been spotted by hunters and "mushroomers."

While walking down the trail, quite a distance from the excavation, Nate happened to spot a piece of the fuel gasket with part of the hose still attached. And away from the bomb crater about 150 meters, next to the stream, was a tree that had fallen down. It was a great big tree and had been there a long time. The blast could have blown it down in the direction it laid. Underneath the huge trunk, I found a bent, ragged piece of the exhaust system. Later on, somebody came through the site and told us that this was where an engine had been found, near the stream.

One morning, Udo and Inge Doerr had telephoned us saying they planned to go to the crash site that day. In an e-mail exchange before leaving Nebraska, we planned to meet with them in person in Austria. While waiting for them to show up, we watched the team dig and screen—and dig and dig and dig—around the bottom of tree trunks. Every ounce of dirt was picked off the exposed roots. Still attached by the tap root, some trees wobbled and leaned. Often, the spindly ones fell over, but every effort was made to preserve the area's trees.

The pit crew removed eight to ten inches of dirt in most grids, the depth determined when Gunny, the EOD tech, scanned the area with the metal detector. No hits with the detector meant virgin soil—deep enough. Because the area was environmentally protected, machines were prohibited, so the team employed old-fashioned, physical back labor. We felt helpless while we sat and watched.

Dad walked off in the woods by himself. I could see him. He wore his JPAC ball cap, leaned against a tree, and scanned the treetops.

I figured Stan, or whoever might have been flying the plane, needed about two hundred feet of altitude to make the open area, Mr. Auer's meadow, at the top of the ridge. The plane hit the spruce tree and went down. It was close. The plane could have fallen apart, or with only two engines and trying to make a turn or gain some altitude, the plane could have stalled. Some questions were answered, but then we had more. It would have been like threading a needle to have had enough room on that field to get the plane stopped.

The urge to turn back the clock and change things overcame me again. However, history had been written.

The Doerrs did not show up at the site, so we phoned them from the hotel at the end of the work day. They had been to Vostenhof but took a different trail and couldn't find the right area, so we made arrangements to meet in the hotel lobby that evening.

Pleased to finally meet them, we expressed our gratitude for their interest and research that helped our search progress. Their English was good—much better than our German.

They were the link in putting everything together to get to Austria.

Harold E. Dwyer, Udo Doerr, Inge Doerr, Darlene Dwyer.
Photo taken in Wiener Neustadt, Austria, in 2006.

"I am originally from Germany, and Inge was born in western Austria," Udo explained. "We were married in 1959 and moved to Wiener Neustadt in 1960 where I was in the textile business running a factory that made bras. We will be celebrating our fiftieth wedding anniversary in 2009. You are invited to our celebration."

The couple had no children of their own but were godparents to Martin and his sister—Martin, the connection to Dave Hughes.

"Nebraska was admitted to the union as the thirty-seventh state in 1867," Udo stated. He recited other information and challenged my retention of fourth-grade Nebraska history. Udo knew my hometown's population was approximately 2,500, and when we mentioned Omaha, he smiled and said, "Warren Buffet."

From earlier correspondence, Inge had written about losing her younger brother when he was six-and-a-half years old. A bomb from a B-17 dropped on her family home. It devastated the family, especially her mother. The ravages of war distinguished between no one.

Inge's eyes brimmed with tears as she gazed into my eyes and said, "When Martin asked us to help research the May 10, 1944, crash, I did so because of my Christian heart. I knew I could be forgiving and help with Martin's request."

Inge asked Dad about Granddad and Grandma Dwyer. She said to Dad, "This is good for you."

I believed it was a healing process for her also. She had some bridges to cross; I think in the long run, meeting us and being part of the process helped her too. Udo showed me on a map his understanding of how Stan's plane circled over Vostenhof. He asked me about my impressions at the crash site. I told him I was humbled.

Udo and Inge are why the people of Austria have the reputation of being so hospitable and friendly. After our forty-five-minute conversation, it seemed like we were old friends.

Occasionally, the team had a day off from excavating, often due to rainy weather. On those days, Nate and Mom played cards while Melissa and I window-shopped and browsed the boutiques. Dad watched John Wayne television movies in German. It turns out that Fred Flintstone and friends are bilingual. Moreover, those nonworking days were used for sightseeing—including Mr. Brettner's museum—and catching up on socializing, reading, sleeping, and e-mailing. To be up to speed when he arrived, Rick had requested that I e-mail him often with an update. It was a stretch to e-mail daily. Every other day or two was manageable.

Besides Rick, the e-mail list of recipients was growing and included Stanley's crewmen Eugene Parker and George Mitchell, other friends, and especially our oldest daughter, Sarah, home in Nebraska with her husband and their two young daughters. My three sisters, unable to make the trip due to scheduling conflicts, received the updates as well. They then forwarded them to their friends. Cousin Mary Ellen also followed the excavation's progress. She and her two daughters planned to travel to the crash site that September.

At first, Hotel Zentral, on the central *platz* near the vendors selling their colorful wares and the lively outdoor musical performances, offered the most reliable Internet—with a German version of our familiar keyboard. Eventually, I detected the strongest Internet signal on the patio at Hotel Corvinus, so I began e-mailing from our hotel even though they charged by the minute. Whether hanging out on the patio or in the lobby, team members relaxed. Recovery specialists Guillermo Richards, Robert Danford, and Dave Zeitz talked about their families. And Danny Frye showed us pictures of his infant son and wife back in Hawaii, where team members are stationed during their three-year JPAC tour.

"We try to limit team members to about four deployments a year, which gets into about 140 days deployed a year," Johnie Webb had once told me. "MOS—Military Occupational Specialists—like your medics, your explosive ordnance disposal technicians ... those guys deploy over two hundred days a year simply because of the demand for their skills."

Meanwhile, word got around about the Vostenhof excavation, so the team's skills were practically on display for local residents and any other interested persons. Relevant information came from different sources, often unexpectedly. A man named Wolfgang Losos came to have a look. "I was in the German army for many years," he said. "I joined the army two days after my seventeenth birthday. I started out as a pilot but had poor vision. I talked an officer into helping me memorize the eye chart. I flew for a while but then was grounded when they learned of my poor eyesight.

"My father was an ace pilot for the Luftwaffe, and my grandfather was a Nazi party leader in his town. When the trains stopped there on the way to the camps, my grandfather pulled off ten or twelve people to work in the fields. Eventually, those people would disappear, and then ten or twelve more would be pulled off another train. After the war, one person returned to the town and thanked Grandfather for taking him off the train and saving his life.

"Grandfather believed the extermination camps were work camps. They were tightly secured, and people did not know what was going on."

Wolfgang, who'd spent years hunting the countryside for missing German fighter pilots, showed Doc what he thought were seatbelt harnesses near the grids. Wolfgang returned on other days with his wife, who brought her homemade desserts for the team. Over the next few weeks, Wolfgang periodically checked in on developments at the crash site. And before we departed Austria, he shared information from a page of map defenses. Pointing to one location, he stated to Dad, "This is probably the antiaircraft battery that hit your brother's plane."

As a local attraction, another side benefit of a JPAC excavation in any country was generating new leads for future cases.

Historian Dr. Jakob Mayer drove approximately four hundred miles from his home in Innsbruck to meet people who professionally searched for missing service personnel.

In a conversation with Dr. Mayer, he asked me how American boys became pilots during World War II. I told him we volunteered. There was IQ testing, boot camp, military training, and hours of flight training.

He replied, "The Nazis, to inspire their German fighter pilots, used propaganda and told them that all rich guys were American pilots coming over here to drop bombs."

Dr. Mayer shared his extensive research on crashes, and JPAC, of course, was interested in any crashes associated with missing crewmen. Also, he was motivated to organize something similar to JPAC in Austria.

Without a doubt, JPAC's work fascinated almost everyone. We witnessed from front-row seats the extent to which the United States government goes to honor its promise to bring home the missing.

Johnie Webb once told me, "Americans value life and value people as individuals. We value the life of that person. There's a saying in the military— we take care of our own basically from cradle to grave.

"It's the American culture, but American families expect closure. When a loved one passes away, they expect to have closure—to lay that person to rest. For those families where an individual never came home, they didn't have closure. In our culture, if a person dies, we need to be able to have a proper burial, to be able to go out and visit that person on special occasions or honor that person on Memorial Day or Veterans Day—to honor them for the sacrifice they made to our country. The whole mind-set we have is totally different from most of the rest of the world.

"The Brits, for example, didn't bring their war dead back home. Countries that followed British rule—for example, the Australians—don't bring their dead back home either. They leave them where they died.

"We did a recovery of one of our aircraft in Papua New Guinea. An Australian flight officer flew on that aircraft, and we recovered him and identified him. The Australians wouldn't take him back. To this day, he's buried in Arlington National Cemetery. But, you're beginning to see that whole attitude change in a number of countries.

"In Vietnam, the Vietnamese really didn't care. Now, things are changing because of local conscience. When one of our teams goes to Vietnam, we hire anywhere from twenty-five to one hundred local villagers. They come out and work for us for thirty days and see the efforts we go to trying to recover just one guy. Those villagers go back to their province officials saying, 'Wait a minute, I just spent thirty days working with the Americans trying to recover one of their soldiers. You know, my father never came back home from the Vietnam War, so what are you doing to try to return him to my family?'

"Recently, South Korea spent ninety days working with JPAC, and the result was that they built a brand-new central identification laboratory in South Korea, a permanent command, to recover and identify soldiers from the Korean War."

Johnie Webb's prophetic statement made earlier about the excavation—
"You can't even imagine and will be absolutely amazed"—was simply an
understatement. Taking one day at a time was about all we could process.

Often when Dad, Mom, and I arrived at the site, we looked up the slope
from the muddy, narrow road to watch the excavation.

On the hillside, colored pin flags marking metal debris spanned out and
fingered downward from the bomb crater. Blue and orange flags poked up
everywhere and trailed down to where we stood.

And the bomb crater grid deepened, penetrating hard layers of earth.
Time and again, Gunny detected hits with the metal detector, so the pit crew,
taking turns, repeatedly raised the pick axe above their heads and slammed
it into the hard earth. Gunny swept the metal detector over the grid. More
beeping. Then Doc, steady, patient, and vigilant, sat on the ground in the pit,
carefully scraping away earth with small tools.

"It's a good thing we don't have all anthropologists digging," Major Legler,
on his twelfth and last excavation, said in jest. "We'd be here forever."

Each crash site presents unique challenges. Typically, the impact crater
harbors the cockpit area and—hopefully—remains.

*At Vostenhof, the impact crater was the bomb crater, and it was a hell of an
explosion. By the looks of the pieces of metal coming out of the grids and scattered
on the hillside, you could tell the ferocity of the explosion. The team dug a huge
hole in one area of the bomb-crater grid, about four feet deep and fifteen feet
across. Besides buckets of bomb fragments, they dug up some fabric, snaps, and
one huge chunk of armor plate about one-fourth-inch thick and roughly a foot
square. That piece of armor plate had been ripped apart to about two-thirds its
normal size. Armor plate, as I recalled, reinforced the back of the pilot and copilot
seats. One time, Wolfgang Losos visited the crash site carrying a diagram of the
armor plating on a B-17—the diagram the Germans had used to train their
fighter pilots. Everything added up. The team was finding stuff close to where
Stan would have been sitting.*

Completed grids were nothing more than barren, brown earth, some with
exposed bare tree roots, which twisted and gnarled like tentacles. Another
screening station had been built uphill, making a total of ten screens.

*The screening stations were like swing sets. They usually consisted of an
A-frame structure on one or both ends with the screening trays attached overhead
to the center bar, swinging back and forth. The slope at the crash site was
about forty-five degrees, even steeper closer to the upper ridge. With the second
screening station positioned uphill, the team hauled the buckets of soil from the*

grids up steps made from dirt-filled burlap sacks. I can't imagine excavating at a forty-five-degree angle. The dirt residue from the screens fell into a pile on a blue tarp, barricaded by a retaining wall made of filled burlap bags. At the right time, that dirt pile was pushed downhill and back into an excavated grid. The replaced soil covered any exposed tree roots, and the attempt was to return the hillside to as normal a state as possible. The team worked hard. It was all very labor intensive.

Yet as they worked, the screeners sometimes casually conversed and every now and then played invented word games. Occasionally, team members bantered back and forth, and one time, while passing off a heavy bucket of dug-up earth, I heard Brad joke with Frederick. "If you get a tattoo, I'll get one too."

On one particular day, I was observing Rodney Acasio, the team medic, scoop dirt. He told me about his three sons and that his qualifications exceeded those of a physician's assistant. Then Rodney paused and watched as an elderly man walked up the hill with some of his family. At times, it must have seemed like working in front of an audience. Rodney even once quipped, "You should have brought a guestbook for everyone to sign." But the popularity of this site had its advantages.

The excavated bomb crater.

Frederick approached the elderly man. Translated, Johann Piringer, a local farmer, described what he saw as an eyewitness on May 10, 1944. "I was thirteen years old. At my family farm nearby, I saw the plane fly past me, smoking, burning, headed to a clearing, an open area. I thought maybe the wind caught the wing or prevented it from staying 'on course.' Then the plane, flying at an angle, crashed.

"The crash was followed by an explosion. I ran from my farm and through the trees, and I was one of the first ones to arrive here at the crash. I saw an arm from a white man with a watch on the wrist and a decapitated head from a black man."

Singed body parts, no doubt. In 1944, the Tuskegee Airmen, flying P-51 fighters, were America's only black airmen.

"The area was still smoldering and smoking, and I was afraid to go closer," Johann continued. "I stayed at the bottom of the hill, scared. As people started to come, especially the MP, I ran away. Four more times that day, I returned to the site to show other people.

"There were lots of scattered airplane parts. Within two to three days, all the big parts were carried off by the Germans."

While we were listening to Johann, Udo and Inge arrived at the crash site. We greeted them. Johann continued to tell his story in German. And then there were at least two German conversations, English conversations, a translated German conversation, and an excavation in progress involving an eighteen-member JPAC team. My head practically swiveled. As I stood at the crash site, it reminded me of walking into a crowded room filled with commotion and not being sure where to focus. It was nearly impossible to absorb everything happening on the hillside—I didn't want to miss anything but tuned in to the English conversation.

Examining the collection of unearthed artifacts at Dr. Silverstein's station, Udo remarked, "War is a terrible thing. War is war. What we must learn, people come together, but governments cannot."

Commenting on their recent visit to Auschwitz, Udo told Dr. Silverstein, "Do not go—it is terrible. It is unbelievable that something like that happened in the middle of the twentieth century."

"It is unbelievable that we come together, that we meet," Inge said to us. "We have the same destination. There were many little steps to get here. It's God's gift." Inge left some homemade sweets as she and Udo departed.

Translated by Frederick, I asked Johann if he could show us where he stood on the hillside at his farm.

In response to Dad's request, Johann and his wife invited us to their farm. So some of us piled into two vehicles to drive there. Mom rode in the back seat wedged between Johann and his wife, Josefa. Josef, their son, drove, and I sat next to him in the front passenger seat. They spoke German; we spoke English. However, photos speak a universal language, and Josef's photo on the dashboard of his sons triggered our "conversation" of hand motions, smiles, and "yah, yah."

Johann Piringer, Harold E. Dwyer, Kay (Dwyer) Hughes.
Photo taken near Vostenhof, Austria, in 2006.

Approximately two kilometers from the crash site, the way the crow flies, we stood on a grassy slope near Johann's farm. Standing on the hill, we stared down on a neighbor's house. Derrick Goode, the team photographer, documented the scene while Frederick translated for Johann. "I was standing about here." Then Johann gestured in the opposite direction, past his farmhouse. "The pilot, I assumed," he continued, "figured he didn't have the altitude to clear that distant mountain."

"So then I saw your brother's plane curve around the area," Johann motioned and continued. "He flew eye level right in front of me, right there near the neighbor's house, curving to miss it."

Frederick translated Johann's low German dialect fluently. Johann offered the group something to drink. Derrick lowered his camera and, in English, politely declined. But before anything further was said, Frederick clued us in.

"This is a big deal for this family to have us to their home. This is a once-in-a-lifetime experience for them. Let's accept his invitation."

In German, Frederick accepted the invitation for the group.

Johann smiled and said, "Super."

Frederick was more than a translator. He helped us understand the culture—what was acceptable and what was not.

As we sat around the kitchen table—more like an L-shaped wooden booth—drinking juice, Frederick gave us a heads-up. He said, "The soup bowls at our places indicate that there's more than drinks, and the knife and fork at each place setting mean that we are in for a treat." We savored a delicious, authentic, five-course Austrian meal—ham, spicy sausage, dumplings, sauerkraut, salad, and warm homemade apple strudel.

Sitting next to me, Frederick leaned closer, lowered his voice, and said, "This kraut isn't from a can." As we feasted, we remembered the hard-at-work JPAC crew with only sack lunches provided by the hotel. But more than the food, it was the friendship of the family, their warmth, sincerity, and generosity along with Johann's willingness to share his story that defined the experience.

Josef's wife, Johanna, and three of their four sons, along with Josefa, served us and worked in the kitchen while we ate. After the meal, Johann moved from where he sat, walked around the table, and slid in the bench to sit next to Dad. His face beamed. His broad smile accentuated his rosy red cheeks.

"I am happy to have you in my home, to have Americans visit," Johann said. "The crash happened around noon time—like now—when we're eating."

We thanked our hosts. "*Danke schoen.*" Josefa genuinely wanted to communicate and continued to converse with me in German. Her eyes spoke for her, and I could only smile, nod my head, and repeat, "Yah, yah."

Johann walked us back to the crash site—down trails, through the woods, through the tangle of shrubs, across streams—similar to the way he ran to the crash site on May 10, 1944. In sixty-two years, the woods had grown denser with nature hiding the scars, but people still remembered that defining day.

Johann was probably the last one to see Stan's plane. We stood on the spot where he was standing when the airplane flew by. It flew by in about a four- or five-second span, from right to left, down through the valley and over a small hill. And from Johann's testimony, we knew that the airplane had circled to the left and was under control until the last moments of flight. My theory about the open field was feasible.

Whenever we drove back and forth between Vostenhof and Wiener Neustadt, I observed the terrain. Near Vostenhof the countryside was hilly and more wooded. Closer to Wiener Neustadt the lay of the land was flatter, with large, treeless areas of farm ground. I can only speculate what Stan's situation was in the last minutes of flight. If he was alive, his hands were full in the cockpit. They were out of formation; German fighters were attacking; oxygen was cut off; there were injured crew members; two engines were on fire; they were losing altitude, and things happened quickly up there. If he'd been a little higher, a forty- or fifty-degree turn might have put them over that flatter terrain for a belly landing. But German fighters were all around, and there were more prominent things on his mind than where the heck he was going to put the airplane down if he had to. We'll never know. We had a few more pieces to add to the puzzle.

Eyewitness testimony continued to reveal the 1940s' wartime scenario. And many of the local people often arrived at the crash site early in the morning before we showed up. So Dad rallied Mom, Melissa, Nate, and me to get there first thing, too, in order to meet these early birds and any eyewitnesses who stopped through.

Often the scenario at the crash site included a group gathered around Dr. Silverstein's desk to watch him inspect the team's findings. The soil at the crash site yielded more clues to the mystery. Markus Reisner, an officer in the Austrian armed forces who had written the book, returned to the site, bringing another historian named Rudolf Beisteiner.

Standing at Dr. Silverstein's desk with Markus, I examined one little piece that I recognized as part of the grid work on an E6B computer. That piece would have been lying on the navigator's desk, down below and forward of the pilot's seat. More life-support evidence had turned up; there were many flak armor plates from our flak jackets, a buckle, fabric, an earphone piece, as well as other material evidence and personal effects, such as buttons, snaps, eyelets, leather fragments, and a possible watchband piece. Dr. Silverstein and I examined what we thought was a piece of a throat "mike."

Markus commented about the dime that had been unearthed earlier in the excavation. "It's like a sign."

And then he continued, "In the spring of 1944, on May 10, it was one of the biggest operations of the United States Army Air Forces in the European theater. There was fierce resistance from the German air force and German antiaircraft, so about thirty bombers and four fighter planes were shot down that day. About 120 Americans died, and another 170 became POWs. Four planes were shot down in the area south of Wiener Neustadt, and one of the planes was the plane of Stan."

Markus had personally met and interviewed one of those POWs, Colonel Jacob E. Smart, vintage B-17 pilot and past commanding officer of the 97th Bomb Group. Colonel Smart, making his twenty-ninth and supposedly last mission on May 10, 1944—the same mission Stanley had flown in—was in command of the lead group in the formation.

Markus recounted the story that Smart had related to him.

As we were in the last one or two minutes of the approach to the target Wiener Neustadt, we encountered the first salvos of exploding flak. The first bursts were in front and a little left of us but at exactly our altitude, which was unusual for the very first rounds. The dark gray-black explosive clouds told us that we must be getting hit by large caliber flak. Major Hill [copilot] threw me one of those, "Oh, Boy!" looks, but said nothing.

I had one of our oldest model parachutes, one that went on the chest. Although it would be difficult to steer the plane, I reached under my seat, got it and put it on. I could hear little pieces of flak hitting the plane, but that was nothing unusual, just the notification that we were being shot at.

The bombardier said, "One minute to bombs away."

I heard over the intercom one of my crew members moan and then yell, "Christ."

I concentrated on the instruments and the bombardier reports, "Thirty seconds to bombs away." Suddenly, the world around me exploded. We had been hit. There was a big explosion, a glaring fireball, and I was covered in flames. It seemed like a gigantic fist had come up and hit us with centrifugal force. I felt the blast of wind and realized I had been thrown outside the plane. Suddenly I felt deep pains in my legs and back, and it grew dark about me. Flak was exploding again, and I realized with terrible fear that I had been hit with the shrapnel. Blood from the wounds in my head flowed into my eyes, and I could see only through a red veil, but it seemed to me that for a short time I could see, from outside, into the damaged plane, and I believed I could see one or two people actually in the cockpit. That all happened in a couple seconds, and the next thing that came to me was that I was whirling uncontrollably in the air and falling to earth. On my back, I reached to my chest to see if my parachute was still there. Relieved, such was the case. I tried to get rid of the flak vest which I still had on, but at the same time realized the whirling was making me lose consciousness. I grabbed the opening ring of the parachute and pulled. The chute opened with a jerk. I was whirling, turning; the parachute lines were turning like I was under a whirling umbrella, going in a circle. One look at the ground told me that I was at a height of about one thousand meters.[40]

Markus said, "Colonel Smart was one of three surviving crewmen from his plane."

My mind flip-flopped from the 1940s to 2006 and the excavation at hand. The excavation progressed, and time passed quickly. Team Sergeant Chris Bunnell's daily schedule hung on a pine tree. Every hour, the team rotated jobs—digging in the pit and shoveling dirt into buckets, or passing off buckets of dirt uphill in the bucket brigade, or screening tediously through dirt and debris.

Mom, always a trouper, sometimes observed the ongoing excavation. At other times, she stayed back at the parking area, reading or sitting with Melissa on the bench next to Mr. Auer's field and taking in the beautiful scenery. Mom, designated as our welcome party, communicated with Mr. Auer and others using hand signals along with German words and phrases she remembered hearing her mom and uncles use when she was growing up.

Then, at about noon, she switched roles—from "international relations" to delivery lady. With our lunch in a backpack and her walking stick in hand, Mom hiked to the crash site for a picnic lunch. Following Melissa and Nate's lead, some team members called her "Grandma," or "Grandma DD," and besides just my kids, a few called me "Mom."

The hotel prepared sack lunches for the team, but we shopped at the local grocery store, the *Billa*, a small market of about five aisles with well-stocked shelves displaying things we recognized, even Pringles. But sometimes we never knew exactly what we were getting. We preferred grainy mustard for our sandwiches; yet ketchup, mustards, and mayonnaise were sold in toothpastelike tubes and labeled, of course, in German. Even the tube coloring gave no hint to its contents. Our first mustard purchase was a guess. The second time, we got it right after a young man in the market with limited English helped us. Our attempt to be inconspicuous had failed, again. Because of our limited knowledge of German and lack of *Billa* checkout protocol, sooner or later, like the Pringles on the shelf, we were recognized. And when we ate our lunch at the crash site, weren't we surprised that the bottled water we'd bought was fizzy—carbonated?

Lunch break for the team meant eating, playing hacky sack, reading, visiting, smoking, or maybe sneaking in a nap on a hammock strung between trees. The recovery in Austria may have seemed like a vacation compared to rappelling cliffs and recovery work in other treacherous terrain and adverse climates. In the remote jungles of Southeast Asia, team members deploy with self-packed food and sleep in elevated quarters, away from poisonous, creepy-crawling critters. Underwater recoveries, excavations in the Himalayas, and sometimes a country's political environment present other unique challenges and risks for JPAC teams.

"There are risks in everything, but not especially here," Dr. Silverstein said. "Cluster bombs are all over Southeast Asia. In other areas of the world, we've dug up five-hundred-pound bombs and moved them, dealt with poisonous snakes, and taken helicopters into tight places, sometimes not even landing but getting as close as possible and then jumping from the helicopter with our gear."

Yet all risks cannot be calculated. JPAC has lost eight individuals while attempting to bring home the missing. One team leader was killed when his group was ambushed, and another time, seven Americans died in a helicopter crash. Their work is not done without cost.

Whatever the obstacles and challenges of a recovery, the teams focus on their missions. And one might wonder why the JPAC team members are willing to risk their lives to complete these missions. Perhaps it is partly because they themselves have seen war firsthand.

As current active duty military, almost everyone on the JPAC team has served in Afghanistan or Iraq or Bosnia—or two or all three—and some harbor personal, private stories which motivate them to bring closure to those who still nurse unhealed wounds of war.

"War is not something we like to remember, but sometimes we have no choice," Kili Bald Eagle commented. He offered one explanation for their willingness to serve. He simply stated, "We're mining for fellow countrymen."

Reminders of war are scattered across Austria—around the world, for that matter. Stanley's crash site was peaceful—birds chirped, squirrels chattered, and a couple of white butterflies noiselessly fluttered around that valley. Bombers no longer rumbled overhead, antiaircraft guns were silent, but internally and externally, visible and invisible scars of war still exist. In 1944, a sixty-five-thousand-pound, four-engine bomber exploded at that spot; trace remnants remained. JPAC was moving half a hillside in search of bone fragments and/or teeth from two missing soldiers. Yet Stanley Dwyer and John Boros were only two of seventy-eight thousand American World War II MIAs. Thinking about the sacrifices that so many have made and are still making, I wonder why so many of us live our lives often sweating the small stuff.

Why do we invest time fretting and stewing about seemingly insignificant things—a football score, p.s. (petty "stuff"), burnt toast, and the weather? Cold Nebraska winters are nothing compared to the eight-hour missions in subzero temperatures that aircrews endured. Stanley described some mission details in one letter, "You as tail gunner would have cold perspiration on your brow in thirty-below air. You as a pilot would forget the danger of the tons of high octane gasoline in your wings or the explosive charge in your cargo.

Instead, when the gunner reported rocket or twenty-millimeter cannon fire, you would pray that no missile find a human target."

When considering the whole scheme of life, some of our worries and complaints aren't worth the effort. Acknowledging what's important in life, I count my blessings. I'm humbled thinking about the soldiers who have sacrificed for our freedom. Some sacrificed everything.

14

ᴄᴍᴄ

You Are Not Forgotten

One becomes attached to his crew, and his greatest desire, next to the
accomplishment of his purpose, is to return his boys to ten worrying mothers ...
—Stanley N. Dwyer in a letter dated April 22, 1944

Days slipped by. Without a calendar to dictate the schedule, we lost track of
time. The team was focused and worked diligently—sweating, digging, and
sifting through soil, grid after grid. The seemingly daily stream of onlookers
and eyewitnesses tapered over time. Still, we never knew what to expect.

One day, a man stopped to observe and told about serving with a German
SS panzer tank unit on D-Day—the second wave. Dr. Silverstein made the
point, "D-Day from the other side."

And Augustin Stranz, professionally a tailor, unofficially the town historian,
had recorded parts of Austria's history, "from the other side," for his area in two
published volumes. He kept his research at his tailor shop, the shop we drove past
every day on the way to the crash site, near the intersection with the statues.

I said, "*Gruss Gott, Herr Stranz*." Frederick had explained to me the
proper greeting. As Mr. Stranz turned the pages in his notebooks, translated,
he said, "Over the years, I heard the stories. After a while, I started recording
information, and I interviewed eyewitnesses to the Vostenhof crash. Many
explained the way Stanley's plane, under 'control,' curved over the area."

Mr. Stranz walked with us past the two statues on the corner near his
home and down the intersecting street to the Pottschach cemetery. He pointed
to a white cross atop a granite base. Several names were inscribed on the
black headstone, including misspelled Francis Gilhooley, Prescott Piper, and
William Olfenius, other deceased crewmen on Stanley's plane.

I remember a story about one name on the grave marker, the name of a
fifteen-year-old boy also buried in the common grave. It seems the boy was

conscripted into the German army and sent to the front. He couldn't take it and deserted to go back home. As the story went, the Germans captured him and executed him for deserting.

The three deceased crewmen's IDPFs I had requested from the archives, which took several months to reach me, included pages of information not found in Stanley's IDPF. It seemed AGRS garnered even more details from their field investigations in Austria in 1948.

In 1948, Franz Pogacnik, the undertaker, was interviewed by AGRS. He stated:

> With a horse cart and three caskets, I drove to Buerg, and in the company of Gendarmerie-Wachtmeister Exner, I picked up the remains of one dead flyer at Thann. Exner took the identification papers, and we placed the body in one of the caskets. Then we drove farther over to Vostenhof to the place of the crash at Buerg where we did the same with the other flyers. One of the deceased, who seemed to have bailed out, lay on top of the hill, above the Saubachgraben [the small stream valley] ... The second flyer lay at the bottom of the Saubach and was not visibly injured. Exner, who had the identification papers of the flyers, wrote the names and numbers on each casket. The deceased were placed in the marked caskets and the caskets closed. The caskets were buried at the cemetery of Pottschach, and wooden crosses with the names were placed above each.
>
> I certify with my best knowledge that the names of the pilots have been placed to the right casket, and therefore no mistake about the identification was possible.

"Sergeant William Olfenius, the tail gunner, bailed out on fire before the crash," Mr. Stranz noted. "His parachute was on fire too. He hit the ground in the meadow near Thann."

A statement from Karl Essl, the cemetery attendant, related:

> On 11 May 1944 I received orders ... to dig a grave for three American flyers ... the grave to be so that the three caskets could be placed side by side ... All three caskets had the names and numbers written on. The caskets were buried and registered in the cemetery records. Then the grave was closed ... three wooden crosses with the names and identification numbers were made. In the presence of the administrator, the crosses were placed above the caskets so there could not be any mistakes about who the remains were. After placing

365

the crosses, I received orders from the administrator to take care of the grave, which order I carried out.

Josef Wagner's testimony added:

> Four dud bombs lay underneath the plane wreckage. At the place of the crash, I saw the body of one flyer without his head; one hand was also missing, probably because of the explosion. This flyer laid about one hundred meters from the place. Close to him laid another flyer that had a parachute in his hands, and his body seemed not to be destroyed. A Dr. Goldinger from Pottschach came to the place but only found that the flyer was dead.
>
> After a few months, the parts of the plane and the disarmed bombs were removed by the German military ... I can certify to my best knowledge that, except the two dead flyers, there were no other flyers near the scene of the crash or underneath the plane or in the vicinity. I was two to three weeks together with other guards on duty at the place, and we searched the surroundings thoroughly by orders, but no other person could be found. I am a hunter and tenant of this district, but also later when I went hunting there, I could not discover another person.
>
> To my opinion, it is impossible that there could have been more than the two bodies that had been found. I also know that nobody was in the plane wreckage when it was removed by the German military.

And like a sock that keeps bunching up in your shoe, we couldn't ignore another unanswerable question—were buried crewmen body parts commingled?

Mr. Pogacnik, Mr. Essl, Mr. Wagner, and Mr. Exner were no longer living. However, Kurt Exner, son of the mentioned Mr. Exner, visited the crash site during the excavation. Unfortunately, we missed meeting him; however, Dr. Silverstein recorded their conversation, "As a thirteen-year-old boy in 1944, he saw one of two bodies on the site. One tire was found in the stream by some boys who took it for a reward. Many records were destroyed so the Russians wouldn't capture them. He'd also found photos of the incident in the estate of his deceased parents."

Udo had mentioned the miserable times in parts of Austria during the Russian occupation after the war. "During those ten years," he said, "there was little economic development. Austria is at least ten years behind."

"The Russians in the area wanted watches ... then women," Mr. Stranz explained. "The children and old people were left alone; the people in between had to be careful. Women went to hide. The SS came to farmers' homes at night and took food. The next morning, the Soviets came to the farmers' homes to steal, and everything was gone. The farmers explained that they had given to the Germans, or the Russians would have shot them."

Eventually, when AGRS accounted for servicemen in 1948, Prescott Piper and William Olfenius were disinterred from the Pottschach cemetery for final interment at Neuville-en-Condroz United States Military Cemetery in Belgium. Francis Gilhooley's family had requested that their son's remains be returned to the United States. Navigator Gilhooley is buried in New York, easing his mother's fear about not knowing where her son was buried.

"During the exhuming process of the three Americans," Mr. Stranz said, "the cemetery Pottschach was blocked for the local people by the Russian military."

The disinterment process by AGRS personnel involved an identification checklist, including physical characteristics, personal effects found with the remains, and dental records and tooth chart comparisons, if available. In the case of Prescott Piper, his IDPF stated, "Although available dental information for T/Sgt. Piper is inadequate for a positive tooth chart comparison, there is definite negative comparison with dental records of the two unaccounted-for crew members, T/Sgt. Boros and 2/Lt. Dwyer. Heights of these two men are also in disagreement with estimated height of remains tentatively identified as Piper." Therefore, favorable comparisons with "no contradictory evidence" for the three crewmen were ascertained. Corresponding dog tags were never recovered.

Mr. Stranz and Felix Rameder, two of several local historians, exchanged information; the latter had mailed Eugene Parker a piece of the crashed plane. In my attempt to contact Mr. Rameder, his daughter Beatrix had responded. And when we were in Austria, she invited us to her home in Breitenbrunn, fifty kilometers east of Wiener Neustadt near Lake Neusiedl.

"It is a landmark the airmen knew very well," she said. The lake is located near the initial point for bombing missions to Wiener Neustadt. Our map referenced the lake as Neusiedlersee, on the eastern border of Austria, near Rust.

Mom, Dad, Melissa, Nate, and I had already taken a short, adventurous sightseeing trip to Rust, noted for nearby vineyards and a stork population that perched on their scraggly nests that hung over chimney tops. We drove to Breitenbrunn the same way we had driven to Rust—off the beaten path with Major Legler's lifesaving, detailed atlas and plenty of backseat drivers. We were lost—well, we knew where we were, just not how to get where we were going—but we admired the charm of rural Austria.

As we sipped wine on the patio with Beatrix and her husband, Michael, Beatrix said, "My father received your letters at a difficult time. In his last months, he was not interested in his air war research anymore. My mother and I do not have the knowledge my father had, so we cannot give you any firsthand information.

"As a young boy during the air war, the bombers flying overhead with their vapor trails were an amazing sight to my father. He wanted to meet the people who flew them. His research took him to the villages where the crash sites were, and he located overgrown antiaircraft gun positions in the woods or cornfields. I went with him as interpreter to a bomb group reunion in Chicago where he was a guest speaker. My father would have been very happy about the excavation."

And the excavation progressed in grids above the bomb crater. Dr. Silverstein theorized that the thrust of the crash and the bomb blast threw debris in that direction too. In grids upslope, a possible parachute clip, eyelets, pieces of leather, and other evidence were exposed.

Moreover, not only did we lose track of time, we were out of touch with world news. But, we decided we hadn't missed much—except for one thing that Frederick brought to our attention a few days before Melissa and Nate flew home. The liquid bomb scare at Heathrow caused turmoil in airline travel as well as the imposition of more travel restrictions. Bantering as they worked, somebody on the team envisioned a new airline called "Air Natural," where all passengers would fly naked, which of course, triggered lively and colorful commentary and revived an earlier discussion about other imaginative business proposals.

But before Melissa and Nate departed, the team planned a going-away dinner at the Greek restaurant. In Wiener Neustadt, there are a variety of ethnic restaurants. Someone on the team said, "When eighteen of us land in a town and everyone goes their own way, we find out where most everything is located." Everything but laundromats. Laundromats were a figment of the imagination, but Mom came prepared with laundry detergent. The sinks in our hotel rooms substituted for washing machines until we discovered a reasonably priced "send out" laundry service. So the discovered Greek restaurant—that's not its official name, but it was how our group identified it—was a favorite.

The atmosphere, the authentic food—especially the lamb—the licorice-flavored Ouzo, and sitting around long, L-shaped, arranged tables in a party room talking and laughing with the team depicted the evening.

Team Sergeant Bunnell presented Melissa and Nate with SpongeBob SquarePants backpacks. He said, "We feel like we're part of your family. It's an honor to have the family here."

"It's my turn to do some 'corrupting,'" Dr. Silverstein said to the kids, "so I'm giving you these chocolate eggs with a toy inside. They're illegal in the United States, of course, because kids would choke on the small toy."

"It's an honor for us to be here," Melissa said.

"Thank you for your work," Nate added.

Then Dad pushed his chair back and stood in front of the arched wall next to an art niche and displayed statue, a row of pilsner glasses filled with tea-colored beer lined the center of the table. All eyes watched him, and everyone listened. He stood next to Mom, seated in her chair, and recited a poem called "I Live in These United States," written by his father in 1961. I didn't know Dad had committed Granddad's poem to memory.

> Outside tonight, it's ten below,
> And hand-in-hand with that is snow;
> A swirling, sifting, drifting flour
> Is piling deeper by the hour.
> But here within, the Andiron Twins
> Have kept a fire to toast my shins;
> It both reflects, and radiates,
> The life in these United States.
>
> With unlocked door and undrawn blind,
> I think my thoughts, and speak my mind.
> My neighbor there across the way,
> May also think and have his say.
> Each night, I lay me down to sleep
> Without a fear. And then down deep
> Within my soul I thank the Fates
> I live in these United States.
>
> In this free land we have no dread
> Of knock at night, or heavy tread.
> I know I'll not be led away
> And disappear, for what I say.
> I know I'll not be made a slave,
> And at the last, dig my own grave.
> To me, no man on earth dictates—
> I live in these United States!
>
> I need no dole—I ask no bread;
> I'll take my liberty instead.
> With it, I'll go where choice shall lead,
> And get the bread—and every need.
> I'll earn these things for me and mine

The while I'm serving thee and thine.
It works that way where each man rates—
I live in these United States!

I'll always thank my lucky stars
For this fair land of food, and cars,
And lights, and rights that ease the load
As we folks journey down the road.
And I thank my God for eyes to view
That Grand Old Red and White and Blue
That waves on high, and guards the gates!
I live in these United States!

"I'm proud of all you guys," Dad concluded. "I loved the army life. Whether you do or not, I don't know, but that's the way it affected me."

Melissa and Nate, not ready to leave Austria, flew west to Nebraska while Rick was en route to Austria. Meanwhile, Markus Reisner, on vacation, picked Dad, Mom, and me up at the crash site for a tour of Wiener Neustadt, but not before more personal effects—another "Burst-of-Glory" button from a uniform—showed up in a screen. More onlookers stopped and watched the detailed work of the Americans as the team continued to excavate for their missing comrades. One man, Mr. Eisbacher, was six years old in 1944. Translated, he said, "My ninety-year-old mother has forgotten a lot but remembers going to the funeral of deceased crewmen at Pottschach. She remembers seeing two open caskets, and the local pastor did the ceremony."

So, the four of us rode in Markus's four-wheel drive vehicle up the muddy, narrow road coming out of the wooded valley by Vostenhof's landmark castle.

Markus backtracked to Wiener Neustadt, driving past cornfields and a lone countryside church—almost an island in the middle of a sea of green corn plants with tan tassels—its tall spire pointing toward the heavens. The sunflower fields—big, yellow heads turned toward the sun—reminded me of Kansas. Traffic slowed, and local villagers, cycling or walking to do their shopping, crowded out the black-and-white picture in my mind of long-ago food lines. Dad's fantasy was seeing Stanley come walking out of the mist; my fantasy was seeing an elderly man, his stature similar to that of Granddad's and Dad's, walking down the sidewalk in a nearby village.

"Wiener Neustadt was the seventh-most bombed city in World War II," Markus told us. "Back then, the town's population was approximately fifty thousand. Today, it is about forty thousand. Prior to the war, the town consisted of maybe four thousand homes and buildings. Around fourteen buildings stood at war's end. Many of the city's inhabitants, a population reduced to mostly women, children, and the elderly, were forced out of the city into the countryside, possibly finding temporary housing with some relatives. After the war, people returned and built the town again."

One target on May 10, 1944, was the factory that produced one-third of Hitler's Messerschmitt 109s, a German fighter. Markus pointed to where the factory once stood.

"After the tenth of May," Markus replied, "it was said that one of the two factories was completely destroyed. With repeated bombings, by the end of May 1944, both factories were completely destroyed. It was clear that those two factories had to be destroyed for you to win the war."

Markus trained with the Austrian special operation forces, whose barracks are located on the former Luftwaffe air base by Wiener Neustadt. Some glider aircraft and all-terrain vehicles used parts of the base, but much of it was abandoned. The original entrance, runways, and other buildings remained. We looked down a round opening to an underground cement bunker—the bunkers used during an air raid by the Germans. The prisoners doing forced labor took cover in a shallow, grassy trench about a foot deep.

A bomb crater from American-dropped bombs, overgrown with weeds, left a shallow hole near what remained of the foundation of an antiaircraft position— the war from the ground perspective.

"On May 10, twenty antiaircraft batteries surrounded Wiener Neustadt," Markus continued. "About ninety to one hundred antiaircraft guns were ready for action, many manned by fourteen- and fifteen-year-old boys, forced to serve with the home front antiaircraft units. For the bomber crews, in order to bomb the city, they had to fly through nearly one hundred explosions around you. In reports I've read, American crew members couldn't believe they flew through that hell."

One report in Stan's IDPF stated that the wind on May 10, 1944, blew out of the northwest at forty knots, or about fifty miles per hour. To reach their target, the formations were flying right into the wind, which slowed them down to about one hundred miles per hour. At that speed, the gunners on the ground had a whole lot of time to fire a whole lot of shells at the planes. They were easy targets for the guns on the ground.

"The entire formation flew over Neusiedlersee," Markus said. "After a final turn, it flew on a west-northwest heading in the direction of Wiener Neustadt. The accuracy of the flak fire was exact."

Some groups in the bomber formation "repositioned," and Stan's 463rd group had slipped in as part of the first wave. Naturally, after the bombers came off the bomb run, the German fighters were waiting.

"Some planes were first hit on the approach to Wiener Neustadt," Markus said. "After they dropped the bombs, they tried to follow the formation, but because of the loss of one or two engines, they became stragglers. The bombers were attacked repeatedly by fifty German fighters. Stan's group, the 463rd, was shot up really badly that day. Fighter escorts were not able to give them cover, and when Stan's plane fell back, they didn't have cover from the other planes of the formation. Stan's group lost seven planes, the most the group experienced for any one day in the entire war. Of the seventy crewmen on board those seven downed B-17s, twenty-one were killed, and forty-nine were taken prisoner."

I caught myself thinking, *if only.*

Markus thought he knew which German pilot hit Stan's plane. I'd like to meet the guy, but apparently he's passed on.

Markus explained, "I think in Stan's case, he tried to control the plane and was assisted by his technician, John Boros, but the plane was too close to the ground. From research, it is my understanding that they dropped part of their bomb load—six of the twelve bombs. It was very dangerous if there was a belly landing of the plane."

Like I've said before, a lot of it was luck, and a lot of it was timing.

Rick arrived in Wiener Neustadt the night of the team birthday party for Eric Ahlstrand, Brad Thompson, Tuni Amani, and Kili Bald Eagle, complete with cake, tall, pointed party hats, and a lively rendition of "Happy Birthday." When Rick went to the crash site for the first time, he got on board quickly. The team had excavated nine grids. We watched Jennifer, on her hands and knees, scratching dirt away from tree roots and picking off every morsel before she swept the loose dirt into a pile in the completed grid.

Moved again, the ten screens were lined up side by side on the sloped hillside. Our meager contribution consisted of leaning against a tree trunk, facing uphill, and watching everyone else work—until Rick grabbed an extra shovel, and Dad filled a gap in the bucket brigade line. Screeners, some wearing an earpiece attached to an iPod, dumped a bucket of dirt into the mesh tray. When they shook their screens, the rocks, dirt, and debris sliding back and forth sounded like fingernails scratching a screen door. Fine dirt filtered through the mesh. It reminded me of sifting flour. *Scratch, scratch, scratch*—more particles sprinkled to the ground.

Screeners, hunched over a screen, pawed through the collection of debris. With one glove off and one glove on, whatever their style, they sorted out obvious pieces and either tossed them away or dropped the evidence into a bucket for Dr. Silverstein's examination. With the bare hand, screeners scrutinized countless stones, twigs, and tree roots.

"There is a different feel between rock, bark, bone, and teeth," Jennifer said. "Sometimes teeth turn green."

If in doubt, a screener placed the artifact in the evidence bucket or asked the anthropologist for his analysis. When nothing of significance remained in the tray, the screener tipped it to the side and dumped the leftovers onto individual piles of debris. Ten piles of dirt resembling giant anthills collected for backfill.

Looking around, JPAC was faced with a monumental task. I wished my dad could have joined us, but maybe he was taking it all in. The thought crossed my mind that they may not find any remains, but they were giving it a try. Some of the grids weren't producing much.

"Sometimes at excavations, we find nothing for two weeks," team members commented.

Doc was optimistic. "If there are remains, we're in the right spot to find some teeth," he said. "The difficult part of this mission is the secondary explosion. It didn't leave much evidence behind. The German army may have carried off remains when they removed wreckage, and animals could have gnawed on bones, scattering them. What is troublesome is that people have been picking through the wreckage for a long time. After two months, flesh is gone, and the rest could have been taken away. But, in many instances, we find something at the end."

Kili Bald Eagle and Dave Hansen showed us the telltale signs they watch for when digging in a grid. When dirt changed color or got darker, it was a sign that something had disturbed that area of earth.

"The bomb blast uprooted trees," Dr. Silverstein said. He theorized, "'Stuff' washed and filled in where the roots had once existed, creating a pocket and a good place to find remains or other personal effects."

Screeners are searching for the remains of missing servicemen
Stanley Dwyer and John Boros. Photo taken by Christian Feigl.

Trees were uprooted; lives were too. And survival was foremost, whether
the person was a crewman in the air or someone on the ground. The ravages of
war knew no borders and distinguished between no one. Inge understood.

"I was born in 1934, a premature baby weighing only two kilos," Inge said.
"I lived with my mother and father near Feldkirch, in the region of Vorarlberg
in western Austria, with my brother, Elmar. On October 1, 1943, my family
was traumatized when a bomb from an American B-17 hit our home and
killed my six-and-one-half-year-old brother. The house was destroyed, and
we had nothing."

For Inge's mother, misfortune had struck again. Already suffering from
the loss of a one-year-old and firstborn daughter and the death of yet another
infant son in 1933, she was devastated by another tragedy. It eventually
became too much for her to bear. She ended her life.

"It was difficult, but I managed to get over it and live my life," Inge
said.

Udo and Inge welcomed Mom, Dad, Rick, and me to their home, and
other evenings we dined together at restaurants, drinking wine and visiting
about their perspective of our story.

"Martin, my 'nephew,'" Inge said, "studied in America, in Ann Arbor,
Michigan, and there he had an American friend, Dave Hughes. In 1998,
Martin asked me to help him with a story that happened in the war ... an

airplane crash near Wiener Neustadt, maybe near Vostenhof. I did not know of Vostenhof. I was not born in this area.

"I made several phone calls. I called Vienna for information and Wiener Neustadt and then was told to call a woman who worked in the archives. I wanted to help. I checked everything. The woman who worked in the archives had changed her name and moved away from Wiener Neustadt. When I called, she happened to be home from her worldwide travels. She knew a little something and referred me to Mr. Stranz.

"Udo and I drove to meet Mr. Stranz. He showed us his records and the information where the plane crashed. One of the names listed was Stanley Dwyer."

"The beginning of the story is good, and the end will be good, whatever the conclusion may be," Udo said.

While standing at the crash site, I explained to Inge and Udo how, in my opinion, Stan needed about ten seconds to reach the open field, but the plane probably came apart on him.

"Your brother did the right thing for his character and his crew," Inge remarked. "The people who died in our house had the same bad luck as the people who were in the plane."

Dad said to Inge, "I grieve more for you than for me.

Under the circumstances, we were very sorry about Inge's brother. Soldiers in the line of fire realize what the consequences might be. The loss of a youngster is tragic. A six-and-a-half-year-old boy is a six-and-a-half-year-old boy. An army man is an army man, and he knows the dangers.

Inge hugged Dad and said, "No, no, no. After sixty years, I can forgive. You are a very sympathetic older man for my older person. It is unbelievable that we should meet. It is good for my soul and good for your soul. We are from Austria; you are from Nebraska. It is incredible and important that we come together. It is supposed to be. We have similar experiences."

Nevertheless, the reality of war was all around and unending. One rainy day, some of the team congregated at the bar in the hotel lobby—nothing peculiar, only it was midmorning. Gunny was drowning his sorrows. Too old for a babysitter, he had requested "mansitters"—Eric Ahlstrand and Dave Zeitz.

Gunny—Gunnery Sergeant Kris Donald—had received "the" phone call. His best friend, Marine Staff Sergeant Dwayne E. Williams, another

EOD tech, had been killed in Iraq, disabling a roadside bomb. Unlike any remote news headline, a firsthand account rattled a reality check. More than another name or another statistic, Willie, the "Golden Boy," was like a brother to Gunny. He was a great friend and person, son, husband, and father. Gunny was inconsolable. Words were inadequate. Only Chivas Regal could temporarily mask his grievous pain. Gunny compared it to sixty-two years ago—the same mess—another soldier blown up by a bomb. It sure put life into perspective.

It's always a tough deal. For me, it's been sixty-two years, and that dampens your feelings a little bit. I can probably look at it from a more practical view now. It was meaningful to be at the site, searching for remains, getting a clearer picture of what happened to Stan on May 10, 1944. Another eyewitness showed up and remembered standing on a hill near the cemetery in Pottschach on May 10 and seeing a plane break apart. He pointed to an area down the narrow road, away from the bomb crater, opposite the direction where I found the piece of exhaust. And he remembered the tail section with two dead bodies. His account was inconsistent with the others, but Dr. Silverstein still checked out all the leads. Gunny searched the area with the metal detector and pinpointed where four sections of the brake drum, the slightly bent cooling jacket to a .50 caliber machine gun barrel, and a distorted spring from the machine gun were buried. If I remember correctly, the coiled springs were attached from overhead to the machine guns in the nose of the plane for easy maneuvering.

Aircraft wreckage scattered all over made it hard to reconstruct events and strategize. The breech of a machine gun was found on the surface, covered by leaves near the bomb crater. It was about twenty-four inches long and six inches wide and approximately one-eighth-inch thick. On one edge, a bullet had penetrated the metal and left a jagged edge where it exited. The bullet hit with too great a force to have been shot out of a gun. Hundreds of expended cartridges were found at the site, the casings blown out the side—perhaps when the heat set them off.

However, the breech of the machine gun disclosed a serial number. The serial number traced back to Stan's plane, number 685, not 804, which we resolved with Markus as a mix-up with the German records. Still, the most encouraging items were the personal effects. They were still showing up, mostly near the grids around the bomb crater.

Somehow, the crash site evoked peace, a place for reflecting and remembering. There we summarized and speculated about answers to the decades-old question of what happened to Stanley—answers that eluded Granddad and Grandma. If only Granddad and Grandma had known with more certainty the circumstances of Stanley's fate.

And the folks, it seemed, were distraught that there wasn't something tangible for them to bury in Kansas. That's what we were hunting for, and hopefully we could still accomplish the mission.

What was waiting for us at the journey's end? My motto was "One day at a time," but I started to think ahead.

Meanwhile, Markus spearheaded the search for monument companies. Several days before, Markus stood with a group of people that had congregated around Dr. Silverstein's "desk." At that time Dad and I were discussing with Doc the possibility of leaving a memorial marker at the site. Markus had said, "I can help find a stone maker." Thank goodness for his offer. So another day, he drove the four of us from our hotel to the crash site to meet with a monument maker or stone mason. We appreciated Markus's help.

"It's for Stan and his comrades," Markus said. "It's good for Stan's soul."

Markus translated and introduced us to Gerald Hofbauer. Because Mr. Hofbauer is a very muscular man, almost as thick as he is wide, and for other obvious reasons, Markus nicknamed him "the Viking."

Translated, Mr. Hofbauer asked, "Do you want a blue stone or a green stone?"

The four of us exchanged confused glances. Markus said something. This seemed to be just another business transaction for Mr. Hofbauer. We nodded our heads, and Dad answered, "Blue."

A vague translated version of size, wording suggestions, cost, and transporting were determined. We needed permission from landowner Mr. Auer for the memorial to sit on his land at the crash site, and we understood Mr. Hofbauer's desire to erect the memorial before we, the family, left the country.

And then, just a few days later, with only a week left in Austria, Dad and Mom walked with Udo and Inge from the crash site up the muddy road to the castle. "The Viking," unannounced, was parked by the castle, deliberating delivery of the two-ton blue rock strapped to his backhoe.

In the meantime, unaware of "the Viking's" arrival, Rick and I had hiked the less-than-a-mile path to our car parked at Mr. Auer's field, momentarily stopping at the nearby apple orchard to pick, oddly enough, not just one but five four-leaf clovers clumped together. We drove to the castle to pick up Mom and Dad, but then we scrambled in different directions. Udo and Dad walked down the narrow road back to the crash site, Inge and I rode with "the Viking," and the backhoe driver followed. Rick backtracked to the parking area to find Dr. Silverstein and Major Legler in order to get their input on the stone's placement. Mom thought she could help by flagging down any JPAC vehicles driving past the castle.

Major Legler and Doc traversed down the hill to the crash site just in time to direct the stone's placement. "The Viking" was a big, burly man like Bluto, Popeye's nemesis. Our mouths dropped open as the erratic rookie backhoe operator jerked the backhoe's arm, which swung around, bumping "the Viking," knocking him to the ground. In almost one continuous motion, he rolled to his feet, brushed himself off, and assured us that he was okay.

Udo and Inge offered suggestions in German while Rick looked for Mom. Therefore, we only had to contain Dad. Major Legler stuck to him like glue as Dad itched to help "the Viking" move the dangling blue boulder into position. Mr. Auer and his son stopped and commented how well the stone went with the surroundings. "The Viking" had his vision. Since we were only in the way, we left him to his work. Besides, I was almost a nervous wreck watching Dad hover near the boulder dangling from a strap, the strap that was connected to the backhoe arm, the backhoe arm that was controlled by an inexperienced operator. So we returned to the hotel.

JPAC's work continued in the evenings at the hotel. Well … some work, some play. One time Kili Bald Eagle had picked "Grandma DD" wildflowers and left them in her mailbox at the hotel lobby. Frederick translated local newspaper articles about the excavation for me, and he returned phone messages from even more eyewitnesses. After reading about the recovery project, people had called the hotel to pass on information to the Americans. Some of what they described about the crash and the crewmen was secondhand, while some of it was from personal memory, and much of it was consistent with other acquired testimony.

One man told Frederick, "Everyone, particularly the women in this area, suffered immeasurably during the Russian occupation. An invasion by the Huns would have been preferable to the invasion by the Red Army. If it had not been for the Marshall Plan, everyone here would have starved. For that help, we are truly thankful to the Americans."

Often, a group gathered on the patio. The church bells chimed, marking the quarter hour. One evening, while Doc and Derrick photographed and documented findings from the site, Rick and some of the team puffed fine cigars. I sent e-mails and whiffed cigar smoke.

"Your e-mails are probably in the hands of Chinese intelligence," Doc said, half-joking.

Dad stepped inside to join Mom in the lobby with the congregation at the bar.

Cigars didn't appeal to me. When I was in about third grade, I walked from the farm where we lived to school in Glasco, Kansas. Coming home one day along Highway 24, I found a cigar in a cellophane wrapper. So I stowed it away until the weekend, when Mom and Dad would go to town to shop. I smoked that puppy clear

*down, and then, midafternoon, before they came home, I went to the icebox to eat
lemons or something to get rid of the bad taste in my mouth and the odor. That night,
I ran a fever and got sicker than a son of a gun. Mom called the doctor to come out,
and he gave me some medicine. After he left, I had to fess up. The next day, when
the doctor returned, he smiled and said, "That's not all he did. He's got scarlet fever."
Back in those days, people with scarlet fever were quarantined. So the sign went on
the door, and Stan moved in with another family for about two weeks.*

Derrick continued to photograph evidence and said, "While I shopped
at an antique store in Wiener Neustadt to buy a gift for my wife, the store
owner, knowing I was an American, said that everyone locally is talking about
the excavation because of newspaper coverage. It is rumored that the locals in
Vostenhof possess personal items from the crewmen."

The small-town rumor mill is a universal phenomenon even in Austria.
Information circulates in small towns everywhere—sometimes there's a hint of
truth to the information, and sometimes it's fabricated. Stanley even remarked
in one letter, "Can't depend much on what you hear aboard ship. It's worse
than what you can hear over the backyard fence in a small town."

So we brainstormed about the best approach to request the return of
possible crew members' personal items. When Mr. Stranz stopped at the
excavation site, he suggested using the newspapers and possibly asking the
mayor for help. On another evening, our request was mentioned at the Rotary
meeting in Wiener Neustadt.

"Dr. Silverstein and Harold joined me for the Rotary meeting," Rick said.
"The members, all men, met in the pub at Hartigs. Some drank cocktails and
smoked cigars or pipes. The group was called in to a meeting room for dinner
and the program. The president of the club spoke in English and introduced and
welcomed us. Dr. Silverstein told the group about the excavation. The program
speaker, in German, narrated as he showed slides of his trip to Mongolia.
About halfway through the program, Harold sneezed, and one of his hearing
aids blew out of his ear and landed under the table. Harold whispered to me,
'Forget about the damned thing.' But, I bent over and looked under the table
and our chairs and found it for him so he could maybe wear it another day. That
Rotary meeting was the first time in many months he'd even worn his hearing
aids. Harold always said, 'Hearing aids are for old people.' Other than that
incident, I'll remember the meeting because it was a good Rotary experience,
and everywhere, Austrian people were generous and hospitable."

Yet the search for remains as well as personal items continued. The team had
reached their halfway point of the excavation, and Major Legler reported to

Hawaii, "This is a heartening experience for everyone with the family here and a success story."

Even so, the story continued to unfold. In a scheduled evening interview, Dr. Silverstein told reporter Christian Feigl, "One objective is to explore certain parts of the crash site with the highest probability of remains, and we're not done exploring. The team leaves when they've dug in all areas that may produce something and when we're sure we have everything. The very small pieces of leather indicate the intensity of the blast."

And then, every once in a while, a larger piece of leather, possibly from a boot, turned up and boosted morale. The team found many small pieces of leather and several buttons. Walking around the crash site, I liked to look up to the top part of the trees to see if something was lodged in the pine needles.

The crashed bomber, it seemed, had been swallowed up as part of the landscape. Promising life-support materials—remnants of war—like a possibly melted nylon cord from a parachute, a possible leather strap, and a small metal plate from the plane's alarm system, showed up in grids eleven and twelve.

"Melted plastic looks like bone," Dr. Silverstein explained. "One of the tricks with melted plastic is you have perfect little circles or regular air bubbles not seen in bone. We take things back to the lab just to make sure."

The remnants of a four-engine B-17 bomber that crashed near Vostenhof, Austria, on May 10, 1944. Large pieces of wreckage were hauled off by the Germans soon after the crash. JPAC photo—Derrick Goode, photographer.

Occasionally, bones and bone fragments were dug up. They were mostly animal bones—inconclusive until scientists at the lab in Hawaii conducted an osteological analysis. Each excavated grid was photographed, and survey equipment documented grid coordinates. Buckets of dug-up ACW—aircraft wreckage—were stacked near Dr. Silverstein's workstation. Dr. Silverstein collected other fragments on his desk. Many times, Derrick arranged selected artifacts on a small cloth and photographed the evidence. One day while he worked, Derrick asked me, "When should parents stop checking their child's homework?" Derrick continued working, carefully positioning and arranging the unearthed artifacts, and we visited parent to parent about homework. Juggling work and family took on a new meaning.

At one point, Derrick documented all the ACW from the buckets which was laid out and grouped into piles on a blue plastic tarp—all two hundred pounds of leftover remnants from an over sixty-five-thousand-pound Flying Fortress.

On another return visit to the crash site, Johann Piringer invited the four of us and Frederick for coffee. Rick had not met the Piringer family.

Again, we stood with Johann on the hillside next to his farm looking down on the neighbor's house below. It began to rain. "Stanley's plane just missed that house," Johann emphasized. From our uphill vantage point, we again heard how the smoking plane had flown barely above his eye level.

"The Piringers' farmyard reminded me of simpler times," Rick said. "It was like my aunt and uncle's place in the 1950s. The Piringers' yard was neat and clean, and we walked through the barn to enter their home."

As we gathered around the table, drinking coffee and eating homemade sweets, Rick showed them recent photos of our farm buildings, machinery, and corn crops in Nebraska. Josef asked Rick how the combine worked. I thought Rick might start with page one of the owner's manual, in English, of course. Frederick knew nothing about farming. He remarked, "We didn't learn the words 'corn head,' 'snout,' 'silo,' and 'bushel' in any German classes." And it was not easy translating and describing unfamiliar machinery and alien concepts.

But worldwide, farmers must be on the same wavelength. Rick made hand motions and pencil sketches, and with Josef's limited English, the two communicated. The scene reminded me of a description in a letter Stanley had written home from Cuba. Stanley wrote, "Some of the motions we go through to help us speak to them are wows."

With daughter Sarah's help at home in Nebraska, Rick came to Austria prepared. We presented the Piringer family with a book about Nebraska.

Johann Piringer indicates the path of the crippled B-17 he witnessed on May 10, 1944. According to Johann, the smoking plane, flying treetop high, maneuvered to barely miss his neighbor's home in the background.

Johann grinned and said, "Super."

As we exchanged addresses, the Piringer family, in turn, gave us a picture book of their area of Austria. Then Dad took off his JPAC ball cap and handed it to Johann.

Johann is probably the last guy who saw Stan alive, only he didn't know it at the time. To me, it's really meaningful to talk to somebody who saw the crash and knew what happened.

In the meantime, "the Viking" met his deadline, and the plaque for the memorial stone was ready for placement with four days to spare. Late one afternoon, Markus once again drove the four of us to the crash site in order to finalize our transaction with the stone mason. Mr. Stranz joined us.

The plaque was different from our familiar bronze-type plaques. Mr. Hofbauer had inscribed the following on a polished slab of dark gray granite, highlighting the names in gold:

IN MEMORY
OF THE FALLEN CREW
MEMBERS OF AN AMERICAN
B-17 BOMBER
WHICH CRASHED HERE
ON 10ᵀᴴ MAY 1944

1 LT STANLEY N. DWYER
SGT JOHN J. BOROS
2 LT FRANCIS G. GILHOOLEY
SGT PRESCOTT C. PIPER
SGT WILLIAM OLFENIUS

"YOU ARE NOT FORGOTTEN"
USA JPAC RECOVERY TEAM
AUG/SEP 2006

DEDICATED
BY THE FAMILY OF STANLEY DWYER

Markus and Rick positioned and held the plaque against the memorial stone while "the Viking" screwed it in place. I watched for Dad's reaction. He said nothing.

I was concerned that the two screws holding the plaque on the stone wouldn't last. Mr. Hofbauer assured me that it was very secure. I said that in our country, it might last about two days before someone might attempt to steal it. So he convinced me that such wouldn't be the case in Austria.

Then Mr. Hofbauer made some final adjustments. Before permanently securing the plaque with the bottom screw, Dad said, "Wait. It's not level."

Dad stood back and observed as Markus and Rick shifted the granite slab slightly left and then right.

With the plaque level and permanently mounted on the stone, Dad smiled.

Mr. Stranz snapped photos and said, "Super."

"It is good that the United States government, after sixty years, still looks for missing soldiers," Mr. Hofbauer commented.

That evening, the four of us dined with Markus. He chose a restaurant serving traditional Austrian fare. We all agreed that the memorial stone was impressive and a fitting tribute to the fallen crew.

Tailor and historian Augustin Stranz and Harold E. Dwyer.
Photo taken near Vostenhof, Austria, in 2006.

At dinner, Markus repeated what "the Viking" had told him earlier. "The Viking" said, "It was an honor to make this memorial for the crew. I am glad to meet the family."

Our last weekend in Austria arrived. We could have used ten more hours in each day, but we had one day, Saturday, to plan the memorial dedication.

Frederick made a few morning phone calls to inform people of the dedication on Sunday, August 27. Dad wondered if we needed somebody to play taps, so I called Markus on his "handy" (i.e., cell phone).

"Oh, you need a 'bug-gler?'" Markus asked.

We needed a bugler. By evening, Markus, true to form, had one lined up.

Frederick saved the day and accompanied us to the florist and elsewhere. By now, we knew our way on the curved roads to the Piringer farm, and then Frederick left Mr. Stranz a note in his mailbox and translated to Mr. Auer and his son the date and time of the memorial dedication.

That same day, we had an "assignment" from Dr. Silverstein. Johanna Stipsits from Ternitz had mailed a letter to Dad and Mom at the hotel. "I

384

would help you to find your brother fall," she wrote. "Excuse my English. I cannot speak in English, only a little write. I have seen the wreck and the right hand." Leaving no stone unturned, Dr. Silverstein had asked us to follow-up on the correspondence and visit Johanna Stipsits. We'd driven through Ternitz every day on the way to Vostenhof—now we had to locate her home.

Johanna sat next to her husband, Ignaz, and made hand motions. Frederick translated. She said, "The bombers flew over on their way back from missions. I was fourteen and one-half at the time of the crash. I went to the site with a bunch of friends. The front part of the plane was split from the back part. In the front part, I saw a black right hand protruding. I remember wings on the ground but no tail section."

Johanna served us juice and was pleased to tell her story to someone. However, details were inconsistent with the Vostenhof crash, so she rode in our car and directed us to her described crash site, which turned out to be the one near Sieding, about two miles direct route from the Vostenhof site. Mrs. Stipsits reminded me of my grandmother Coplen. She hugged us and gave me a red rose picked from her garden.

Next, we located the church in Pottschach, the one Mrs. Stipsits recommended, and we arrived just as a young priest pulled up in his car. In the absence of the regular priest, he agreed to attend the memorial dedication in an official capacity. We also discussed the rumor that locals might possess crew members' personal items. Perhaps a church announcement was appropriate.

So back at the hotel, after a stop at the crash site, Frederick made more phone calls and suggested we follow custom and serve cake after the memorial dedication. It was Saturday evening. Shops were closed for the weekend, and Udo was picking us up for dinner. We were running out of time.

Inge, under the weather that evening, stayed home. It wasn't the same without her.

On the way to the restaurant "in the mountains," Udo gave us a tour of the countryside and quaint villages and stopped at an elaborately ornate, eight-hundred-year-old church alongside a road the Romans once traveled. Then he wound his way left and then right and then left and right, around hairpin turn after hairpin turn. My stomach felt woozy. Udo drove up the mountain to about three thousand feet and stopped at a restaurant called *Kohlroserlhaus*, where we dined. Despite being from different countries and cultures, we shared more similarities than differences—even similar perspectives on many current issues. Besides the good food, good conversation, and good company, the view was spectacular.

Wiener Neustadt was visible in the distant haze, and farther east, we could make out Neusiedlersee on the horizon. From that elevation, we looked down on the farm fields and red-tiled roofs. The fields resembled a patchwork quilt and were planted right up the hillside to the tree line. To the right was Neunkirchen, followed by Wimpassing, Ternitz, Pottschach, and, in the hills, Vostenhof.

It gave us an idea of the "view" Stan had when flying over the area under very different conditions. The land below was pretty flat ground—an easy place to put an airplane down if you had to, assuming it was under control. A few weeks before, Mr. Piringer's neighbor, a commercial airline pilot, offered to fly me over the area, retracing Stan's route. I never took the ride.

The following day, Sunday, August 27, 2006, started out gloomily, both the weather and our moods. It was the day of the memorial dedication, and it was like the day of a funeral. All day, rain threatened. Still not giving up on Frederick's cake suggestion, the four of us hustled to find a café that was open on Sunday and one that sold whole cakes. The third time was a charm. As Rick parallel parked the car, a young gal walked—and bounced—along the sidewalk. Momentarily, Dad cut through the gloom and asked, "Rick, did you even notice her hair color?"

So we were off to Vostenhof with cakes and hotel-borrowed serving pieces. After stopping in Wimpassing at the florist, we arrived at the site. It looked different. The team had groomed around and behind the memorial stone, and led by Dave Zeitz, a rock border had been formed between the stone and the narrow road. Next to the large memorial stone was a matching small, flat rock. Gerald Hofbauer, "the Viking," had placed it there with a permanently attached lantern and a candle burning inside—a big man with a big heart. Our flower arrangement sat in front of the memorial on a flat rock Rick pulled out of the stream.

And along with the team, local people congregated for the dedication. The clouds thickened. Rain seemed imminent. Inge brought flowers from her garden, and Wolfgang Losos and his wife placed another lit candle next to the lantern. The scene was set, and the four o'clock hour arrived.

Major Legler, wearing his signature faded red ball cap, welcomed the gathering of approximately forty-five people. "We are here to officially place this memorial marker for the soldiers who crashed here in a B-17 over sixty years ago," he said. "We'd like to thank everyone who helped in the recovery effort, starting with the historical research and continuing through to the recovery that you see behind me. Because of your hard work and your dedication, all this was possible. In addition, I'd like to thank our new friends and all the support we have received from the Austrian government."

Team member Rodney Acasio read from the Second Letter of Maccabees 12:42–46, followed by words from the young priest, Leopold Selhofer. He first spoke in German and then in English, "In the name of the Father, Son, and Holy Spirit. Amen. Family Dwyer, members of the United States Army, we are here to bless this memorial stone. As human beings, our lives are marked from the past, from this moment, and in the future. We have possibilities to remember moments of history. This stone here is one possibility to have a memorial of somebody. It is a small but important sign of memory. It intends to be a sign of our faith in God that everybody is remembered in God—that God forgets nobody. We have here the words 'you are not forgotten,' and in God, they are not forgotten. Here in this valley is a sign of God's love to us and to our descendents ..."

Side by side, the Austrians and Americans prayed the familiar Lord's Prayer in a way I had never heard. Half of those gathered recited in German, the other half in English. Unlikely sixty-two years ago, now we prayed together for five young American men who perished on once-enemy territory.

Dad stood off to one side of the memorial stone, and Udo quietly slipped through the group of people to stand next to him. Dr. Silverstein expressed his thanks and continued, "On behalf of our government, it is my solemn duty to bring home our country's missing servicemen. It is incredible to believe we were at war with these people because we have developed such friendships. Without the sacrifices by soldiers and this country's people, we wouldn't have peace now. The dream of a better world can come true because of what they did."

When we spoke, we said a sentence or two in English, followed by Frederick's translation. "The B-17 bomber that crashed here on May 10, 1944, flew out of Foggia, Italy, with a ten-man crew," I said. "Five crewmen bailed out and survived. Five young men perished at or near this site. William Olfenius was nineteen years old, born February 7, 1925. He was the tail gunner from New York. Prescott Piper, the togglier-bombardier, was born on January 18, 1918, and resided in Illinois. Originally buried in Pottschach, Olfenius and Piper are now buried in Belgium. Francis G. Gilhooley, the navigator, was born on October 10, 1920, and came from Brooklyn, New York. His wife's name was Eleanor. His final resting place is in New York near his family.

"Two crewmen's remains were never recovered from this crash site. John J. Boros was born on October 6, 1911, and served as the flight engineer. He and his wife, Stella, lived in New York.

"Stanley Naismeth Dwyer was born October 26, 1916, in Kansas. His parents, my grandparents, were Harold W. and Ellen Dwyer. Stanley's older sister, Aileen, passed away this past June at the age of ninety-one. His younger brother is Harold Dwyer."

After placing the red rose from Johanna Stipsits's garden on the memorial stone, I rejoined Rick and Mom in the crowd. Inge stood next to me and held my hand.

I expressed my appreciation to everyone and told those gathered that Stan had left home when I was fourteen. We grew up in Kansas, and Stan had a typical childhood playing basketball and baseball, even playing on a minor league team. Stan graduated from college with a degree in broadcasting and journalism. Our country was recovering from the stock market crash, and there weren't many jobs, so he signed on as a merchant marine. He signed on with Standard Oil sailing on the SS India Arrow. *At one port where their tanker was anchored offshore in South America, Stan and some buddies threw barrels overboard, made a raft, and swam ashore. For a short time in 1941, Stan was a radio announcer in Nebraska. On December 8, 1941, Stan entered the army and later joined the United States Army Air Corps. On May 10, 1944, his life ended here.*

I offered a prayer for Sergeant Boros, another fallen crewman. Boros remained behind to help fellow injured crewmen. If Stan was injured or dead, it's possible Boros could have jumped in the right seat, the copilot's seat, and flown the plane. The plane was ten seconds short of the open area above the ridge.

The dedication continued. Major Legler stepped forward and stood next to the memorial stone.

"Let's have a moment of silence," Major Legler said. "Also remember Dwayne "Willie" Williams, who was killed in Iraq this past week and was a comrade of one of JPAC's team members." Major Legler then removed his red cap, the signal to the bugler, Andreas Poropatits.

The sound from his trumpet was clear. "Day is done ..." The most beautiful, mellow tone of taps rang throughout the valley. I can still hear it.

After the dedication, we complimented Andreas. Markus had contacted him the day before, on Saturday, asking him to play taps. Not knowing what taps was, Andreas called a friend in Vienna, who in turn called a friend in the United States. He played it perfectly.

And Major Legler and I chuckled about him being the only one who wore his cap during the Lord's Prayer. Before the dedication began, Major Legler and I worked out the signal for Andreas to begin taps. So when the prayer began, I saw Major Legler hesitate, but his ball cap stayed on.

People mingled and conversed, and Mom served cake from her makeshift buffet table, concocted from buckets and a screen.

Markus Ladek, the local game warden who often checked in on the excavation and volunteered site security because of curious souvenir seekers, brought his mother, Maria, to the ceremony. Translated, she told Kay and me about coming through the area about thirty minutes after the crash. The plane was still smoking. She told how young children straddled the unexploded bombs, riding them like a horse. She also remembered sheep walking on the bombs and the noise their hooves made on the metal. Maria grieved and felt bad for the young men who would never get to go home again and see their families. She broke down and couldn't tell any more of her story.

More stories, more perspectives, and more than pages in a history book, it was the human side of war.

All the Austrian people we met were caring people who knew something and wanted to help.

Those people shared their perspective of the war, stories of their missing, stories of their sacrifices, their sufferings, their losses, their survival. I once heard our local funeral director P. R. Farmer repeat his own mortician father's "philosophy of funeral service." His father's philosophy was, "Rich or poor, young or old, no matter what walk in life, the grief is all the same."

Again, we thanked "the Viking" for his fine workmanship, and I'll always remember my conversation with Udo and Inge.

Standing on the hillside near a barren excavated grid, I asked Udo about their fiftieth wedding anniversary celebration in 2009. "Udo, what day were you married?"

With an impish smile, he said, "You'd better ask Inge."

"Our anniversary date is October 26," Inge said.

As we stood at the crash site, I replied, "Inge, October 26 is also Stanley's birthday."

Inge shook her head and said, "It is unbelievable that we should meet. Unbelievable."

As we left the crash site, it began to rain. The air smelled fresh and clean. I noticed a sense of peace had come over Dad.

The ceremony was moving and important, possibly a replacement for a funeral, if it comes to that.

After the service, several team members accepted our invitation to dinner at Hartigs, our favorite restaurant since Mom, Dad, and I first dined there with Udo and Inge and Dr. Silverstein in what seemed like a long time ago.

Danford, Brad, and Danny repeated, "This is the first time for a family at an excavation. We like the personal touch it gives. It's been a good experience for us."

"It's relaxing for us with the family around, seeing the interaction," Bald Eagle said. "Harold, I watch you at the site, looking into Doc's screen and the pit area, not judging the team, just knowing you've waited so long,"

Photo taken after the memorial dedication on August 27, 2006, at the Vostenhof crash site. From left to right: Rick Hughes, Kay (Dwyer) Hughes, Dr. Jay Silverstein, Darlene Dwyer, Major Mike Legler, Harold E. Dwyer.

I told him I wasn't judging. I just held those guys and that gal in highest esteem.

"Harold deserves this," Jennifer said. "He didn't know his older brother; he was taken from him."

Dave Hansen commented, "All the easy crash sites have been excavated. The hard ones are left. But if there is anything to find, JPAC will find it. We do not like to leave anyone behind. They need to go home because they earned that trip home."

We still hoped to bring Stanley home. Yet our journey—the family—to Austria was drawing to a close, but the team would continue excavating for two more weeks. Still no day was the same. The day after the ceremony, Karl Teigl came to the crash site and told his version of May 10, 1944.

"I was fourteen at the time of the crash," Mr. Teigl said. "During the raid, I was in my aunt's basement in Wimpassing. We heard the explosion, and afterward, it got quiet. I saw a plume of smoke and followed it to the crash site. There were many animals in the forest. Everything was smoking, and the trees were stripped. It's hard to remember after sixty years. About one hour after the crash, my buddies and I came to collect casings to reuse the metal."

Mr. Teigl carried a book showing a broken tail section of a B-17, which he remembered being up the slope on the other side of the creek. However, the markings on the tail section were different from Stanley's group's markings. He mentioned seeing a piece of skin—with hair—bloodied and charred next to a broken machine gun lying in the open on the other slope. Also, another vivid memory was the crewman he saw hanging from a parachute in the trees uphill from the impact crater, on the ridge top.

The small valley reminded me of a skateboard park. Down one slope was the crash site, and across the flat area was the narrow road, tangle of shrubs, and the stream. The incline on the other side was a much steeper wooded hillside with a different landowner.

Whether or not Dr. Silverstein harbored any preconceived notions, all leads were investigated. Gunny stepped away from his screen and grabbed his metal detector to scan the slope on the other side. There, the forest floor had absorbed bomb frag, and more flak jacket metal plates littered the surface. Rick noticed a partially buried black glove sticking out of the ground.

It looked like the military-issue flying gloves we wore. The threads were deteriorated; it had been there awhile. Dr. Silverstein bagged it for further examination and indicated that the soil from around the glove would also be tested at the CIL for phosphorus, which is decomposed bone.

"Since life-support and other material evidence have turned up on this slope, there is a possibility of remains," Dr. Silverstein explained. "I have an obligation to explore any areas where there could possibly be remains and will recommend this site be left 'open.' I will recommend it be put on the operational calendar for next year, which means another team would come and reopen the site to totally complete the excavation."

We'd already witnessed firsthand the backbreaking work one team exerted to find two missing servicemen. Their unsurpassed efforts reflected the commitment of our government to honor its promise that no fallen comrade is left behind.

And now JPAC would consider sending a second team? So the direction of our unscripted journey was still unpredictable. Privately, I had confided with Rick, "Why were we led here? To find remains? For the memorial dedication?"

Even with the possibility of a return trip, it was time to pack, throw our wilted flower bouquets from Inge away, and say our good-byes to our Austrian friends and the team. Markus and Udo and Inge came to the hotel to bid farewell to the four of us.

As we drank beer, Markus requested that I send him a copy of one of Stanley's letters whenever we corresponded. Then he asked, "How did your family meet Inge?" So Markus heard more about the many coincidences of our search.

"I was just lucky I met Mr. Stranz," Inge said. "Mr. Stranz was the only really helpful source, and I'm glad we could help the family. We are really friends, and it is really great that Austria and America came together."

"It's fate," Markus added. He raised his glass. "To Stan! *Prost!*"

It was cool, as usual, and rainy as Mom, Dad, Rick, and I drove to the crash site for one last visit. Riding in the car, we commented about the rainbow fragments that appeared and disappeared in the sky. Already moving and screening dirt, the mood of the team was evident by the level of chatter. Dr. Silverstein sorted pieces of miniscule evidence into small piles on his "desk." Momentum perked up when a large, round fuel cap, inscribed ENG NO. 3 FUEL, was dug out of grid thirteen. Then a bucketful of debris was carefully uncovered using trowels. Disappointingly, the debris was later determined to be unrelated to the crash. However, the team remained steadfast. No one ever complained. For the team's sake and all their hard work, we hoped they would find what they had come for too.

"Did you see the little rainbows?" I asked Jennifer, who was sweeping down a grid. She only nodded and gave me one of those funny looks. I didn't understand the look until weeks later when I received JPAC photos from Derrick.

And at the memorial stone, the candle in the lantern still flickered, and the flowers remained fresh. The team worked on the partially cleared hillside in the background. I tried to imagine the scenario on May 10, 1944. We stood and took it all in. For me, I felt an unexplainable connection at the crash site.

To be at the spot where my brother perished was very meaningful. JPAC put forth a tremendous effort, and we still hoped they would find something we could take home to accomplish what the folks couldn't. However, I understood the situation. It was worth every bit being there.

I had brought some red crepe paper poppies from home and purposely had put one in my jacket pocket. The red poppy is a symbol of the sacrifice of military men and women. Hospitalized American veterans make the flowers that the American Legion Auxiliary sells for the veterans' benefit. Years before, Grandma actively served in the auxiliary. As a young girl, around Memorial Day, I went with Grandma to greet people outside the Hested's store in downtown Hastings and sold poppies. But back then, I didn't understand why or know the flower's significance. Before walking away from the crash site, I attached the red poppy to the screw cap on the memorial plaque—for Grandma.

On our last night in Austria, the Greek restaurant was once again the venue for the final team dinner. We were in the same room as before—the one with curved walls and niches with statues—and again pilsner glasses with iced tea-colored beer were lined up down the middle of the table, along with a red, white, and blue centerpiece Dad furnished.

Somebody clinked a glass with a fork. Chris Bunnell addressed the group, saying, "Thanks, everybody, for coming out. We wish the family good-bye. It's been awhile. We've gotten to know all four of you, and I feel close to you. This feels like a big family, and Harold, you're just like my grandfather. I wish you could stay until we go. And right after we're done here, the restaurant owner wants a photo of all of us for his wall."

"Okay," Dad remarked. "But there's one condition to that photo, and we'll tell you what it is pretty soon."

Laughter competed with the background music.

"Rick and Kay, please come forward," Sergeant Sweet ordered.

"Move it," somebody chided.

"I have to say it's been a pleasure," Jennifer continued. "Our missions usually start with paperwork. We study the case, the name of the person we're looking for, and the incident which occurred. This is a great opportunity. This doesn't happen; we do not have family members go out with us. Meeting the family has brought a lot more to all of us. We've gotten to know Stanley, and that means a lot to us. Harold, you came by it honestly. Your brother was ornery just like you, and Kay, you're just like your father. Your husband says you are persistent, which is what it takes to make our missions go—family members pushing, asking questions, wanting to know what happened. To actually have you here has meant so much for each and every one of us. It hits home to all of us because we've seen what it has done to your family. So it's special, and we appreciate what you've done for us."

Jennifer presented me with a team photo taken at the memorial and said, "This is a small token of our appreciation. As time goes by, you may remember names and places, but sometimes the faces fade away."

As I looked at those eighteen faces on the photo, I could only think about what each one of them had done for us.

"Thank you," I said.

"Group hug." Jennifer laughed and said.

"Kay, hold it up," Dad requested.

"Speech," somebody added.

"When we began our search to find Stanley in 1998," I said, "we had no idea it would come to this experience. And because of you, it has really been a lifetime experience for us. We cannot thank you enough for your dedication and the thorough work you do at the site. We appreciate your hard work and are glad we could observe. It's been our privilege to meet all of you and know each one of you personally. All of you have shared a special part of our family history, and we are grateful. When you are in Nebraska, please call us and come visit. We want to see you again. I guess we can go home now knowing Stanley is in very good hands. Dad gave you a glimpse of Stanley at the memorial dedication, and I would like to read a letter—one of three hundred letters found in Stanley's trunk. Harrison Summers, who sent the letter to Granddad, was one of Stanley's professors at K-State College and a friend Stanley stayed in contact with while a merchant marine."

The restaurant background music played, and I read:

HARRISON B. SUMMERS

57 East 88th Street, New York, N. Y.

June 12th 1944

Mr Harold Dwyer
906 West 6th Street
Hastings Nebraska

Dear Mr Dwyer:

We were all sorry to hear that Stanley is
reported missing in action over Austria. More than sorry;
Stanley is someone whom all of us think of as a very close
friend. As you know, he visited with us often during the
time he worked for Standard, and we were glad to have him
with us a couple of times at least after he was in uniform.

While the news that he is missing is distressing,
I refuse to feel that it is completely bad. I have known
of so many cases in which men in the Air Force have been reported missing and have later been reported as prisoners that
I think as you do that the chances are at least 50-50 that
we'll have better news, some day.

Meantime, I know you'll want to read the following
letter that we received from Stan only a few weeks ago --
it was written on April 22nd. We thought that he had expressed
himself and his feelings so beautifully that both Mrs Summers
and I took the letter to our respective offices on different
days, and showed it to our friends. Here it is, except for
his opening reference to a letter of mine which had finally
reached him . . .

"'Here' is Italy. It is a disappointment to the
visitor, but then we didn't come here to visit. Best
place to be is the canvas home. It's not an outstanding
example of modern architecture, but its conveniences are
products of our own initiative and handiwork and therefore
a source of no little amount of pride. The typewriter I
brought along makes the home complete, and I have an idea
that time would hang heavy if it were not for the pleasure
I get out of pecking. My co-pilot offered no little
amount of criticism to my bringing the machine, but has
since seen the hand-writing on the key-board, and uses it
about as much as I do.

"Italy is void. It is but land and people and stone
buildings. Everything else the Germans took, including
clothing, food, live-stock -- and soap. In their wake is
a womb wherein grows filth and poverty and disease. Even
the rich are poor, for there is nothing to buy. The
native, with cities to rebuild, soil to till, and faith
in life to have restored, waits on the lea side of a
crumbled stone wall, waits either for peace or for death.

-2-

There is school, it is said, but only for the more
fortunate.   Thousands of urchins, parentless and homeless, live only on the kindness of American troops.
And when the war is over, the cost to America of recreating civilization will be great.   Italy is only
one of many countries in like circumstance.

"Combat is interesting.   It holds the excitement
of a college football game multiplied to world-wide
scope.   Returns from victory are tangible and real, and
accomplshment gives one an unequalled sense of satisfaction.   But the cost is great, and it will take a lifetime to disso.ve the mental, physical, spiritual and
financial mortgage.

"You should go on a bomber mission.   You would
feel a tenseness in the air when the navigator announces
over the interphone,'Flak at 12 o'clock.'   You would see
the wingmen edge closer into position on the lead ship
when fighters attacked from the rear.   You as tail
gunner would have cold perspiration on your brow in
thirty-below air.   You as a pilot would forget the danger
of the tons of high octane gasoline in your wings, or the
explosive charge in your cargo.   Instead, when the gunner
reported rocket or twenty-millimeter cannon fire, you would
pray that no missle find a human target.   One becomes
attached to his crew, and his greatest desire, next to the
accomplishment of his purpose, is to return his boys to
ten worrying mothers after the time has been served.   Too,
no matter how intense the fighting, one finds himself
taking a moment from his job to make sure that his buddy
in another plane is still in formation.

"And you haven't loved, Doc, until amidst machine gun
fire you have heard from a crew member, or seen, the intent
approach of a P-38 toward the Messerschmidts on your tail,
and seconds later 'heard' the silence of your own guns.   It
is a thrill I shall never forget.   The thirty-eights that
are coming over now are without the camouflage paint, and
their silver beauty as they form vapor trails in the blue
sky while covering a bomber formation is without comparison.

"My literal candle is not burning as high as my fig-
urative one.   And tomorrow is another day.   So .. kindest
regards to all the researchers!

                         Sincerely,

                              Stan."

     I think that is a letter you'll want to keep.   It is
one of which any parent should be very proud.   It typifies
Stan; it shows much more than most letters I've received from
friends across the water, what he thinks about -- and more
than that, that he understands things, and feels.   I'm glad

-3-

that I'm able to send the copy along to you -- and you'll
forgive me, I'm sure, if I keep the original myself.

Stan's a boy of whom you must be very proud; one I'm
proud to have had as a student, and still to hold dear as
a friend.   Dorothy, Bob, Leda and I all join in hoping
that one day, we'll have good news about him from you.

Sincerely,

Harry Summers

(to Stan, "Doc.")

P S - Pvt Gervaise V Keogh's address is:
    32 885 747 Battery B 534 AAA
    Battalion (AW) M   APO 464 % Postmaster, New York

*Frederick noted Stan's foresight of the Marshall Plan. Stan was eight years
older than I was when he served, and his grasp of the situation was more mature
than mine.*

Dr. Silverstein stepped forward and said, "The eloquence of Stan is a
hard act to follow. How about all four of you come up? Obviously it's been
a very powerful thing for us. Stanley knew what his mission was, and our
mission is to bring him home. As tokens of our appreciation, I have a couple
of JPAC tie tacks for Rick and Harold's next Rotary meeting. We were a bit
conspicuous, being the only ones without ties. And one other token I have.
Anthropologists like to share forensic anthropology coins with those directly
involved in a recovery. I have one for you, Harold—a somewhat grim-looking
coin—for providing B-17 expertise in the field. And there's another one for
you, Kay, for providing research about the men we were looking for. For
Darlene, I have a gift to remind you of the good impression you made here in
Wiener Neustadt, something to put on your shelf. Put a little Ouzo in it and
remember where you have been."

"Well, I've got a few things to say here," Dad said. "I hate good-byes, so
I may as well lighten it up. A couple of nuns were driving down the road and
ran out of gas, so one of them walked to the filling station. Well, the attendant

said, 'By golly, we've had three or four people run out of gas. I don't have anything to put gas in for you to carry. But wait a minute. I'll go in and ask the missus if she's got a container.' He comes back with a bedpan and says, 'This is all I've got.' He puts some gas in it for the nun, and she returns to the car. As she's pouring the gas in the car from the bedpan, another car drives up and screeches to a stop. The guy driving said, 'Do you see what I see? If that car runs, I'm turning Catholic!'

"You all know how we feel about you. So, dad gum, if you don't call or yell when you come through our part of the country, why, I'm going to be upset.

"In reference to the picture for the owner, Rick's going to help hand out some stuff. We'd like everyone to wear these hats for the photo."

Rick presented Jennifer with a Nebraska Husker T-shirt and the rest of the team with red or black Nebraska Husker ball caps. Texas Longhorn burnt orange ball caps were reluctantly exchanged for Husker gear, and Georgia Bulldog fans sheepishly curled the bill of their new black *N* caps. The evidence hangs on the wall at the Greek restaurant in Wiener Neustadt, Austria.

In the meantime, reporter Christian Feigl waited at the hotel for his interview.

"It's been a special honor to be with the family," Dr. Silverstein told Christian. "Morale has been exceptionally high this excavation. Usually, after three weeks on a mountain, we start to feel stressed. Everyone always wants to do their best to find what's there. This time, I can see the team is trying extra hard from the inspiration of family being here. I am a little more concerned that we're going to find what we want. We have no bones or teeth yet, but until we are done, we don't know what we'll find."

Following the interview, Chris Bunnell summoned team members at the hotel to present Dad with his going-away present.

The plaque the team gave me hangs in our family room at the top of the order in prime location. Stan's photo in uniform, my service picture, and the JPAC team photo are on the plaque, and I slipped the ENG NO. 3 FUEL cap in behind the attached piece of machine gun breech. The plaque reminds me most of the trip and the great group of guys and one gal involved. It's a treasure.

Dad wrote to Johnie Webb, "We are very grateful to be born in a country that spends the effort to recover long-lost servicemen and servicewomen who gave their very last for our way of life. From Dr. Jay Silverstein, Major Legler, and the rest of the group, it was a first-class group of people and a pleasure to be with them. As good representatives of their respective services, their attitudes and good American spirit impressed the local folk and us. With or without remains, it rates an A-plus."

From left to right: Frederick Smith, Dr. Jay Silverstein, Jennifer Sweet, Tony San Luis, Guillermo Richards, Chris Bunnell, Kris Donald, Harold E. Dwyer, Rodney Acasio.

On board the train, Mom, Dad, Rick, and I waved good-bye to Major Legler, Dr. Silverstein, Rodney Acasio, Dave Hansen, Tuni Amani, Tony San Luis, and Frederick Smith standing on the station platform. Everyone had included us as part of the team. I was reluctant to go home without Stanley. But maybe something would still turn up.

When we departed Austria, we gave up our front-row seats to the ongoing excavation. But we departed with answered questions, new friends, more personal stories, other perspectives, and an appreciation of our government's efforts to resolve the fate of two missing soldiers. In fact, I thought about what Dad had said when we arrived in Austria. "Expect nothing—and anything more would be great." Our journey to Austria had surpassed all expectations.

The 2006 JPAC recovery team.
Standing, left to right: Master Sergeant Frederick Smith, linguist; Staff Sergeant Derrick Goode, photographer; Staff Sergeant Eric Ahlstrand, recovery specialist; Sergeant David Zeitz, recovery specialist; Sergeant Robert Danford, recovery specialist; Major Michael Legler, team leader; Sergeant Bradley Thompson, recovery specialist; Dr. Jay Silverstein, recovery leader; Sergeant David Hansen, recovery specialist; Sergeant Tuni Amani, recovery specialist; Sergeant Kili Bald Eagle, recovery specialist; Sergeant Guillermo Richards, recovery specialist.
Kneeling, left to right: Staff Sergeant Anthony San Luis, recovery specialist; Staff Sergeant Jennifer Sweet, mortuary affairs; Staff Sergeant William Frye, recovery specialist; Gunnery Sergeant Kristopher Donald, EOD tech; Sergeant First Class Christopher Bunnell, team sergeant; Master Sergeant Rodney Acasio, medic.
JPAC photo—Derrrick Goode, photographer

15

A Life of Its Own

But the cost is great, and it will take a lifetime to dissolve the
mental, physical, spiritual, and financial mortgage.
—Stanley N. Dwyer in a letter dated April 22, 1944

Somewhere on the drive between the airport and home, reality set in. Physically in Nebraska, Rick and I wished we were still in Austria. Then, soon after reality set in, the daily routine cluttered my mind. Even so, every day, I thought about our unforgettable experience, the connection at the crash site, and the JPAC team still working in Austria.

"Just an update," Dr. Silverstein e-mailed.

We have moved excavations down to the lower portion of the grid and are moving toward the southwest corner area to wrap up for this season ... I cannot close the site; we will be back here next summer. There is the far side of the valley, and the metal detector survey below the crater came up with seatbelt parts and a lot of the thick Plexiglas (from the nose).

Today, just at the close of work (before Markus showed up with a case of beer for the guys), we found a U.S. Army (Eagle and Shield emblem) plastic button made of red plastic. Quite strange, and I do wonder if it had been coated in something more metallic before ... It is a mystery. Perhaps your dad has an idea.

I bought flowers today for Mrs. Auer. Her son said she is not expected to survive more than another week or two.

Dr. Silverstein wrote another day:

Today, working in that bottom corner, we found two bits of leather and three zipper parts as well as the usual flak plates and snaps … Tomorrow we will try to pay the Auer family for the use of their land.

Oh, and your cookies arrived, thanks from all!

Before our suitcases were unpacked, correspondence with our new Austrian friends began its unending flow back and forth. To this day, with translators standing by on each end, Mr. Stranz sends his letters in German, and I write to him in English.

"Today we have been at the crash site," Udo and Inge e-mailed. "I brought Stanley a wreath of pine. I did it by myself. What a peaceful and silent place."

Again, Dr. Silverstein e-mailed, "the latest headlines and gossip from Wiener Neustadt."

Doc wrote:

A general, Dr. Reinhard Mang, stopped by while we were not there. He left his card with a note and a wreath at the monument. The note reads, "My greatest respect to all who gave their lives for their country!"

Markus [Ladek] brought the guys a case of beer which he chilled in the stream. [He] also brought *Herr* Stranz back for a farewell. We all had a beer together and a photo session. *Herr* Brettner and Chris, the reporter, showed up, as well as *Herr* Piringer, who was proudly showing off the JPAC hat your father had given him. It so impressed the reporter that he kindly asked for a hat for his collection, as well.

Our last few grids did yield another uniform button … the plain, four-hole sewing button used on U.S. uniforms, and bits of leather, including a shoe piece with a lace tie fitting. I do think there is still a good chance of recovering remains at this site; it will just take time. As long as we keep finding things directly associated with the crew, I believe we should keep expanding the area.

We have patched up the hillside so that from the road you would not even know there had been an excavation. We set cement markers so the next team can match up the grid and begin right where we left off.

Wolfgang Losos came by yesterday and brought us a wonderful rum-coffee whipped-cream cake. He unraveled that melted mess of plastic we could not identify, the one that had the battery-looking piece attached to it. It appears to be a flare parachute. I had mentioned that possibility to your father, but he wasn't sure.

We miss you all. The team was a little low after you all left, but the thought of going home has reanimated them.

Around mid-September, after a six-week mission, the team returned to their families in Hawaii—for a while, anyway—before deploying on yet another JPAC recovery mission somewhere in the world.

"As much as we liked Austria, we were getting homesick and missed our families," Rodney Acasio e-mailed.

I am so glad that I got to meet your family. As many have already stated, it makes our missions worthwhile having the family on site while searching for our fallen comrades. The blood, sweat, and tears we endure [do not] go unnoticed when family members witness firsthand what JPAC members encounter on our missions ... Please let the rest of the POW/MIA community know that JPAC professionals are dedicated and are willing to sacrifice to bring our comrades home. I hope that what you have witnessed and the friendships you made will echo throughout to the other families still waiting for answers of their lost loved ones. Stanley was one of them, but will not be the last ... Until they are home!

Excavated grids in 2006. JPAC photo—Derrick Goode, photographer

"I started carrying a jagged piece of metal from the crash site in my pocket," Rick e-mailed back.

It reminds me of Stanley and his crew trying to "land" the B-17. I like to think that he lands it in the field above the ridge, but that didn't happen. It reminds me of all the wonderful people we met on the mission, especially the JPAC team—the chatter on the hillside, laughing and listening to your adventures while consuming an adult beverage or smoking a fine cigar, and your company and conversation over a tasty Austrian meal. When I touch the metal in my pocket, I think of the memorial stone, the crew members, and all servicemen who've fought for our country. Anyone who puts their life on the line while serving is, in my mind, a hero.

The dime went to the Central Identification Lab; however, we shipped home some other plane parts uncovered at the site, including some of the bullets, the ones that didn't have explosives in them. I keep one of the bullets in my pocket for a good luck charm.

As I mentioned before, the general population is relatively unaware of JPAC, and in this instance, the Boros family probably wouldn't have knowledge of JPAC excavating the site in Vostenhof or that there's a memorial stone marking where John Boros lost his life. Furthermore, in conversations with others about our search for Stanley and JPAC's efforts, funding for excavations sometimes entered the discussion.

In the late 1990s, a Senator Smith proposed legislation to fund recovery efforts devoted to the South Pacific. Later, the efforts were expanded to more World War II recoveries in general. I'd like to take my hat off to him. I'm sure many people think the money is probably wasted, but to the next of kin, it isn't.

"When you talk about money," Johnie Webb said, "it angers me to no end. It is clear that people who ask about money don't have a loved one who never came back home, because if they did, they would never think about the money. You can't put a price on that life.

"As a Vietnam veteran, there were a couple times when I wasn't sure I was coming back. One day, we were in a really serious ambush. I had six five-thousand-gallon fuel tankers on fire—fuel was running down along the ditches, and flames were everywhere. I didn't know if I'd be going home. I hoped that somebody would be doing this for my family. I'd hate for my family to think that nobody cared. I think it goes to what this country is all about, who we are as a nation—that we do value life, and we do value individuals.

"The moral fiber of our country is eroding every day. If we ever lose this, the ability to put forth the effort to bring people back home, we've lost a big part of who we are as a country. If we had enough money to send them into battle, we've got enough money to try to bring them home.

"One particular story reminds me why we do what we do. There's a box on my desk with a POW bracelet in it. The name on the bracelet is that of a young NCO killed on a helicopter during the Vietnam War. I got to know his mother and father very well. They were patriotic Americans, but over the years, they became very angry at their government because their son never came home.

Every year at the National League of Families meeting, I'd visit with the father. He'd say, 'Well, Johnie, when are you bringing my son back home? I don't want a bag of bones. I didn't give you a bag of bones. I gave you my son, and I want my son back and won't take anything less.'

"So I kept talking to him. Then, one year, JPAC went to the crash site and recovered some remains. And that year, as he always did, the father asked, 'Well, Johnie, when are you going to bring my son back home?'

"I told him, 'We went to his crash site and recovered some remains, so you need to prepare yourself. I'm going to return everything of your son that I can.'

"Well, he got very upset and said, 'I told you, I don't want any damned bones. That's not what I gave the army.'

"I talked to him several times. We talked for hours over drinks when I repeated, 'You need to prepare yourself.'

"A couple of months later, we identified his son and sent him home. I thought, 'Oh, boy. This isn't going to go well. Last time I saw the father, he was still angry with me.'

"However, soon after the young man's big military funeral, I received a little brown envelope in the mail with something in it. A very plain card with a POW/MIA logo on the front read, 'Johnie, I just want to thank you for all you have done for me and my family. We can never do enough to repay you for everything you have done. As a small token of my appreciation, this is my son's POW/MIA bracelet that I've worn for twenty-plus years and have never taken off. It's yours to keep.'

"Many countries don't look up to us anymore like they used to, but on this one issue, they do look up to us. They know we do it right."

After we'd been home several weeks, Derrick's CD of photos arrived from Hawaii. When the rainbow photo popped up on my computer screen, I immediately remembered our last day in Austria and Jennifer's "look."

Derrick had photographed a full-spectrum rainbow that arched unbroken, end to end, across the sky near the crash site. I couldn't remember ever seeing a more perfect and vivid rainbow. It gave me goose bumps. Our experience in Austria and at the crash site came rushing back, and Rick and I reflected on our search for Stanley. What was the ending of our journey? Our journey seemed to have a life of its own.

Yet, without remains, had we come full circle? Whether or not Stanley's crash site would be on JPAC's operational schedule again the next year hadn't been determined. Some sites require repeat field recoveries, and an existing site receives some priority in the selection process. So, while we anticipated Part II, we continued to digest Part I.

Extended family met in Scottsville, Kansas, to pay our last respects to Aunt Aileen. Her ashes were buried next to Grandma, her mother, in the Dwyer family plot. Cousin Mary Ellen and her two daughters, Sherry and Karena, had recently returned from Austria. They, too, went to the crash site but just missed connecting with the JPAC crew.

As the graveside committal concluded, Mary Ellen sprinkled dirt from Stanley's crash site on Aunt Aileen's and Grandma's and Granddad's graves. *Ashes to ashes, dust to dust,* I thought.

After the celebration of Aunt Aileen's life, Dad, Mom, Rick, and I compared Austria notes with Mary Ellen and Karena.

They had seen the memorial stone in Austria, so we talked about the memorial dedication. I told them about Maria, who was at the crash site on May 10, 1944, and how she remembered the little girls riding the unexploded bombs like sawhorses. I explained how Maria broke down telling us her story about the young men there that would never get to go home.

Karena offered some insight from a personal experience over ten years before.

"Mom and I decided to take a different direction home one day," Karena said. "As we came around a corner, there was an accident scene. It had just happened. One car sat haphazardly amid some trash and glass in the road, and another was facing a hill off the side of the road. We felt the strong need to pull over and help. Someone motioned to a woman inside the car facing the hill. I remember getting in the car from the driver's side to see if she was awake or what she needed. She had a trickle of blood coming from the side of her mouth, and no expression showed through her slightly opened eyelids.

"A man outside the car, with blood on his forehead, begged us to help her. He paced around the two cars. The whole feeling was of confusion and panic. Then the woman lay on the cold ground after being pulled from the car through the driver's side. Mom and another lady did CPR on her. The man with blood on his head was helpless and pleaded with them not to stop.

"More onlookers circled and desperately paced. So much energy and will was focused on the woman. Eyes searched the road for a glimmer of lights, and we listened for screaming sirens, some kind of help. Then the first tiny snowflakes of that winter fell. A female paramedic took my mother's place. We were dismissed to the side of the road to watch in the cold.

"When they gave up on saving the woman, she was left on the side of the road—shirt open, lifeless, and uncovered. Quietly, we waited a long time to see some kind of white sheet like a final signal of death. It never came. We waited for some kind of explanation. That never came either. Time marched on with one less person. Awkwardly, we just gave up waiting and left. An inescapable, abstract, dark sadness clung to us like a shadow no one else could see.

"We wanted to know more about the woman. Who was she? We watched the obituaries the following days and surmised from one that the woman's name was Lucille, and the man with the bloody forehead was her husband. It was important for us to personalize the experience, but that's all I remember learning about her life. I can still 'see' her death in my mind's eye like it happened a few weeks ago.

"Maybe the people that found Stanley's plane went through something similar and had a connection with the dead men they 'met.' My experience was nothing like the carnage they came upon. It seems like they were caring with the remains, seeing that the crewmen were buried and respected. Like our family, hopefully they now have a new 'light' in which to see the plane crash. The kindness and concern they showed then mean the world to families they never expected to meet. And maybe the memorial dedication and meeting the family helped them personalize their experience."

The Austrians we met were caring and helpful, and many knew or wanted to know the circumstances of May 10, 1944. When we were in Austria, a man by the name of Kurt Rieder had visited the crash site a few times, but we always missed meeting him. After we returned home, Kurt e-mailed us.

> I'm a copilot at Tyrolean Airways in Austria and fly a Dash 8 turboprop aircraft. I flew my first two hundred hours in the area of Wiener Neustadt. I learned the area in detail from above, also the crash site at Vostenhof. If you come back to Austria, it would be a pleasure for me to take you by plane above that site.
>
> I was always interested in planes, archeology, and especially World War II. My granddad lost two brothers in that war. One is

KIA and the other is MIA somewhere at the eastern front in Russia. We never found any hints about his remains.

I visited the crash place and tried to help him [Dr. Silverstein] identify some parts they'd found. I even offered to help him dig, but that wasn't allowed by the law ... I went back to the area mushrooming, and while looking for them, I can have an eye on other parts. I came back to that place again and again. Unfortunately, we never met.

On some days I found parts of the bomber far away from the crater, and since Dr. Silverstein told me he was interested in where the parts were blown away when the plane crashed, I just marked them.

When we were in Austria, Dad explored the hillside at the crash site. One time he found a "mysterious" arrow made from stones that pointed to aircraft wreckage. So, it was Kurt who had made that stone arrow to mark scattered airplane parts.

Kurt continued:

A few days before Jay Silverstein and the guys left Austria, I found an interesting part of the fuselage [in] the grass between the crater and the place where the JPAC guys parked their cars ... about two hundred meters away from the crater. There were no rivets on it, only tracks of welding on the inner side that was painted green.

I've just started working on a model B-17G ... and would like to make it look like the plane which crashed at Vostenhof.

Both Eugene Parker and Don Pratt confirmed the color of the plane. It was olive drab camouflage, and from underneath, it was grayish aluminum, not shiny metal.

Kurt was interested in the whole story about Stan, so we exchanged several e-mails. From the mission information we provided, he tried to piece together what happened to Stan on May 10, 1944, from a pilot's perspective of the area. Then Kurt plotted on a map what he thought was the possible flight path of Stan's plane, noting the locations where the crewmen that had bailed out were picked up. It was a small-scale map of the area, in German, which did show Vostenhof and surrounding villages. After Kurt took into account eyewitness Johann Piringer's version of observing the plane from his farm, he e-mailed us a revised flight path. The revised map was an actual photo of the area that Kurt had taken from the cockpit of his Dash 8.

Kurt and I posed similar questions but still could only speculate about Stan's flight path and what happened during the last minutes of flight. Some answers, more questions. I still think the airplane was trying to get back to the open space, but something gave out about ten seconds before they got there. Even though the flight path after the bomb run was generally to the south-southwest, Stan's plane was in a left turn headed east-northeast just before the crash. It's possible that a bomb exploded just before contact with the ground, explaining the extent of scattered pieces of the airplane. A view from the air might clear it up.

Dad e-mailed Kurt, "JPAC has scheduled another team back to Austria approximately August 1, 2007. That is the word we hear at this end. I must caution that it is still a military operation, and anything can happen to a schedule. But if they go back, we would like to return. Then I could fly over the area."

Kurt's maps refined our perspective of May 10, 1944, and even more of the story unraveled as time went on.

After Markus Reisner returned from a six-month tour to Afghanistan, he wrote:

> I instructed some of my friends to look for more evidence in your certain case. A week after my return, I got a call from a friend who visited with a man about the fightings at the end of the war around Wiener Neustadt. The man stated he has a pistol in his custody which was found at the crash place of an American B-17 bomber at Vostenhof. The pistol, an American 1911 Colt Cal .45 Browning, was found by locals after the crash. After some reservation, the man handed over the serial number of the pistol to my friend.

For my crew, I remember being issued pistols as our own personal property. If so, I'm sure they were issued by serial number. Eugene Parker didn't recall carrying a handgun and thought it possible that only their officers were issued a .45. That would be something if it happened to be Stan's pistol.

The Air Force Historical Research Agency at Maxwell Air Force Base archives some of the Fifteenth Air Force records. I was informed that any log recording the issuance of weapons was not maintained as permanent records. I preferred a different answer to my question. The .45 could have been a vital link to a possible identification, so just to be sure, I checked with the Colt Collectors Association about tracing the assignment of weapons to individuals. No dice—"an impossible task," so they said.

JPAC also followed the lead to the same dead end. "Serial numbers on machine guns are difficult to trace," Johnie Webb said, "and it's nearly impossible to find any records of weapons issued to personnel during World War II."

Nonetheless, a return trip to Austria was penciled in on our calendars, and we daydreamed about weekend visits to Austria to pay our respects at the memorial and to share a meal with our Austrian friends. Even though thousands of miles separated us, letters and e-mails connected our worlds. Johanna Stipsits enclosed a cross-stitched lavender pouch with her Christmas card, and Johann Piringer's grandson, Thomas, sent and received their English e-mails.

"Today we have been at the memorial," Udo and Inge e-mailed. "For one short moment a sunbeam fell at the plate, and it seemed like a mirror. Every visit for us is a special emotion when we reflect that on this place sixty-two years ago, five young men are fallen. And we are thinking about you, and we hear your voices."

Closer to home, next door in Cheyenne, Wyoming, at a family update, Mom, Dad, Rick, and I met with Johnie Webb and noted the scheduled date of the Vostenhof excavation on his calendar.

"We don't give up easy," Johnie Webb said.

More than we could ever express, we appreciated JPAC's efforts. We never expected a second team.

"World War II families are always appreciative because they never thought anybody would be doing anything for them," Johnie Webb said. "That's true of a lot of Korean War families; however, we're finding that Korean War families, because their war was considered the forgotten war and nobody cared, are angry that they're not getting parity with the level of effort with what we're doing with the Vietnam War."

Field recoveries were called off in North Korea in 2005 because of the political discord between our two countries. North Korea had opened their doors to JPAC in 1996. Between 1996 and 2005, the remains of over two hundred American soldiers had been recovered.

"The majority of our losses are in North Korea," Johnie continued. "But if I can't get into North Korea, I can't get into North Korea. To give you an idea, for the Vietnam War alone, there are about 190 sites we have approved for excavation, and we're approaching approval for about fifty sites from World War II. But right now, we identify more from World War II; however, we try to keep it fair and somewhat consistent."

Hopefully, the names of Stanley Dwyer and John Boros would be added to the list of identified World War II servicemen. And while organizing letters and memorabilia in Stanley's trunk, I filed Huretta Wright's photo along with some other pictures. Would she want to know what we'd learned about

Stanley's fate? Her life had moved on since May 10, 1944, so would she even remember Stanley?

After making some assumptions, a time-consuming trip into cyberspace yielded a marriage certificate for Huretta, divorce proceedings, another possible marriage certificate, and then the trail seemed to vanish. I was ready to cross the search for Huretta off my list.

And George Mitchell would never know the outcome of our journey. Even though he wanted to regain his strength to travel to Nebraska, George passed away less than a year after we visited him in Hanover, New Hampshire. But George's motto, "Keep the flame burning," still resonated.

George's friend and caretaker, Mr. Milne, wrote:

> George was always reluctant to talk of his war experience, but some years ago, when I applied for his veteran/POW benefits, I had to do a great deal of research. I had only heard George speak of his pilot, Stan, so that is where I began. That process finally got George to open up about the war culminating with your visit ...
>
> We both enjoyed the e-mail diary of your trip to Austria ... We spent a great deal of time his last weeks recalling his memories of Stan and his other comrades. I have no doubt he came to a peace with the war years ... May George and Stanley know the peace they deserve.

Meanwhile, from Austria, Kurt Rieder e-mailed on July 2:

> Today evening I visited the crash place at Vostenhof. I was surprised finding all these screens and barriers again—JPAC must be back. Unfortunately, it was too late in the afternoon and raining so nobody was there. Are you sure they were scheduled for the end of July?

Somewhere, wires crossed or schedules changed. Dad and I hustled to expedite our travel plans. Rick would follow later. Even though plans changed, Mom, suffering from a sinus infection, had already decided to stay home, and my sisters also wavered.

The abrupt schedule change affected one other person—Peter Soby. Pete, a photojournalist, had read a brief article in the *Omaha World Herald* about our search for Stanley. Intrigued, he called and met us and heard the long version of the journey. Pete offered to tell the story of Stanley and JPAC's efforts in short-form documentary, which necessitated travel to Austria for film footage and interviews. Neither JPAC nor the family nor Pete wanted to turn the excavation into a dog and pony show with media, cameras, and all the

411

hoopla. Following protocol, Pete and JPAC's public relations people worked out the details. And Pete, the only one of his crew, worked his magic and eked seven days out of his work and personal schedule for a visit to Vostenhof.

Dad and I arrived at Vostenhof, driving directly from Vienna. The closer we got to Vostenhof, Mt. Schneeberg, in the distance, beckoned. Every time I saw Schneeberg's rounded, rocky mountaintop, I thought of its twin—Mt. Baldy—a similarly shaped, barren, and flattened mountaintop near Grand Lake, Colorado, where Mom and Dad have a cabin. Colorado. Stanley had expressed his thoughts several times about the Rocky Mountain State. "I'd like to live there if I could, or at least near there."

We exited the Autobahn. The sunflower fields and cornfields gave the impression of a Midwest countryside. We continued off the beaten path and drove through familiar villages, passing manicured yards and everything-in-its-place homes and cottages. We circled our landmark—the colorful and picture-perfect flower garden roundabout. Finding our way to the crash site was like riding a bike—once you know how, you never forget. The peaceful serenity at the crash site was undeniable, and I felt that connection. Inge's wreath leaned up against the memorial stone. Another red crepe paper poppy I had sent Udo and Inge was faded but still attached to the screw cap.

If a guy had to pick a place, you couldn't do any better than right there.

The JPAC team already had a ten-day start, and they were moving dirt—lots of dirt. They dripped with perspiration because it was hot and dry. A wheelbarrow under each screen caught the sifted soil. A full wheelbarrow was then dumped on one huge backfill dirt pile. That pile was barricaded with dirt-filled burlap bags. Looking uphill, wood stakes and orange tape outlined—like a crime scene—the area excavated the year before. The current recovery team expanded the grid system from the taped-off area, mostly downhill.

Anthropologist and recovery leader Dr. Andrew Tyrrell led the nine-member recovery team. Right off the bat, Andy expressed his theories about the remains of the two missing crewmen. The possibility of Stanley and John's remains being removed from the crash site by locals and buried in an isolated grave concerned him. After a search of the local cemetery records, Andy learned that four of the five unknowns in the disinterred crewmen's common grave were German soldiers, but who was the fifth? And somehow, Gilhooley and Piper spilled out of the plane at the last minute; one partially intact body was found at the top of the ridge, and the other was found on the lower slope. Could John and Stanley have escaped before the crash and been buried elsewhere, or did they ride it in? Since the Vostenhof area of Austria was occupied by the Russians after the war, what was the likelihood of Russian soldiers burying one or two sets of American remains in a Russian-marked or unmarked mass grave? Always more questions.

Besides Andy, the other team members were Marine Captain Alex Vanston, the team leader; Staff Sergeant Edward Lee, team sergeant; Staff Sergeant John Johnson, EOD tech; Staff Sergeant Jody Ohmer, medic; Staff Sergeant Arian Church, photographer; Sergeant Mark Boyer, supply tech; and civilian Peter Weichselbraun, the linguist from Vienna hired by JPAC. Peter's wife, Judann, originally from Colorado, occasionally did some translating and screening. The day Dad and I arrived, repeat team member Kili Bald Eagle flew home to Hawaii due to a family emergency.

Excavating just below the bomb crater, the team had found pieces of gauges from the navigator's compartment, more flak jacket plates, some leather, snaps, shoelace string, Plexiglas, and a clip from a Mae West life vest.

The 2007 JPAC recovery team.
Back row from left to right: Staff Sergeant J. R. Johnson (John), EOD tech;
Peter Weichselbraun, linguist; Dr. A. J. Tyrrell (Andrew), anthropologist
and recovery leader; Staff Sergeant J. L. Ohmer (Jody), medic.
Front row from left to right: Sergeant M. A. Boyer (Mark), recovery NCO;
Staff Sergeant E. C. Lee (Edward), team sergeant; Staff Sergeant A. C. Church
(Arian), photographer; Captain A. J. Vanston (Alexander), team leader.

"The flak plates could have come from any of ten flak vests on board," Andy said. "The leather from a boot is a little more specific, something possibly related to the pilot or flight engineer. That's what we're looking for now."

Dad and I walked down the shaded, dusty, narrow road to where the cooling barrel of the machine gun was unearthed the previous year. While trying to get our bearings, two white butterflies flitted in and out of the shadows.

I wanted to snoop around that area, which was quite a distance from the bomb crater. Mentally, I had noted a pile of wood next to the road where the machine gun piece was found, along with the piece of spring coil and some brake drum. The spring coil meant the machine gun came from the nose of Stan's plane. My thought was if his plane had been burning from about twenty-three thousand feet, did it come apart before it crashed? It makes you wonder, too, about the possibility of an explosion before the crash. More theories and more questions.

Before we left the crash site, Alex Vanston, the team leader, asked Dad and me, "Did you screen last year?"

"No," we both said.

"If you want to screen," Alex continued, "we would train you and show you what to look for."

At last, we had the opportunity to pitch in and physically help with the task of bringing home the missing.

By the time we checked in to our rooms at Hotel Corvinus in Wiener Neustadt, Udo and Inge had left fragrant lavender in my room with a note that read, "To your 'second home.'" There was a familiarity in the surroundings, and Dad and I recognized employees' faces at the hotel's front desk. Other than the music of popular American hit tunes I grew up with, the lobby was quiet. The JPAC team had already relocated to an army training center in the town of Seebenstein fifteen miles from Wiener Neustadt.

The bells at the church down the street from the hotel clanged, marking the quarter hour, and for the remainder of the first day, we kept moving, fighting off the urge and need to sleep. At the train station one block from the hotel, Dad worked the ATM machine, and while waiting, I soon understood how someone could fall asleep standing up. The bakery, where we'd bought sticky, sweet pastries to feed the team working at the site the year before, was still located in the station. So we repeated the gesture for the second team.

Dad and I lost a day—we thought it was Wednesday when it was actually Thursday. Nonetheless, back in Austria for another field recovery, the philosophy remained the same—take one day at a time for yet another unique experience all its own.

My hair was combing into place nicely, and jokingly, I told Kay that it was a good sign. But I was optimistic about a good trip. The JPAC team was making a lot of progress, and the dry conditions seemed to be ideal for screening. They knew what they were doing.

And so Dad and I were recruited to screen. After dumping a bucket of dirt onto the screening tray, we shook it. *Scratch, scratch, scratch.* Debris slid back and forth on the mesh screens. Then, with laserlike focus, we inspected every fragment, large or small. Dad and I both wore gloves. Experienced screeners made it look easy. We caught on, but our tempo was slow. I didn't want to miss a thing.

I always like to help. Being able to screen, looking for my brother's remains, made the whole trip.

"Screening is the most important," Andy instructed. "With screening, you can systematically recover physical evidence. Bone is fibrous, and the textures on the outside look like those of wood."

While shaking a screen, Eddie, the team sergeant who had been in Baghdad when the statue of Saddam toppled, said, "Do you hear it—the sound of metal pieces in the screen? If you find something you think is important, hold on to it and show it to Dr. Tyrrell. He'll let you know how significant or insignificant something is. To me, everything is pretty significant. It's a piece of something that just may help put the rest of the puzzle together."

Someone on the team, usually Eddie, checked our screens before we dumped them.

Dr. Andy Tyrrell, in his British accent, explained, "The soil here is very hard, so the plane didn't create a large hole when it crashed, just a small shallow impression. Most of that was probably created by the explosion after the crash. The bedrock predates the crash, and nothing penetrated it. We're removing material that's developed since the crash. A large amount of material was highly fragmented and scattered across a very large area, and of course, that includes the crew members that were on board the plane at the time.

"When we find life-support materials—a generic term for material associated with the crew—we excavate a two-meter boundary around that area, and if remains are found, the area is extended to four meters to get the fullest possible recovery of the material. I must ensure that the evidence we find remains stable and doesn't deteriorate from the point of recovery to analysis back at the laboratory in Hawaii."

Linguist Peter Weichselbraun drove to the site every day from his home in Vienna, and he served double duty. Stepping away from his screen, he translated Hans Selhofer's version as an eyewitness. "I was an eight-year-old boy in 1944," Mr. Selhofer told us. "I came to the site the second or third day after the crash. It was roped off, and there were some large pieces. I lived at Burg 27, at the inn where the windows were shattered from the explosion."

He motioned with his hands toward the top of the ridge, the area above the excavation. The inn was located beyond that area. We speculated whether the explosion was above the ridge, therefore breaking the windows of the inn, or if there was a secondary explosion after the crash. It is something we'll never know, but it is part of the mystery.

Markus Reisner, Mr. Stranz, Mr. Brettner, Udo and Inge, and the Piringer family had already visited the site in the days before our arrival in Austria. Then Udo and Inge contacted Dad and me to go out to dinner. They were a welcome sight. We ate *wiener schnitzel*, drank wine, and talked for hours.

"During the war, I lived in Stuttgart, Germany," Udo said. "As a fifteen-year-old, I was part of the Hitler Youth. After the war, I would have to get up at 4:00 a.m. to go stand in line and wait four to five hours to get food. It was terrible times. We now know Hitler was evil. We were not just victims of the bombings; we were victims of our government.

"Before the war, the majority of Austrians wanted Hitler to come to Austria. Times were bad in Austria, and Hitler promised the people economic prosperity. Under Hitler's rule, the people did not know what his motives were."

"Then the Russian occupation from 1945 to 1955 was not good for this country," Inge explained. "Our wedding day is celebrated on the same day as the Austria National Day, October 26. We were married in 1959, but on that date in 1955, all foreign soldiers left Austria, which was especially important for the Russian occupation zone. In that zone, which included part of Vienna and the surrounding areas, there was no development, which was opposite the American, British, and French zones."

"But it is unbelievable that we should meet," Inge repeated. "We are from Austria, and you are from Nebraska, and it is important we come together. It is supposed to be. It is good for my soul and good for your [Harold] soul."

We sure would like to reciprocate their hospitality; however, Inge, traumatized by the bombing of her home during the war and the loss of her brother, doesn't fly. So in addition to the United States atlas we sent them, I introduced them to our part of the country with a subscription to NEBRASKAland *magazine.*

"It is important for us to go to the crash site often and think about the young boys who gave their lives," Udo said.

The JPAC team had permission to drive to the crash site down the isolated narrow, dusty road, and eventually, we followed suit. Along with a candle to burn in the lantern, Dad and I brought paper napkins to clean the lantern glass and tidy up around the memorial. General Flowers, JPAC commander, was in Austria and stopped by the site for a visit.

I thought it was a good gesture for him to come out and see the troops. When he found out I was from Hastings, Nebraska, he mentioned that his college team played football against the Hastings College team years ago. It's a small world. The general shook everyone's hand—the JPAC team working and all the locals that were there, including Augustin Stranz.

"Super," Mr. Stranz said as he photographed the event for his research records. Instead of his usual hour walk to the site from his home, MariaLoise Thannhauser, the vice mayor of the village, drove Mr. Stranz and translated our conversation. Mr. Stranz was interested in knowing more about the search from our side, and then he said, "I believe the bomb or bombs exploded after the crash. In my records, I have a handwritten note from Otto Mali, a man who reported that a bomb went off after he went running to the crash site."

The general observed the excavating work. As team leader, Alex explained to the general, "The recovery team is being environmentally conscientious, not using heavy equipment. We cannot take all the trees down and will restore the area to the way it was." Because of some rare, strangely grotesque black and yellow salamanders and other amphibians, the excavation site was in a protected area.

And so, without heavy equipment, backbreaking manual labor was the means of excavation. By then, the pit crew dug up ground on flatter terrain in the trees downslope from the bomb crater. They breathed dust, tasted dust, and it coated their sweaty, exposed skin. Even in the heat, the team stayed motivated and worked hard to achieve their goal of excavating thirty to forty square meters per day.

As we screened, Jody, the team medic, said, "We never know how the weather is going to be, and we only have so much time in country, so we have to stay on a time line."

"That means we have to sustain at least thirty square meters a day," Eddie added. "It's a pretty demanding job, so we've got to switch it up. I don't care how good of shape you're in; you're going to get tired. It's hot, and the dust might bother you, but these are pretty ideal conditions for what we're doing right now."

"We're looking for anything like buttons, snaps, anything out of the ordinary that doesn't look too much like a basic rock," Jody said. "What keeps everybody motivated is that we're trying to help find missing people. Sometimes you find a lot, and sometimes you find hardly anything when you're screening. Everybody has their own way to be motivated. You could find a tooth or human remains at any time during the day, and it makes you feel good to find things that will help people close areas of their past and help them move on with their lives."

Pete Soby, a salt-of-the-earth kind of guy, arrived in Austria and hit the ground running. A whirlwind four days of interviewing and filming gave him an up-close and personal look at JPAC's demanding work that supports their worldwide mission of bringing home the missing. Pete met many local Austrians and got a glimpse of the network of personal stories linked with our search for Stanley. JPAC Public Affairs Deputy Director Troy Kitch teamed up with Pete and also joined in the excavation work.

With his camera steadied on his shoulder and squinting into the plastic eyepiece, Pete filmed Andy sitting on the hillside at the site, balancing a screen on his knees and prudently inspecting small pieces of unearthed debris. "I ensure the work is done to satisfactory standards, not only to meet our own accreditation standards, but to make sure we are doing the job correctly so we can all go home and sleep well at night," Andy said. "Most of the large, easily identifiable pieces of wreckage would have been carted away and put in recycling very soon after the crash because the Germans were very short on material at the end of the war. Our major objective is to find remains so we can identify those remains, but pieces like the life support help answer questions too. So it gives me hope."

Andy was optimistic about a piece of radio headset uncovered in one grid. It resembled a piece from a small antenna.

I explained to him that, unfortunately, the piece of headphone was not unique to the pilot. Those types of headsets were worn during low-altitude flying. Since the May 10, 1944, mission was high altitude, Stan would have been wearing his leather helmet with the headset "built in." Communication throughout the plane was done with the low-altitude headset; therefore, there could have been ten of that kind on the plane. Small leather fragments turned up, possibly from a uniform or something else inside the plane.

Team members sometimes ate "to go" McDonald's hamburgers from nearby Wimpassing. During one lunch break at the site's "break room"—a table and some chairs protected with a tarp for a backdrop on one side and another tarp overhead—I opened a PowerPoint presentation on my computer about our search for Stanley. As requested, Dad and I explained our journey. Peter, the linguist, looked at the squished black letters on the page of Stanley's

MACR. Instead of our interpretation of "Vostenhof," the crash location read "Foestenhof," the old German spelling of Vostenhof.

Nevertheless, sixty-three years later, in a surreal episode in Austria at the place where his brother's life ended, Dad told the team about Stanley while they viewed photos of Stanley growing up in Kansas.

I've told this story several times. Stan liked to fish. One time, he caught a large catfish on the Solomon River that runs west of Asherville, Kansas. You know how fish stories go—it was probably about a twenty-pound fish. Anyway, Mom cooked it up and put it out on a table for the whole town to feast on.

I told the gathered JPAC team that being at the crash site where his life ended—it's hallowed ground for the Dwyer family. And the amazing part is how, over the years, everything fell in place. If this is the end of the journey, then we're satisfied. We're grateful to be here—all because of the efforts of JPAC. It gives us a good feeling.

While Dad was off walking the perimeter of the site and hunting for physical remnants of war, other stories surfaced. Linguist Peter and I met another man. Translated, he said, "In 1944, I was five years old. I came here after the crash with my grandfather. We wanted to get some rounds from a machine gun, but the police had roped the area off. The crewman down low looked like he was asleep. Grandfather felt the fabric of his uniform, and it was good-quality fabric. People were curious, and everyone was encouraged to look around for useful items—raw materials and bone for soap—which we delivered to the school for collection."

I must have had a funny look on my face. The man said in English, "No, no, just animal bone, not human bone." He stepped closer to me and said, "I'll tell you, my father was a Nazi. It was unlucky times."

That was the way of the world back then. In desperate wartime survival mode, how do you respond to dire circumstances?

At the end of another workday, while the team packed their gear and loaded into their van, Johann Piringer, his son, grandson, and some friends arrived at the crash site. Dad perked up, shook hands, and Mr. Piringer's eyes twinkled, and his broad smile emphasized his rosy cheeks.

"I wondered who that guy was hugging Harold," Pete Soby said. "Then I was introduced to Johann. Harold and Johann acted like two people who had been boyhood friends."

Pete positioned his camera. Thomas, the grandson, translated.

"I think about this nearly every day," Johann answered Pete Soby's question. "There was not really a fire because the bombs blew out the fire. There was just a lot of smoke. I didn't see anyone jumping out of the plane."

We were invited to the Piringer home for cake and drinks.

Johann's story became fine-tuned every time I heard it. Once again, from the hillside near his home, Johann explained to Pete what he saw on May 10, 1944. It became clear that my brother's plane was between Johann and his neighbor's house—the house the plane actually curved to miss—not on the other side of the house. The plane, within four hundred yards of Johann, flew at treetop height.

"I will never forget it," Johann said. "I was standing right here, and then I ran down the hill. The pilot was good. That was the house where he was flying low to the ground, very low to the ground. He didn't hit the house; he saved lives and didn't drop the bombs."

I didn't realize the plane was so close and so low to the ground. So he did turn and missed that house and probably saved the people inside. I imagined myself in the left seat of the airplane and wondered if Stan had any other options besides what happened, which is all supposition. He almost made it. I'd say he was within two hundred feet of making it to the ridge he was going back to. There had to be quite a bit of stress with one side burning hard ever since they were hit with flak at approximately twenty-three thousand feet. Anyhow, he came close to making it.

"Did you see anyone in the plane?" I asked Johann.

"No, no," he answered. "I looked up, and it was gliding. I saw it smoking."

While Dad walked to the farmyard with Johann, Pete shot more footage of the small valley. I pointed out to Pete the hidden crash site between where we stood and the hills in the background. Then I walked to the farmyard and looked around for Dad. Someone pointed to the secluded picnic table in the shade. When I peered around the screen of trees, with wine glasses held high, Dad and Johann toasted, "*Prost.*" I didn't need a translator to understand the expression on their faces. I was a little uneasy thinking about my eighty-two-year-old dad drinking wine on an empty stomach and barely hydrated.

Small groves of trees protected two sides of the picnic table area, and branches arching overhead shaded the table and affected the temperature. Pete put his camera away and joined the group. Thomas joined the party, too, and translated.

"My American slang confused Thomas," Pete said. "I think I said, 'Oh, that's bad.' So then Harold tried to explain to Thomas that sometimes kids say 'that's bad,' but they really mean something is good. When Harold's glass was nearly empty, Johann filled it up."

After the second bottle of wine, Dad toasted Johann. "To my other brother." Dad put his arm around Mrs. Piringer, Josefa, sitting next to him and said, "That makes you my sister."

Josefa served cake, and Pete helped Dad's cause by drinking wine too. I guess I was the party pooper. Being the designated driver, I guzzled juice and water. *Prost!* Josefa went to the house and brought out sausages and more snacks and laughed when she showed Pete and me the worms from the cherries floating in a bottle of her home brew.

"We were fearful of the American fighter pilots because they strafed homes and haystacks," Johann said.

Dad explained, "The fighter pilots' objective was to eliminate the enemy, and sometimes antiaircraft guns were hidden in haystacks."

"After the war, the Russians occupied, and we didn't know whether we were safe or not," Johann told us. "It was horrible times. One day, some of my family and I were almost shot by the Russians, but I wasn't afraid. We lived here one day to another."

"*Prost,*" Johann toasted with Dad after he opened a third bottle of wine. "I am always happy to be with you. We have the same attitude. Come back again."

"It was incredible sitting and drinking with two eighty-year-old guys," Pete said. "Johann and Harold did not speak each other's language, but they could understand each other with hand signals and expressions. For Harold, Johann was the last guy who saw his brother. And Johann probably thought, 'Hey, I'm the last guy who saw Harold's brother.' The light that went off in their eyes was what made their incredible bond."

That night, I made sure Dad got to bed. That night was also a first—the first time I'd ever seen him in that condition. In the middle of the night, more than once, I tiptoed down the hall of the hotel in my pajamas to Dad's room to check on him. The air conditioner in his room worked overtime, but the air conditioner in my room didn't work at all. It was like stepping out of the Sahara Desert and into the North Pole all in a matter of thirty steps. I missed Mom for a lot of reasons, and that night was one time.

As imagined, Dad was not too perky the next day, so he rested at the hotel. But by evening, we went for dinner. Near the hotel are remnants of a twenty-five-foot-tall stone wall—crumbling, broken sections of wall which, centuries before, had surrounded and protected the town. That was before bombers clouded the sky—penetrating the front line—and bombs rained on the city. They say mostly women rebuilt the demolished city. Narrow cobblestone alleyways intersected one-lane streets. Dad and I stepped around gathered groups of people on wide sidewalks and saw our reflections as we peered into shop windows. Arched passageways led to still more cafés and shops. A newly opened ice cream shop became another favorite. Yellow, green, gray, and red stucco buildings with steep-pitched, red-tiled roofs and blooming window boxes outlined the central *platz*. The twin towers of the eight-hundred-year-old stone cathedral, one of the few structures that remained standing in Wiener Neustadt after World War II, projected above all buildings.

We dined at Café Siegl and first ordered water. "No gas, please." Even though it was "wet," drinking carbonated water is an acquired taste. We preferred ours "regular."

I thought about Pete's interviews earlier that day at the crash site. Alex told Pete, "The team has good morale. As team leader, I set little goals and try to stay positive."

"You have to have a little self-motivation," Eddie added. "But a lot of times, we keep each other going by laughing with each other and cracking jokes."

Other days, we, too, laughed at their humor. And Arian, the team photographer and the only female on the team, often was on the receiving end of the jesting and jokes.

"Since she had grown up with a bunch of brothers," Peter Weichselbraun remarked later, "her retorts were not timid at all."

And most days while the team worked, they played made-up word games.

Alex had challenged Dad, Pete, and me to become members of their make-believe Kelly Green Village "club."

"There are no hopes, dreams, or wishes in the Kelly Green Village," Alex said. "There are also apples but no oranges, teeth but no mouths, puppies but no dogs, kangaroos but no joeys, Halloween but no Christmas, and Allah but no Jesus."

On the drive from Vostenhof back to Wiener Neustadt, Pete Soby and I repeated the clues and racked our brains. No hopes, dreams, or wishes … terror but no fear … floors, walls, and roofs, but no ceilings.

That night during dinner at Siegl's patio area, Dad and I put on our thinking caps. In order to join the "club," we had to solve the riddle and come up with five more examples. While we ate, we watched mothers pushing strollers around the *platz*, while older children laughed and chased each other. I repeated the clues out loud; then we caught on. Later that evening, we tried out one of our clues on Pete—pepper but no salt.

"You figured it out?" Pete asked.

Every day was still an adventure. Starting work early in the cool morning, the team practically mowed through the dirt, sometimes achieving the goal of forty meters by midafternoon. Usually, it was hotter than blazes by noon. Music played aloud at the site, almost setting the tempo for the pit crew.

"What kind of music do you like?" Mark Boyer asked me.

"I grew up with the sounds of the Beach Boys and Motown," I answered.

"Our music is probably just noise to you," he said.

I smiled. The same kind of noise Mom and Dad probably considered Motown.

Except for the standing trees with exposed roots, the bald hillside had been excavated down to the memorial stone and tree line above the narrow road. The pit crew scooped and dumped dirt into the buckets and hauled them from the lower grids across to the screens set up downhill. While they sifted, screeners played an alphabet game. I showed Andy a piece of dark leather the size of my palm with an eyelet or snap on it. I wondered who might have worn the leather article or piece of boot.

The grids down low were yielding less and less. Andy conferred with Dad. "We found this. It looks like a handle of something. It might be the charging handle of a machine gun. Do you think so?"

I examined another piece of something. It's hard to know for sure where on the plane it came from.

When the time was right, I offered the required five new clues for membership to the Kelly Green Village "club." "Butter but no bread," I said. "Coffee but no cream, moon but no stars, streets but no cars, and kiss but no lips." Dad smiled and said, "Booze but no hangover."

No official membership cards were issued, but Alex said, "Here's another one to solve. It's at the beginning of eternity and the end of time, at the beginning of the end and the end of every place."

Markus Ladek, the local game warden, came by the site again and showed me the mechanism the antiaircraft units used to set the altitude on their gun shells. The mechanism, the ballistic cap, was a fine piece of workmanship. The gun battery chief was responsible for measuring the range and calculating the speed and angles of the artillery they aimed at Allied bombers. Near the end of the war, the Germans were running out of fuel, but it seemed they had plenty of ammunition.

Markus drove Dad, Pete Soby, and me up to a plateau to look down over the valley. The heat made Dad a little weary. In the distance to the right, we saw Mr. Auer's home and the open, sloped field above the crash site. In the opposite direction, Markus pointed to a castle in the hazy distance, the area of Stixenstein near where Eugene Parker had been picked up after he bailed out. The distance between the two, the castle and the crash site, was only about three to four miles via a direct line—closer than we imagined. But, according to eyewitness accounts, Stanley's plane, flying in a southwesterly direction, circled back before it crashed on the hillside. On our back roads tour, Markus noted that his mother, Maria, had lived in those hills during the Russian occupation, when the women went to hide. And then he pointed southwest.

"For the airmen, home was that way—over the mountains," Markus said.

The bomber boys of the Fifteenth Air Force knew their way home to Italy. Many made it there. Some didn't.

And back at the crash site, Mr. Stranz told Pete Soby in an interview, "It was a surprise to the Austrian people when the Fifteenth Air Force from Italy began bombing their cities. Hermann Goering told the Austrian people that Austria was the Third Reich's air raid shelter—no one could ever reach it.

"One should not forget it was not the U.S.A. that declared war on Hitler but that Hitler declared war on the U.S.A. after Pearl Harbor. If the search reveals bones or teeth, then the family can bury the remains at the family grave at home, and he would be much closer. This is understandable. People from here have gone to Stalingrad to look for the graves of deceased husbands, fathers, and brothers, or just to visit the monument there. It is quite understandable for the memorial to be erected here by relatives. Family members lost their lives at this spot. It is super that the U.S.A. makes this effort, even if it is a long time past."

In another interview, Inge told her story to Pete Soby and concluded by saying, "This is the story about Inge, my soul. It's my life. Although it was difficult at times, it was possible to live my life. I found my husband. I found my peace now. I am at peace."

"Me too," Dad said to Inge as he hugged her.

"I live in freedom," Inge continued. "My life became great, and I live in freedom. Not many people can say 'I live in freedom.'"

"Unfortunately, the whole world forgets," Udo commented. "This has been a great process of learning because all the problems from the war came back to the surface. Both sides suffered, but before I read Markus Reisner's book, I knew everything from just one perspective. In Europe, the German and Austrian public knew a single-sided view—that only we suffered from the outcome of the war. But that is wrong. The Americans have suffered too."

One day, if or when Markus's one-thousand-plus-page book is translated to English, I'd like to read it. Curious, I once asked Markus what the message was from his book. "It's on you to decide your future," he answered.

Udo continued, "And most important, if America did not enter the war, we would not sit here right now. We would have a dictatorship in Europe, and it would be completely different. It was our own fault, not the Americans' fault, that they bombed. Only through fighting can you repress governments that are trying to take control. You can't take over a dictator with words or sanctions, but with war."

"Why should young Americans die here?" Inge questioned.

"Here at the crash site, it is a calm place," Udo continued. "In the wintertime, it is lovely here. It's a good place for remembering. We do not like to think about the horrible times, but think about the good times now. We come to the memorial and say a prayer and hope that it brings peace to everyone and the family."

"God bless America," Inge remarked.

And what was it Stanley wrote about war? "It will take a lifetime to dissolve the mental, physical, spiritual, and financial mortgage."

"For me," Andy said, "an important part of JPAC's mission is the renewed interest, a public reminder of the story of what that person did, that we don't forget what was asked of those people and what they did for us. It's incredibly important for us to keep being reminded of that fact. One thing that keeps this job interesting is the fact that I'm constantly encountering stories about people and about incredible events and things other people went through."

War was reality for millions, and the stories of suffering and sacrifice were endless.

Living in Vienna, Peter Weichselbraun, the linguist, had read about the previous year's excavation and knew the circumstances. He said, "I was contacted purely accidentally through a chain of acquaintances who asked if I would be interested and available to work on short notice as a linguist for the JPAC team. I immediately agreed.

"The strong motivation to agree lay in my own family history that flashed back into my memory. The first husband of my mother was home to spend Christmas 1940 with his wife and his four-month-old daughter. Later that year, he was wounded as a motorbike messenger in the advance on Leningrad. In a letter to my mother, he stated that he was worried that she would not recognize him or want him anymore as he 'looks different.' It seems that half of his face was blasted off as he had ridden onto a land mine. His worries turned out to be futile. The hospital tents, clearly marked as Red Cross, were bombed, and my mother was informed in 'proud grievance' that she was a 'warrior's widow.' She was close to twenty-two.

"One of my mother's rarely mentioned wishes was to eventually travel to the Leningrad area and at least visit the large war cemetery there. It never came to that. My mother raised my sister alone throughout the war years and married my father in the late 1940s."

The cost of war, in foreign "currency," too, yet the grief's the same.

"Pictures I'd seen on CNN came to mind—pictures of young women in their early twenties saying good-bye to their husbands outside Texas bases," Peter continued. "The father of my American-born wife, Judann, joined to go to war in Korea when he was nineteen.

"I reckoned the emotional element of my small (and late) contribution to the possible peace of one or two American families and to the possible recovery of their missing family members would far outweigh the assumed nuisance of spending a traditional vacation month in a remote forest with assumed mosquito and tick attacks.

"Well, in a remote forest, there's not a lot of interpretation to do. The physical labor is challenging for someone expecting to be a linguist, but in the context of the task, very, very satisfactory."

"It's a pretty interesting journey Stanley has you taking," Pete Soby commented to us. "The people you have met ... the lives that have been touched ... it is amazing."

It's been an amazing journey. We think the world of the people we met in Austria.

And no matter where you travel or what sights you see, it's the people you meet along the journey's way—and Stanley would be included on the list—that you remember. Our unplanned journey was a humbling experience. Among other things, it intertwined history and the lives of ordinary people. And our journey had its own life. So we held on for an unpredictable ending.

At the crash site, visitors were few and far between. Dardis McNamee, a reporter from *The Vienna Review* and friend of Peter's wife, Judann, scheduled an interview. Father Leopold, who conducted the memorial dedication the year before, stopped at the site. And Dad and I finally met Kurt Rieder. Kurt showed Andy the spot near the bomb crater where he had found a piece of what he thought was part of a pilot or copilot seat, but it was no longer there.

"For World War II cases, this is an unusually large crash site," Andy explained. "It is similar to sites excavated in Vietnam—fast movers that scatter across a large area. The secondary explosion here at the site scattered and fragmented everything. It is difficult, also, when a long amount of time elapses between the event and now. We have a general idea of what happened soon after the crash. What transpired in the last sixty-some years is hard to determine. It is hard to reconstruct what happened and develop a strategy. Basically, this has become a search by excavation. We're searching a large area, hoping to find remains."

When Kurt wasn't flying, he spent his time off searching remote areas for crash sites. Flying over the site with Kurt didn't work out, but he explored the area with Kay and Pete Soby before joining us for a team barbecue in Seebenstein, at the team's living quarters, the same place we'd toasted Marine Captain Vanston's birthday.

Markus Reisner's vacation time didn't coincide with the 2007 excavation schedule, but he arranged to join the group at the barbecue. Arian, the team photographer, talked about her infant son at home in Hawaii, and John Johnson told snippets of an EOD tech's responsibilities as an attachment to the Secret Service and State Department. Team Sergeant Eddie retired early in order to be rested for the demanding work at the site.

"This is the first time a family has ever come out," Mark Boyer said. "It's good to hear their side of things and the story and history surrounding the people you're looking for. America doesn't forget the people that have come before."

Markus said, "It's good, especially for the people in the armed forces. If you get killed, at least years later, a branch will look for your remains and bring them back."

Andy said, "Our missions give today's military assurance, when they are called to go into combat, of how far their government will go to find them if they find themselves, heaven forbid, in this kind of situation."

Markus had e-mailed me during his six-month tour in Afghanistan. He told Pete Soby, "I worked in Psychological Operations, and it was a challenge—let's say it that way. I worked a lot with the Americans, and I have deep respect for the work you guys do. It was a good experience to see that against all the voices you hear all over the world, you guys tried to make it better for the Afghan people."

After only a few days in Austria, Pete Soby returned to Nebraska, Rick arrived in Wiener Neustadt, and Dad was running out of steam. Restless nights in a freezing cold hotel room, as well as the heat during the day, zapped his energy. Our room reservations at Hotel Corvinus could not be extended. We anticipated a last-minute cancellation to continue our stay there, but that didn't happen. Instead, we relocated, with Kurt's help, to Hotel Freizeittempel near the airport. Their efficient room air conditioners kept Dad comfortable, and he liked the nearby McDonald's. The lady at the front desk described the wireless accessibility. She said, "It goes through the air in the room." And it was reliable at no extra cost.

Occasionally, Rick and I stopped at Mr. Stranz's tailor shop. We traded research and photos. Mr. Stranz gave me statements from other eyewitnesses. And without the linguist, we communicated with hand motions and gestures, saying "yah, yah." Translated remarks from eyewitness Otto Mali read, "One of the B-17s, which one could see from afar, broke out of the formation, lost height, and seemed by its flight to be in a drunken state. My grandmother, who stood farther away from the house, yelled at my grandfather and me that we should get out of the house quickly because the plane was coming directly toward us. The plane circled a couple times over Gasteil and Tanaschach [in the area over Saubachgraben and west of Pottschach]. Grandmother feared it would hit the trees and then strike our house. The pilot apparently recognized the same thing and tried to avoid the crash by getting a motor started and got the plane back up by doing that, made a right turn, and crashed into the nearby woods. The Ehrenboeck family, visitors at the neighbor's house, stood in front of the house and watched the event. Mr. Ehrenboeck and I decided to search for the crashed plane ... As we were on the way to the disaster site, there was a large explosion near us. We immediately sought cover in the trees for protection from falling debris. A short time later, there were other explosions, and then we found ourselves 150 meters from the crash. It was a horrible sight. At the edge of the crater lay one dead American soldier, who apparently had a hand ripped off. On the other side of the slope, there was a parachute hanging in a tree with a dead soldier ... Mr. Ehrenboeck and I were the first ones at the miserable site, and it was impossible to offer any help."

Another page from eyewitness Josef Teix read, "It was Wednesday, May 10, 1944, we sat in our parents' home, Gasteil 16, ready for lunch ... Around 11:00 a.m. the radio was interrupted by a cuckoo call (alert) ... A little later, one heard the sirens howl, another air raid alert ... We went to the cellar for the first time. Many splinters of flak and rounds from the cannons made staying in the open very dangerous. Standing in the open cellar door, we watched what was happening. All at once, there was a deafening roar, and smoke came over our house. It was a burning bomber ... But with the explosions coming from the bombs, we soon went back into the cellar. At first we believed the plane must have landed in our field. Then we saw a cloud of smoke from Voestenhof ... My brother Ludwig and I went out toward the smoke and immediately found the crash site. Of course, it was not totally safe because we did not know if there were still unexploded bombs to be found ... We saw two dead soldiers ... Parts of the plane were strewn all over. One of the four motors had been thrown by the explosion a short way into the meadow near Saubach. Both of us immediately began to look if there might be something to salvage. In the meantime, the police from the Pottschach office showed up and closed off access to the crash site ... After that, almost every day we went to Saubach looking for something that we could secretly carry home in our pants pockets. What interested us most was the isolation of the motor and its cables from which we made a stone catapult." (When I was back home in Nebraska and rereading the translated eyewitness reports, I wondered if Johann Piringer knew either of these men. Johann confirmed in an e-mail that he knew both men. On May 10, 1944, Josef Teix was his neighbor and lived in the house Stanley's plane curved to miss.)

We were always hopeful that some remark from an eyewitness would give another clue and more answers.

From the information of all eyewitnesses, we could piece together darn near most everything of Stan's mission up to the last moments of flight. And it was evident that the crash site had been picked over, which supported Andy's theory of remains being removed from the crash site.

Whenever I found bones in the extended perimeter at the site, I flagged them for Andy. Most of it was animal bone, but Andy bagged some osseous material laying on top of the ground above the crater and at the edge of the excavated area. Andy first thought it was animal bone, but lab tests in Hawaii would make the final determination. The grid was then expanded.

The team had moved uphill, about two-thirds of the way to the top ridge, and excavated on a considerably steeper incline. The hillside remained slippery even in the dusty, dry conditions. A screening station was set up on the incline and draped with some netting, providing shade. Rick learned the mechanics of screening.

Rick said, "Even though it's repetitive work, you have to stay focused and pay attention to tiny details. You couldn't let anything slip by. It was good to participate rather than standing around watching everyone else work. I always hoped that I would find something significant."

Again, Andy sat on the sloped ground and sorted the unearthed artifacts deposited in his screen. I joined him and watched as he inspected piece after piece. He explained, "Dog tags are much more resistant to environmental conditions. I look for rolled edges on any metal pieces that are found. It is a bit of a mystery to me why nothing is showing up."

I had been thinking about one of Andy's theories, the one concerning whether or not Stanley and John escaped the plane before it crashed or if they rode it in.

While Andy examined some twisted metal, I commented, "If I know the character of Dad, Granddad, and Stanley from his letters, my opinion is, dead or alive, Stanley rode it in. And it seems John Boros, heroically, stayed behind to help his comrade." Then I asked Andy, "Did they vaporize?"

"It is incredibly hard to destroy an entire human body," Andy said. "There will still be fragmented pieces, and under harsh environmental conditions, it will take proportionally less time to decompose the bone. At this juncture, I have to determine when to say enough is enough and sleep at night with the decision."

"Rick and I have discussed why we were led here," I said. "Was it to find remains, to erect the memorial stone, or what? It's a daunting challenge to explain it all or even understand everything, but considering the big picture, the healing and peace people have experienced is profound."

"The dead don't bury themselves," Andy said. "Ultimately, it's all for the living."

Yet it was obvious that JPAC didn't give up easily.

"The odds of finding anything at sites over sixty years old are stacked against you," Eddie said. "But there's always a chance you will find something. It just depends on where it's located and how much activity has been in that area. But you always go into it optimistically thinking you are going to find something. Because you never know—the next bucket you dump into the screen might be the one that's going to do it for everybody."

Alex said, "Finding remains can come any time on a mission, and we try to stay positive. If you find something, it is a great feeling. It brings it all together, and we know we've done something to make a difference. But if no remains are found, it's not failure because we have exhausted all means possible. We go home knowing that we tried. Here at this site, there is not much to find. Even so, time, distance, and cost are not factors because you can't put a price on the sacrifice of a human life."

However, little by little, Dad became antsy and was ready to go home.

It was so damned hot. I was uncomfortable and not feeling good. I had somewhat made up my mind that they were not going to find anything. There wasn't much more we could do.

Meanwhile, meeting the Valenta family boosted our moods. One evening, Dad, Rick, and I dined at Mom's favorite café, Hobl and Scher, in Wiener Neustadt. The restaurant is located in one of the fourteen buildings that withstood the city's wartime destruction.

When Darlene and I ate at the café the year before, our waiter Marco talked about acting, his horse, and his participation in Civil War reenactments. I hadn't forgotten about him. Marco recognized me again the second year and invited us to have dinner with his family. At their home, with a John Wayne plate collection hanging on the wall, you could tell his mother, Beatrix, was a big John Wayne fan and an American Indian buff. Marco showed us his four or five complete Civil War uniforms. Marco knew more about the American Civil War, and Beatrix knew more about Indian wars in our country, than the three of us combined.

Front and center in their home in Neunkirchen, a floor model jukebox played American golden oldies. We met Marco's dad, Rudy, and Marco's sister, Karin. Beatrix—her official Indian name is "One Who Walks with the Buffalos"—showed us her Indian-beaded deerskin clothing that she had made, as well as photo albums of their travel in the United States to places like Ft. Kearny, Nebraska, as well as South Dakota, Wyoming, and Montana.

Over dinner on one of the evenings we spent with them, neighbors Wolfgang and Susi joined with the Valentas and discussed their favorite topic—America—and anticipated their next trip to our country. Our mission to Austria was to uncover part of their country's past history, but we felt like we were at home.

Wolfgang shared his grandfather's Nazi papers and other documents he had picked up at yard sales. "The German Reich required people to record their heritage for five generations to make sure there was no evidence of Jewish roots," Wolfgang said. "The document to prove your Aryan heritage was called *Ahnenpass.*"

"The Iron Cross was awarded to soldiers for success on the battlefield," Beatrix said. "The Mother's Cross was blue with white enamel and was given to women having many children for Hitler."

Beatrix explained that if a woman had four to five children, part of the Mother's Cross was bronze. Part of the cross was silver if a woman had six to seven children, and the cross was decorated with gold if a woman had eight or more children.

"The German and Austrian people were more afraid of Hitler's SS than of the enemy," Karin added. "Hitler allowed the SS to do anything."

The discussion continued into the evening. They recounted more of their country's history and were interested in our search, eagerly visiting the crash site another day.

"I know it is possible for people to live on in the hearts of the ones who know them, and I thank God for that," Karin said.

The excavation continued upslope on steep terrain way above the crater. It was still dusty and dirty but a little cooler. Markus Reisner stopped by the site a time or two. Markus had his theory about the crash. He concluded, "Stan, still at the controls and maybe assisted by Boros, tried for a last time to get full power on all engines to avoid hitting the trees before touching the heavy plane down on its belly in the meadow. Already too slow, the plane stalled and roared to the ground.

"There was no huge crater because when the plane impacted it was not impacting at a vertical angle but a more flattened azimuth. If the plane had crashed in a vertical angle, there would have been a deeper crater. The bombs would have gone through the cockpit and penetrated the soil at least for several meters before exploding. But it was not like that. The plane came in nearly 'parallel' to the slope and the ground before it went into a stall and nose-dived over the left or right wing into the ground. The fuselage disintegrated on impact. The bombs ended up 'on top' of the soil and didn't explode immediately. The safety pins were already removed, but the propellers of the fuses were still fixed because the bombs hadn't gone through the air and gotten 'hot.' The crash was followed by an explosion of the gas in the tanks and that ignited the bombs. The trees around the crater were put down by a shock wave caused by exploding bombs—bombs laying on the surface."

Team members continued to dig up ACW, but no life-support materials or evidence directly associated with the two missing crewmen was found. Eventually, the lower grids were swept down, photographed, and documented before they were backfilled—more backbreaking work. One bucket or wheelbarrow at a time, the huge pile of sifted soil disappeared. The bucket brigade passed off buckets, and the last person in line heaved the dirt downhill. Using rakes and hoes, the team spread the dirt over the expanse of excavated grids and tamped it around naked tree roots. The pace continued.

"The plan is to move across the stream, to the other side of the valley where the flyer's glove was found last year, and excavate four or so grids to see what might result," Andy said. "The excavation is focusing on areas where we're most likely to find remains, but with this site, it is difficult to put a limit on where it begins and ends. We are less likely to find a concentration of remains the farther out we extend. Therefore, the question is when to close the site. Are we getting anything more for the level of effort?"

So, our time—Dad, Rick, and my time—in Austria was coming to an end. Dad had a brief bout with the "green apple quick step," which cancelled our tour to Hitler's Eagle's Nest and, on top of everything else, swayed our decision to go home a few days sooner than planned. While Dad rested at the hotel, Rick and I went to the crash site. As we drove past the floral roundabout landmark, I pointed to the Russian cemetery Pete Soby and I previously searched out—a small plot with mass graves and headstones we couldn't read.

Rick and I stayed at the site after the team left. We sat together on a hard boulder while I had a meltdown. When the breeze moved the treetops, sunlight streaked through the valley. Birds chirped, and chatty squirrels scampered among the trees. The calm of the forest was momentarily interrupted by a deep, rumbling noise that grew louder as it came closer.

"It's a logging truck," Rick said.

In an imagined flashback to May 10, 1944, the roar of Stanley's plane in the valley must have been deafening, consuming the serenity and silencing the sounds of nature. But instead of dwelling on that scenario, we reflected on the peacefulness at the crash site and our journey and search for Stanley. Remains were elusive, and unanswered questions persisted, but maybe in another realm, Granddad and Grandma knew all the answers. We sensed that Stanley and John Boros were somewhere. But where? They were in our hearts and minds, of course, as well as in the hearts and minds of those who'd indirectly been introduced to both of them. One thing went without saying—Stanley's memory was alive.

It was time to say our good-byes to all of our kind and caring Austrian friends and the JPAC team. We went to visit Johanna Stipsits, without the linguist, and we bumbled through the German-English barricade. Once she recognized us, she greeted us with open arms and a big hug, exclaiming, "Nebraska." Somehow, she communicated that her husband, Ignaz, was hospitalized. Johanna called her son on his cell phone, and he explained to me, in English, his father's serious condition. Ignaz passed on within days, and Johanna mailed us a notice from the funeral service.

And Udo and Inge stopped by our hotel before we went to the team dinner.

Looking into Dad's eyes, Inge softly cradled his cheeks in her hands and said, "I thank God I met you. Have a good life."

Old enemies, new friends. Surely that was the way it is supposed to work—in our case anyhow.

"You are my adopted sister. I have no sister," Inge said to me while we hugged.

Inge's unselfishness and forgiving heart gave our search life. I am grateful that our paths in life crossed. Udo and Inge's friendship is a unique treasure. Because of their generosity, support, and loving spirits, our lives changed, and, we believe, Austrians and Americans together found peace.

"*Servus,*" Udo and Inge said to us.

"*Servus,*" we replied.

Then the team joined us for dinner on the back patio of Hartigs in Wiener Neustadt. Markus Reisner, sitting next to Dad, sketched out the home he was building. Everyone visited and joked. Judann even showed me the children's book she had illustrated.

"To freedom and those who fought the fight," Rick toasted.

The team added yet another dimension to our search to find Stanley, and I thanked them for their service to our country and for all their hard work.

The team presented Dad with a plaque that read:

433

In recognition of outstanding support, this certificate of appreciation is awarded to the Dwyer family. This certificate is in recognition of the outstanding support you provided to Recovery Team-Two, Joint POW/MIA Accounting Command, during Recovery Mission 07-01EU in Vostenhof, Austria. The presentation you shared with the team allowed us to meet 1st Lt. Stanley Dwyer and served to personalize this recovery mission in a way recovery teams rarely experience. Additionally, your presence on the site served as a constant reminder of the importance of our efforts. The support you provided was vital to our mission of returning our nation's fallen heroes to their families with honor. Dated: This 27th day of July 2007.

"We're just going to say thank you," Dad said. "You've done what you can, and we're appreciative of the effort. I have nothing but respect for you and hope you can continue with your job of bringing home the missing."

The excavation expanded to four marked-off grids on the other slope, a much steeper slope, a challenge even for the most sure-footed. Nothing much was showing up in the screens. Melancholy set in as Dad, Rick, and I stood at the memorial one last time, but the time had come to leave the hallowed ground. I reflected, *we came close but couldn't get it done.*

Deep in thought, Dad walked off down the narrow dirt road. When Rick and I joined him, he said, "We did what we could. So be it."

One last time, I glanced up the slope to the top of the ridge where sunshine peeked between the trees next to Mr. Auer's open field. I lamented about what Dad had said several times, "Stan almost made it." When we returned to Nebraska, I explained the scenario to friend Steve Einsel in Hastings, and he commented, "Stanley did make it. He didn't back out of the ship and let it crash wherever. He laid down his life to protect people unknown to him in enemy territory. Another generation is playing joyfully in the field because of Stanley. Though painful for Stanley's father, he knew what his son did. It was his finest day, but Stanley lost his life making it."

16

◦◦◦

"Coming Back to Kansas"

I'll be a midwesterner by choice, not by inheritance or something else.
—Stanley N. Dwyer in a letter dated April 21, 1940

Back home in Nebraska, I sorted through more odds and ends in Stanley's trunk and still detected a slightly smoky, musty odor. I read and reread some letters. Janice Cuthbertson wrote Granddad from California on August 6, 1945:

> I won't try to comfort you. Even if I knew how, it wouldn't help. I just want to thank you for writing to me so generously these past many months, and now that the last vestige of hope seems to be gone, to beg you to believe as I do: that up there in that ship, Stan found his "happy ending."

Of course, the folks wanted to bring Stan's remains back to this country. And our search evolved to where we hoped we would have something to bury and bring my brother back to Kansas.

Even though my folks lived the last thirty or so years of their lives in Nebraska, Dad was a Kansas man from start to finish and didn't mind showing it. In about 1945, he wrote a tune titled "Coming Back to Kansas," and dedicated it "to each and every Kansas man and woman in uniform, and to my two bomber pilot sons, Stanley Dwyer, missing in action the past ten months, and Harold E. Dwyer, on duty somewhere overseas."

> I am coming back to Kansas,
> She's my first and bestest flame.
> She's a little short on shoreline,
> But I love her just the same.
> When we've sunk the other navy

As we're doing true to form,
I'll be coming back to Kansas,
She's a port in any storm.
Land of built-in sunny skies,
Where we grow our own supplies;
Where a man, if he half tries,
Can always live until he dies.
Then I think I'll anchor me
There midway from sea to sea.
That spot suits me to a T ...
Dear Kansas Land!

I am coming back to Kansas,
And I'll bring this foxhole, too,
To be sure of solid comfort
When the day's work is all thru.
She's a land of milk and honey,
More of real and less pretend.
I'll be coming back to Kansas,
Right below the rainbow end.
When we've polished off these yegs;
Broken them from sucking eggs,
Please believe me, these old pegs
Will work as wings instead of legs.
Then I'll marry my best gal;
Dig in there with my best pal,
Just halfway from Maine to Cal ...
In Kansas Land.

I'll be coming back to Kansas,
When this global war is o'er,
But for now we're flying missions,
Pole to pole and shore to shore.
On we drone, alone,
We're on our own till rendezvous or base.
We're a world, apart, a planet
Revving on thru endless space.
Here we hobnob with the stars;
Pal around with Old Man Mars;
Show the Pleiades our scars,
But watch our p's and q's and r's.

436

And we sometimes, winging thru,
Twist a comet's tail or two.
But I always think of you …
Dear Pal of Mine.

Dad went so far as donating to a journalism memorial fund at K-State College, and I vaguely remembered the service Dad and I attended in Manhattan, Kansas, in the '50s. There were some papers in Stan's trunk about the journalism memorial fund. Supposedly, pictures of the K-State journalism students and graduates who were war casualties hung in Kedzie Hall on the campus. It was dated information, so Darlene, Rick, Kay, and I made a trip to Manhattan, Kansas, to see what we could find.

Darlene and Rick waited in the car while Kay and I, once again, walked into the right office in Kedzie Hall, the Journalism College—Stan's old stomping grounds. After walking the halls and looking for a plaque and some photos called the "Honor Roll," we stood in front of an office door.

Dad said, "Let's ask her."

Journalism Professor Gloria Freeland took immediate interest in our mission, made several phone calls, and eventually—after she and husband Art Vaughan sorted through storage closets during spring break—located a bronze plaque in the campus chapel. Since both Gloria and Art have stories to tell of their own and others' genealogical adventures, they understood and were curious about our journey.

Gloria e-mailed me what she'd written for her *Snapshots* column published in the *Riley Countian*, "First, if our military can spend hours in remote places searching through mounds of rubble to locate a trace of a lost serviceman, what are a few hours in a cozy office? Second, Stanley was a young man who gave all he had to serve his country, so setting aside some time to honor that service doesn't seem like much to me."

Kansas State University, previously named Kansas State College, solicited donations for a World War II memorial to be constructed on campus. Stanley and his other colleagues who perished in the war would be honored and memorialized by their alma mater. Unable to attend the groundbreaking of the memorial, I almost kicked myself when I realized, after the fact, that soil from various individual graves and cemeteries was collected in a wooden box and symbolically placed beneath the memorial as part of its foundation. I guess the dirt I bagged from Stanley's crash site would be saved for another day.

Coming full circle would mean burying Stan's remains in the Scottsville, Kansas, cemetery. We didn't have the official word from JPAC, yet we were pretty sure we were not going to have any remains. Coming back to Kansas—it probably meant we would put up a monument or headstone for Stan at the cemetery in Kansas where my folks and sis are buried.

When that happens, following Cousin Mary Ellen's example, the dirt I have from the Austria crash site will be sprinkled over the family graves.

The JPAC teams tried hard. No one is left behind if it is physically possible. They moved a lot of dirt and put a lot of effort into it. We got two crews, and we're very thankful for that. They're probably as disappointed as we are that they didn't come up with anything.

Christmas Day. Josef and Johann Piringer relight the lantern at the Vostenhof crash site memorial. Photo courtesy of Johann Piringer.

"A lot of debris was removed right after the crash," Johnie Webb said. "Clearly, people have been through the area. It's a mystery because, even if someone had been in there, usually small fragments are still found. I think they are somewhere. I've been to too many crash sites, and we should have found something."

When the recovery at Vostenhof was completed, the combined work of both JPAC teams excavated approximately half a football field (see Appendix F). It seemed like they had moved half the hillside.

Meanwhile, Austria was only a thought away, or an e-mail, or even a letter from Mr. Stranz along with his winter scene photos of the memorial and forest area. And I kept thinking about our conversation with Wolfgang, Beatrix's neighbor. He'd shown us and told us about the old German papers and documents he had found at yard sales in Austria. Therefore, I often wondered what, if anything, from the crash site might appear at a sale. Maybe Stanley's or John Boros's dog tags?

It would be a small miracle if anything substantial would ever come up, but considering all the other coincidences, who knew? Even if somebody had picked something up and put it in their attic to pass on, the next generation, not knowing what it was, might throw it out.

It was a long shot, but in an e-mail exchange with Beatrix, I mentioned the possibility of crewmen's dog tags showing up at yard sales.

"Every Saturday, Susi and I go to flea markets," Beatrix wrote. "Maybe we can find some personal items from American soldiers. We'll have a look."

The Piringer family e-mailed, "A few days ago, we got our first copy of the magazine you are sending us and in which we love to browse and enjoy the pictures of your land. Attached we send a photo at which we drink to you and your health. *Prost!*"

Johann's family sent another e-mail, including photos taken at the snowy crash site. One photo showed the five red poppies I'd sent Udo and Inge hanging from a branch of greenery slipped between the memorial stone and plaque. Some of the Piringer family pictures, taken on Christmas Day, told a story. "Brother" Johann, solemnly holding his illuminated lantern, stood in the snow next to the memorial stone. It appeared that Johann relit the candle in the memorial's lantern, then he and his son Josef posed there together. "We got your great Christmas card with your family on it," they wrote. "We see it as a special present and put it under the Christmas tree. A peaceful Christmastime to you all from Family Piringer."

"We are just back from the crash site," Udo and Inge e-mailed. "We brought the soldiers a wreath of pine and a candle for the New Year and said our prayers. Snow is there and the little stream is frozen. We could see a few little pines on the place where JPAC has worked. Maybe Mr. Auer has planted those young trees. And we thought again what a horrible incident happened sixty-four years ago and what nice people we have found here. When we are there, we are very close to you. We never forget you."

439

Several months passed, and Johnie Webb sent the teams' final reports. We understood almost everything. Anthropologist Dr. Andy Tyrrell's theory regarding the identification of the unknowns interred with the three deceased crewmen was resolved. According to Peter Weichselbraun, the cemetery records revealed all five unknowns were of German origin. And, from the report, Pottschach cemetery records were not available for the time period during the Russian occupation. And the material report on the glove was inconclusive.

What about the graves in the Russian cemetery Pete Soby and I found? At another one of Dad's 34th Bomb Group reunions, Dad, Mom, Rick, and I met John Gray, an analyst and field researcher for the DPMO's U.S.-Russia Joint Commission on Prisoners of War/Missing in Action group. I had previously sent a request to the National Archives for any Russian text dealing with World War II losses in the Vostenhof vicinity. In light of my request, John Gray told me, "Russian documents pertaining to your request, if they even exist, could possibly be in the central military archives at Podolsk, Russia, or in the KGB archives. Records for mass graves are probably nonexistent because the Russians didn't care. So much is out of our control." However, he forwarded my request to four Russian nationals—researchers in the former enemy country—for review.

I e-mailed John a photo of a headstone from one mass grave located at the Russian cemetery near the crash site in Austria. John translated it to read, "High Glory to the heroes who have fallen in battle for honor, freedom, and the independence of our great country."

"Recently, an American was extracted from a mass grave site in Hungary," John said, "and pulling teeth is like a church picnic compared to what we had to do to get the information on the Hungary site."

"We're having a little difficulty getting the Russians to cooperate right now," Johnie Webb later told me.

Nevertheless, according to JPAC's final report and Johnie Webb, the crash site was "closed," which meant unless new information turned up regarding the remains of the two missing crewmen, there would be no further excavation work. But the dime was returned to us, something tangible and meaningful from the crash site, and something that connects us to Stanley. And now, I think twice whenever I take a dime out of my billfold. Stanley is not forgotten.

So, were we at the end of the road? The perceived sentiment was one of "hanging in limbo." Had we dotted all *i*'s and crossed all *t*'s? We assumed that any more information to uncover was in Austria, and the prevailing thought was the remote chance that Stanley's remains were buried someplace else as an "unknown" or in an unmarked grave. However, we were at a disadvantage living thousands of miles away and not speaking the language or knowing the culture.

In order to denote the second recovery team in 2007, Markus Reisner and "the Viking" agreed on a slight engraving change to the memorial plaque. Then Markus e-mailed a follow-up to the mystery of the crewman's pistol:

> I talked to the guy who found the .45 at the crash site. He said he found the pistol about twenty to twenty-five years ago. And now the thrilling thing of it. He said he is 100 percent sure that close to the pistol he found some remains of a piece of scalp with some hair on it. I questioned him several times, and he always insisted that he was correct.

Markus's news was intriguing and made us wonder again how much more information was "out there."

In a phone conversation with Johnie Webb, he said, "It is still possible, after many years, to find soft tissue below the surface, especially if the area was saturated with fuel, because petroleum preserves biological material. There are a couple of pieces on this case we're still working on."

"I spread the word that the Dwyer family is still interested in learning more about the fate of the two crew members," Markus said. "The Austrian people (young and middle-aged) are open, that's for sure. The older ones, especially in the country, are more silent. So, maybe over time, more news will come out. I don't know. The important thing is that his family presented Stan with a local memorial. This will always bring his death back to the people who pass by."

Furthermore, the powers that be seemed to be at work again. One day, my friend Steve told me that there was a man by the name of Malcolm who wanted to meet us. Malcolm and Steve had recently met through a mutual acquaintance. Since Malcolm resided in Vienna, he had read about JPAC's efforts at the crash site, and because Steve knew our side of the story, the connection was made.

"Malcolm would indeed like to help with various investigative assessments," Steve said. "Malcolm is not doing this for any other reason than his desire to help you in this tremendous undertaking. Malcolm was quick to memorialize the thoughts that his father, too, fought the Second World War, with all the suffering that entailed for his family, and now, he just simply wants to help—as it is right and proper to do so. It seems to me as if Providence is simply playing a very beneficial hand in your family's search for Stanley."

In a conference call with Kay and me, I asked Malcolm to assist and follow up on loose ends and any new leads in Austria. It was great to have him on board.

"War does funny things to people," Malcolm said. "Memories and fears are quite long in Austria. I am honored to be entrusted with a small part of this task and feel that in doing so, I can also reflect my father's respect for those who didn't make it back."

And still, the journey seemed to have its own life. Malcolm's interest and assistance was appreciated. He certainly was in the right place to talk to people, hear earlier statements, and follow any new leads, plus he had the skills and ability to connect any dots. JPAC would be notified of any further information.

"I get e-mails daily from families who have researched, looking for more leads," Johnie Webb said in a phone call. "We want resolution."

So if something of significance turned up, that would be the icing on the cake. Nonetheless, we were feeling satisfied that we gave it our best shot.

Some things we'll just never know but are part of the story. You've got to be satisfied. What else can you be? The government tried hard, and we've explored about every avenue that we possibly could to see if we could find some remains. In my brother's case, you have to believe he was sitting on a five-hundred-pound bomb when it went off. The immediate circumstances before that don't really make much difference—that's the way it was. But you can readily see why, after over sixty years, there are not many remains to be found. That's the history of a lot of soldiers that were close to explosions. It was fulfilling to be at the crash site. If we get nothing more than the memorial in Austria, then that is good enough. We tried. We feel most grateful for the good old U.S.A. to put forth the effort.

Without conclusive answers and without remains of their son to bury, Granddad and Grandma filled the void with hope. And now, without a trace of remains, we relied on answers. Answers were the trump card.

Pete Soby and his co-producer, Brian Mastre, attended a DPMO family update in Chicago and interviewed Ambassador Charles A. Ray, then director of DPMO and deputy assistant secretary of defense for POW/Missing Personnel Affairs. Mr. Ray said, "For a lot of families, getting answers represents a form of closure. Most families realize that, after passage of so much time and because of the particular circumstances of the loss, we're not going to get physical remains returned. But, if we can come up with a logical, coherent answer as to what happened and why those remains are inaccessible, that's a form of closure too. And so I wouldn't say that failure to get remains is failing to get closure. Failure to get remains, in some cases, is understandable, and not just World War II but in Vietnam with high-performance aircraft. If you've ever seen footage of what happens when aircraft going at a high speed meets a solid object, there's very little left, and people realize that.

"Therefore, it's not just the location and recovery of remains that's important. It's the filling in the story, filling in the blanks, this gap in the family history—what happened to this family member who went away and then suddenly wasn't there anymore. I'm reminded constantly when I meet people that until a family gets answers, this never goes away for them. It's a family that has something missing; they have a hole in that family they want filled in.

"People are surprised and pleased that there's an element of government that would do something which reaches out to help families achieve closure. Truly, government is for the people. What we do is for the people. It's for the people who sacrificed. We're honoring the sacrifice they made. It's for the families. The families gave. The families give their sons and now, as we see from casualty lists in Iraq and Afghanistan, increasingly, their daughters, and we owe them something other than a tax bill. We owe them some repayment for what they've given. I just think that the minimum level of responsibility for government is to honor when people give. We should be prepared to give back.

"We're honoring what they gave the country, but in a general way, it's for the American people, as well, because what we do serves to remind people in this country that the freedoms we take for granted weren't free. They came at a very high cost. The freedoms that we enjoy in this country were, in fact, purchased by the blood of patriots, and we [our organization] are a constant reminder to people of just how fragile these freedoms can be and just what it costs to get them.

"I've always had the feeling that governments are supposed to exist to serve the people, not the other way around. And so, when someone has gone out and sacrificed that much for a country, it's the tab the government gets for repayment for that service."

To visit the crash site after so many years and to piece together what we could of Stan's last mission brought closure for me. Like I've said before, being at the crash site where his life ended ... that's hallowed ground for the Dwyer family. And to erect the monument at the crash site puts a nice final touch to be remembered for as long as I live. It's been an amazing journey ... amazing in how, over the years, everything fell in place. It just seems like it was supposed to happen, and we're glad it did.

Reflecting back, the memorial dedication in Austria offered finality—the kind of feeling you get after a funeral. It provided an ending—for the living, anyway—a point from which to move forward.

Dave and Jane Hughes agreed, "Sometimes it's the process that's more important than the end result."

Over ten years ago, opportunity knocked one day in my kitchen. It was the right place and the right time. And God opened doors. The process led us down an unseen trail, filled in many pages of the unfinished chapter of our family history, and the serendipitous experience exceeded anything we could have ever been tempted to predict or plan. Remains became the hoped-for end result. Yet the answers and insight we learned about the May 10, 1944, mission and Stanley's fate far outweighed the mystery of decades-old unanswered questions that at one time eluded Grandma and Granddad and the family. Besides, one other dimension of our search was to know Stanley, and the process—the journey especially—set the stage for the discovery of Stanley, the person.

I now know my brother better than I ever did.

In addition, this experience provided Dad closure; however, for me, it was more of a discovery, a unique way to know Stanley, the uncle I never knew.

Stanley was not tucked away in his trunk anymore. Now, instead of a fading memory, Stanley's memory is alive. Stanley is not forgotten. He became the catalyst. Because of him, people found peace, made reconciliations, and came to terms with their scars of war. It seems Stanley made a difference for people and friends he knew as well as those who met him along the journey's way. Lives have changed, mine included.

I've heard it said somewhere, "It's not how a person dies, but how they live."

Stan loved his country and had a strong sense of right and wrong, just like our dad. From some of his merchant marine escapades, Stan certainly was adventuresome and wasn't going to let life pass him by. He made the most of the circumstances in which he was placed and created opportunities for himself. And he understood the value of education both inside and outside the classroom. He was poorer than a church mouse, but he didn't let that stand in the way of his ambitions. He aspired to be a broadcaster. With his foresight, it would have been real interesting to see where and what he would have gone on to if he had survived the war.

In Stanley's words, a timeless thought, "Ah, yes, money is fine; it will buy fine clothes and cars, etc., but it can't buy the satisfaction one derives from accomplishments through his own efforts, the thrill of seeing one's self work gradually from the bottom to the top."

Stanley embodied the Midwest work ethic. And in his twenty-seven short years on earth, he accomplished much and earned the respect of those who knew him and those who came to know him.

I remember Dr. Silverstein commenting that they'd heard so much about Stan that they almost felt like he could walk out of the hotel room and meet us.

Dr. Silverstein said, "There's every indication, from witness statements, from what we saw archeologically, what the survivors said, and statements you collected, that Stan Dwyer and John Boros performed heroically, and they ended up sacrificing their lives in order to save their crew and their aircraft. I have nothing but the greatest admiration for those guys."

Stanley may have been poorer than a church mouse, but he was rich in character. He was a wholesome young man with a sense of humor. He modeled integrity, seemed to be a quiet leader, and cared for his family and fellow man. Stanley had a refreshing perspective and optimism, and throughout all three hundred plus of the letters he wrote, he didn't complain. The way Stanley lived his life is an inspiration to me.

"I'd like to sit down and drink a beer with Stanley," Pete Soby said.

"And smoke a fine cigar," Rick added.

Janice Cuthbertson wrote in a letter to Granddad, "I would do well to pattern my life after some of the ideals Stan stood for."

Again, the words of Stanley's friend, Ralph Lauper, came to mind. "They just don't make medals heavy enough to fit men like my friend Stan. I came to learn that personal honor and integrity were to him as valuable as life itself. He proved that to me one day in a bomber over Austria. He could have cleared the ship if he had been content to give his crew less of a chance, but he knew why he took over command of those men and that ship, and by heaven, he lived up to the trust. What more can a man do?"

The search was winding down, or so we thought. So far, we hadn't attended one of Stanley's 463rd Bomb Group reunions. Yet, in the fall of 2008, Dad's 34th Bomb Group celebrated their twenty-fifth and final reunion in Washington, D.C. Several family members made the trip. It's humbling to hear an esteemed veteran tell a story or two about a mission, recount the tireless work of the ground crew, or recall the trauma of life in a POW camp or the fear and suspense of evading the enemy with the help of partisans. It's one more way to keep life in perspective. Indeed, their service and sacrifice should always be acknowledged and remembered.

While we were in D.C. for the reunion, Rick and I liked to eat breakfast at a small, cafeteria-style diner next to our hotel located near the nation's capital's historic monuments, memorials, and Arlington Cemetery. We carried our trays and sat down at a long table with veteran Ken Paxton and his wife, Kathleen. The man sitting next to me wasn't wearing an "official" name tag of the 34th Bomb Group, so I introduced myself and asked him if he was a veteran attending the reunion.

"Yes," he said. "My name is Bill Cheek."

We made small talk, and then I asked Bill, "What position were you?"

"I was a tail gunner on the B-17," he said.

"Oh, you were like a rearview mirror back there in the plane all by yourself," I commented.

"Yes, I crawled along a narrow catwalk from the waist of the plane to the rear and sat on a piece of wood shaped like a bicycle seat—it had a little padding—with my knees folded under and behind me. For a nineteen-year-old, it wasn't too much effort. It was just me in the back of the plane with my two machine guns mounted side by side.

"There was this one mission; it was April 7, 1945. After we dropped the bombs on an ammunition dump in Gustrow, northwest of Berlin, we made a turn to fly back to England. Our plane was the trailing one in the formation, tail-end Charlie. I had just relaxed from the strain of going over the target when I noticed tracers in the air from at least two other gunners on other bombers in our group. I wondered what they were shooting at. Then I began to see a German Me 109 fighter coming in straight and level toward me. If you can picture it way back at the end of the plane, the German fighter was coming at us from high. The gunners in the other bombers had a different profile—they saw him curling down into a dive. All I saw was the round area of his engine and a straight line on either side for his wings. And oddly enough, my pilot or copilot hadn't given any warning over the intercom about bandits in the area. But every gunner's obligation is to protect his plane and his crew.

"The rate of closure between a fighter and us was very fast. Our airspeed was around 160 miles per hour, whereas the fighter was probably flying maybe three hundred miles per hour. There wasn't much time for me to do anything, but I squeezed off three short bursts real easy. The German fighter plane flew right beneath us, and I saw the German pilot's head—he'd been hit—leaning against his canopy as he passed underneath, just missing us. My ball turret gunner followed the fighter down, and it crashed.

"It all happened in a matter of a few seconds. There was no time to think about it; you just react or you don't live to tell about it. To me, it was obvious the fighter pilot's intent was to ram our plane. He hadn't fired at us because I didn't see the flashing from the guns in his wings. Yet, for twenty-five years or more, I still wondered why he was coming in on us and not firing. Eventually, I heard a little bit about German fighter pilots ramming the bombers that day like Japanese kamikaze pilots in the Pacific, but for some reason, the Eighth Air Force never mentioned much about ramming.

"I'm hoping to talk to someone else here at the reunion that flew on that mission."

Well, I happened to know someone who did fly on the April 7, 1945, mission to Gustrow—Dad. Dad had written his version to his friend Don.

After I read the book The Last Flight of the Luftwaffe *and their suicide attacks on the Eighth Air Force, 7 April, 1945, I looked in my flying log book. The date seemed familiar, so I began putting two and two together. Sure enough, it all finally added up.*

"April 7, 1945—Field order 1914A. Target for today—Gustrow, Gy." That didn't mean much to the assembled 34th Bomb Group crewmen who were to fly the mission that day. What the briefing officer said next did get most everybody's attention. "You don't have two extra groups of P-51s assigned for top cover just to give them practice." That meant fighter opposition—and quite a bit of it was expected. We flew the mission—eight hours by my log book—and yes, we did see some German fighters. One especially came right in front of us from right to left and blew up about two hundred yards in front. Just after the explosion, a P-51 crossed right where he had been. He had blown him up right in front of us, which was kind of strange because no airplane, enemy or friendly, turned his nose toward the bomber stream without being fired on. The Germans had captured enough Allied aircraft that they sometimes used them to get at the 17s and 24s. But this guy was hot on the tail of the 109 and wasn't about to lose his "kill" because a bunch of gunners were going to be firing at him. He made it.

The other incident happened when we were in formation, and I was flying on the right side of our element leader. I glanced over my left shoulder and saw a 109 coming at us from the eight o'clock position, from high above with his guns blinking. I looked back to the airplane that I was flying off of to make sure we were holding our position in the formation, and then I glanced back at the fighter. He was still coming in, but the guns were not firing. I took my eyes off him for another look at the 17 we were flying off of and glanced back once more at the German fighter. He was much closer but had rolled left and was headed down. He didn't ram, for which I am really grateful. I saw two enemy fighters make a pass at the group ahead, and they each got a 17—both bombers blew up right in formation. Other than that, the mission was routine, and we returned safely to England.

The pilot of that 109 decided at the last minute that there was more to life than taking out another 17, especially that late in the war. In the book that I mentioned, the last mission of the Luftwaffe was flown by what was left of the pilot pool—some young, inexperienced guys just barely able to get the ship in the air, plus all of the old-timers that were left. And it should be noted that those pilots all volunteered for the mission. Their briefing officer said they expected a 90 percent casualty rate, which turned out to be overestimated. They were given just sixty rounds of ammo with the orders to ram when they were out of ammo. Since the Germans were running out of planes, fuel, and pilots, it was their last-ditch effort to knock out our bombers. The German loss rate was about 67 percent—approximately 104 fighter planes. The Eighth Air Force lost close to twenty planes, but when you add it up, with nine-men crews on the bombers, our casualty losses were higher. It took sixty-plus years to realize how close we were to being one of the unlucky ones.

So I told Bill, "I'll have to introduce you to my dad, Harold Dwyer. He flew on the April 7 mission."

I mentioned to Bill the book that Dad had read about the *Luftwaffe*, and Bill told me about a declassified narrative he had of the mission, but he did not have it with him. So we exchanged addresses.

Bill said, "I live in the hills of North Carolina in the summer and Lakeland, Florida, in the winter."

The wheels in my head started to turn. *Lakeland, Florida.* "Bill," I said. "This might seem like a crazy question, but do you know of a Huretta Wright that lives or lived in Lakeland?"

"Are you serious?" he asked.

"Yes."

"I went to high school with Huretta Wright," Bill answered. "We worked on the high school paper together."

I stared at Rick, who was sitting across the table from Bill. Bill's response nearly took my breath away. Bill knew Huretta and believed she was still alive. Rick and I tried to give him an abbreviated version—if there is one—of the Stanley-and-Huretta connection and why I asked the question.

My response was, "For Pete's sake." There are three hundred million people in this country. What were the odds that Rick and Kay would eat breakfast with someone who knew Huretta?

Later, when Dad and Bill met and discussed the April 7 mission, Bill agreed to be an intermediary and make our introduction to Huretta. Would Huretta want to revisit her past? There seemed to be a little life left in our journey. I guess it never was our game plan. Our chance acquaintance with Bill reminded us, again, that instead of constantly steering the journey's course, we were often just passengers—along for the ride and going with the flow.

A couple of months later, Bill called me and said, "Huretta was receptive to your request to contact her, and she is waiting for your call. It seems she had been very much in love with Stanley and thought her life would have been completely different if they'd been together."

Dad suggested I make the first contact.

I had to carefully think it through. The challenge was whether or not and how to explain some background information about Grandma and Granddad's loss, our ten-plus-year search for Stanley, including finding her letters, well—it doesn't fit in a nutshell. The search was because of Stanley and about Stanley—and his relationship with Huretta—so that, more or less, became the focus of our first conversation.

"After I talked to Bill, I thought maybe I'd lost my mind," Huretta said. "I told my sister Vetra [who Stanley had mentioned in a letter to his folks], 'You're not going to believe my phone call.' I wondered if I'd had a vision or if it really happened.

"I met Stanley when I worked for the city. I ended up working there for thirty-five years. There were many different groups in and out of Lakeland training, even British cadets. Our family entertained quite a few—just friendships, no romance—and Mother was delighted to feed them.

"I knew Stan's plane crashed and felt he had gone down with the plane. Stan would have been the last one off the plane. He would not have gotten off unless everyone else was off first. We knew of other crashes; it happened frequently, even in the wooded training areas of Florida.

"I was in love with Stan, but he never came home. Stan was easygoing but could put his foot down if he had to. My fourth husband was the most like Stan—a little laid-back. I kept trying, but the best one got away. It was unfair Stan was gone."

I called Huretta a few times so she didn't think we were a flash in the pan. Getting to know Stan's girlfriend was another link to getting to know him better. Eventually, Darlene and I got some of our health issues behind us, so we traveled to Florida and met Huretta.

The morning sun drenched south Florida. Soaking in the warmth, Dad, Mom, Rick, Pete Soby, Brian Mastre, and I stood outside a brick house on a corner in Lakeland, Florida. The welcome mat said, "Wipe your paws." Dad rang the doorbell. No answer. He pushed the button again. Then he knocked on the wrought iron storm door.

A petite lady stood in the doorway. In her 1940s' portrait that I had found in Stanley's trunk, she styled her hair in loose curls—dark curls. The dark curls had grown white.

"Hello," Dad said. "Are you Huretta?"

"And you are Stanley's brother?" Huretta asked. "Your first name is what?"

I told her my name was Harold and introduced everyone else.

"Hello, Huretta." I shook her hand. "I have talked to you on the phone."
"We are friends, then, aren't we?"
"Yes, we're friends."
Bill Cheek walked up the sidewalk.

I introduced Bill to Pete and Brian and told them he was the one guy in three hundred million—that's how we found Huretta.

We gathered in Huretta's living room to visit.

Bill said, "In our senior year of high school, Huretta was the editor of our school newspaper, and I was the business manager."

"Did you and Stanley know you each had writing interests?" I asked Huretta.

"Stan had a broadcast journalism degree from K-State," Rick added. "Did he talk about his future plans?"

"I think the main thing he was concerned with right then was going, getting it done, and coming home," Huretta answered. "Stan and I dated a lot. The time we spent together was rather short—two or three hours—because they would have to get back to the base. Sometimes we went to the officers' club, sometimes we went to the movies, and sometimes we went to the USO and danced."

"Was Stanley a good dancer?" I asked.

"Oh, I don't know," she said. "We just liked holding each other. Who cared if you danced or not?"

"Did you think about getting married before he left?" Brian asked while Pete recorded with his camera.

Huretta laughed and said, "I did; he didn't. Our plans were he would come back to Lakeland, and we would be married. The plans were not anything that would say this was set in iron. I am sure he felt like where he was going, he had no assurance on what would happen with him. But he did say he loved me, and I told him I loved him. Actually, Stan didn't want to plan too far ahead in his life. I don't know if it was because I was younger than him. I don't know what Stan's age was then. I was eighteen and knew he was older."

Brian read part of a letter Stanley had written to his folks. Stanley's wrote:

Of course during the stay I have spent no little amount of time with a sweet little girl here. Have been going with her since the first week we had time off. Have grown quite attached to her and will miss her when I'm gone. And I might add that she is rather fond of the old man. To the extent that she would have liked to have spent these few days honeymooning. She's got an awfully nice family, all of which thought about as much of me as she did …

Huretta laughed. "That sounds like Stan," she said. "He was a really super guy. I've been married four times, and believe me, he was a super guy. I guess I kept looking and never found him the second time around. My sister kept saying that she was looking for someone like him. I remember I hadn't had a letter from Stan, and they seemed to come pretty regularly. A lot of troops came through Drane Field, and we were more accustomed to not hearing, or girls not hearing, from someone. You didn't immediately jump to a conclusion that it was the end of the world. You didn't get used to it, but you weren't surprised. You were waiting, hoping the next mail was going to bring something that would tell you 'we are okay.' I guess everybody hoped and prayed that every plane that went over there, that the whole crew would come back safe and sound. I think Jule finally called me and told me she had gotten some word from Pete, the copilot. When you get old, you don't remember all these things."

Huretta Wright and Stanley in Lakeland, Florida, in 1944.

Like Huretta, the folks had a lot of hope at the end of the war when the POWs were liberated. I explained about our search, what we could piece together right before the crash, and how the JPAC teams had excavated for his remains. Darlene had brought some pictures.

Dad showed Huretta and Bill a photo of the memorial stone at the crash site and said to them, "That's probably all we are going to get out of this situation. There's the bomb crater there. That's where the bombs went off."

"There probably wasn't much left," Huretta commented.

"One of the first things they dug out when they started excavating was a 1916 dime, an American dime," Dad told her. "We think Stan had it in his pocket."

"A good luck piece?" Huretta asked.

"Yes, a good luck piece," he answered. "Nineteen sixteen was his date of birth, and my dad was a coin collector, and he always had Stan looking for coins when he traveled around the country."

"Now that's a miracle," Huretta said. "I can't figure out how in the world they could find a dime out there with everything. It's hard to believe. Stan was born in 1916? I was born in 1925. He was nine years older than me." She smiled at Dad and said, "Gosh, I was dating an old man. I didn't know that. Too bad he isn't here. I would get him for that."

Mom gave some other photos to Dad and said, "Here are pictures of your dad, Stanley, and you."

Bill asked Huretta, "Do you see any resemblance in Harold Dwyer and Stanley?"

"Yes, I do," Huretta replied. "He [Harold] is like me. Harold and I both look older than we did back then." Then she looked around the room and said, "Now I have a picture somewhere where Stan looks more like I remember him than this picture. I thought that picture was on one of these tables."

Mom looked through a stack of curled photos on the coffee table by the sofa. On a table in the corner, another small, curled, black-and-white picture lay on top of a paperback book. I picked it up and handed it to Dad.

"Do you recognize that lady?" he asked Huretta.

"That's the picture of Stan and me here in Lakeland," Huretta said. "I think we were walking around the lake."

"So that's you in the photo?" I asked. "I've seen that picture in Stanley's trunk but could never figure it out." It made sense—the tropical foliage and Stanley in uniform with his arm around a girl. Pieces of the puzzle still continued to fall into place.

"How hard was it to move on?" Brian asked.

"I guess I didn't believe in the beginning he was not coming back," Huretta answered. "I guess there was always the thought he had bailed out like Pete. Stan was the nicest and sweetest person I knew. He was easygoing but could certainly stand up on his own. Nobody was going to push him around, except the Germans." Huretta's eyes twinkled. She smiled and said, "You had a wonderful man in your family."

Unpretentious like many of his comrades who lived to be old men, twenty-seven-year-old Stanley, in all his humility, would probably wonder about all the attention.

Mary Ellen had once heard her mom, Aileen, remark, "Stanley would probably roll over in his grave if he knew about all the fuss."

Stanley's story is but one of thousands, all part of the history of our country and the world. As a grateful nation, we, the people, should always remember the cost of our freedom. Freedom isn't free—those words should never become cliché. The cost of war in human lives is incalculable.

May 10, 2009. Sixty-five years after Stanley's B-17 crashed near Vostenhof, Austria, Markus Reisner pays his respects to the fallen soldiers.
Photo courtesy of Markus Reisner.

Ambassador Charles A. Ray said, "As a veteran, I've had comrades who paid the ultimate price. When you fall on a foreign battlefield and they don't find you, you've lost more than your life; you've lost your existence; you've lost your very identity, and that's a heavy price to pay. And I think Americans do a disservice to those people who bought this freedom for them by not being aware of it. I think Americans need to be reminded, though, that everything comes with a price—the freedom to shop and the freedom to own physical material things, the freedom to express your opinion without fear of being sent to a Gulag didn't come free. It came at a cost."

Whenever we received photos and e-mails from Austria, it was almost like being there all over again. Markus Reisner e-mailed, "The world is small, and souls are even closer."

While writing this manuscript, we observed Mother's Day, Sunday, May 10, 2009. The date also had other significance—the sixty-fifth anniversary of the day Stanley's B-17 was shot down over Austria. Prior to the beginning of our journey, that date triggered private reflection for Dad. Our journey started in 1998, and since, we've noted, in private and other various ways, twelve such dates. Usually, a little internal alarm clock subtly signals the 4:00/5:00 a.m. hour.

On May 10, 2008, I awoke before five in the morning, which was about the time Stan was killed sixty-four years earlier. I went out to the patio and sat in the rain with a cup of coffee and had a nice little chat with him. I hope in the "hereafter," the mental signals got through to Stan. Who knows? The memories are all good, and it made me feel better.

May 10, 2009, was highlighted with e-mails, photos from Austria, and a letter too.

One e-mail from Udo and Inge read:

At noon, we have been on crash site and found there a bunch of forget-me-nots and a candle was burning. Forget-me-nots are also blowing around the stone. We brought bunches of pine, our prayer, and our thoughts for this special day. So you can see that other people also do not forget these soldiers.

Johanna Stipsits sent a letter, and she enclosed a photo of herself taken standing next to the memorial stone. It seems she was responsible for the forget-me-nots. Johanna wrote, "I would plant flowers. It is so dark. Flowers are dead. So sorry."

Markus Reisner also e-mailed:

I visited the crash place, sixty-five years after the crash. It was heavily raining in the late afternoon, so I made a walk from the castle to the place. The wood was steaming from the passing rain, and so the whole scene had an atmosphere. I spoke some words in my mind at the memorial and made a look around at the crash site. The small candle in the little glass box at the bottom of the memorial was already burning. A sign that the site was already visited earlier in the day. The site was full of fresh grass which was still heavily wet from the rain.

I think it is allowed to say that Stan and his comrade have found their peace in this part of the world, far from their home. It's their grave, and the memorial is their tombstone—visible for everyone who is crossing by. That means it is not an unknown grave; it has a place, and it is named. That's more than thousands of soldiers have who are missing in oceans, the jungles, deserts, woods, and all the places where humans used to fight against each other in an often senseless war.

We were with Udo and Inge in spirit when they celebrated their golden wedding anniversary on October 26, 2009. "At 26 October we have been at the crash site to light a candle," Udo and Inge e-mailed. "The stone is becoming a light green patina. There we are always very near to you. And when we get *NEBRASKAland,* we are in Nebraska, which is so far away."

So when we put Stan's monument down in the cemetery in Scottsville, Kansas, that will probably be the end of the journey—the end of the physical part of it—but not the end of the memories.

Stanley's Purple Heart was tucked down in his trunk along with an accompanying certificate signed by President Harry Truman. The certificate states:

In Grateful Memory of 1st Lt. Stanley N. Dwyer who died in the service of his country in the Mediterranean Area. He stands in the unbroken line of patriots who have dared to die that freedom might live, and grow, and increase its blessings. Freedom lives, and through it, he lives—in a way that humbles the undertakings of most men.

The Tomb Guards at Arlington National Cemetery have a motto, "Soldiers never die until they are forgotten. Tomb Guards never forget." Like Tomb Guards, we won't forget either. Stanley Naismeth Dwyer is not forgotten. Even though we close one chapter of family history, another chapter begins. Stanley's memory is alive. This is his story. This is Stanley's legacy.

EPILOGUE

◦№◦

Tuesday, May 10, 2011

Vostenhof, Austria—"We are just coming from Vostenhof where we laid down a new wreath and your red paper flower [poppy]," Udo and Inge e-mailed on May 10, 2011. "Also, we prayed for the soldiers who lost their lives in the war. We hope there never will be war in the future."

Beatrix Valenta also e-mailed from Austria on May 10, 2011. "Sixty-seven years are gone. We visited the crash site today and brought flowers and a candle ... commemorated to Stan and the others."

Scottsville, Kansas—The same time Beatrix pressed the send button on her computer, Stanley Dwyer's family and their friends gathered at the Scottsville Community Church to honor his life. The circle was closing.

Granddad had written a revised version of his original song "Coming Back to Kansas," and my sisters Jan and Lori sang the uplifting melody, "I am coming back to Kansas ever home sweet home to me." Symbolically, Stanley was coming home—back to Kansas. After sixty-seven years, it was time.

"There is a time for everything, and a season for every activity under heaven," my sister Sue read from Ecclesiastes 3.

Pastor Barry Rempp officiated, "For Stanley Dwyer there was a time to be born; his time to die, by our standards, came much too early. It came in another kind of time—a time for war ... The times change, but God always knows what time it is. Right now it's time to give thanks for the life of Stanley Dwyer—to be grateful for his service, to honor his memory, and to celebrate his life that is held in the eternal grace of God."

Cousin Mary Ellen read from the Gospel John, "My command is this: Love each other as I have loved you. Greater love has no one than this, that he lay down his life for his friends."

Pastor Eugene Parker stood at the pulpit in the Scottsville Community Church and said this about his fellow comrade, "Stanley wasn't out for only himself; he was out for each and every one of us ... I'm not the hero here. Stanley and the crew that didn't make it are the heroes. God bless them."

And Pastor Rempp continued, "You [the family] have been given the gift of a legacy of a man who unselfishly and courageously risked himself for others—for his family, his crew, his nation, and the people of other nations that had fallen under the Nazi onslaught … You have lived in ways that add worth to the sacrifices of those who died in defense of our freedom … You have honored Stanley's death; indeed, you have honored his life and given him a legacy."

Dad and I reflected on Stanley's life in our eulogies. Whenever I look at the entire Dwyer family, little things remind me of Stanley—maybe it's someone's reddish hair or creative abilities, or their love of sports or being left-handed and even a left-handed first baseman, or someone who is ornery or likes to play Chinese checkers. But Stanley was probably the only one in our family who had climbed a coconut tree in the middle of the night. Stanley had a sense of humor, an easygoing style, an attitude of caring for others, a strong work ethic, a desire to be a lifelong learner, and he was disciplined and humble. And whenever family members emulate these characteristics, it seems Stanley's spirit is in our midst.

At the Scottsville Cemetery, Dad, surrounded by family and friends, stood near Stanley's headstone. That marker—contemplated for years—had recently been placed on the Dwyer plot. And with Dad's help, Chloe and Allie, two of Stanley's great-great-nieces, pushed their star-spangled pinwheels into the ground next to Stanley's headstone inscribed with the words, "You are not forgotten." Stanley's great-great-nephew, Elijah, delighted at the whirling blur of red, white, and blue.

Pastor Rempp stated, "The manner of Stanley Dwyer's death has left us with no body to commit to the ground. What we do have, however, is soil from the crash site near Vostenhof, Austria. You are all invited to come forward, take a handful of soil that Kay has in the yellow bag, and scatter it on this grave site." Dad was the first to sprinkle dirt from his brother's crash site on the family graves. American flags fluttered in the Kansas wind as Pastor Rempp prayed, "Loving God, in whose eternal care are all your people, we trust in you. This soil, gathered from the place where Stanley Dwyer died and where his physical body returned to the elements of the earth, is something tangible—something we can touch and hold—to represent Stanley's earthly remains. Earth to earth, ashes to ashes, dust to dust; in the faith of Jesus Christ, we place this soil from a hill far away into the soil of home, entrusting Stanley Dwyer to your loving care, and humbly acknowledging that he has been in your care all along—in life, in death, in all the intervening years until now, and forever. Amen."

The wind carried the beautiful mellow tone of taps across the Kansas prairie. As the last note faded—"God is nigh"—a silver P-51 approached. It shimmered in the sun, soared upward, and rolled over—a "Little Friend's" parting salute to another fallen World War II hero.

Stanley Dwyer is home. Our journey culminated in Kansas. The memorial stone with the plaque that we had erected at the crash site in Austria is a meaningful and an everlasting tribute that commemorates Stanley and his fallen crew. Grandma and Granddad always wanted to bring their son's remains back to Kansas to bury in the plot they'd reserved for him next to their graves. So now, the ceremony in this country brought Stanley back home to Kansas.

After the service in Kansas, I felt complete closure. I felt my body relaxing. I've always heard of closure, and for me, beginning in Austria, one led to the other. It's more meaningful than you could ever imagine. I'm just tickled that everybody could be in Scottsville to participate. It's been a long journey for my folks and me and our family, and what a journey. It's been very good. It seems the journey has come to an end now, the physical part, but not the end of the memories of Stan.

Pastor Rempp concluded the service, "In the church I serve, we often quote Gracie Allen and say, 'Never place a period where God has placed a comma.' I think that's what God is doing here. God has placed a comma. There's more to this story yet. Today is a comma in Stanley's ongoing legacy."

I've thought about what reporters Nayeli Urquiza and Dardis McNamee from *The Vienna Review* wrote in their article about our search for Stanley, "World War II did not end in 1945—at least not for the Dwyer family of Hastings, Nebraska." I think that in Kansas on May 10, 2011, World War II ended for the Dwyer family. We have come full circle. And endings lead to beginnings.

Appendix A

Duty post: Air Base Command A(e)1/XVII Flight Command

Place: Wiener Neustadt

Date: May 13/44

Time of downing: May 10/44-11.45 hrs.

Place of impact; 2 km SW of Pesstenhof

How captured: Downed by flak

Plane type: Boeing B 17 F

Plane marking: Could not be identified

Assignment number: Could not be identified

Photo equipment: None found

Radio frequencies: None found

Condition of airplane: 100% destroyed. - (Plane detonated on impact with
                                          complete bomb load.)

3 dead recovered:
          1. Prescott G. Piper   16079053 T43-43 A
          2. Francis Gilhvolay   0-814293 T43 A
          3. Olfenius   32869413 T43-43 A
Buried on May 14/44 in Community cemetery Pottschach.

APPENDIX B

Printed with permission from Microsoft.

APPENDIX C

LITTLE ONION

Verse: I won a dozen trophies when I was a lad
           I stole all the hearts that the pretty girls had
           I've been quite a guy it is plain to see
           Yet a measly little onion was the downfall of me.

Chorus: A. I was feeling so blue
           Cause my gal ran away
           But I didn't want a soul to know,
           I was playing a part
           From the start of the day
           And I didn't let a broken heart show,
        B. But when I walked through the garden,
           Pulled you from the ground,
           The tears went tumbling downward
           And the news went round and round,
           Little onion, why did you make me cry?
        A. All my friends know it now
           Yes, it's all over town
           What a silly fool she made of me,
           Cause the tears wouldn't stop
           They just kept dropping down
           Like the raindrops from a leaf-covered tree,
        C. For when I walked through the garden
           You got in my eye,
           Little onion, why did you make me cry?

                                   ---Stanley N. Dwyer

THE MAN IN THE MOON

The man in the moon sang a love song
From a star-studded stage high above,
And the song was inspired
By two hearts that were fired
With the flame of an unspoken love.

The man in the moon sang a love song
And the breeze in the trees played the tune;
As the sound filled the air
And the leaves bowed in prayer
I was lost in the song of the moon.

You never said a thing that night,
Any words would have been out of place,
Yet you gave your heart and soul to me
When you lingered in my embrace.

The man in the moon sang a love song,
Then he smiled down at lovers confessed,
And the song lingered on
Though we parted at dawn
And the moon sailed away to the west.

————Dwyer

IN THE SHADOWS OF MY HEART

Verse: Behind this pretending smile of mine
In a world apart
No one knows what is hidden
In the shadows of a lonely heart.

Chorus: A. In the shadows of my heart
In silent deep
A faded love of summer lies
In restless sleep.
A. In the shadows of my heart
Where love was found
The answer to my lovers call
Makes not a sound.
B. From the very start
I would tell my heart
This affair wasn't meant to be,
Then she went away
On an autumn day
But my heart wouldn't listen to me.
A. In the shadows of my heart
Love waits in vain
The one I cherished long ago
To come again.

---Stanley N. Dwyer

DO YOUR LOVIN' TONIGHT

Verse: Yesterday you dreamed of a beautiful love
          That tomorrow would come your way,
          So open your eyes, give your heart a break
          Tomorrow is here today.

Chorus: A. Do your lovin' tonight,
           Don't put it off till tomorrow,
           Waiting will only bring sorrow,
           For tomorrow never comes.
        A. Do your lovin' tonight,
           That's what this evening was made for,
           That's what a new moon has stayed for,
           For tomorrow never comes.
        B. Can't you see the love in those big blue eyes,
           Can't you grow up, be a man,
           If you can't, soon you'll realize
           There's another one waiting who can.
        A. Do your lovin' tonight,
           Don't keep a woman awaitin',
           You will be lost hesitatin',
           For tomorrow never comes.

                         ---Stanley N. Dwyer

APPENDIX D

There's a Job For Every American

Stanley N. Dwyer
1139 N. Denver
Hastings, Nebraska

There's a job for ev'ry A-me-ri-can In the ranks of the na-tion'l guard, So we'll stay over here lest we should ne-glect The weeds in our own back yard. O-ver here we'll work, o-ver here we'll fight, With an ar-dor be-yond com-pare, A hun-dred mil-lion strong to pro-tect our land, But not a man for the bat-tle o-ver there. There's a

465

job for e-v'ry A-me-ri-can In the work-shop of Li-ber-ty, To pro-

tect and de-fend the shores that sur-round The soul of De-moc-ra-cy. O-ver

here we'll work, o-ver here we'll fight, With the rest of the he-mis-phere, We'll

keep the home fires burning For the sake of our loved ones o-ver here.

APPENDIX E

O   Give Us Wings

Respectfully dedicated   to

Stanley N. Dwyer

O give us wings--
Wings to soar with
Wings to carry us into the aeroform fluid
Wings to carry us up over the highest mountain
Where our bodies may soar with our spirits,
Far above the toils of earth,
Where we can truer preceive our universe below.

O give us wings--
Wings of the eagle
That we may clean the skies of tyrants,
Wings of the falcon
So that we may defeat all who would prey upon the weak,
Wings of the gull
So that we may fly peacefully, surely silently,
     To preform our mission,
Wings of a dove
So that when peace is won,
We may bring help, food, and comfort to the world
     From the skies.

And give us wings--
Wings of free men--
For only free men can know
The thrill of conquering space,
And rise with their wings
Nearer the stars and God.
                    Theron Newell
               3/10/43

APPENDIX F

Final Search and Recovery Report: CIL 2007-137

ARCHAEOLOGICAL FINDINGS

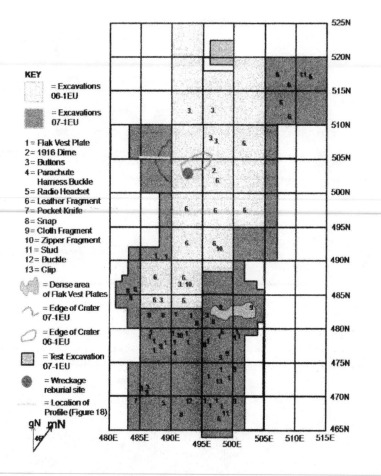

Figure 17. Plan map of units excavated during 06-1EU (Search and Recovery Report: CIL 2006-130) and 07-1EU on the northern side of Saubach Graben showing the recovery locations of pertinent material evidence, and crater. Grid squares represent 5-x-5 m.

ENDNOTES

[1]Christine Hatt, *Documenting the Past: The Second World War 1939-45.* London, England: Evans Brothers Limited, 2001.

[2]Dick Patterson, "Memories of World War II," *Historical News, Adams County Historical Society* 28 (1995) 4:2.

[3]Charles Seerveld quoted material from Camden NJ Merchant Marine Memorial – SS India Arrow website http://www.dvrbs.com/ccwd-ww2/WW2-MM-CLSeerveld.htm.

[4]Camden NJ Merchant Marine Memorial – SS India Arrow website http://www.dvrbs.com/ccwd-ww2/WW2-MM-CLSeerveld.htm.

[5]Website information written by Charles Seerveld http://www.dvrbs.com/ccwd-ww2/WW2-MM-CLSeerveld.htm.

[6]Website information written by Charles Seerveld http://www.dvrbs.com/ccwd-ww2/WW2-MM-CLSeerveld.htm.

[7]*Hastings Daily Tribune,* "Allied Pilots Not Laughing At Germans Now, Rogers Says," October 4, 1943.

[8]*Hastings Daily Tribune,* "Eighth Still Short of Goal," October 5, 1943.

[9]*Hastings Daily Tribune,* "Arsenal City Is Bombed," October 4, 1943.

[10]*Hastings Daily Tribune,* "Hannover Is Target Again," October 9, 1943.

[11]*Hastings Daily Tribune,* "Tons of Bombs Over Europe," October 4, 1943.

[12]*Hastings Daily Tribune,* "Soviets Intend to Drive On," October 8, 1943.

[13]*Hastings Daily Tribune,* "Germany on Edge of Ruin," November 6, 1943.

[14]*Hastings Daily Tribune,* "Two Years After Jap Sneak American Position Is Good," Louis F. Keemle, December 7, 1943.

[15]*Hastings Daily Tribune,* "Eisenhower Declares 'We Will Win the War in 1944' as Germans Are Pushed Back on Major Fronts," December 27, 1943.

[16]*The Fighting 463rd,* Narrative by Harold Rubin, circa 1946, n.p.

[17]*The Fighting 463rd,* Narrative by Harold Rubin, circa 1946, n.p.

[18]Carl B. Cassidy, *Allyn's Irish Orphans.* Lime Springs, Iowa: Carl Cassidy, 1946.

[19]*The Fighting 463rd,* Narrative by Harold Rubin, circa 1946, n.p.

[20]Kenn C. Rust, *Fifteenth Air Force Story ... in World War II. Historical Aviation Album.* Terre Haute, Indiana: SunShine House, Inc., 1976.

[21]*The Fighting 463rd,* Narrative by Harold Rubin, circa 1946, n.p.

[22]*The Fighting 463rd,* Narrative by Harold Rubin, circa 1946, n.p.

[23]*Hastings Daily Tribune,* "Air Giants Strike a 2-Pronged Raid," April 13, 1944.

[24]Fifteenth Air Force WWII Combat Chronology from Eugene Parker, n.p., n.d.

[25]Alexander Jefferson, *Red Tail Captured, Red Tail Free.* New York, New York: Fordham University Press, 2005.

[26]Carl B. Cassidy, *Allyn's Irish Orphans.* Lime Springs, Iowa: Carl Cassidy, 1946.

[27]*The Fighting 463rd,* Narrative by Harold Rubin, circa 1946, n.p.

[28]*Hastings Daily Tribune,* "'Hour of Liberation is Near,' Chained Peoples of Europe Told; Air Giants Roar On," May 1, 1944.

[29]Carl B. Cassidy, *Allyn's Irish Orphans.* Lime Springs, Iowa: Carl Cassidy, 1946.

[30]*The Fighting 463rd,* Narrative by Harold Rubin, circa 1946, n.p.

[31]*The Fighting 463rd,* Narrative by Harold Rubin, circa 1946, n.p.

[32]*The Fighting 463rd,* Narrative by Harold Rubin, circa 1946, n.p.

[33]*The Fighting 463rd,* Narrative by Harold Rubin, circa 1946, n.p.

[34]*The Fighting 463rd,* Narrative by Harold Rubin, circa 1946, n.p.

[35]775th Bombardment Squadron (H), Office of the Historical Officer, Unit history of the 775th Bombardment Squadron from the period 1 May 1944 to 1 June 1944, n.p., n.d.

[36]Carl B. Cassidy, *Allyn's Irish Orphans.* Lime Springs, Iowa: Carl Cassidy, 1946.

[37]JPAC Fact Sheet – 1, Fall 2005, JPAC Public Affairs.

[38]Joint POW/MIA Accounting Command Video, JPAC 2005 Command Video.

[39]Joint POW/MIA Accounting Command Video, JPAC 2005 Command Video.

[40]Markus Reisner, *Bomben auf Wiener Neustadt.* Copyright Eigenverlag Mag. (FH) Markus Reisner, 2006.